Praise for *Great Faith, Great Wis*

The three Pure Land sutras are a body of M
comparatively early, which for centuries have
spiritual life of Far Eastern Buddhism. They describe the Pure Land of Amitābha or Amitāyus, the Buddha of Infinite Light and Eternal Life, and being products of the Mahāyāna imagination, it is to the imagination rather than to the understanding that they appeal. Ratnaguna therefore has much to say about the imagination, and about the way in which it can be developed. He beautifully explores these ancient texts, bringing out their significance for us today. For him, the development of the imagination forms an integral part of the spiritual life, as does the development of both faith and wisdom.

As the names of two of the sutras suggest, the Pure Land is a realm of supreme happiness. It is also a realm of transcendent beauty. By repeating with faith the name of Amitābha or Amitāyus one can achieve nirvana in the Pure Land and hear the dharma from his lips. Ratnaguna draws some fascinating parallels between the Pure Land sutras and passages in certain earlier Buddhist scriptures. *Great Faith, Great Wisdom* is a ground-breaking work and it will appeal not only to Buddhists, particularly Mahāyāna Buddhists, but also to artists, poets, archetypal psychologists and historians of art.

Urgyen Sangharakshita, founder of the Triratna Buddhist Community

The three Pure Land sutras are among the most significant texts of Mahāyāna Buddhism, having inspired the traditions of China, Japan, Tibet and other East Asian countries in devotion to Amitābha Buddha. Magnificent in their literary style, these texts are foundational to the Pure Land schools of Jōdo Shin-shū and Jōdo-shū, the largest Buddhist schools of modern Japan, as well as to their antecedents in China. This book offers a fresh exploration of the texts, drawing directly on new translations by Śraddhāpa, which, unlike many commonly used, are based on Sanskrit rather than Chinese versions of the sutra. These, together with Ratnaguna's commentary, bring new perspectives on the traditional material, interpreting them in ways that make them particularly accessible and applicable to Western practitioners.

In locating these sutras as an aid to developing the imaginative faculty, Ratnaguna shows how their rich imagery evokes expansive mind-states which take us beyond the personal story into the greater realms of spiritual truth. As a departure from traditional Japanese interpretations, this book, with its detailed textual referencing, offers important new insights into the scriptures. It will appeal both to those seeking to understand the heart of Mahāyāna devotion and to scholars of Pure Land Buddhism keen to embrace new perspectives.

Caroline Brazier, course leader, Tariki Trust, author of *Buddhist Psychology* and *The Other Buddhism: Amida Comes West*

Several experiments in neuroscience have found that what we experience as "reality" or "imagination" are not two entirely separate entities but parts of a continuum, a gradient where our brains blend present sensations, memories, and expectations in order to generate meaningful experiences. Therefore, our daily life exists in a kind of fuzzy perceptual world, partly real and partly imaginary. In this fuzzy world, "reality" gives us the feeling of grounding and connectedness with the "here and now", while "imagination" provides us with the goals and values that give meaning to reality. In *Great Faith, Great Wisdom* Ratnaguna and Śraddhāpa guide us in a fascinating journey around the paradox of the imaginative worlds found in the Mahayana cosmology. Imagination plays a crucial role in this tradition since the universe imagined by the Mahayana is not just an imaginary universe like many other cosmological worldviews, but also a kind of meta-imaginative world where imagination is also a meditative tool to attain different levels of experience. This blend of imaginary worlds and imaginative meditative practice makes this book very interesting reading, not only to Buddhists but to anyone interested in the role of imagination in different cultures.

Professor Luiz Carlos Serramo Lopez
Laboratory of Behavioural Ecology and Psychobiology
Federal University of Paraiba-Joao Pessoa

Unshackled by the binding orthodoxy often found in East Asian Buddhism, the European authors of *Great Faith, Great Wisdom* offer perspectives that are refreshingly insightful and novel. By stressing the value of "imagination" over "understanding", the book shows why Pure Land Buddhism has been a dominant stream of Mahayana Buddhism for two millennia. Readers will be fascinated by dimensions and sensibilities beyond the usual doctrines and meditations that the West has come to associate with Buddhism.

Kenneth Kenshin Tanaka
Professor, Musashino University, Tokyo
President, International Association of Shin Buddhist Studies,
author of *The Dawn of Chinese Pure Land Doctrine*

Great Faith, Great Wisdom offers a lively translation and thoughtful, readable commentary, inviting a rethinking of the role of imagination in Buddhism. It is a welcome contribution.

David L. McMahan, Charles A. Dana Professor of Religious Studies,
Franklin & Marshall College, Lancaster, Pennsylvania, author of
Empty Vision: Metaphor and Visionary Imagery in Mahayana Buddhism

Great Faith, Great Wisdom

Also by Ratnaguna

The Art of Reflection

Great Faith, Great Wisdom

Practice and Awakening in the Pure Land Sutras of Mahāyāna Buddhism

Ratnaguna and Śraddhāpa

Windhorse Publications

Published by
Windhorse Publications
169 Mill Road
Cambridge
CB1 3AN
UK

info@windhorsepublications.com
windhorsepublications.com

Cover design by Dhammarati
Typesetting and layout by Ruth Rudd

Printed by Bell & Bain Ltd, Glasgow

British Library Cataloguing in Publication Data:
A catalogue record for this book is available from the British Library.

ISBN: 978-1-909314-56-6

Contents

About the authors

Ratnaguna has been an ordained member of the Triratna Buddhist Order for forty years. He is a director of Breathworks – a project that is dedicated to helping people with long-term pain to live well with their condition, using mindfulness and meditation. He also teaches at the Manchester Buddhist Centre and at other centres in the UK and Europe.

Śraddhāpa is also a member of the Triratna Buddhist Order. He studied Scandinavian languages and translation at the University of Edinburgh and University College London, and is currently studying for an MPhil in Sanskrit. He lives and works in Norway and teaches at the Oslo Buddhist Centre.

Gratitude

This book is a labour of love, in fact the product of many labours of love. The first were the sutras on which this book is based. Who the authors were we will never know, as they attributed their words to the Buddha. What wonderful works of the imagination they left us. Then there is Śraddhāpa, who, when I told him of my intention to write this book, immediately offered to compose new translations of the sutras. Working with his translations has been an education and a joy. Birgit Barten read and commented on every draft of every chapter as I wrote them, and with her great eye for detail pointed out grammatical errors, confusing passages, and unnecessary repetitions. Vidyadevi, my editor, did more of the same but also gently and skilfully suggested more elegant ways of expressing myself, and occasionally just did the work herself. Without the input from those two the book would be a lot poorer. I'd also like to thank Paramartha, who bought me the reproduction of the Taima mandala – a painting of the pure land – that has inspired me greatly; my teacher, Urgyen Sangharakshita, whose commentaries on other Mahāyāna sutras inspired me to write these commentaries; Priyananda, director of Windhorse Publications, who always had faith in the project when others doubted it, and worked hard to make sure it was realized; and finally, of course, the Buddha, without whom none of this would have happened.

Ratnaguna
October 2015

Publisher's acknowledgements

Windhorse Publications wishes to gratefully acknowledge a grant from the Triratna European Chairs' Assembly Fund towards the production of this book.

We also wish to acknowledge and thank the individual donors who gave to the book's production via our 'Sponsor-a-book' campaign.

Triratna
European Chairs Assembly

Audio downloads

Great Faith, Great Wisdom has been produced with an accompanying reading by Ratnaguna of the translations of the three Pure Land sutras. This is available as a free download, and can be streamed directly from the web or downloaded in MP3 format.

Please go to bit.ly/greatfaithgreatwisdom or windhorsepublications.com/great-faith-great-wisdom-audio.

Introduction

The three texts explored in this book are Mahāyāna sutras. Mahāyāna means "Great Vehicle" or "Great Way", and is the collective noun for a number of Buddhist texts, ideas, and practices that arose a few hundred years after the death of the Buddha. "Sutra" means "discourse" (literally "string" or "thread"). Mahāyāna sutras are often highly imaginative, describing spiritual teachings and experiences through stories, images, poems, supernatural events, and great beings in other worlds, separated from us by tracts of time and space so vast as to be unimaginable. The authors of the Mahāyāna sutras reimagined the Buddha's teachings, releasing them from their geographical and historical locations and lovingly placing them in a limitless, magical cosmos. In particular they tell of bodhisattvas – heroic beings who vow to gain Enlightenment for the sake of all beings, practise the Dharma (the teachings of the Buddha) for countless lifetimes, teaching and helping innumerable people along the way, perfecting their positive qualities and wisdom until, in their final lives, they become buddhas, spiritually presiding over world systems like great kings.

The Pure Land sutras describe such a world system millions of world systems to the west of ours, called Sukhāvatī – the Realm of Utmost Happiness – in which a Buddha called Amitāyus or Amitābha lives and teaches. You might ask why the sutras do that. Most people read Buddhist texts – if they read them at all – for their doctrinal content. They look for teachings that tell them how to live, how they can become happier, what to do to be sure of a favourable rebirth, how to meditate, how to gain Enlightenment. These sutras have a different purpose. They are works of the imagination, and reading them, or, better, listening to them being read, is a practice in awakening the imagination. Luis O. Gomez puts it very well in his book *The Land of Bliss*, which is a translation and study of two of these texts:

> As I read the two Sukhāvatīvyūha Sutras, I see in them not only documents of Buddhist history and statements of Buddhist doctrine, not only claims to religious truth, but also works of the literary imagination. It is impossible for me to read them without thinking of Dante and the Western literary tradition of journeys to the underworld and visions of heaven and hell. ... Thus, I like to imagine these two sutras as somewhere between the works of poets, visionaries, and theologians. ... Although we, in Asia as well as in the West, tend to overemphasise the doctrinal content of Buddhist sutras, traditional commentaries on the sutras did not ignore their literary nature.[1]

Webster's dictionary defines imagination as "an act or process of forming a conscious idea or mental image of something never before wholly perceived in reality by the imaginer". The Pure Land sutras ask us to imagine a whole world never before wholly perceived in reality by the imaginer: a world in which trees are made of gold, silver, and jewels, lotuses many miles in diameter grow in ponds lined with gold, magical birds sing the Buddha's teachings, and the golden Buddha Amitāyus radiates light that fills the whole universe. But, again, why awaken the imagination? What does the imagination have to do with the path to Enlightenment? In an article on the eleventh-century Sufi philosopher and mystic al-Ghazâlî, Aaron Hughes provides an answer: "The imagination is the faculty that experiences and expresses in sensible form that which is essentially inexpressible."[2] This captures very well, I think, the way the Pure Land sutras work: they attempt to express in sensible form that which is essentially inexpressible – Awakening or Enlightenment. By reading or listening to the sutras, or visualizing their descriptions of Sukhāvatī and Amitābha, we are, in turn, enabled to experience Awakening, or at least something of it. Put in simpler language, they don't tell us the truth in words and ideas, they show it to us in images, and we access that truth by imagining those images.

Sukhāvatī is not *just* an image though. The sutras speak of it as if it were an objectively existing realm into which it's possible to be reborn – in fact the main purpose of imagining it is to cultivate the desire to be born there. This presents a problem for the majority of Westerners, even many Western Buddhists, who don't believe in or are agnostic about rebirth. Can these texts have any meaning for them? I believe they can. Being works of the imagination, they can be read symbolically as well as literally, or we might say imaginatively as well as literally.

On the literal level, Sukhāvatī is an objectively existing realm, and the spiritual life consists in cultivating the necessary faith, ethical purity, and concentration of mind to be reborn there. On the imaginative level Sukhāvatī is a symbol of Awakening (nirvana), and the spiritual life consists in cultivating the necessary faith and so on to realize it in this life. Buddhists throughout history have interpreted Sukhāvatī in both ways. An example of the imaginative interpretation is found in the Zen master Hakuin's "Song of Meditation":

> *The Pure Land paradise is not far ...*
> *Nirvāṇa is clear before him,*
> *This very place the Lotus Paradise,*
> *This very body the Buddha.*[3]

I suspect that Buddhists in the past didn't hold a hard and fast distinction between the literal and the imaginative. They tried to awaken in the present life but knew that if they didn't get that far they could be born in Sukhāvatī in their next life. In fact, they would perhaps have been puzzled by the way we divide the literal and the imaginative and then make them mutually exclusive. We might think that Sukhāvatī is either a place in which we can be born in our next life or a state that can be experienced in this life. I believe that the authors of these sutras, and the people they were writing for, simply wouldn't have seen the world in that way. For them, symbols, metaphors, supernatural stories, and myths were not a different kind of truth from what we call literal truth. They lived in a spiritual or animistic world in which states of mind and places were not separate categories. To be born in Sukhāvatī was to experience deep insight, and to gain insight was to glimpse Sukhāvatī.

When I say insight, I'm referring to a word used in the ancient Indian Buddhist texts: *vipassanā*. *Passanā* means "to see", and *vi-* is an emphatic prefix, so *vipassanā* means "to *really* see". Here *seeing* is a metaphor for spiritual understanding or realization, as expressed in another phrase the Buddha often used – "knowing and seeing things as they really are". "Knowing" refers to the fact that understanding is involved in the experience and "seeing" to the fact that that understanding is not merely cognitive – it's a direct *perception*. Buddhist texts often describe this experience in terms of clarity: without insight everything is dark and murky, and with insight everything is seen with razor-sharp clarity. However, perceiving reality is not simply a matter of accurately receiving objective data from the world, but one of perceiving the world more imaginatively or, we might say, imagining it more vividly. The

Buddha himself spoke of insight as clarity of vision, but he often gave imaginative examples of what this clear seeing is like. For instance:

> It is just as if there were a gem, a beryl, pure, excellent, well cut into eight facets, clear, bright, unflawed, perfect in every respect, strung on a blue, yellow, red, white or orange cord. A man with good eyesight, taking it in his hand and inspecting it, would describe it as such. ... Just as if, Sire, in the midst of the mountains there were a pond, clear as a polished mirror, where a man with good eyesight standing on the bank could see oyster-shells, gravel banks, and shoals of fish, on the move or stationary ... just so, with mind concentrated, he knows.[4]

These similes express not only clarity of vision ("good eyesight") but also beauty, delight, and wonder. The part imagination plays in the experience of insight becomes clearer if we take one of the Buddha's central teachings: everything in this world is impermanent. To *really see* this is not the same as seeing an object in front of you very clearly and distinctly. To see impermanence requires imagination, because the things and people around us are relatively stable and consistent, and that stability and consistency gives the illusion of permanence. We have to see beyond the present moment to understand their impermanence, which involves the imagination.[5] In a Mahāyāna sutra called the *Vajracchedikā Prajñāpāramitā*, the Buddha gave a series of similes to help us to see, that is, to really understand – realize, feel, and embody – impermanence. He said that we should contemplate our existence in this "fleeting world" to be "like a tiny drop of dew, or a bubble floating in a stream, like a flash of lightning in a summer cloud".[6] These similes work by comparing our lives – which continue over a number of decades – with things that last for just a few hours or even a second. The Buddha could have said the same thing more prosaically by pointing out that our lives are actually very short and that they'll go past much more quickly than we think. But he does so with the help of beautiful images, so that we experience the juxtaposition of the brevity of our lives with beauty. We see the tiny, delicate drop of dew, for instance, and feel its fragility, its oh-so-short existence, its gorgeous liquid beauty, and we feel our life to be somehow like that drop of dew. We also realize, I would suggest, that it's OK for that drop of dew, that bubble, that lightning flash, to come and go, to be impermanent. Part of the precious beauty of such things is surely their transience. We relish the beauty of the drop of dew all the more for knowing that in an hour it will no longer be there, and, along with that, we get the message that it's somehow OK for us to be impermanent too. Life is like that. It comes and goes. That's its nature. There is no problem. In other words, imagining the drop of dew, the bubble, and the lightning flash enables us to let go of – or at least loosen our grip on – our identification with our own particular, individual existence. Imagination in this sense is not the seeing of imaginary things but *the faculty that perceives reality*.

To say that imagination is the faculty that perceives reality is to speak metaphorically. Imagination in this sense isn't a faculty like memory, reason, or speech, it's a particular state of mind that is attuned to – in harmony with – truth or reality or, to use a less abstract term, the way things are. When the Buddha met someone he would often give what's called a "graduated discourse", talking first about generosity and its benefits, then morality and the heavenly realms, the dangers of indulging in desires, and the benefits of renunciation. Only then, if he could see that his listener was ready, would he give them a "wisdom" teaching, that is, something about the way things are. The ancient Pali suttas ("sutta" is the Pali form of the Sanskrit "sutra") use a stock formula to indicate the readiness of the listener's mind.[7] They say something like:

> and then, when the Buddha saw that [his listener's] mind was ready: malleable, unbiased, exalted, and clear; then he taught them the way things are.[8]

I've written that the suttas say "something like" this because much is lost in the translation, and I want now to reclaim some of what was lost by looking at each of the original Pali terms and bringing out their fuller meanings. It's worth doing this because this short passage not only tells us something important about the state of mind in which wisdom is most likely to arise but also gives us a clue to understanding the Pure Land sutras.

The word translated as "mind" is *citta*, which means "heart" as much as "mind": the experience of insight is as much a "change of heart" as it is a knowing of something. *Citta* therefore means something like mindset, attitude, disposition, or inclination. The word translated as "ready" is *kalla*, which also means "prepared", so we could translate *kalla-citta* as "a mind prepared" (to know and see things as they really are). The next four terms tell us what this state of mind is like.

The first quality of the prepared mind is *mudu*, which means "soft, gentle, tender", and therefore "pliable, malleable, flexible, workable", so we could say that this state of mind is receptive, responsive, sensitive.

If it weren't for its negative connotation of gullibility I would say impressionable, which brings to my mind the image of a wax seal receiving the impress of the emblem. *Mudu-citta* is a mind softened, not resisting the truth, but ready to receive its impress.

The next dimension of that mind is *vinīvaraṇā* – unbiased, unobstructed, or unprejudiced, and therefore open-minded, able, and willing to see things in a new way. Some translators have "free from the hindrances" here, referring to the five negative states that prevent one from entering into meditative absorption or dhyāna, these five negative states being desire for sense experience, animosity, anxiety/remorse, lethargy, and doubt/indecision. This throws an interesting light on the state of mind prepared to receive the truth; it's apparently very close to the state of dhyāna. In the introduction to his translation of the *Bodhicaryāvatāra* Dr Marion Matics writes evocatively of dhyāna as an experience that allows the meditator "to pass through the door of the mind to other regions of experience than those provided by the common faculties of thought and sense perception".[9] In a word, the imagination.

The third aspect of a mind ready for insight is *udagga* – exalted, elated, exultant. This is the natural outcome of an unbiased, unobstructed mind. If we understand the previous quality in its more technical sense of freedom from the five hindrances, we can see why this is so. Speaking of a man in whom the five hindrances are absent, the Buddha said that "gladness arises in him, from gladness comes delight, from the delight in his mind his body is tranquillised, with a tranquil body he feels joy, and with joy his mind is concentrated".[10]

The final quality of the mind ready to receive wisdom is *pasanna* (not to be confused with the word we've already encountered – *passanā*, "to see"). *Pasanna* has quite a wide range of meaning – clear, bright, happy, gladdened, pleased; specifically "pleased in one's conscience", to quote the Pali–English dictionary. We might say then that *pasanna* is the happiness of a clear conscience, and it therefore also means "virtuous, good". The Buddha was not able to guide everyone he met to this state of readiness and, when he could not do so, one of the reasons for this was the person's lack of virtue. The simplest formulation of the path to Awakening is the threefold way, the first stage of which is the practice of ethics. This prepares the mind for the next stage, which is meditative concentration,[11] and this in turn prepares the mind for the third stage – wisdom. If a virtuous person were lucky enough to meet the Buddha, he or she would be guided to meditative concentration and wisdom simply by listening to the Buddha speak about the path to Awakening.

This offers us another insight into the first quality of a mind ready for wisdom – *mudu-citta*, which can also be translated as "tender-hearted", that is, sensitive to the pleasures and pains of other living beings. This sensitivity to all of life is the basis of ethics, which, as we've seen, is a necessary condition for the gaining of wisdom.

Finally, *pasanna* also means "trust, belief, faith". Let's remind ourselves that this state of mind has arisen towards the end of the Buddha's graduated discourse, by which time the listener will have developed a degree of trust and confidence in the Buddha. He or she will have a sense that this man has their best interests at heart, that he knows something important, and that he can help them to know it too. And they *want* to know it. There are many dimensions to faith, but one of them is *desire*. A mind ready for wisdom *wants* wisdom, more than anything else in the world.

Let's just review the qualities of the mind prepared to receive the truth: flexible, malleable, workable, receptive, responsive, sensitive; unbiased, unprejudiced, unobstructed, open, free of negative emotion; exultant, elated, joyful, delighted, inspired; with the happiness of a clear conscience, bright, pure, trusting, believing, desiring wisdom. It's this state of mind I'll be referring to when I use the terms "imagination", "the imaginative faculty", "the imaginal faculty", or "the imaginal realm".

Once the Buddha has seen that his auditor's mind is ready, he teaches them the Dharma, the truth, and the texts invariably then say

> just as a clean cloth, free of stains, would properly absorb a dye, in the same way, as [the listener] sat there, the dustless, stainless Dhamma eye arose within him or her.[12]

Notice how imaginatively that is expressed: the clean cloth is the mind ready to receive wisdom, and the dye is wisdom, colouring the purified mind. The opening of the "Dhamma eye" is a simile for insight or wisdom, and is contrasted in the texts to the "fleshy" or physical eye. To see with the Dhamma eye is to see things as they really are, not in the sense of an accurate perception of physical objects, but in the sense of an imaginative understanding of them.

Before the encounter between the Buddha and his listener is over, one final thing always happens: the listener "goes for refuge" to the Buddha, to his teaching, and to those of his disciples who have also gained deep insight, and he or she asks the Buddha to accept him or her as a disciple "for as long as life shall last". (The Buddha, his teaching, and those disciples who have deep insight are collectively known as the

Three Jewels – the Buddha, Dharma, and Sangha. To go for refuge to them means to commit oneself to practising the Buddha's teaching.) The feeling of trust and confidence in the Buddha has been confirmed and deepened by their own insight, and they now possess *unshakeable faith*.

I wrote above that reading or listening to the Pure Land sutras is a practice in awakening the imagination, and we're now in a position to see what this means a little more precisely and from a more traditional point of view. Their purpose is to lead us through the sequence described above, although they do that through imagery rather than through conceptual teachings. How this works will become clear as you read this book, but I can say immediately that the Pure Land sutras emphasize the emotional dimension of the experience rather than the cognitive. Faith and wisdom are the two sides of the same gold coin and, whereas most Buddhist schools (and most Western Buddhists) speak of insight mainly in terms of understanding, the Pure Land sutras (and, I suspect, most Eastern Buddhists) conceive of it more as a change of heart. Towards the end of the *Longer Sukhāvatīvyūhaḥ Sūtra* the Buddha says:

It takes a long time to attain the wisdom which has faith
as its goal.
You should rouse your energy to attain this goal.

The phrase "the wisdom which has faith as its goal" is a compound Sanskrit term – that is, it is a word made up of three words[13] – which the translator says can also be interpreted as "the wisdom which has faith as its object", "the wisdom which is concerned with faith", or "the wisdom which is motivated by faith". The last of these interpretations makes wisdom the goal and faith the means, while the other translations put them the other way round, which I think is closer to the position of the Pure Land sutras. Of course insight does have a cognitive dimension, but contemporary Western Buddhists tend to overemphasize that, so that it's easy to get the impression that it's the only dimension: insight is knowledge. The Pure Land sutras – in common with many other Mahāyāna sutras – emphasize the emotional dimension.

I've been referring to the sutras as the three Pure Land sutras, but this is not a very precise description. Firstly, Sukhāvatī is not *the* pure land, but just one among many. It would be more accurate to call them the Happy Land sutras. The term "pure land" was first applied to these texts by the sixth-century Chinese teacher and writer Tanluan, and that name stuck. Secondly, a fourth sutra is sometimes included – the *Pratyutpannabuddha Saṃmukhāvasthita Samādhi Sūtra* – the *Sutra of the*

Meditation of Being in the Presence of all Buddhas.[14] I decided not to include this sutra in my explorations, mainly for reasons of space.

Of the three sutras we will be exploring, two are called *Sukhāvatīvyūhaḥ – Evocation on the Abundance of the Wonders of Sukhāvatī*. One of these is only a few pages long while the other is several dozen pages, so one is called the *Shorter* and the other the *Longer Sukhāvatīvyūhaḥ Sūtra*. It is thought that they were written in the region of India's north-west frontier (present-day Pakistan) in around AD 100–200. There isn't a consensus among scholars as to which was the earlier of the two. There are two surviving versions of the *Shorter Sūtra*, in Sanskrit and Chinese, and seven versions of the *Longer Sūtra*, one in Sanskrit, one in Tibetan, and five in Chinese. The translations in this book are of the Sanskrit versions, and my commentaries are based on those. The third sutra has only survived in its Chinese form, and its provenance is unknown. It purports to be a translation from an Indian language; it seems likely that it was in fact composed in Chinese, probably in the fourth or fifth century AD, but probably from earlier Indian material. Its full title is *Fó shuō guān wúliàngshòufó jīng – The Sūtra on the Visualization of the Buddha Amitāyus*. It is sometimes called the *Amitāyur-dhyāna Sūtra* – a loose Sanskrit translation from the Chinese – and it's known in English variously as the *Meditation, Contemplation*, or *Visualization Sūtra*, all of which are translations of its abbreviated title, the *Guān Jīng*.

This book is divided into four parts: the first three parts consist of my commentaries on the sutras, while the fourth comprises new English translations by Dharmacārī Śraddhāpa. The reason my commentaries are placed before the translations is because readers new to Mahāyāna sutras almost inevitably find them baffling, boring, or frustrating, coming as they do from very different cultures from their own, written for ritual purposes rather than for silent, solitary reading, and containing numerous references to ideas and practices with which many readers are unfamiliar. If you are such a reader, reading the commentaries first will help you to understand and enjoy the sutras. If you already have some experience of reading Mahāyāna sutras, you may prefer to read the sutras before my commentaries. Some readers may be content to read only the commentaries – they make sense on their own – but I hope that the commentaries will inspire them to go on to read the sutras themselves.

Part One is a commentary on the *Shorter Sukhāvatīvyūhaḥ Sūtra*, Part Two is about the *Longer Sutra*, and Part Three is on the *Guān Jīng*. I've arranged them in this order because doing so makes narrative sense:

the *Shorter Sukhāvatīvyūhaḥ Sutra* briefly describes Sukhāvatī and tells us how to be born there; the *Longer Sutra* recounts the "mythic history" of Sukhāvatī and describes the Buddha Amitābha, the land, and the beings who live there in much more detail; and the *Guān Jīng* begins with a story of great suffering in this world, showing the relevance of the Sukhāvatī myth to human life, shot through as it is with suffering, and then describes *how* to visualize Sukhāvatī and Amitābha in great detail.

Living with these sutras for the past year and a half – reading them, thinking about them, writing down my thoughts, reflecting further, meditating, revising my original thoughts, visualizing the sections I happened to be writing about, reflecting and revising and writing again, and finally trying to turn my chaotic thoughts into order and my clumsy prose into pleasing English – has been very hard work, although very absorbing and enjoyable. There was another layer to the work too. When I told Śraddhāpa of my plan to write the book, he proposed making new translations of the sutras that could perhaps be published as a companion volume. (In the event, Windhorse Publications decided to publish them both in one volume.) Obviously this meant writing my commentaries based on Śraddhāpa's translations, but by that time I had already started writing, using another translation, and I wanted to continue. Śraddhāpa never caught up with me, and so began a rather convoluted and laborious process of writing my commentaries and some time later receiving Śraddhāpa's translations and revising what I'd written. On occasions a passage in Śraddhāpa's translation gave a different meaning from the translation that I'd written about, and this would entail my not only revising but rewriting parts of the commentary. Not an efficient way of writing a book, but a very good way to get to know the sutras!

And it has been wonderful to get to know them better. I thought I knew them pretty well before I started writing the book but, as I read them more closely, reflected on them, and wrote about them, I learnt, understood, and imagined much more than I had previously seen. In this way, writing about them has been much more than just work; it's been a spiritual practice, in fact my main spiritual practice these past eighteen months. Writing about the sutras has been very good for me, and I hope it will benefit others too. In Chapter 7 I comment on a line from one of the sutras to the effect that one should not only practise the Dharma but also encourage others to do so too. I hope that reading this book will inspire you to read the texts and practise the Dharma.

You may be wondering who I am to be writing a commentary on these sutras. I am not an academic scholar, nor am I a "Pure Land

Buddhist" – that is, I don't belong to any particular Pure Land school. I'm a Buddhist, practising within an ecumenical tradition, interested in and inspired by these sutras. Although I have the greatest respect for the great Pure Land teachers of the past, who have stimulated, excited, puzzled, inspired, and surprised me in almost equal measure, I didn't want to read the sutras through the lens of the Pure Land traditions, but to look directly at them and – to mix metaphors – let them speak for themselves. A friend of mine who plays the violin says that when she plays a piece of music she tries not to impose her own "interpretation" onto the music, but tries instead to express what she thinks were the intentions of the composer. Similarly, I have tried to understand what the sutras seem to be saying and to explicate those meanings in ways that I think contemporary readers will be able to relate to and enjoy.

The question of the validity of my interpretations may trouble some readers. What gives me the authority to interpret them in the way that I do? How true are my interpretations to the intentions of the authors of the sutras? In answer I will quote the literary critic John Carey, from his book *What Good Are the Arts?*

> Like all criticism of art or literature my judgements are camouflaged autobiography, arising from a lifetime's encounters with words and people that are mostly far too complicated for me to unravel. They may, of course, persuade some or all of my readers, and I hope they do. But this will not show that they are true, only that they are persuasive. We cannot talk of truth and falsehood except where proof is available, and where proof is available persuasion is not needed.[15]

I would only add that my "camouflaged autobiography" arises not only from a lifetime's encounters with words and people, but also from the best part of a lifetime of Buddhist practice and reflection, imperfect though that practice and reflection undoubtedly have been.

Whether or not you are persuaded by my interpretations, they are not to be taken as definitive. A definitive interpretation of an imaginative work is neither possible nor desirable. I once heard a story about St Augustine, which I haven't been able to verify, but, whether true or not, it's a good story. Someone once pointed out to him that his interpretation of a passage from the Bible differed from that of another bishop. He replied, "Good. The more interpretations the better."

Part One

The Shorter Sūtra on the Abundance of Wonderful Qualities Which Adorn Sukhāvatī

Chapter One

The state of happiness

All three of the sutras we're exploring begin with the words "This is what I have heard." This prompts the question "Who has heard?" Who is the narrator? In the early Buddhist texts, such as those found in the Pali canon, most sutras begin with these words. Tradition has it that the Buddha's closest disciple, Ānanda, committed to memory everything he heard the Buddha teach, and, if he wasn't present, the Buddha would later repeat what he'd said to him. Ānanda apparently had the aural equivalent of a photographic memory – he remembered everything he heard. This meant that when the Buddha died Ānanda was the repository of nearly all of the Buddha's teachings. So when we see these words it means that what follows is to be trusted as the words of the Buddha – buddhavacana. Ānanda heard them, and he is narrating this sutra to us.

The Pali suttas were originally spoken, and then passed on from person to person, generation to generation, by word of mouth. Early Buddhism was an oral tradition or, to be more precise, a number of oral traditions, which were written down a few hundred years later. Mahāyāna sutras may also have begun as oral creations, but almost certainly not spoken by the Buddha.[16] So why do they begin with these words, "This is what I have heard"? The obvious reason would be to give them legitimacy. When people read these words, the authors presumably thought, they would take what followed to be the Buddha's own teaching. On the face of it, from a contemporary literary point of view, this seems to be a deception, although the authors may not have seen it like that.

We have no way of knowing now, almost two thousand years after they were composed, how the authors viewed their use of the phrase "This is what I have heard" at the beginning of their sutras. They may have interpreted it quite broadly. Actually, not even all of the Pali suttas were spoken by the Buddha, even though they begin with these words. There are many in which someone other than the Buddha teaches. Often the Buddha later "certifies" these teachings by saying that they are in agreement with his own, thus giving them the status of *buddhavacana*, but not always. For instance, a monk named Uttara gave a teaching to some other monks, after which he was asked whether what he'd just said was his own extemporaneous invention or a saying of the Buddha. In reply Uttara used the analogy of a great pile of grain, from which many people take small amounts away with them. Asked where the grain they are carrying came from, they answer that it came from that great pile of grain. Uttara then remarks:

> In the same way, whatever is well said is a saying of the Blessed One, the Worthy One, the Rightly Self-awakened One. Adopting it again and again from there do we and others speak.[17]

The import of this is that any teaching of the Dharma is buddhavacana – the word of the Buddha – irrespective of who the speaker is. This is a very liberal interpretation and one that is potentially confusing or even damaging. Surely not everything that's "well said" is a teaching of the Buddha? Luckily, the Buddha gave a list of criteria to help us distinguish between that which is not in accordance with his teaching and that which is. Speaking to someone named Upāli, he said:

> Those doctrines, Upāli, of which you may know "These doctrines lead one not to complete disenchantment (with the world), nor to dispassion, nor to ending (of suffering), nor to tranquillity, nor to understanding, nor to awakening, nor to the cool (Nirvana)" – regard them definitely as not the Dharma, not the discipline, not the word of the Teacher. Those doctrines of which you may know "These doctrines lead to complete disenchantment (with the world), dispassion, ending (of suffering), tranquillity, understanding, awakening, the cool" – regard them unreservedly as the Dharma, the doctrine, the word of the Teacher.[18]

The teachings, in other words, have their own intrinsic authority – if they help us to grow towards Awakening they should be regarded as buddhavacana – and so don't need the extrinsic authority of the Buddha to "certify" them.

This gives rise to another possibility. Perhaps the authors of these texts, rather than Ānanda, had heard the Buddha teach them? But how could they possibly have done so, living as they did a few hundred years after his death? One Mahāyāna sutra, related to those we're exploring in this book, recommends the practice of visualizing a buddha in meditation, and states that with continued practice the visualized buddha becomes so real to the meditator that he or she can ask him questions, which he will answer.[19] An imagined buddha speaking to the meditator! It's possible then that these sutras were narrated to the authors in an imaginal realm. Not everyone will accept this explanation, of course. Can we really give the teachings of a visualized buddha the same status as those of the human, historical Buddha? Is an imagined buddha really a buddha? Is he another being, "visiting" the meditator, or is he an aspect of the meditator's consciousness, a kind of buddha archetype?

These are interesting questions and the answers you give will determine how you approach these sutras. I would guess that Mahāyāna Buddhists from the East in days gone by would have considered a visualized buddha to be a real being. Contemporary Buddhists, especially Westerners, will be more inclined to regard him as an aspect of their own consciousness. There is also a third possibility, but I'm going to leave that to the next chapter.

For now let's return to the sutra. It begins with the Buddha – the human, historical Buddha. He is staying in Prince Jeta's Grove, in Anāthapiṇḍada's Park, and with him are 1,250 monks, all of them arhats, that is, they are all enlightened. Some are mentioned by name, for instance Mahāmaudgalyāyana, Mahākāśyapa, Revata, the Buddha's half-brother Nanda, his cousin and closest disciple Ānanda, and his son Rāhula. Also present are an unspecified number of bodhisattvas, including the youthful prince of the Dharma, Mañjuśrī, and Ajita, also known as Maitreya, the "Friendly One". Finally, many hundreds of thousands of devas – gods – including Indra and Brahmā Sahāṃpati, are also present.

This is a fairly standard way for a Mahāyāna sutra to begin, with its mixture of history and myth. Historically the Buddha often did stay at Anāthapiṇḍada's Park, and the named monks were in fact his disciples. However, the bodhisattvas mentioned are mythical figures and with these we begin to move from history to myth – from early Buddhism to the Mahāyāna. And then there are the gods. The authors of Mahāyāna sutras liked to surround the Buddha with tens of thousands, even hundreds of thousands, of beings, human and non-human. They liked to place the Buddha in a cosmic arena. He might be teaching one of his disciples, just as he does in the older, Pali suttas, but thousands of beings will be looking on and listening in. It's as if the authors were saying that, although the Buddha was human, and he could therefore only teach a few people at a time, in another sense – in a deeper kind of reality – his teaching was a cosmic event that affected not only those to whom he was speaking directly. When the Buddha spoke the universe changed.

But I want to begin our exploration by focusing on the second sentence of the sutra:

> Once, the Blessed One was staying in Śrāvastī, in Jeta's Grove, in Anāthapiṇḍada's Park.

I wonder why the author chose to situate the Buddha here. Of course it could simply be that he or she had to place the Buddha somewhere and this was as good a place as any; the Buddha did spend quite a lot of time here after all. I like to think there may be another reason, though – something to do with the story of the park and its owner.

Anāthapiṇḍada (also known as Anāthapiṇḍika) was a prominent lay follower of the Buddha. A wealthy businessman, his given name was Sudatta, but everyone knew him by his "nickname" Anāthapiṇḍada – the "Feeder of the Poor". His first meeting with the Buddha was remarkable. He was visiting the city of Rājagṛha on business and was staying with his sister, who was married to another wealthy businessman. Now, usually when Anāthapiṇḍada visited, his brother-in-law would put aside whatever he happened to be doing and receive him with all due hospitality. But on this occasion he was preoccupied, busily ordering his servants about, obviously getting the house ready for an important event, and consequently he gave his guest scant attention. Eventually he was able to free himself from his duties and sat down to talk with his old friend. Naturally Anāthapiṇḍada asked what was going on. Was he getting married (it seems that he wasn't monogamous), or preparing for a great sacrifice? Or had he invited King Bimbisāra and his court for a meal? No, his brother-in-law told him, it was none of these things. He'd actually invited the Buddha and his disciples for a meal the following day.

Just the sound of the word "Buddha" electrified Anāthapiṇḍada. "What? Did you say the Buddha?"

"Yes, I said the Buddha."

Anāthapiṇḍada was so amazed that he asked again – "What? Did you say the Buddha?"

Once again his friend replied, "Yes, I said the Buddha."

And a third time, "What? Did you say the Buddha?"

"Yes, I said the Buddha."

"It's hard indeed to find in the world even the sound of the word 'Buddha'. Is it possible for me to meet him now, at this very moment?"

"No, but you can meet him tomorrow morning, when he comes here."

Anāthapiṇḍada woke three times in the night thinking it must be morning, but each time was disappointed when he realized it was still night-time. The third time he woke he'd had enough of waiting and decided to get up and go to find the Buddha. He knew that the Buddha was staying outside the city walls in a place called the Cool Grove, and this meant that he'd have to go through the city gates and beyond, a dangerous undertaking at night. Out in the wilderness, in the dark, he was overcome by fear and nearly turned back. He faced his fear though and continued on, and at dawn he found the Cool Grove. There was the Buddha, slowly walking back and forth, no doubt reflecting on something. When he saw Anāthapiṇḍada he stopped walking, sat down, and called to him: "Come, Sudatta." Delighted that the Buddha called him by his name, Anāthapiṇḍada approached and prostrated himself at the Buddha's feet. The Buddha then taught him the Dharma, and in a little time Anāthapiṇḍada gained deep insight. He then asked the Buddha to accept him as a lay disciple, which the Buddha did.[20]

This story illustrates two of the most important themes of this and the two other sutras we're exploring: faith and the potentiality of the name of the Buddha. As soon as Anāthapiṇḍada hears the word "Buddha" – apparently for the first time – a tremendous faith arises in him. He wants to meet him immediately and cannot wait until the morning. His faith is strong enough to wake him in the night and compel him to face his fear by going outside the city walls in search of him. I wonder why he had such a strong response to simply hearing the word "Buddha". Of course he would have known what the word meant – "Awakened One" – and this may have been what so excited him. I remember watching a TV documentary about the novelist Lawrence Durrell when I was seventeen or eighteen years old. In an interview he said something to the effect that "most people are asleep". He didn't mean asleep in the literal sense; he meant that, even though they might be literally awake, metaphorically they are asleep. This statement had quite a strong effect on me – nothing like the effect that the word "Buddha" had on Anāthapiṇḍada, but still, an effect. I remember being puzzled by it – in what way were most people asleep? – but I also remember feeling that he'd said something very important, and that I wanted to understand it. If I was asleep I wanted to know what it was like to be awake. I wanted to wake up.

As we explore these sutras we'll discover that the name of the Buddha – not the historical Buddha, but one called Amitāyus or Amitābha – is very important indeed. Hearing his name, bearing it in mind, saying it repeatedly, meditating on it, is a central practice in these texts and has – according to the sutra – profound effects. It is, in fact, a way of gaining insight, a way of waking up.

When the Buddha sees Anāthapiṇḍada approaching him in the Cool Grove he calls him by his name, Sudatta. There are two puzzles here: how did he know his name, and why did he use his given name rather than his nickname? Well, we don't know, but the Buddha calling him by his "real" name suggests to me that he really saw him, recognized him for who he really was. There's a nice symmetry here. Just as Anāthapiṇḍada "recognized" the Buddha by hearing his name, the Buddha recognizes Anāthapiṇḍada by knowing, and saying, his name, Sudatta. The relationship we have with the Buddha – if we have a relationship at all – is often experienced as one-sided. We "know" the Buddha through his teachings, through paintings and statues, perhaps through visualizing him, but does he know us? Does he, can he, have a relationship with us? The idea that I mentioned above, about receiving teachings from a visualized buddha, suggests that our relationship with him may not have to be one-sided. Perhaps the Buddha – whoever or whatever you consider him to be – is able to "see" us, to know us, and to give us appropriate teachings. In saying this I don't mean to suggest that there really is a buddha "out there" literally giving us teachings, nor do I mean that the visualized buddha is merely a figment of our imagination. What I mean I'll explain in the next chapter.

Let's return now to the sutra. After the introduction the Buddha rather abruptly turns to Śāriputra – one of his two chief disciples – and says:

> To the west, Śāriputra, there is a buddha-field, a world system, named Sukhāvatī which lies beyond countless hundreds of thousands of other buddha-fields. At the present time, a tathāgata, an arhat, a perfectly awakened buddha named Amitāyus dwells there, teaching the Dharma. Why do you think, Śāriputra, that world system is called "Sukhāvatī", the "Realm of Happiness"? In that world system, Śāriputra, in Sukhāvatī, living beings experience no physical or mental suffering, and there are endless causes of happiness. This is why that world system is called "Sukhāvatī", the "Realm of Happiness".

This is our first introduction to Sukhāvatī and Amitāyus, and, before the Buddha goes into any more detail, already there are three key ideas that need a little explanation. Firstly, buddha-fields. A buddha-field is a world system in which a buddha lives and teaches. "Field" here has a metaphorical meaning, as when we speak of the field of economics, or an electric field. A buddha-field is the area in which a buddha has an influence. This is, according to Mahāyāna doctrine, a massive area – not just a land or world, but a world system, something like a galaxy. So, given how large buddha-fields are, "beyond countless hundreds of thousands of other buddha-fields" is a very, very long way away. Not all worlds have buddhas residing in them, but of those that do there are two kinds: pure and impure. A pure buddha-field is one in which there is no suffering, mental or physical. Sukhāvatī, as we've seen, is a pure buddha-field. An impure buddha-field is one in which the inhabitants suffer in various ways. We live in an impure buddha-field, clearly.

The second key idea in the Buddha's statement is that Amitāyus' buddha-field is called Sukhāvatī, which is translated here as the "Realm of Happiness". The Buddha said on a number of occasions that he taught for one reason only, to alleviate suffering – *dukkha*. A more positive way of putting this would be to say that he taught to help us to cultivate happiness – *sukha*. Sukha has a very wide range of meaning. It means any kind of pleasure, physical or mental; it means worldly happiness, it means spiritual happiness, and it means the happiness of Awakening. Before he eventually reached Awakening – Buddhahood – Śākyamuni tried a number of spiritual practices current in India. Some of these were extreme ascetic practices, such as fasting to the point of starvation, sleeping out of doors in the winter and staying in direct sunlight in the hot season, standing or squatting continuously, and sleeping on a bed of spikes. He practised these for six years, almost starving himself to death in the process, but eventually he came to the conclusion that they weren't helping him in his quest for Awakening. He gave them up and began to ponder what he should do next. He remembered a time when he was still a boy, sitting under a rose-apple tree, watching his father till a field. He was apparently in one of those states so familiar to children – a simple, innocent delight in being alive. Reflecting on this childhood experience, he intuited that it was somehow significant in his quest for Awakening. Suffering didn't take him any closer to Awakening – perhaps happiness would. The rest, as they say, is history. He began to eat properly, regained his health, began to meditate once again, experiencing the happiness and pleasure of the dhyānas – absorbed meditative states – and in a little time attained his goal: Awakening.

Pleasure and happiness, the Buddha realized, were important elements in the leading of the spiritual life. Without them our spiritual life will wither and die. Not all pleasure – or happiness – is good for us in the long term though. Here's the Buddha, from a text called the *Sutta Nipāta*:

> *If one, longing for sensual pleasure, achieves it,*
> *yes, he's enraptured at heart. The mortal gets what he wants.*
> *But if for that person – longing, desiring – the pleasures diminish,*
> *he's shattered, as if shot with an arrow.*[21]

Pursuing sensual pleasures sometimes works in the short term, but those pleasures can so easily turn to pain, as I'm sure you know from bitter experience. In another text, the well-known *Dhammapada*, the Buddha says this:

> If by renouncing a limited happiness [or pleasure – *sukha*] one would see an abundant happiness, let the spiritually mature person, having regard to the abundant happiness, sacrifice the limited happiness.[22]

You could say that the whole of the Buddha's teaching is a means to help us move from a limited to an abundant happiness. In another text he distinguished twelve levels of happiness – from the most limited to the most abundant.[23] There are three principal levels, and each of these is divided into four – let's call them sublevels. The principal levels are worldly, unworldly, and still greater unworldly happiness. The four sublevels are joy, happiness, equanimity, and freedom.

Worldly happiness is the happiness and pleasure we derive from our physical senses: sight, sound, smell, taste, and touch. The first level of worldly happiness is *pīti* – joy, delight, zest, exuberance. It's a kind of excited happiness, the kind you might feel when you're in love, or when you've just acquired something you've been longing for, or when you've unexpectedly come into some money. The second level is *sukha* – here meaning a deeper, more lasting happiness. It may be the kind of quiet happiness that occurs when the feeling of being in love calms down to a more mature feeling of companionship, or when you feel the satisfaction of a job well done, or experience the contentment of walking in the countryside on a beautiful day. The third level is *upekkha* – equanimity; a deep sense of ease, an unshakeable serenity. You may have met someone who possesses this level of happiness. Nothing seems to shake them, nothing seems to get them down. It's as if they are being nourished from some subterranean spring deep inside them. The fourth level of worldly happiness is freedom – *vimutti* – a kind of sitting loose to worldly happiness and pleasure. You enjoy it when it comes your way but you aren't bothered when you lose it. When we have that attitude to pleasure we enjoy it all the more if and when it comes. At this level the happiness we feel comes from the fact that we're not attached to it. We don't mind whether or not we experience pleasure, whether or not we have possessions, whether or not we are successful. Not that we don't care, but we don't mind.

The second principal level is unworldly happiness. This is the happiness and pleasure experienced through meditative absorption – dhyāna. It's "unworldly" because it's not dependent on the five physical senses. It's the happiness of the mind. The first level of unworldly happiness – joy – is experienced in the first and second dhyānas. The first dhyāna is in fact a state of sustained, absorbed joy and pleasure. You're so absorbed in the experience that there's hardly any thinking involved. We can have this experience outside meditation of course, especially when we're doing something that we enjoy: reading a good book, listening to music, dancing, gardening, having a really good conversation, playing football, or whatever. It doesn't always occur, but sometimes we become so absorbed in the activity that everything else – the past, the future – drops away and we're suddenly totally present. And that is very enjoyable. The second dhyāna is an intensification of that experience. Now you're so concentrated that thoughts disappear altogether. You're just left with quiet, still, serene, pure joyfulness. With the second level of unworldly happiness we enter the third dhyāna, which is an even stiller, quieter, more serene, and pure happiness than that experienced in the previous dhyānas. The third level of unworldly happiness is reached in the fourth dhyāna, where happiness becomes equanimity. This is a state of profound and complete contentment, deeply satisfying, in which you're poised in utter stillness.

These experiences are known as the four dhyānas of the world of form. The next level of unworldly happiness – freedom – occurs in the four dhyānas of the formless world. These are very sublime mental states, quite out of my experience, so I'm unable to say very much about them. I'll simply mention their names, which are wonderfully evocative:

the sphere of infinite space, the sphere of infinite consciousness, the sphere of no-thingness, and the sphere of neither perception-nor-non-perception.

The third principal level – still greater unworldly happiness – is the happiness that comes with insight into the Dharma – Awakening. The joy, happiness, equanimity, and freedom experienced at this level all arise when the practitioner reflects on the fact that he or she is no longer bound by greed, hatred, and delusion.

The way to ascend these levels of happiness is to renounce or let go of the relatively limited happiness we might currently possess: giving up the happiness of the five senses for the happiness of meditation; giving up the happiness of meditation for the still greater happiness of wisdom; letting go of an excited kind of joy to move into a deeper, more settled happiness; letting go of that to move into an even deeper and wider equanimity; and finally giving even that up for the happiness of complete freedom. William Blake's poem "Eternity" describes this very well:

He who binds to himself a joy
Does the wingèd life destroy;
But he who kisses the joy as it flies
Lives in eternity's sunrise.[24]

To live in Sukhāvatī is to live in eternity's sunrise – a place of pure happiness with no attachment, no binding oneself to it. The happiness of meditation and of wisdom. It's true that the happiness of Sukhāvatī is described in material terms, as we'll soon see – jewel trees, lotus ponds, and tinkling bells – but we should bear in mind that the sutra is not a doctrinal exposition but a work of the imagination. The material pleasures described symbolize spiritual and transcendental happiness.

The third key idea in the Buddha's opening statement is that the name of the buddha who lives in Sukhāvatī is Amitāyus, or Amitābha. "Amita" means "measureless, boundless, infinite"; "āyus" means "life", and "ābha" means "light". So he's "Measureless Life" or "Measureless Light". Boundless time and boundless space. Eternity and infinity. He is what's called a celestial, transcendental, or mythical buddha, which means that he's not perceivable by the five physical senses, but is perceived by the sixth sense, the mind. Yes, in Buddhism there are six senses. Just as the eye, for instance, perceives objects that can be seen, so the mind perceives objects that can be thought or imagined. To say that Amitāyus is perceived by the mind sense doesn't mean that he is just a figment of the imagination though. This raises some questions. What is the mind? And what does it mean to imagine? We'll be exploring these questions in the following chapters.

However, there is another, more practical question you might ask: why do we need a celestial buddha at all when we already have a "real" – human – buddha? After all, Śākyamuni is the buddha of our buddha-field. Why do we need another buddha? One possible reason is that the Buddhists who lived after Śākyamuni missed him. In a sense they had only two of the Three Jewels – the Dharma and the Sangha. They wanted the Buddha Jewel too. Of course they could talk about him, think about him, perhaps read about him, but they wanted to have a relationship with him, and they wanted to feel that he had a relationship with them. They wanted to have the kind of relationship with the Buddha that Anāthapiṇḍada had with him. So they meditated on him. They practised a meditation called *buddhānussati* – reflection or recollection of the Buddha. This was a practice recommended and taught by the Buddha himself, in which the meditator reflects on a list of the Buddha's qualities. Later this became a visualization practice, the Buddha's qualities being expressed in his physical appearance. No doubt after a while those who practised *buddhānussati* began to see the Buddha in a very vivid way, so life-like that they "saw" him just as if they could see him standing before them with their physical eyes. Now meditation, like artistic expression, tends to have a life of its own. We might start out by trying to visualize the Buddha as we imagine him to be with our conscious mind, or we might try to visualize a painting or statue that we like, but if we become absorbed in this practice he may suddenly appear to us in a startlingly different form, a form that we've never seen or imagined before, as if he were a real being who has "come" to us of his own volition. This may be how celestial or mythical buddhas such as Amitāyus came about, through practitioners' experience of the Buddha in meditation.

Let's return to the sutra. After this opening statement the Buddha goes on to describe Sukhāvatī. It's enclosed on all sides, he says, with seven railings and seven rows of palm trees, with nets of small bells hanging from them. Everything is made of seven precious substances: gold, silver, lapis lazuli, quartz, ruby, emerald, and coral. There are lotus ponds everywhere, brimming with cool, clear, sweet water and lined with golden sand. Each pond is surrounded by jewel trees made of the seven precious substances. The lotuses that grow there are preternaturally large – "as big as cartwheels" – and are of four different colours: blue, yellow, red, and white. The ground is golden and showers of heavenly flowers rain down three times during the day and three times in the night.

You may be wondering what the meaning and purpose of this description might be. Although the sutra seems to be describing an objectively existing world, actually it is describing a meditation practice. The scholar and translator Paul Harrison puts it very well when he writes that these texts shouldn't be understood

> as descriptions of something already existing, but as blueprints for something which is to be constructed in the mind ... as a template for visualization. ... Thus texts like this are not to be read, in our usual modern fashion, but performed ... in this light it might be better if we saw them as more like the scripts for plays, or scores for pieces of music.[25]

These are apt metaphors because they suggest practice or rehearsal. An actor wouldn't just read the lines of a part she was rehearsing, but would speak them aloud, trying out different ways of saying them, entering into the part she was going to play. And a musician would play the music on the page over and over, interpreting it in different ways, trying to get as close to the feeling of the music as he could. In a similar way a practitioner of this sutra would imagine the various objects described, practising, rehearsing, seeing, hearing, feeling them again and again. Harrison uses the term "visualization" but, although sight is the predominant sense employed in the practice, others are used too, so I prefer to use the word "imagination". Even this word is not ideal, deriving as it does from the visual sense – image-ination – and if I could I'd use a word that incorporates all of the senses – "sensorialize" perhaps – but such a word doesn't seem to exist in English.

The visualization of Sukhāvatī may have developed from a set of meditation practices taught by the Buddha, called the ten *kasiṇa*s. It's possible in fact that the author – or authors – of the sutra belonged to a community that specialized in these. The first four *kasiṇa*s are the elements earth, water, fire, and air; then there is a second set of four, which are the colours blue, yellow, red, and white; the last two are space and consciousness (or, alternatively, light).[26] The purpose of *kasiṇa* meditation is to concentrate the mind and so enter the meditative absorptions (dhyānas) or, in other words, to experience the second principal level of happiness – unworldly happiness. This process occurs in three stages. Firstly one simply looks at the *kasiṇa* and tries to concentrate one's mind on it. This is known as the preparatory image (*parikamma-nimitta*). After a while one "sees" the *kasiṇa* in the mind's eye; this is the acquired image (*uggaha-nimitta*). At this stage the image is unstable and unclear, but with continued practice it becomes as vivid and steady as the physical object itself, and this is the stage of the counterpart image (*paṭibhāga-nimitta*). With the appearance of the counterpart image one enters neighbourhood or access concentration (*upacāra-samādhi*), so called because it is in the neighbourhood of, and gives access to, the dhyānas.

Of particular interest here are the four colour *kasiṇa*s, which are the same colours as the lotuses in Sukhāvatī and listed in the same order: dark blue, yellow, red, and white. They are described in the following way:

> One sees external forms that are dark blue in colour, dark blue in appearance, of dark blue hue. Just as a flax flower which is dark blue in colour, dark blue in appearance, of dark blue hue, or a Benares cloth smoothed on both sides that is dark blue in colour, dark blue in appearance, of dark blue hue.[27]

The other three colours are described in the same way, except that a different flower is mentioned for each one. The word "blue" is mentioned nine times in this short passage, and when meditating on the *kasiṇa* one is advised to repeat the name of the colour in this way to evoke it more fully in the mind. In the *Shorter Sukhāvatīvyūhaḥ Sūtra* the lotuses are described in almost exactly the same way as are the colour *kasiṇas*:

> Dark blue lotuses grow in these lotus ponds, lotuses dark blue in colour, of dark blue hue, dark blue in appearance. Yellow lotuses grow there, yellow in colour, of yellow hue, yellow in appearance. Red lotuses grow there, red in colour, of red hue, red in appearance. Pure white lotuses grow there, pure white in colour, of pure white hue, pure white in appearance. Many-coloured lotuses grow there, of many colours, of many hues, many-coloured in appearance.

According to the fifth-century Theravada commentator Buddhaghosa, meditating on the colours blue, yellow, and red brings one to the "liberation through the beautiful". This is not the transcendental liberation of Awakening but the experience of dhyāna, which is a temporary release from all that is ugly. Meditating on the colour white apparently results in seeing visible objects with the "divine eye", that is, in the way that a heavenly being (deva) sees.[28] In the Introduction I mentioned two other kinds of eye: the "fleshy" eye, which apprehends physical objects, and the Dhamma eye, which sees the truth of things, for instance that they are impermanent. The divine eye holds a position somewhere between these, as it were. Traditionally it is represented as clairvoyance, and specifically the capacity to see how beings are born as a consequence of their previous actions, that is, in accordance with the law of karma. I'll explain the law of karma in the next chapter but, in this context – seeing visible objects with the divine eye – it seems to represent the awakened imagination. This means that there is a connection between the divine eye and "a mind that is prepared (to see things as they are)". We could perhaps say then that, when the Buddha gave a graduated discourse, he guided his interlocutor from the physical through the divine, to the Dhamma. The three eyes also have a connection with the three principal levels of happiness: those beings who experience only worldly happiness see solely with the physical eye, those who dwell in unworldly happiness see with the physical eye and the divine eye, and those who live in still greater unworldly happiness see with all three eyes.

Of course there is an obvious difference between the *kasiṇa*s and the objects of Sukhāvatī: the *kasiṇa*s are all found in the physical world, whereas the objects in Sukhāvatī are imaginary. Not completely imaginary though – they are recognizable objects from the physical world, but transfigured by the imagination: trees, but made of jewels; lotuses, but the size of cartwheels; and earth that is gold. This is what tends to happen to the counterpart image when the meditator passes from access concentration into dhyāna – it becomes more than simply a very realistic representation of something from the physical world, and is imbued with an archetypal beauty, free of the constraints of the physical.

Buddhaghosa writes:

> The difference between the earlier acquired image and the counterpart image is this. In the acquired image any fault in the kasiṇa is apparent. But the counterpart image appears as if breaking out from the acquired image, and a hundred times, a thousand times more purified, like a looking-glass disc drawn from its case, like a mother-of-pearl dish well washed, like the moon's disk coming out from behind a cloud, like cranes against a thunder cloud.[29]

I know that some people don't like the imagery of Sukhāvatī. They prefer their landscapes to be natural: they like trees to be made of wood, with gnarled brown bark and green leaves (or yellow, red, or brown, depending on the season). They like the ground to be made of earth and rock. If there are to be lotuses they should be of natural size, and the ponds should be lined with mud, not gold. This is to miss the point, though. Sukhāvatī is not an alternative physical world but an imaginal realm in which the objects of the physical world are transformed by the experience of dhyāna.

Psychology and cosmology are closely connected in the Buddhist understanding of existence, as the idea of the divine eye suggests. Our inner worlds reflect our outer worlds and vice versa. Baudelaire wrote "There is no landscape independent of the mind" and we could add that there are no mind states independent of landscape. For instance, according to Buddhist cosmology there are six realms of existence: the human realm, the realm of the gods or heavenly beings, the realm of the jealous gods or titans, the realm of hungry ghosts, the hell realm, and the realm of animals. (Impure buddha-fields include all six of these realms, the latter four of which are realms in which suffering predominates. Pure buddha-fields only include the human and god realms.) Traditionally, Buddhism considers each of these to be objectively existing "worlds" or places. Animals and humans share the same world, of course, but the beings in the other realms live in different "places", or perhaps a better way of saying this is that they live on different levels or planes of existence. To take just one example, gods live in more refined, pleasurable, and beautiful worlds than the one we live in. Because they live on different levels of existence to ours, we are unable to perceive them most of the time, although there are exceptions to this, as we'll see.

The traditional word for a realm of existence is *gati*, which literally means "going". What this signifies is a rebirth – a going to another birth after death. Buddhism teaches that we are reborn into a realm that suits the kind of mental states we most commonly occupy in our present life. So our next life will be a kind of objectification of our inner world in this life. If we live like an animal now, we'll be reborn as one in our next life – we'll go to the animal realm. Conversely, if we live like a god in this life, we'll be reborn as a god. This is not a kind of cosmic system of punishment and reward, it's simply the natural result of the direction we've been taking in this life, carried through to the next. If you live like an animal now, you must want to live like that, so why not become an animal? What does it mean to live like a god in this, human, life? We live like gods when we regularly experience the kind of states of mind that gods experience all the time: that is, joyful, inspired, loving, appreciative, undistracted, absorbed. And how do we regularly experience those states of mind? Through pure ethical practice and meditation. Absorbed meditative states are the inner correlative of god realms, and god realms are the objective expression of absorbed meditative states of mind.

So, although the six realms of existence are considered to be really existing objective worlds, they also symbolize mental states that we can occupy at any given time. We've already seen what it means to inhabit the mental states of gods. Let's now briefly explore the other realms as subjective experience. The jealous gods or titans want what the gods possess but aren't willing to do the necessary work to get it – that work being the practice of ethics, generosity, and meditation. Instead they want to forcibly take it from them by any means. They are embodiments of jealousy, anger, aggression, self-justification, and a sense of entitlement: gods of power, we could say, rather than of love. We can see this mental state manifested also in the human realm – in gangsters, unscrupulous businessmen and bankers, many politicians, and conmen. The character of Tony Soprano in the TV series *The Sopranos* is a very good example of a titan. We too can be occasional titans on a small scale, when, for example, we feel jealous of another's achievements or possessions, when we are domineering in a relationship, or when we are tempted to try to get something at the cost of another's well-being.

The realm of the hungry ghosts is a desolate wasteland and the beings who live there are emaciated except for their stomachs, which are bloated but empty. They continually try to satisfy their extreme craving for food and drink, but their stomachs are so big and their mouths so tiny, they can never get enough. What morsels they do manage to swallow turn to fire in their stomachs. It's a graphic picture of insatiable craving. In the human realm this state is embodied in addiction of every kind – drugs, alcohol, pornography, shopping, you name it. We all experience desire, of course, but the craving embodied by the hungry ghosts is the kind that can't be satisfied, no matter how much is ingested. It's a kind of inner emptiness that can't be filled by anything in the world. "I can't get no ... satisfaction", as Mick Jagger sang. That kind of craving can only be satisfied by going beyond craving – by waking up and gaining Enlightenment.

The hell realm is, obviously, a realm of intense suffering. We've all been there. As Milton has Satan say in *Paradise Lost*: "The mind is its own place, and in itself can make a Heaven of Hell, a Hell of Heaven."[30] Beings are reborn there as a result of extremely unskilful (unethical) behaviour. Like the god realms, there are many levels of hell, many different forms of suffering. In our human world too there are many hells, many of them the result of our unskilful actions, but there are also hells that are visited on us through the unethical behaviour of others: the betrayal of a friend, our partner cheating on us, a conman swindling us of everything we've worked for. There are also the hells of natural disasters – earthquakes, tsunamis, hurricanes, droughts, and famines. And there is the hell of war. To be born into some countries, torn apart by civil war, is to be born into a kind of hell – a hell on earth, as the saying goes. There are also the hells of mental illnesses. There are so many ways to suffer in our impure buddha-field, so many pitfalls and traps, some of which we bring upon ourselves, but many of which occur simply because we've been born into a world where such things happen. Once you fall into a hellish state it can be very hard to get out, and it's very hard to practise the Dharma there because you're likely to be overwhelmed by the suffering.

You may be surprised to learn that the animal realm is, like the others we've just considered, predominantly a realm of suffering, in this case the suffering of a very limited awareness. Animals seem to possess only sense consciousness – they are aware of the world around them but are not self-aware; they are unable to reflect on themselves and their situation. This limitation of consciousness is in itself a kind of suffering – the suffering of very limited horizons. People who embody animal consciousness are only aware of and interested in basic sense pleasure and comfort – food, drink, reproduction. If you're an animal lover you may reject this characterization because some animals, as we know, can be very affectionate, intelligent, and loyal. Animals aren't merely dumb brutes – not all of them anyway. But when we say that a human being "lives like an animal" we mean that they're brutish and perhaps barbaric. We mean that they've turned away from the very thing that makes them human.

And what makes a human being human is self-awareness – the awareness of awareness. With self-awareness we aren't just aware of, say, a bowl of cereal in front of us; we are also aware that we are aware of that bowl of cereal. It's as if awareness has bent back onto itself, is aware of itself, and for this reason it's also called reflexive awareness. This is important because it allows us to reflect on our experience, to ask questions of ourselves, giving us the possibility of changing our habitual reactions. Buddhist practices such as mindfulness and meditation are designed to help us develop this more reflective awareness. Another important aspect of the human realm is that it includes both pain and pleasure, suffering and happiness. This is significant because, if there were only unmitigated suffering, we'd probably be overwhelmed by it, or completely demoralized, which would tend to sap any motivation we might have to practise the Dharma. And if we experienced only pleasure there wouldn't be motivation enough to make the effort to wake up.

Now you might think that last sentence contradicts what I wrote earlier about the importance the Buddha gave to happiness and pleasure. You may have thought then that I was saying the Buddha advocated a life of unalloyed pleasure. But he wasn't a hedonist. Pleasure and happiness are important, but not everything. More important is understanding, insight, wisdom. One of the dangers of pleasure is that it can become so intoxicating that we forget about trying to gain wisdom. Fortunately or unfortunately, the human realm doesn't allow us to indulge in pleasure for very long. Sooner or later we will experience the shock of pain or suffering – a disappointment, toothache, a betrayal, getting stuck in a traffic jam, a misunderstanding with a friend, loneliness, a financial downturn, illness, the death of a loved one – which may wake us from our complacency.

We tend to think that the inner and the outer – the mind and the world – are two very different categories, each in its own realm, each more or less impervious to the other. But perhaps they're not. It seems that there are people who perceive the objective realm that corresponds to their mental state. If, for instance, they experience a god-like state of mind in meditation, they might see gods. This seems to have been very common in the days of the Buddha, and perhaps this is because in the India of that time people didn't make a hard and fast distinction between the mind and the world in the way that we tend to. To them, for something to exist didn't necessarily mean material existence. The Buddha regularly perceived gods and other non-human beings, and often taught them the Dharma; one of his epithets was "the teacher of gods and human beings". This can be problematic for some contemporary Western Buddhists, especially those who like to think that the Buddha was a rational philosopher, and who advocate "secular" Buddhism. Of course it's possible to be a rational philosopher and perceive non-human beings, but these days the word "rational" is wedded to the idea that evidence is only admissible if it can be perceived with one or more of the five physical senses. The Buddha was very rational but he wasn't a rational*ist*. That is, although he had a great respect for reason, he also considered it to be limited, not adequate, on its own, to enable us to perceive the world as it is. For that we need another faculty, which we'll explore in the following chapter.

I've said that gods experience joyful, inspired, loving, appreciative, undistracted, absorbed states of mind all the time. How do such beings see their surroundings? As beautiful. They see beauty everywhere. A beautiful mind lives in a beautiful world. What to me may look like an unremarkable tree, with a brown trunk and dull green leaves under a grey sky, may look to a god like a luminous, wondrous thing of beauty, shimmering in light. Wendell Berry seems to be looking with the eyes of a god in his poem "Grace", the first four lines of which are:

The Wood is shining this morning.
Red. Gold and green. The leaves
Lie on the ground, or fall,
Or hang full of light in the air still.[31]

I remember watching a documentary about the painter David Hockney, who had recently returned to the UK after spending many years living in California. The documentary showed him painting a country lane somewhere near his home town of Bradford. He returned to the same spot over a number of months, painting the lane in different weathers and seasons. At one point he pointed to the sky and guessed that most people would see it as grey (which I did). He then asked the viewer to look more closely and see that it was not simply grey; it had tints of pink, or blue, or purple, depending on factors such as the time of day. And it was true. The sky was not uniformly grey. For a moment I entered Hockney's world: a world of colour – and beauty.[32] This is why, I think, the Buddha describes Sukhāvatī in the sutra: he is describing the world in which a god lives, or the way a god sees the world. Same world, different mind. The realms of existence are perhaps only different worlds to the extent that we perceive the world differently. By describing Sukhāvatī the Buddha is evoking a god-like state of mind, and if we are receptive to it we can enter into that state of mind and perceive the world as a god perceives it.

This implies that we don't merely perceive the world in which we live but that we create it. Even more radically, we could say that perception is not a passive receiving of objective information through the five physical senses but an imaginative creation of the world. When we are in the grip of intense craving, for instance, we don't just enter the world of the hungry ghosts, we create it. We thus live in two dimensions simultaneously – the inner subjective dimension (the mind) and the outer objective dimension (the world) – and they influence one another. For instance, seeing a very attractive person might bring about sexual craving and, conversely, being in a state of sexual craving will probably cause you to see sexy people everywhere you go – people who, when you were in a more contented state the day before, you hadn't noticed. You've created a world of sexy people! By making an effort to notice and appreciate the beauty around us we are creating a world of beauty, a world of the gods.

As I've mentioned before, though, Sukhāvatī is more than just a god realm. This is illustrated by the next section of the sutra, where the Buddha tells Śāriputra that in Sukhāvatī three kinds of birds exist: *haṃsa* geese (mythical birds) as well as curlews and peacocks

> fly down and sing together in harmony, each one with their own unique voice. When they sing, their voices proclaim the five spiritual faculties, the five spiritual powers, and the seven factors of Awakening. When they hear the song of the peacocks, the minds of the living beings who dwell there become absorbed by the Buddha, absorbed by the Dharma, absorbed by the Sangha.

Sukhāvatī possesses all the features of a god realm – light, beauty, pleasure, happiness – but it's also a Buddha realm, or a Dharma realm, or an Awakening realm. It's interesting that the Dharma is only heard; there are no texts or inscriptions in Sukhāvatī. This may reflect the fact that, for the few hundred years previous to this sutra, Buddhism had been an oral tradition, and it was probably largely still so. It's true that the sutras we're exploring were written down, but that would have been a relatively recent development and it's likely that few people in India were able to read at that time. Most people would have heard the sutras, probably in a ritual context, rather than read them. But birds teaching the Dharma? This may seem bizarre, childish, like something from a Disney film. And if you're an attentive reader you may have noticed an apparent contradiction. If the animal realm doesn't exist in pure buddha-fields, what are birds doing there? Well, the Buddha pre-empts that question and tells Śāriputra that they are not real birds but magical apparitions. Even more Disney-esque! How can we take this seriously? It's probably obvious to you by now that I don't take the imagery of Sukhāvatī literally, but in that case what might magical birds teaching the Dharma mean? What truth might they be pointing to?

I wonder whether you've ever been walking in the countryside, or on a meditation retreat, and suddenly found yourself in an unusual and rather lovely state of mind? A state in which you feel so alive, so aware, so sensitive, that you seem to be in communion with everything around you. The trees, grasses, shrubs, flowers, earth, rocks, stones, sky, clouds, birds, animals, insects are no longer separate from you. You feel yourself to be part of the life around you rather than a bystander looking on, as if through a window. There is a kind of significance to everything – nothing is without value. Even the fly that comes to rest on the back of your hand – an insect that usually slightly disgusts you – has, now that you look closely at it, very beautiful eyes. Similarly, you look at the slug and the earthworm as if for the first time, and you realize that their lives are as valuable to them as yours is to you. Nothing is any more important than anything else. Everything around you is as alive, as significant, as you are. You may feel that significance pressing in on you, as if the world was trying to tell you something, something that you kind of know already but haven't listened to intently enough to get the whole meaning. As the writer of the Zen poem *Zenrinkushu* puts it:

Nothing whatever is hidden;
From of old, all is clear as daylight.
An old pine tree preaches wisdom;
And a wild bird is crying out truth.[33]

Sukhāvatī symbolizes this state of mind: a state of utter receptivity to the world, a sensitivity to its life, an appreciation of the beauty and sheer is-ness of everything; the reality of everything. Every single thing is absolutely crystal clear and standing out in its uniqueness, yet at the same time inseparable from everything around it. If only we could see clearly, we'd see that reality. If we could hear, we'd hear it. It's not hidden, it's there right in front of us if only we'd open our eyes, if only we'd wake up.

So perhaps the birds in Sukhāvatī don't literally "teach" conceptual formulations of the Dharma such as the five spiritual faculties; perhaps they squawk or tweet or quack like any other birds, but the people there "hear" their songs as Dharma. When they hear those magical birds their minds "become absorbed by the Buddha, absorbed by the Dharma, absorbed by the Sangha". In this case the Buddha is Amitāyus, the Dharma is the Buddha's teaching, and the Sangha is the community of his disciples, specifically those who have awakened to some extent. Together they are known as the Three Jewels and to be a Buddhist is to go for refuge – to commit oneself – to them. Sukhāvatī is a world in which it's easy to go for refuge to the Buddha, Dharma, and Sangha. Everything there reminds you of the Three Jewels and encourages you to practise. This is a naive way of putting it, of course, as if Sukhāvatī were a magical land that casts a spell on those living there: "Abracadabra! From this day forth your mind will become absorbed by the Three Jewels, and practising the Dharma will be as easy as falling off a log." Actually it's easy for those who live there to go for refuge to the Three Jewels because they are the kind of people who find it easy to go for refuge to the Three Jewels, and Sukhāvatī is the world such people co-create. We could compare it to how a really good musician lives in a world of other musicians and composers, musical instruments, recording studios, concert halls, impresarios, and audiences – a musical world that is sustained by a shared love of music. An unmusical person wouldn't last long in such an environment, nor would they want to. Talking of music, the Buddha goes on to say:

> in that buddha-field, when the wind stirs the rows of palm trees and the nets of small bells which adorn them, they make a delightful sound which soothes the mind. Śariputra, the countless hundreds of thousands of divine musical instruments make a delightful sound which soothes the mind when they are played, and so too do the rows of palm trees and the nets of small bells when the wind stirs them. When the people there hear those sounds, they recollect the Buddha in their bodies, they recollect the Dharma in their bodies, they recollect the Sangha in their bodies.

Towards the beginning of this chapter I wrote about a meditation practice called *buddhānussati*, which consists in recollecting, remembering, or reflecting on – *anussati* – the Buddha's qualities. There are corresponding meditations for the Dharma and Sangha too – *dhammānussati* and *sanghānussati* – and their purpose is to help us go for refuge more deeply to the Three Jewels. On hearing the birds, the minds of living beings become absorbed in the Three Jewels, whereas on hearing the nets of bells they recollect the Three Jewels in their bodies. This suggests a deep pleasure in practising the Dharma, a sensual pleasure felt not only in the mind but also in the body, just as we feel when listening to beautiful music. This reminds me of something the Buddha said about the Dharma being "lovely in its beginning, lovely in its middle, and lovely in its ending".[34] Often in the early texts the hearer doesn't merely "understand" what the Buddha says in a conceptual sense; they are moved by it, and as a result they experience the world totally differently. Pleasure and beauty are inseparable from wisdom.

The idea of pure buddha-fields is a Mahāyāna one, but perhaps it has its origin in the early, Pali texts. There the Buddha taught that there are four stages of wisdom or insight: stream-entry, once-returning, non-returning, and full Awakening. A stream-entrant is assured of Awakening within the next seven lifetimes. A once-returner will awaken in this or the next life (they'll only return – be reborn – once at the most). The non-returner has such deep insight that he or she won't return to the human realm: if they don't achieve Awakening in this life they'll be reborn into one of the pure abodes and become awakened there. A fully awakened being is awakened in this life. (Incidentally, it's possible that the four levels of still greater unworldly happiness – joy, happiness, equanimity, and freedom – refer to these four stages of wisdom, although the Buddha didn't correlate them as far as I know.)

The interesting thing about this scheme, from the point of view of pure buddha-fields, is the stage of the non-returner and their birth into the pure abodes. What are they exactly? To answer this question I need to say a little more about ancient Indian cosmology, according to which there are three levels of existence, sometimes called the triple or threefold world: the world of desire, the world of form, and the formless world. The world of desire is the physical or material world. We live in this world, as do the animals, hungry ghosts, jealous gods, and hell beings. The next two levels make up the worlds of the gods. The world of form is the objectification of the first four dhyānas, and the gods who live there abide in one or another of those dhyānas. The levels of the formless world correspond to the four formless dhyānas. The pure abodes are situated at the highest levels of the world of form – subjectively, in the fourth dhyāna. The difference between the pure abodes and the other god realms is that the beings born into these realms have very deep insight into the Dharma. So deep is their insight that they won't be reborn again but will awaken fully there. Interestingly, it's possible to be born into the god realms of the formless world, which are technically higher than the pure abodes, without any insight. They are higher only in the sense of being more pleasurable, not in the sense of being more awakened. So the pure abodes are, as my teacher once said, "off to the side, as it were". They are, in a sense, specifically Buddhist realms, in that the beings born there have deep insight into the Dharma. The pure abodes then are something like a pure buddha-field.

Something like a pure buddha-field – but not exactly the same. The pure abodes may have been the inspiration, but pure buddha-fields are a development of the idea, not a replica. In the next section of the sutra, the Buddha tells Śāriputra what kinds of beings live in Sukhāvatī:

> That tathāgata has an immeasurably large sangha of śrāvakas who are pure arhats, whose numbers cannot easily be measured. ... Moreover, Śāriputra, the progress of those living beings who are born in the buddha-field of the Tathāgata Amitāyus as pure bodhisattvas will be irreversible, and they will only experience one more birth. The numbers of these bodhisattvas, Śāriputra, cannot easily be measured. It can only be said that there is an immeasurably large innumerable multitude of them.

There are then two kinds of being in Sukhāvatī: arhats – fully awakened beings – and bodhisattvas who are very close to full Awakening ("they will only experience one more birth"). This isn't as simple as it may seem. The kind of Awakening the bodhisattvas are close to is not the same kind of Awakening as the arhats have achieved. To understand this we have to go into a little Buddhist history. Let's start by going right back to the earliest days of Buddhism, when the Buddha was alive. He taught the Dharma, and as a result many people woke up. Some woke to the extent of becoming stream-entrants, others became once-returners, others non-returners, and some woke fully – they became arhats. They woke up to the same extent that the Buddha himself had woken up. At least that's what the Buddha said in the early suttas. Later, perhaps once the Buddha had died, his disciples began to feel that the Buddha's Awakening was qualitatively different from the Awakening of his disciples.

This idea of two different kinds of Awakening was connected to two ways of regarding the Buddha's achievement – human and cosmic. The first way is to see it as something that was achieved in one lifetime: Śākyamuni was born, he left home, took up the spiritual life, and in a few years awakened – he became the Buddha. The second way is to see his Enlightenment as the culmination of an unimaginably long period of practice over innumerable lifetimes. Although it appears to us that he managed to do this in just one life, in reality he had been practising for aeons, and only in his final lifetime did he wake up fully. Legend has it that an unimaginably long time ago he met a former buddha – Dīpaṃkara – and practised his teachings. He could have woken up in that very life and become an arhat, but instead he made a vow to practise for countless lifetimes, and in his final life to become a buddha in a world system in which, up until then, there had been no buddha. He would thus introduce that world to the Dharma. In all of those former lives he is known as a bodhisattva – an Awakening being – determined to gain the full Enlightenment of a buddha, not just for his own sake, but for the benefit of all beings. According to this legend, the Awakening of his disciples – the arhats – is not the same as the Buddha's. Or, more precisely, the motivation is different – the arhats' Awakening was for their own benefit, whereas the Buddha's was to enable everyone else to wake up. It's but a small step to then regard the Awakening experience itself to be different: the Buddha's Enlightenment was compassionate; the arhats' was selfish.

Mahāyāna sutras, such as the ones we're exploring in this book, expound the Great Way (Mahāyāna) leading to the Awakening of a buddha, out of compassion for all living beings. They invite us to eschew the opportunity to wake fully in this life and instead to emulate the Buddha and practise as a bodhisattva over many lifetimes, until we are eventually born in a world system in which there is no buddha. There we wake fully – become a buddha – and introduce the beings there to the Dharma. So, when the sutra says that the bodhisattvas in Sukhāvatī "will only experience one more birth", it's referring to their final birth, when they will become buddhas.

In the earliest Mahāyāna sutras there is no evidence of any antagonism between the followers of these two paths.[35] They are simply presented as two distinct goals that Buddhists can choose between – Awakening in this life as an arhat, or "putting off" your Awakening to become a buddha at a future time. Of course, being Mahāyāna texts, they have a bias towards the latter path and encourage people to follow it, but they don't disparage the arhat path. In the later Mahāyāna sutras there is some antagonism, even animosity, towards those following the arhat path. Reading those sutras can feel a bit like having a quiet chat to a friend when all of a sudden they start ranting about someone else, telling you what a bad person they are. Many of the later sutras use the pejorative term Hīnayāna to refer to those trying to become arhats: *hīna* means "small, mean, low, inferior". Happily, the sutras we're exploring in this book are quite early ones, which means that they are free of any antagonism towards those aiming to become arhats. Sukhāvatī is for all Buddhists, whether Mahāyāna or those following the arhat path. When the Buddha tells Śāriputra about the two kinds of living beings in Sukhāvatī he refers to the arhats as the "sangha of śrāvakas". "Śrāvaka" means "listener" or "hearer", meaning those who listen to the Buddha and are therefore his disciples. Some Mahāyāna sutras refer to the arhat path as the Śrāvakayāna – the Way of the Listener – and I'll use that word for the remainder of this book.

I'll conclude this discussion by saying that I don't believe there are two different kinds of Awakening. In the early Pali suttas the Buddha taught that anyone who follows his teaching can achieve what he achieved, can become as awakened as he was, and I don't see any reason to disagree with him. The idea of two kinds of Awakening arose from the Buddha's early disciples' devotion to him – they felt that he was special, that his Awakening was somehow different from that of those who followed after him – but in positing two kinds of Awakening they departed from his teaching.

Although the author of the sutra believes that there are these two kinds of Enlightenment, he or she also describes a scenario very much like that seen in the early, Pali suttas. There we have the Buddha surrounded by his disciples, simply listening to him and practising what he taught. In Sukhāvatī we see a very similar picture, albeit in an idealized world with a different buddha.

I began this chapter by describing Anāthapiṇḍada's first meeting with the Buddha but I didn't finish the story. The day after his meeting with the Buddha, Anāthapiṇḍada requested something of him. He asked him to spend the next rainy season at Sāvatthī, Anāthapiṇḍada's home town. The Buddha replied indirectly, saying that "tathāgatas delight in solitude" (tathāgata is another name for a buddha). Anāthapiṇḍada took the hint and on his return to Sāvatthī began looking for somewhere outside of the city where the Buddha and his disciples might stay – "easy of approach for folk who wish to see him; not too much frequented by day and free from noise and din at night; a place sheltered from the wind, remote from the haunts of men and suitable for solitude". He soon found the ideal place, a park owned by Prince Jeta. So he approached the prince and asked him to give him the park. The prince was unwilling to give his park away, joking that Anāthapiṇḍada would have to cover the whole park with gold if he wanted it. Anāthapiṇḍada took him at his word and had his servants take gold in carts and spread it across the park. All day they worked and by evening they had covered nearly the whole park. There was just one area still uncovered – a beautiful grove. Anāthapiṇḍada ordered his men to fetch more gold, but the prince had been watching this spectacle and was by now deeply impressed. He told Anāthapiṇḍada to stop his servants, saying, "Don't cover that space. Let it be my gift." And it's in this grove – thereafter called the Jeta Grove – that the Buddha and his followers are staying at the beginning of the sutra.

This may be another reason why the author of this sutra chose to locate it here. Anāthapiṇḍada's Park is the ideal location for the Buddha and his followers, the sangha. It's quiet, pleasant, and beautiful, but also allows the Buddha to keep in touch with people from the nearby villages and the city of Sāvatthī. He can "delight in solitude" but also teach the Dharma. Perfect! Anāthapiṇḍada's Park is a buddha-field, "field" here in the literal sense. Not a pure buddha-field, but about as close as we can get to one in this world.

The description of the Buddha and his assembly that starts this sutra, with the 1,250 monks (all of them arhats), the bodhisattvas, and the tens of thousands of gods, is a reflection or echo of the description of Amitāyus and the beings in Sukhāvatī, "an immeasurably large sangha of śrāvakas who are pure arhats, whose numbers cannot easily be measured" and "an immeasurably large innumerable multitude of [bodhisattvas]". Even the story of the covering of the park with gold can be seen as a reflection of the golden ground of Sukhāvatī.

And so we come to another interpretation of pure buddha-fields: they symbolize the best possible conditions in which to practise the Dharma. In Sukhāvatī everything helps and encourages those living there to practise. In fact, everything in Sukhāvatī is a symbol of practice and its results. The beautiful gardens, the trees, the lotus ponds symbolize the serenity and beauty of dhyāna (meditative absorption) and the songs of the birds and the nets of small bells symbolize the constant recollection of and reflection on the Dharma.

Our lives are full of the things we need to do to stay alive and be as happy as it's possible to be in this world of suffering: we work, we cook, we clean, we shop, we bring up our children, we save for a rainy day. We think, we plan, we fret, we calculate, we hope, we regret. And we are susceptible to craving, aversion, and ignorance, mental states that result in our getting trapped in the realms of the hungry ghosts, the jealous gods, the animals, and the hells. In the midst of all this we try to practise the Dharma. And it's hard. It's easy to forget. It's easy to leave practice for another time, to feel too tired, to go back to sleep, to feel demoralized. Sometimes we're in such a negative state that we can't even think about practising the Dharma. Living in an impure buddha-field is hard because the conditions for practice aren't the best. Often we practise despite the conditions we're in. That's good, but we probably can't do it all the time. So we need to try to find, or create, conditions that are conducive to practice and that inspire us. Going to a class at a local Buddhist centre, meditating with others, going on a retreat, meeting up with friends who are also trying to practise; all these activities are like small, pure buddha-fields in the midst of our impure buddha-field. They help. And we need all the help we can get, don't we?

Chapter Two

Embraced by all the buddhas

So far the Buddha has just been describing Sukhāvatī and its inhabitants. In the next part of the sutra the Buddha refers to people living in this – our – world:

> Living beings, Śāriputra, should cultivate a heartfelt desire for that buddha-field.

Heartfelt desire is quite a strong term, isn't it? The Buddha says that we should really want, really desire, to live in Sukhāvatī. Some people think that the Buddha taught that we shouldn't desire anything, but this is a misunderstanding. Certainly he warned us of the dangers of craving, but not all desiring is craving. The difference between the two is dependent partly on the object that you want and partly on the quality of the wanting. Simply put, craving is the kind of desire that leads (inevitably) to suffering. If you reflect on your own desires and what happened when you pursued them, you'll probably see that some of them caused you to suffer in the long run, while others didn't; some may have contributed to your overall happiness, in fact.

As we saw in Chapter 1, the Buddha said that desiring objects perceived by the five physical senses often causes suffering. (An object can also be a person. Of course they are a subject to themselves, but when we desire them we see them as an object.) The problem with sense objects is that they are *unreliable*. They sometimes give us what we want, but not always. Or they give us what we want at first, but are subject to the law of diminishing returns. Or they turn into something else, or turn against us, or break, or die, or get taken away from us.

So instead of desiring sense objects the Buddha recommended that we cultivate a desire for certain mental, emotional, or spiritual experiences – experiences of meditative absorption; positive emotions such as friendliness, kindness, joy in other people's happiness, compassion for their suffering; and, best of all, wisdom. These are all worth desiring because they give lasting, reliable happiness. There is an important distinction in the Pali language – the language of the ancient Buddhist texts – between *kāma chanda* and *Dhamma chanda*. *Chanda* is desire. *Kāma* is sense pleasure, or an object of sense pleasure (here we return to the idea that the inner subjective sphere – the mind – and the outer objective sphere – the world – are not separate). So *kāma chanda* is desire for sense pleasures. *Dhamma* is the Pali form of Dharma, the Buddha's teaching, or truth or reality. *Dhamma chanda* then is desire for the Buddha's teaching, or the results of practising the Buddha's teaching. This kind of desire is desirable!

The Buddha's reason for recommending that living beings cultivate a heartfelt desire for Sukhāvatī is interesting:

> Why should they do this? They should do this because, in that buddha-field, they will be in the company of good people such as these bodhisattvas.

We should desire to live in Sukhāvatī not because of the golden ground or the jewel trees, the lotus ponds, or the magical birds teaching the Dharma, or the palm trees with their nets of small bells that make such delightful music that the listeners recollect the Three Jewels in their bodies. No, the reason the Buddha gives – the only reason – for cultivating a heartfelt desire to be born in Sukhāvatī is to be in the company of the bodhisattvas who live there, so that we can enjoy spiritual community and spiritual friendship with them. We will also be in the company of śrāvakas of course, but this is a Mahāyāna text, and though it's not antagonistic towards the Śrāvakayāna, it's biased towards the bodhisattvas. Leaving that little bit of partisanship aside, the reason we should cultivate a desire to live in Sukhāvatī is so that we can enjoy spiritual community and spiritual friendship. This echoes something the Buddha said in one of the early Pali texts. One day his closest disciple – and friend – Ānanda said that he thought spiritual friendship was half of the spiritual life. The Buddha replied, "Don't say that Ānanda, don't say that. Spiritual friendship is the whole of the spiritual life."[36] That's pretty close to what the Buddha says here, isn't it? Towards the end of the previous chapter I said that pure buddha-fields symbolize the best possible conditions in which to practise the Dharma, and the single most important of those conditions is spiritual community or friendship. Pure buddha-fields symbolize sangha at its best. We'll explore this idea further in Chapter 6.

Let's look a little closer at the phrase "heartfelt desire". This is *praṇidhāna*, which is often translated as resolution, aspiration, determination, or vow. In the previous chapter I wrote about the cosmic view of the Buddha's achievement: how, an unimaginably long time ago, he made a vow before the Buddha Dīpaṃkara to become a Buddha. This is commonly known as the bodhisattva vow: *praṇidhāna*. Amitāyus – the buddha of Sukhāvatī – also made such a vow; he too resolved to practise over innumerable lifetimes as a bodhisattva, so that he could eventually become a buddha in a world system that knew nothing of the Dharma, teaching the living beings there, purifying that world system, and establishing Sukhāvatī. What's interesting is that the same word is used here, only the object of that heartfelt desire is to be born in Sukhāvatī. There's a neat symmetry here: Amitāyus made a vow or resolution to become a buddha and establish a pure buddha-field and now we need to make a vow or resolution to be born there. Heartfelt desire meets heartfelt desire. There is a difference, of course. Amitāyus' is a heartfelt desire of compassion, whereas ours is one of faith.

Heartfelt desire is a necessary, but not sufficient, condition for rebirth in Sukhāvatī though. Something else is needed:

> Śāriputra, living beings with only a few roots of virtue will not be born in the buddha-field of the Tathāgata Amitāyus.

"Roots of virtue" is a translation of *kuśalamūla, mūla* meaning "root" and *kuśala* meaning "good, wholesome, or virtuous". It also means "skilful", especially in an ethical sense. One word I haven't yet used – and it surprises me that I've got so far without mentioning it – is karma. Everyone has heard of it these days. I just had a look at karma on Wikipedia and found that there are sixteen recorded songs with karma in the title, including songs by John Lennon, Culture Club, Radiohead, Alicia Keys, and the Black Eyed Peas. What does it mean though? Literally it means action, specifically action with an ethical dimension. Just moving a book from the left-hand side of your desk to the right, for instance, doesn't constitute an action in this sense because it's ethically inconsequential. Every action (with an ethical dimension) has an effect. We could say then that an action, in the sense of karma, is that which has an effect. Unethical actions are the expressions of the three unskilful roots: greed, hatred, and delusion; and ethical actions grow from the roots of generosity, friendliness, and awareness. Skilful actions lead to more happiness, pleasure, ease, and freedom, while unskilful actions lead to the opposite. If, for example, I say something unkind to someone, they will probably feel hurt. (Only "probably" because they might mishear me, or take what I meant to be unkind as a compliment, or not care because what I say doesn't matter to them.) There will be an effect on me too. The unkind words that I uttered would have come from an unskilful mental state, and expressing them would have strengthened that state in my mind, which will be unpleasant for me. There will probably be a more long-term effect too, of estranging that person from me and consequently of them withholding their goodwill towards me. If I ever need their help or support in the future they may be unwilling to give it. Now let's consider the opposite scenario. If I say something kind to someone, they will probably feel pleased – it will make them feel good about themselves and a little bit happier. I will also have strengthened a skilful state of mind in myself, so I will also be a little happier. The long-term benefits of my kind words will result in more goodwill and trust between us, probably leading to further kindnesses and therefore more happiness.

I've been discussing the karmic effects of unkind and kind speech, but there is also the arena of physical action to consider. Shoving someone out of the way so that I can get onto a crowded train is obviously unskilful, whereas helping them up after they've fallen over is skilful. And then there's the mind. Thoughts have effects too. If I allow myself to harbour unkind thoughts about someone, those thoughts will have a detrimental effect on me. They will also have a harmful effect on my relationship with that person, even if I don't express my thoughts: they will probably notice that I'm withholding my goodwill towards them and they will probably, in turn, begin to hold back from me, resulting in a cool, perhaps frosty relationship which is unpleasant for both of us. Whatever actions we perform, whether by body, speech, or mind, the most important factor is the mind, because all actions are expressions of our states of mind. The first two verses of the *Dhammapada* put this very clearly:

> Experiences are preceded by mind, led by mind, and produced by mind.
>
> If one speaks or acts with an impure mind, suffering follows even as the cartwheel follows the hoof of the ox (drawing the cart).

> Experiences are preceded by mind, led by mind, and produced by mind.
>
> If one speaks or acts with a pure mind, happiness follows like a shadow that never departs.[37]

There is of course a connection between karma and the six realms of existence. The four painful realms (the hungry ghosts, the jealous gods, the animals, and the hells) are created by unskilful actions of body, speech, and mind. The human realm, which is a mixture of pain and pleasure, is created by both skilful and unskilful acts, while the god realms are created by skilful actions, especially the highly skilful absorbed meditative states of mind. You may remember that impure buddha-fields contain all six realms while pure buddha-fields consist of only the human and god realms. That's why the Buddha says that those with only a few roots of virtue won't be born in Sukhāvatī.

However, it's not as simple as that. The first English translation of this sutra to be published was by F. Max Müller in 1883, and in his translation this sentence reads: "Beings are not born in that Buddha country of the Tathāgata Amitāyus as a reward and result of good works performed in this present life."[38] This seems to be saying exactly the opposite, doesn't it? How can this be? There are three possible explanations: an early copyist of the sutra made a mistake and one of the two versions of this passage is wrong; Müller made a mistake in his translation; or there are two versions of the sutra. There are in fact a number of versions of the sutra, different in a few minor ways, but this is a significant difference: one version tells us that the practice of ethics is an essential condition for birth in Sukhāvatī, and the other says that ethics have nothing to do with it. Actually they can both be right, but, before investigating how, let's look at another condition necessary for rebirth in Sukhāvatī:

> If a child of good family hears the name of the Blessed One, the Tathāgata Amitāyus, and if their minds become absorbed by it – for one night, two nights, three nights, four nights, five nights, six nights, or seven nights – if their minds become undistractedly absorbed by it, then when they die the Tathāgata Amitāyus, surrounded by his sangha of śrāvakas and accompanied by his assembly of bodhisattvas, will appear before them, and they will die with an undistorted mind. When they die, they will be born in the buddha-field of the Tathāgata Amitāyus, in the world system of Sukhāvatī. Therefore Śāriputra, it is with this purpose in view that I say that a child of good family should single-mindedly cultivate a heartfelt desire for that buddha-field in their minds.

So all of this can happen through hearing the name of the Buddha Amitāyus and absorbing the mind in it. I alluded to something like this in the first chapter, where I told the story of Anāthapiṇḍada hearing the word "Buddha" and the amazing effect that had on him. This is the second time in the sutra that we've encountered the idea of the mind becoming absorbed in the Buddha. The first referred to the living beings in Sukhāvatī, who "become absorbed by the Buddha, absorbed by the Dharma, absorbed by the Sangha". The translator tells me that the word he translated as "absorbed" is *manasikāra* – *manasi* meaning "in the mind" and *kāra* "making or doing" – so it's literally something like "making (to be) in the mind". This seems to be a kind of meditation practice then, an aural equivalent of visualization.

One of the differences between the Chinese and the Sanskrit versions of the sutra is that, whereas in the Chinese version the Buddha recommends absorbing the mind in the name of Amitāyus for one to seven *days*, in the Sanskrit version he says *nights*. Why nights? This may be fanciful, but perhaps the fact that Sukhāvatī is situated in the west has some bearing on this. The west is where the sun sets of course, so there's a suggestion of the end of the day perhaps, and the end of the day suggests rest, repose, sleep. This in turn may suggest the end of life: "Come heavy sleep, the image of true death", as John Dowland sang.[39] Perhaps the author of the Sanskrit version of the sutra connected night with death, because the Buddha then tells of the effect of this practice at the moment of death: "the Tathāgata Amitāyus, surrounded by his sangha of śrāvakas and accompanied by his assembly of bodhisattvas, will appear before them, and they will die with an undistorted mind" to be born into Sukhāvatī.

We can of course interpret death here in a metaphorical way, as a *spiritual* death – the death of the old, deluded self, the person who's been metaphorically asleep all their life. Rebirth in Sukhāvatī would then symbolize *spiritual* rather than literal rebirth: the waking up of that person into wisdom. If we interpret this passage metaphorically, the three passages that we've so far looked at in this chapter form a kind of path or sequence:

1. "Heartfelt desire" – faith, going for refuge to the Three Jewels, commitment to practising the Dharma.
2. "Roots of virtue" – the practice of ethics, purifying oneself of unskilful states, developing skilful states, preparing the mind for meditation.
3. "Absorbing the mind undistractedly" in the name of Amitāyus – meditation – absorbed states of mind.
4. At the moment of death, being met by Amitāyus and his retinue.

5. Dying with an "undistorted mind" – spiritual death – insight into the Dharma. The mistaken notion of a fixed and permanent self is seen through.
6. Birth in Sukhāvatī – "spiritual" rebirth – waking from the sleep of ignorance.

However, before interpreting this passage metaphorically we should explore its literal meaning, and to do that we have to return to the subject of karma. You'll remember that I said karma is action that has an effect – the effect being one of either pleasure and happiness or pain and unhappiness. When is the effect felt? Sometimes immediately, as in my example of saying something unkind to someone, with the result that they feel hurt there and then. The effects of our actions are not always instant though (John Lennon's "instant karma" notwithstanding); sometimes they don't manifest for a while. For instance, I may have helped someone out a few years ago. I may have forgotten all about it, but then I get a letter in the post from the person I helped, thanking me, telling me they've never forgotten that act of kindness, it meant so much to them. Happiness floods my being!

According to the Buddha the effects of our actions are not all felt in this life but are carried over into our next life: karma is bound up with rebirth. This is a difficult topic for Westerners who are interested in Buddhism; indeed it's difficult for many contemporary Western Buddhists, who find themselves unable to believe in the doctrine of rebirth. One of the common ideas about Buddhism that Westerners often find attractive is the idea that to be a Buddhist you don't have to *believe* anything; you don't have to take on faith any statements that you can't verify in your own experience. This isn't true, though. Take the Awakening of the Buddha. We are unable to verify this in our own experience. Even if the Buddha were alive today and we met him, we'd be unable to say with any degree of certainty that he was awakened. How would we know? Then, the Buddha taught that others can also awaken. How do we know this is true? Can we verify that statement in our own experience? Only at the point when we awaken. Until then we have to take that idea on faith.

Returning to the topic of rebirth, we can only verify this when we die. It seems that, generally speaking, Eastern Buddhists in the past have believed in rebirth, or at least there doesn't seem to be any evidence of people not believing it in the texts that have survived; there doesn't even seem to have been any debate about it. Contemporary Western

Buddhists often do have a problem with it though, some simply not believing it and others holding an agnostic position. The sutras that we're exploring in this book definitely assume a belief in rebirth. When the Buddha in the sutra talks about being born into Sukhāvatī, I think it's meant to be taken literally. This doesn't preclude our interpreting the texts metaphorically, but to do the text justice we also have to at least look at the literal meaning.

Early Buddhist scholars developed a detailed classification of the different kinds of karma, and it will be helpful for us to look at one of these classifications. In a category called "priority of effect", four kinds of karma are listed in order of the relative potency of their effect. Firstly there's *weighty karma*. Weighty *skilful* karmas are the absorbed meditative states – dhyānas – which result in rebirth in one of the god realms. Weighty *unskilful* karmas are of five kinds: killing an arhat, killing your mother and / or your father, wounding a buddha (tradition has it that it's not possible to kill a buddha), and creating disharmony in the sangha, such that it splits into hostile factions. Any one of these actions results in rebirth in one of the hell realms.

The second is *death-proximate karma*. These are the actions done, words spoken, thoughts thought in the moments immediately before death. They are important because they link this life to the next; the state of mind you are in when you die will have a significant – perhaps a decisive – effect on the kind of being you are reborn as. Because of the passage quoted above about the dying person, as well as another important passage in the third of the three Pure Land sutras – the *Guān Jīng* – Pure Land Buddhists place great emphasis on the moments before death. They believe it's possible in these moments to make a determined effort to be reborn in Sukhāvatī, and, because of the relative strength of death-proximate karma, they believe the consequences of previous unskilful karmas can be cancelled out.

The third is *habitual karma*, actions that we perform over and over again. The more we do them, the easier it is to do them again, which is why it's so hard to give habits up. Neuroscientists tell us that when we do something for the first time we open a neural pathway in the brain. That neural pathway being open, it's now a little easier for us to do that action again. The second time we do it the neural pathway is opened a little more, making it even easier to do it again. Imagine a meadow of long grass: someone walks through it, making a faintly discernible "path". A second person walks the same route and the pathway is now a little more defined. If a number of people follow that route there will be a very definite pathway, much easier to walk along than through the long grass. A habit is an opened neural pathway. Musicians, who have to practise for hours a day, have wide-open neural pathways in a particular part of their brains. Athletes have open neural pathways in different parts of their brains. Hence the phrase "practice makes perfect". Remember though that thoughts are actions too. Thinking the same thought a few times makes it easier to have similar thoughts in the future. The Buddha once said that, whatever someone "frequently thinks and ponders upon, that will become the inclination of their mind",[40] and he warned us not to underestimate the long-term effects of small actions, for they are not inconsequential. Drop by tiny drop, a pot fills with water.[41] Thought by thought, our minds become filled with – what?

The fourth and weakest of the four kinds of karma is *residual karma*. This category is made up of any actions not included in any of the above. This will probably include occasional things that we do but don't repeat or think any more about. Their karmic effect is consequently quite small.

If we now review the conditions necessary for rebirth in Sukhāvatī according to the sutra, we can see that three of these categories will be operative. The first condition is a heartfelt desire to be born there. For this desire to be effective it would have to be ongoing and consistent – a habitual karma. It wouldn't be enough to desire it just once. That would come under the category of residual karma and would be too weak to have any real effect. The practice of ethics ("roots of virtue") would again come under habitual karma – filling the pot with pure water, drop by drop, to change the metaphor. The mind absorbed in the name of Amitāyus could come under two categories: as a meditative absorption it would be a weighty skilful karma, and as a practice done many times, habitual karma. Finally, as the person is dying, death-proximate karma comes into play.

However, there is an argument for saying that karma has nothing to do with rebirth in Sukhāvatī, and to explain this I'm going to return to the two apparently contradictory statements from the sutra that I highlighted earlier. According to one version, "living beings with only a few roots of virtue will not be born in the buddha-field of the Tathāgata Amitāyus." According to the other version, "beings are not born in that Buddha country of the Tathāgata Amitāyus as a reward and result of good works performed in this present life." I've just referred to these as *apparently* contradictory statements because they aren't necessarily so. They can be understood to be two statements about the place of ethics on the Buddhist path, both of which are true. In fact, if I were the author of the sutra I'd include both, like this: "Living beings with only a few roots of virtue will not be born in the buddha-field of the Tathāgata Amitāyus. However, those who are born there are not born there as a reward and result of good works performed in this present life." The first statement tells us that ethical practice is a necessary condition for rebirth in Sukhāvatī, and the second statement qualifies that, although ethical purity is necessary, rebirth in Sukhāvatī is not a *reward* for our good behaviour, and we're not reborn there *because* of our skilful actions. If that were so, Sukhāvatī would be merely a god realm.

No matter how full of pure water our pot may be, at the end of the day it's just a pot of pure water. If we only practised ethics we'd end up as a lovely person: honest, trustworthy, generous, unselfish, kind, but not necessarily wise. If we want to transform that water into the nectar of Enlightenment, another factor is needed – insight. Skilful actions are a necessary, but not sufficient, condition for Awakening. Considering one of the Buddha's simplest formulations of the path to Awakening will help to make this clear. The threefold path is made up of ethics, meditation, and wisdom. The first stage, ethical practice, is an important preparation for meditation because unethical actions have the effect of scattering the mind, disintegrating it, making it hard to focus. Meditation prepares the mind for the third stage, wisdom, because it's only possible to break through our habitually deluded perception and see things as they really are with a concentrated and focused mind. If we practise the first of these three stages only we'll be reborn as a fortunate human being. If we practise the first two stages only we'll be reborn as a god. Only if we have extensive and deep experience of the third stage will we be reborn in Sukhāvatī.

What this implies is that the law of karma only operates within the world, or the six realms of existence. Unskilful actions lead to rebirth in one of the painful realms, skilful actions to the human or god realms, but Awakening is *outside* of those realms. It's *beyond* the world, beyond the six realms. Where's that?

> There is, monks, a condition where there is no earth, no water, no fire, no air; no sphere of infinite space, no sphere of infinite consciousness, no sphere of no-thingness, no sphere of neither-perception-nor-non-perception; neither this world nor another world nor both; neither sun nor moon. Here, monks, I say there is no coming, no going, no staying, no deceasing, no uprising. Not fixed, not movable, it has no support. Just this is the end of suffering.[42]

This remarkable passage was spoken by the Buddha, as reported in one of the most ancient of ancient texts, the *Udāna*. He was talking about the state of complete Awakening. He begins by saying that none of the elements that make up our world is present in the experience – no earth, water, fire, or air. He goes on to say that the formless worlds – represented here by the four formless dhyānas – are not present either, meaning that the non-material worlds are also absent from the experience. Enlightenment occurs "outside" of the phenomenal world. He then says that in the awakened state there is neither "this world" nor "another world", "this world" being this life and "another world" being a future life; he or she is no longer subject to rebirth. (Why that is and what it means we'll see later.)

He goes on to say that in the experience of Awakening there is no sun or moon – no external sources of light. That doesn't mean it's dark though. In a similar passage in another part of the same text the Buddha says, "There gleam no stars, no sun sheds light, there shines no moon, yet there no darkness reigns."[43] Light and dark are features of a world made up of objects able to be seen and whose inhabitants possess the sense of sight. (Incidentally, it's a common misconception that a person blind from birth "lives in darkness", but they don't. If you can't see anything you can't see darkness either. Similarly, bats don't live in darkness. They know nothing of darkness or light; they live in a sonic world. So, when the Buddha says there is no sun or moon, he's saying that the sense of sight does not apply.) The Buddha then says that in the awakened state there is no coming, going, staying, and so on, but, nevertheless, it's not fixed or movable. The Buddha's central insight was that everything that exists does so in dependence on certain conditions, continues to exist for a while (anything from a millisecond to a billion years or more), and then ceases to be. This applies to everything in every world, on every plane of existence. There is not one thing that exists independently of conditions. Here though he seems to be saying that in the experience of Awakening this doesn't apply. We've seen that Awakening occurs dependent on certain conditions – going for refuge to the Three Jewels, the practice of ethics and meditation, spiritual friendship, and so on – but once awakened no further conditions are necessary for its continuation. Hence "it has no support." This, he concludes, is the end of suffering, or, we might say, the beginning of true happiness – sukha.

Yet ... Awakening has to happen *somewhere*. It occurs within the world, or *a* world. The Buddha became the Buddha sitting on the earth, breathing in the air, close to a river on a hot Indian day. So what does the Buddha mean when he says that in the enlightened experience there exists no earth, no air, and so on? He's saying that Awakening can't be compared with anything else because it's like nothing else we've ever experienced. He's emphasizing the discontinuity between Enlightenment and our experience. In theology this is called the approach of the *via negativa*: essentially the approach of saying, "It's not this." However, he also used the *via positiva* approach sometimes, as when, for instance, he compared Awakening to a cool cave or a magic city. The author of the *Sukhāvatīvyūhaḥ Sūtra* clearly prefers the *via positiva* approach; he or she emphasizes the continuity between Enlightenment and our experience. The author is saying, "Look, everything you experience now – trees, flowers, ponds, and birds – imagine all that transformed into this amazing, colourful, richly beautiful world called Sukhāvatī. That's what Awakening is like."

This brings us back to a metaphorical interpretation of the sutra, so let's now consider the death of the practitioner and his or her rebirth in Sukhāvatī as a metaphor for *spiritual* death. Any kind of insight into the Dharma will include the realization that the "self", the "person" having the insight, doesn't exist in the way that we previously thought it did. Up until that moment of insight we assumed that there was a kind of abiding self at the centre of our experience, guiding us, protecting us from danger, pursuing the good things in life, even trying to gain Enlightenment. Now we see that this was a delusion. Now we see that our self is, like all other things in the world, a conditioned thing or event, dependent on other things and events. In a sense "it" doesn't exist. It's not an *enduring* entity, that is, it's not a fixed, unchanging *thing* somewhere inside us. It's more fluid than that, more elusive, changing all the time, having different feelings, different thoughts, different urges from day to day, from moment to moment. I say *having* different feelings and so forth, but that implies that there must be a thing – a self – that *has* those feelings: if there's experience there must be an experiencer; if there's an action there must be an actor. Actually there is just a stream of events – feelings, thoughts, urges – and we assume that there's someone – some fixed point – in the middle of all that. With insight into the Dharma we realize that there is no self, so there is a kind of spiritual death. What actually dies is simply the *illusion* of selfhood, but that is as terrifying a prospect as physical death.

The Buddha says that, if the practitioner absorbs his or her mind undistractedly in the name of Amitāyus, at death he will appear to them, along with his assembly of bodhisattvas and arhats, and they will die with an undistorted mind. Interpreted metaphorically, this implies that absorbing the mind in Amitāyus' name brings about insight into non-selfhood. How? In most Buddhist texts – both Śrāvakayāna and Mahāyāna – this insight comes about from reflecting or meditating on a wisdom teaching: something cognitive, a conceptual expression of the way things are. But there are no wisdom teachings here: there is just the name of Amitāyus. If anything, absorbing one's mind in the name of Amitāyus would seem to be a practice that engenders faith rather than wisdom. In fact, when we look at the sutra as a whole we find that it contains no wisdom teachings at all: no mention of dependent origination or the three characteristics of existence or *śūnyatā*, or anything like that. And, without its distinctive wisdom teachings, Buddhism is no different from other religions that propagate the goal of an everlasting life in heaven. Many Buddhists – ancient and modern – have criticized the *Sukhāvatīvyūhaḥ* sutras for this. Sukhāvatī seems rather like heaven and Amitāyus – Eternal Life! – seems more than a little like God.

The *Shorter Sukhāvatīvyūhaḥ Sūtra* is what I have come to think of as an incomplete teaching. An incomplete teaching is a sutra that doesn't encompass the whole path but focuses on a few elements or even just one aspect of the path. The historical Buddha gave many incomplete teachings. He sometimes spoke just about ethics, or meditation, or the way lay followers should treat family members and servants. He also sometimes described how an awakened person perceives the world, but didn't go on to explain how his listener might gain that perception. Mahāyāna sutras are often incomplete teachings, even though some of them are very long – hundreds of pages long in some cases. You'd think with all those pages the authors should be able to get the whole of the path in, wouldn't you? After all, in the early Pali suttas the Buddha often manages to teach the whole path – ethics, meditation, and wisdom – in just a few paragraphs. The answer to this is that Mahāyāna sutras assume prior knowledge of the early teachings of the Buddha. This is clear from the fact that they mention in passing formulations of the Buddha's early teachings without explaining them. They assume that you are already familiar with them. The *Shorter Sukhāvatīvyūhaḥ Sūtra* mentions three such formulations: those magical birds teach the five spiritual faculties, the five spiritual powers, and the seven factors of Awakening with no further explanation. There would be no point in Mahāyāna sutras simply repeating what the Buddha has already said; people could just go back to the basic teachings as recorded in the early canon for that. The purpose of Mahāyāna sutras is to say something new, something that the Buddha *hasn't* already said, or to draw out the implications of something that he perhaps mentioned but didn't elaborate on. The three Pure Land sutras have something new to say about faith, imagination, and wisdom.

The Buddha's attitude to faith in the early texts is quite consistent: faith is an essential component in the living of the spiritual life, but definitely limited: a necessary stage on the path but not enough, on its own, to bring about Awakening. However, there is a passage in the older texts in which the Buddha seems to give a very different message. The text is the *Sutta Nipāta*, and the passage comes at the end of the fifth and final chapter – "The chapter on the way to the beyond". In this text sixteen Brahmans have been sent by their teacher, Bāvarī, to ask the Buddha a series of questions, Bāvarī himself being too old to make the journey. In an epilogue to the chapter one of the sixteen, Piṅgiya, tells Bāvarī (the text says that he "sang") about the life-changing effect of his meeting the Buddha. Bāvarī then asks him how, considering the intensity of his feelings, he can bear to stay away from the Buddha even for a moment, and Piṅgiya replies:

> *I cannot stay away from him even for a moment ...*
> *I see him with my mind as if with my eye ...*
> *I pass the night revering him.*
> *For that very reason I think there is no staying away*
> *from him.*
> *My faith and joy, mind and mindfulness do not go away*
> *from the teaching of Śākyamuni.*
> *In whatever direction the one of great Wisdom goes,*
> *In that very direction I bow down.*
> *I am old and of feeble strength.*
> *For that very reason my body does not go away to there.*
> *I go constantly on a mental journey,*
> *For my mind, Brahman, is joined to him.*[44]

Piṅgiya says that he passes the night revering the Buddha, which is reminiscent of the passage from the *Shorter Sukhāvatīvyūhaḥ Sūtra* in which the Buddha talks about absorbing the mind in the name of the Buddha Amitāyus "for one night, two nights, three nights, four nights, five nights, six nights, or seven nights". In commenting on that passage I asked why the Buddha stipulates nights, and I suggested a connection between night – and therefore sleep – and death. There's another possible explanation. When we sleep we often dream, and in dreaming we enter the realm of the imagination. Dreams contain the objects and people that we perceive in our waking state, but differently. We may be dreaming of our house, for instance, but at the same time it's not our house. Our dream house may have cellars, whereas our waking house does not. Or it may have extra passages and rooms. Our house in the dream, therefore, is also something else. Is it, perhaps, our mind? Are the cellars, the extra passages and rooms, aspects of ourselves that are not available to our conscious mind? In our dreams the people that we know in our waking state become different too, don't they? They often do or say things that we've never known them to do or say while we are awake, and we'd be very surprised if they did! And sometimes a dream person seems to be a juxtaposition of two people that you know – your mother and the prime minister! What's going on?

Our dreams are of different types too. Sometimes a dream seems to be simply a slightly weird rerun of something that occurred in the day – you were on a train journey in the daytime and the following night you dream about that journey. Some dreams seem to be symbols of something else – you are at your place of work, but it's also the room in which you go to yoga classes, or you have an encounter with someone you know, but they seem to also be a horse! Occasionally we have what some call "big" dreams. A big dream is highly charged with meaning and significance, although we may not be sure exactly what it means, or what its significance is. This is because dreams don't tell us their meaning in conceptual terms. The "language" of dreams is symbols. A symbol is an object or an event that stands for something else. Not in a one-to-one relationship, such as we get on road signs, for instance, with a matchstick person representing a pedestrian. A symbol is not merely a sign. The *meaning* of a dream is often tantalizingly out of reach of our conceptual mind, yet what it's trying to tell us seems to be very important. These two aspects of the dream are connected, of course – if the dream could be explained conceptually it wouldn't be all that important. Some dreams can be "translated" into conceptual terms: "Oh, being back at school and not knowing what the lesson was about means that I'm a bit behind in my work and I need to catch up." Big dreams can't be conceptualized so easily. Their significance is bigger, multifaceted, and multilayered. A big dream tells us that we need to change, we need to become a different person. Returning to the notion of the self, a big dream challenges our current idea of who we are and shows us how limited and limiting that self-view is. Life is stranger, more wonderful, more mysterious, than you – *as you are now* – can admit.

Dreams are intimations of *acintya* – the inconceivable, the unthinkable, the unknowable.

Piṅgiya spends his nights revering the Buddha. I would suggest that this means that he is with the Buddha even while sleeping, even while dreaming, and this suggests that his mind is absorbed – not just his conscious, rational mind, but also his unconscious, non-rational, imaginal mind – in the Buddha. Put like that it sounds like a purely subjective experience, but something strange then occurs, something that suggests that Piṅgiya's experience is not just in his mind. Up to this point Piṅgiya and Bāvarī seem to be talking of the Buddha in his absence, but suddenly the Buddha speaks directly to Piṅgiya:

> *Just as Vakkali was released through faith,*
> *and Bhadrāvudha, along with Alavi-Gotama,*
> *In just the same way you can be set free through faith.*
> *You, Piṅgiya, will go to the far shore of the realm of death.*[45]

The conversation must have taken place in Bāvarī's home, once Piṅgiya and the other Brahman students had returned to report back to their teacher, so the Buddha isn't physically present. It's as if Piṅgiya's inner experience is externalized in the voice of the Buddha. This reminds me of the Mahāyāna sutra I mentioned at the beginning of Chapter 1, which claims that a visualized buddha can become so real to us that he will answer our questions. Of course in this case the buddha that Piṅgiya "visualizes" – "sees" would be a more accurate description – is the human, historical Buddha.

The Buddha confirms Piṅgiya's experience and encourages him by mentioning three other disciples who were released through faith. The first of these is Vakkali. There are a number of slightly differing accounts of Vakkali's life and death in the early texts, but they all agree that he was a very emotional, passionate character. Having once seen the Buddha he couldn't keep his eyes off him, and would follow him everywhere just so that he could look at him. It was as a response to this obsession with the Buddha's form that the Buddha said to Vakkali:

> Enough, Vakkali! What is there to see in this vile body? He who sees Dhamma, Vakkali, sees me; he who sees me sees Dhamma. Truly seeing Dhamma, one sees me; seeing me one sees Dhamma.[46]

That didn't stop Vakkali, though, and he continued to follow the Buddha until one day the Buddha told him to go away. Disconsolate, he made his way to Gṛdhrakūta – the Vultures' Peak. One account says that he was going to take his life by jumping from the peak, but that the Buddha, knowing what was on his mind, appeared to him and gave him a short teaching. Vakkali, delighted, rose into the air and gained Enlightenment. Another, less magical, account says he went to Gṛdhrakūta to meditate but was unable to gain insight because of his highly emotional nature. The Buddha later visited him and encouraged him with a short teaching, after which Vakkali gained Enlightenment. The Buddha later proclaimed him to be foremost of his disciples released through faith, and this may be why he is mentioned by name at the beginning of this sutra.

Returning to Piṅgiya, there are two terms in the Pali verses translated here as "released through faith". The first is *muttasaddho. Saddhā* means faith and *mutta* is "released, set free". The second term is *pamuñcassu saddhaṃ. Pamuñca* means "loosening, setting free or loose". The Buddha seems to be telling Piṅgiya that his faith alone is enough to "set him free", or, in other words, to awaken. This seems to contradict what he said elsewhere, as when, for instance, he tells another Brahman that faith

> may turn out in two different ways ... something may be fully accepted out of faith, yet it may be empty, hollow, and false; but something else may not be fully accepted out of faith, yet it may be factual, true, and unmistaken.[47]

Having faith in something doesn't necessarily mean it's true (although it also doesn't necessarily mean it's false). This doesn't stop the Buddha from then telling that same Brahman that, once he's found a teacher he can trust, he should "place faith in him" and "filled with faith" listen to and practise his teachings. This epitomizes the Buddha's predominant attitude to faith as found in the early sutras – essential as it is on the path to Awakening, it can only be provisional.

The author of the *Shorter Sukhāvatīvyūhaḥ Sūtra* is aware of this because he or she has the magical birds proclaim the five spiritual faculties and the five spiritual powers (the latter are simply the former fully developed). They are faith, energy, mindfulness, meditation, and wisdom. There are two ways of regarding this list. It can be seen as a sequence, a graduated path, starting with faith and ending with wisdom, or it can be seen as a set of qualities to be developed simultaneously. Seen in this second way, mindfulness is the central faculty with a pair of faculties on either side (faith and energy to one side, meditation and wisdom to the other). Even better is to imagine it as a four-pointed star, with faith and wisdom at opposite points, energy and meditation at the other opposite points, and mindfulness in the middle. These pairs need to be in balance – energy needs to be balanced by meditation and vice versa, while faith needs to be balanced by wisdom and vice versa (wisdom in this case being a conceptual understanding of the Dharma, not the wisdom of direct seeing, which does not need to be balanced by anything). Mindfulness is the faculty that notices and corrects any imbalances. When understood as a sequence, faith is the first step on the path and wisdom the destination. When understood as a set of qualities to be developed simultaneously, faith has to be "balanced" by wisdom. Either way, faith is not sufficient, on its own, for Awakening.

Yet what the Buddha says to Piṅgiya suggests that it is. There is, I believe, a resolution to this apparent contradiction: there are different kinds, or levels, of faith. We can compare faith here with wisdom. The Buddha spoke about wisdom in at least two different ways: as *insight into* and as *knowledge of* the Dharma. These are two very different kinds of wisdom, the first being a direct seeing or knowing of the way things are, the second an intellectual understanding of the Buddha's teachings. In another formulation wisdom has *three* levels: wisdom through hearing, through reflecting, and through meditating. The first two levels are usually understood to be levels of intellectual understanding – reflection yielding a deeper understanding of what's been "heard" or learnt – and the third level corresponds to insight. I think there are also levels of faith that correspond to the different levels of wisdom. We can begin by identifying two levels: faith as an intuitive grasp of the truth of a teaching and faith as a direct knowing of the way things are (although experienced not cognitively, but imaginatively).

The realization of the truth of the Buddha's teachings (insight or Awakening) is a direct seeing or knowing of the way things are, *free of concepts*. In other words, it's not an *intellectual* awakening. To communicate this experience the Buddha used concepts to describe and evoke the experience, as well as to teach practices whereby we may also have that experience. But the concepts are not the experience. The Buddha seems to be telling Piṅgiya that there is another, non-conceptual way to access that experience.

One of my teacher's teachers, Dilgo Khyentse Rinpoche, identified four levels of faith:

> First, clear faith refers to the joy and clarity and change in our perceptions that we experience when we hear about the qualities

> of the Three Jewels and the lives of the Buddha and the great teachers. "Longing faith" is experienced when we think about the latter and are filled with a great desire to know more about their qualities and to acquire these ourselves. "Confident faith" comes through practising the Dharma, when we acquire complete confidence in the truth of the teachings and the enlightenment of the Buddha. Finally, when faith has become so much a part of ourselves that even if our lives were at risk we could never give it up, it has become "irreversible faith".[48]

He doesn't say in this quotation at which level of faith wisdom arises. Certainly the fourth level would have to be informed by wisdom and it's possible that the third level is too. What's important here is the idea that faith is not just a single experience – it is multilevelled.

We have to be careful about what conclusions we draw from this. Piṅgiya had previously heard the Buddha answer a number of questions – two of them from himself – so he'd heard quite a lot of conceptual teachings by the time he declared his faith to his teacher Bāvarī. It's possible that he'd had an experience of insight on listening to the Buddha, in which case his faith would have been informed by wisdom. That perhaps gives rise to a question: how much do we need to know to gain insight? That probably depends on the person. Some people seem to need to know a lot, others not so much. We all definitely need to know *something*, but probably not very much. We need to know about the importance of ethical practice and how to go about that. We need to know how to meditate, and we need to know something about the way an awakened person sees the world: that everything comes into existence in dependence on conditions and ceases to be once those conditions are no longer present. This being so, all conditioned things are ultimately unsatisfactory and impermanent, and all things whatsoever are without substantial (independent) existence. The Buddha's immediate disciples probably didn't know very much more than that. They grasped the essentials and then practised. Mahāyāna sutras, as I've said, assume knowledge of the early teachings. The author of the *Shorter Sukhāvatīvyūhaḥ Sūtra* assumes that the reader (or listener) already knows what the Buddha taught and is practising it, so there's no need to repeat it. What he or she is interested in is helping the reader to experience the "release through faith".

The next section of the text is quite long and begins:

> Just as I praise Sukhāvatī, Śāriputra, so too, to the east, as many buddhas, as many blessed ones as there are grains of sand in the River Ganges praise their buddha-fields. Led by the Tathāgata Akṣobhya, ... the Tathāgata Merudhvaja, ... the Tathāgata Mahāmeru, ... the Tathāgata Meruprabhāsa, ... and the Tathāgata Mañjudhvaja, ... they each cover their own buddha-field with their tongue, and then describe it. You should trust in this discourse on the Dharma called "Embraced by all the buddhas', which praises inconceivable good qualities.

Before saying anything else about this passage I will just comment on what seems a bizarre image – that of each buddha covering his buddha-field with his tongue. The tongue represents speech, so what this means is that each buddha teaches the beings who live in his buddha-field. The Buddha goes on to say that in the west, south, and north, as well as in the nadir and the zenith (below and above us), there are "as many buddhas ... as there are grains of sand in the River Ganges", mentioning some of these buddhas by name. So, in all directions, throughout the whole of space, there are buddhas and buddha-fields.

As I wrote in the previous chapter, in the earliest days of Buddhism there was just the Buddha – a human being who had awoken fully. Soon after his death a myth began to grow that the Buddha was the last in a line of buddhas. At first six previous buddhas were identified, each of them living an unimaginably long time before the buddha who followed him. Later, more buddhas were enumerated – fourteen, twenty-three, and more – and then a future buddha was added, Maitreya, who, you may remember, is mentioned under his other name of Ajita at the beginning of this sutra. So, many buddhas of the past, one of the present, and one in the future in this, our buddha-field. Buddhist cosmology began to expand, though. Firstly, our immediate universe began to be called "the three thousand great-thousand world-realm", consisting of one billion smaller worlds. Later still it expanded to include innumerable world systems in all directions of space. Many of these world systems had buddhas living and teaching in them, and these are known as buddha-fields. So there was a development from one (present) buddha, to many in the past and the future, and then to many buddhas existing simultaneously in different regions of an infinitely large universe.

What are we to make of this? Are we expected to believe that these buddhas of the past literally existed, and that innumerable buddhas literally exist right now, as individual (human) beings? That would be what's called a naive realist interpretation. Should we instead take these buddhas to be non-existent, simply figments of someone's imagination? That would be a non-realist interpretation. There is a third possibility, one that I promised to mention in the previous chapter, called the critical realist interpretation.[49] This interpretation takes the idea of different buddhas, with individual names such as Akṣobhya, Merudhvaja, and so on, to represent what we might call the buddha principle – or the possibility of Awakening – at work in the universe. In his book *The Dawn of Chinese Pure Land Doctrine* Kenneth K. Tanaka writes:

> Under this view, the Buddhist cosmos is not an objective and material but a subjective and spiritual reality. The transcendent Buddhas and their realms that fill the universe are concretized expressions of the eternal Buddha-principle (dharma), which as the basic reality of the universe is ever active to lead all beings to enlightenment. In other words, the universe is the domain of the Buddhas and is, thus, fashioned and sustained by their work to lead beings to enlightenment.[50]

Incidentally, this interpretation solves the "problem" of Amitāyus' eternal life: he doesn't literally live forever but personifies the ever-present buddha principle. But then who says (apart from Kenneth Tanaka) that "the basic reality of the universe" is "the eternal Buddha-principle", which is "ever active to lead all beings to enlightenment"? Well, that is a matter of belief. It can't be proved or disproved. It is, after all, an interpretation. The poet William Wordsworth wasn't a Buddhist and in his poem "Lines composed a few miles above Tintern Abbey" he wasn't referring to innumerable buddhas living in all directions of space, but he does seem to be expressing a similar idea:

> *And I have felt*
> *A presence that disturbs me with the joy*
> *Of elevated thoughts; a sense sublime*
> *Of something far more deeply interfused,*
> *Whose dwelling is the light of setting suns,*
> *And the round ocean and the living air,*
> *And the blue sky, and in the mind of man:*
> *A motion and a spirit, that impels*
> *All thinking things, all objects of all thought,*
> *And rolls through all things.*[51]

I guess this is what the authors of Mahāyāna sutras, such as the *Longer Sukhāvatīvyūhaḥ Sūtra*, were giving expression to when they wrote about innumerable buddhas residing in all the directions of space. Of course they may not have seen it like this. They may well have held what I've called the naive realist interpretation – that these buddhas exist literally in the way that you and I exist as individual persons. I personally don't hold this view, and I don't think it's necessary to hold it in order to appreciate the sutra or to have faith in it. Whether you take these buddhas literally or metaphorically depends to a certain extent on the culture in which you grew up. Traditional cultures tend to have a naive realist view of the world, whereas contemporary cultures are critical of this view, as expressed in the very term that I've been using – naive realism – which is somewhat pejorative. I hope I'm not being a cultural chauvinist by using that term. Actually I have no problem with people taking these buddhas literally, it's just that I'm unable to do so myself. Being unable to take them literally, I try to understand what I think the authors of these sutras are saying above and beyond our cultural differences. That is, I'm quite sure they are saying something important about the nature of the spiritual life, which they've expressed in the terms that were current in their culture, but which I have to transpose into my own terms. And it seems to me that what they are saying is this: the universe, or something in the universe, is somehow acting on us, encouraging us to awaken. This is expressed especially in the phrase "embraced by all the buddhas", which strongly suggests (in the critical realist interpretation) some outside force acting on us.

This was a new idea in Buddhism. As far as I know the historical Buddha never spoke in these terms, never suggested that the path to Awakening included being embraced by buddhas from other world systems, or opening ourselves to some kind of buddha principle. On the contrary, he spoke of the importance of relying on our own efforts, emphasizing that no one else could do the work for us. So is this new idea still Buddhism? Some would say not. I think it is, and I'll explain why.

A few hundred years after this sutra was written, a Chinese devotee and teacher of the Pure Land sutras introduced the terms "self-power" and "other-power", or "self-help" and "outside-help". In doing so Tanluan gave to Pure Land Buddhism its most distinctive doctrine. Self-power, or self-help, refers to the efforts that we, as individuals, have to make in practising the Buddha's teachings. Other-power, or outside-help, refers to the receiving of Amitāyus' compassion and wisdom. Self-power is active, other-power is receptive, and Tanluan taught that both are necessary if one is to be born into Sukhāvatī. As we've seen, the Buddha seemed only to teach self-power, so why this new teaching? All new doctrines are attempts to solve problems, and the problem Tanluan had was a widespread belief current in Chinese Buddhism at the time he lived: the idea of the three ages or epochs of the Dharma. According to this, in the first age, at the time when the Buddha lived and taught, people were able to understand his teachings (the Dharma), put them into practice, and gain Enlightenment. In the second age people were able to understand the Dharma and practise it, but Awakening (in this life) was no longer possible. In the third age people are unable to understand or practise the Dharma. There are differing opinions as to the length of these ages, some sutras stating, for instance, that the first age lasted 1,000 years while others say 500. Whatever the exact time frames, the central idea is clear: the further we are from the time of the Buddha, the harder it becomes to understand, practise, and awaken. Consequently, people living at the time of the Buddha were able to practise and awaken by self-power alone, but by the time of Tanluan, who lived about 1,000 years after the Buddha, self-power was not enough – other-power was also necessary.

Later, Japanese Pure Land teachers such as Hōnen and Shinran took the idea of reliance on other-power to its extreme, believing that people were no longer able to practise from their own motivation, and that the only thing they could do was to rely totally on other-power. This was because they believed they had entered the third age of the Dharma, in which the practice of the Dharma was no longer possible.

The belief in the three ages of the Dharma is a form of determinism, that is, the belief that everything that happens must happen as it does and cannot happen in any other way. But there is no *a priori* reason to suppose that the further we live from the time of the Buddha, the harder it is to practise and understand the Dharma, or to awaken. Of course, meeting the Buddha and being taught directly by him would have been a great advantage, but, if that were the issue, then people who lived just a few years after the time of the Buddha would have been at the same disadvantage as those who live 2,500 years later. If I look to my own experience and observation of my contemporaries, people do seem to be able to practise and understand the Dharma, and some people I know seem to have had significant insights, which is supposed to be impossible in the third age of the Dharma. The idea of an inexorable decline of the Dharma, as the doctrine of the three ages proposes, seems then not to be rational or borne out in experience, and is probably simply an expression of the common tendency to believe that things were better in the past. However, Tanluan *did* believe in the three ages of the Dharma, and he believed that he was living in the third age, so his doctrine of other-power is at least partly a response to that. If it was no longer possible to practise the Dharma, what could people do instead? Ask for help. Surrender to other-power. Pierre Hadot introduces the very interesting idea of creative mistakes in his book *Philosophy as a Way of Life*. He writes:

> Very often, mistakes and misunderstandings have brought about important evolutions in the history of philosophy. In particular, they have caused new ideas to appear.[52]

I think Tanluan's doctrine of other-power can be regarded as a creative mistake, that is, a creative response to a mistaken idea.

For Tanluan and the later Pure Land teachers, both Chinese and Japanese, other-power was regarded as the "easy" path to Awakening, especially suitable for those living in the latter ages of the Dharma, or too weak to practise by their own motivation. Tanluan, for instance, wrote that other-power is for "an inferior person, who cannot even mount on a donkey (with his own strength)".[53]

Although the terms "self-power" and "other-power" are not found in any of the three Pure Land sutras, it's possible to read them into the *Shorter Sukhāvatīvyūhaḥ Sūtra*. Under the heading of self-power we can put "cultivating a heartfelt desire" for Sukhāvatī (going for refuge), the growing of roots of virtue (the practice of ethics), and the absorbing of the mind undistractedly in the name of Amitāyus (meditation). Under the heading of other-power we can identify the moment of death when Amitāyus, along with his retinue of arhats and bodhisattvas, appears before the practitioner, as well as the section we're currently exploring, with the vision of innumerable buddhas in all directions, and the Buddha's suggestion that this text be called "Embraced by all the buddhas". Notice though that other-power here is *not* regarded as a method for those unable to understand and practise the Dharma or for "inferior" persons, but makes its appearance after the practitioner has gone for refuge and practised ethics and meditation – in other words, after a period of self-power practice. Looked at in this way, dependence on other-power seems to be an "advanced" practice or experience.

My teacher, Urgyen Sangharakshita, has suggested a reason for this. In a letter to his disciples about his travels in North America and Australasia, he wrote that he'd recently read a book about Pure

Land Buddhism and Zen in which the author had connected the self-power approach with the spiritually more advanced, and the other-power approach with the spiritually less advanced. Sangharakshita disagreed with this, saying that in his opinion the path of dependence on self-power is for the spiritually less advanced, and the path of dependence on other-power for the spiritually more advanced. A friend of mine wrote to Sangharakshita asking him why he thought this. Here is his reply:

> My remark about the path of dependence upon self-power being for the spiritually less advanced and the path of dependence upon other-power being for the spiritually more advanced is deliberately provocative and intended to invite reflection. In the ordinary activities of life we are accustomed to making an effort. There are all sorts of things that we want, and we work hard to get them. In all this we rely upon our own efforts, i.e. on self-power. When we take up the spiritual life we naturally tend to adopt a similar approach. We seek to "gain" wisdom or "attain" Enlightenment. The path of self-power therefore makes fewer demands of us, inasmuch as it is in accordance with our natural human tendency and does not require a fundamental shift in this respect. For this reason I say that the path of dependence on self-power is for the spiritually less advanced. As for the path of dependence on other-power being for the spiritually more advanced, this is because in order to follow this path one has to surrender to the other-power, which means giving up one's self-power. Such surrender, or complete letting go of self-power, is extremely difficult, directly opposed as it is to our natural human tendency. Hence I say that the path of dependence on other-power is for the spiritually more advanced.[54]

Letting go of self-power in the highest sense is tantamount to letting go of the deluded idea of a fixed and separate self. At this level it represents the beginning of the process of Awakening, the beginning of the transcendental path. "Transcendental" translates the Pali word *lokottara*, which is made up of two words: *loka* meaning "world", and *uttara* meaning "above or beyond". The path to Awakening is divided into two "paths" – the first is "mundane", by which I mean that, at this level, practice is not yet informed by deep insight into the Dharma, while the second, supramundane, path begins with that insight. These two paths correspond to the second and third principal levels of happiness that we explored in the first chapter – unworldly and still greater unworldly happiness.

But what *is* other-power? Specifically, who or what is the "other", and what does "power" mean? For Tanluan and the later Pure Land masters the "other" is Amitāyus, and the "power" is his wisdom and compassion being transferred to us. The word "power" is misleading though because it means, according to the Cambridge online dictionary, "the ability to control people and events", and Amitāyus does not control people or events. A better word would be "influence".

If, like me, you don't believe that celestial buddhas such as Amitāyus literally exist, what might other-power be in that case? It helps if we consider its counterpart, self-power, which is essentially self-motivation or -volition. Other-power is motivation or volition that does not come from the self. We may therefore assume that it comes from somewhere else, from some other agency outside the self, but that would be a mistake; other-power is not other in that sense. It's not other than – opposed to – the self. If it was, it would still be operating within the mistaken notion of a duality of self and other, which would mean it would be mundane. One way of understanding it is that it's other than the deluded mind, which sees things in terms of self and other. Other-power is the way things are – open, free of mental constructs, without self or substantiality – impinging on a consciousness entranced by the notion of a fixed and separate self. Because we are trapped in the self/other dualism though, we can't help conceiving of other-power as coming to us from the outside. In the first chapter I described a state of mind that you may have experienced, perhaps when you were walking in the countryside or on a retreat, in which you feel that "everything around you is as alive, as significant, as you are. You may feel that significance pressing in on you, as if the world was trying to tell you something, something that you kind of know already but haven't listened to intently enough to get the whole meaning." The suggestion here is that the environment itself is a kind of being "trying to tell you something", just as the poet of the *Zenrinkushu* wrote of an old pine tree preaching wisdom and a wild bird crying out truth, and Wordsworth of "a presence ... a sense sublime ... whose dwelling is the light of setting suns".

Here, other-power is experienced as a kind of non-personal, or perhaps suprapersonal, force or influence. Someone steeped in a spiritual tradition, however, may feel other-power coming not from their general environment but from a significant symbol from their tradition. The writer of this sutra may well have experienced other-power as coming from buddhas in all the directions of space. These buddhas represent the principle of Awakening – the eternal buddha principle – in the form of beings, persons. That's probably why some of those buddhas are mentioned by name, a name identifying the buddha as an individual person rather than as a stereotype. This sutra focuses on just one of those buddhas – Amitāyus – and, as we've seen, hearing his name and absorbing one's mind in it is an important spiritual practice. Perhaps one of the reasons for this is that it enables us to feel a personal connection with him, just as we do when we hear the name of a friend. In this case other-power is felt not as an abstract force but as Amitāyus' compassionate mind.

Wisdom doesn't exist outside of wise persons. In the early days of Buddhism, when it was still an oral tradition, the only way people would have learnt the Dharma was directly from a person. The exchange would have been personal. Afterwards the hearer would associate what they'd learnt with that person, and they would feel grateful to them. Śāriputra, one of the Buddha's chief disciples – and the one whom the Buddha is addressing in this sutra – first learnt the Dharma from Aśvajit, one of the Buddha's first disciples. On listening to Aśvajit he had a deep insight into the Dharma and reached the first of the four stages of Awakening – stream-entry. Soon afterwards – on listening to the Buddha – he awoke fully, he became an arhat. For the rest of his life, just before lying down to sleep at night, he would bow down in the direction in which Aśvajit happened to be at that time. For Śāriputra, the Dharma and Aśvajit were inextricably linked for the rest of his life, just as the person of the Buddha was linked to the Dharma for Piṅgiya. For them the Dharma was embodied in a person, or persons.

Reading Buddhist texts is one step away from this personal connection. Of course a book has been written by a person, but it's harder to feel that personal connection with the written word than with someone we've met. A person is always *embodied* and we can probably only feel a full connection with someone when we are in physical contact with them. If we only read books about the Dharma, we can tend to think of it as something abstract and impersonal, whereas for those living in an oral society it would have been concrete and personal. This is one reason why listening to spoken texts is a better way of being exposed to them: the person reciting the text stands in for the voice of the writer and allows us to feel that human connection more strongly. Having said that, it *is* possible to feel a personal connection with a writer by reading alone. I've become aware of a growing feeling of sympathy for whoever it was who wrote this sutra as I've read and reread it, reflected on and written about it these last two months. I'm only in physical contact with words on a screen, words that aren't even the author's own words, as they've been translated from his or her language to mine, but, somehow, through those dark grey shapes on a light grey background, I feel in contact with their author.

Having talked about those buddhas, and having mentioned thirty-nine of them by name, the Buddha continues:

> Śāriputra, why do you think that this discourse on the Dharma is called "Embraced by all the buddhas"? Those children of good family, Śāriputra, who hear the title of this discourse on the Dharma and who bear in mind the names of those buddhas, those blessed ones which it mentions, will all be embraced by the buddhas, and their progress towards unsurpassed, perfect Awakening will become irreversible.

"Irreversible" is the stage at which one has entered the supramundane path, never to fall back. Being embraced by all the buddhas is tantamount to deep insight into the Dharma. Just as it's possible for an awakened being to say "I am awakened" and for that to make some kind of sense even though there's no "I" that is awakened, so it's possible to say "I have been embraced by all the buddhas" even though there are no buddhas outside of the awakened mind. Self and other are both products of a deluded mind, and at this level of insight the distinction between the two starts to dissolve. At the beginning of the first chapter I mentioned a Mahāyāna sutra which states that, after repeatedly visualizing a buddha, it's possible to ask questions and receive answers from that buddha. The sutra then continues:

> Where does this Buddha come from and where am I going? As I think of this Buddha, he comes from nowhere and I am going nowhere. As I think of the realm of desire, the realm of form and the formless realm, these three realms are formed by my mind. I can see what I think of. The mind forms a Buddha for itself to see; the mind is the Buddha mind. As my mind forms the Buddha, my mind is the Buddha.[55]

Returning to the *Shorter Sukhāvatīvyūhaḥ Sūtra*, the Buddha then says

> Therefore, Śāriputra, you should have faith in me and in these other buddhas, these other blessed ones. Trust in us. Do not doubt us.

If we interpret this in the critical realist way, the Buddha is asking us to have faith and trust in the "eternal Buddha-principle", that is, the potential for Awakening that we all possess, but also the active, "embracing" influence of the awakened mind – other-power. In Chapter 4 we'll explore further the idea of trust in the buddha principle.

> Śāriputra, just as I praise the inconceivable good qualities of those buddhas, those blessed ones, so too Śāriputra, those buddhas, those blessed ones praise my inconceivable good qualities. "The Blessed One Śākyamuni, the king of the Śākyans, has done something which is very difficult to do. In the world system called Earth, he has attained unsurpassed perfect Awakening, and taught the Dharma to the whole of that unreceptive world, in a degenerate age, to degenerate beings with degenerate views, degenerate lifespans, and degenerate defilements."

Having posited two kinds of buddha-field, pure and impure, Mahāyāna Buddhists then had the problem of how to explain the fact that "our" buddha, Śākyamuni, presides over an impure buddha-field. Other buddhas had purified their world systems, so why hadn't Śākyamuni purified his? Did this reflect badly on him? Was he perhaps not as good a buddha as the others? One Mahāyāna text solved this problem by stating that this world is in fact pure, and that it only appears to be impure due to the impurity of the minds of those living here.[56] The author of the *Shorter Sukhāvatīvyūhaḥ Sutra* solves the problem in a different way, by saying that ours is a very difficult world system to purify! The buddhas from pure buddha-fields declare that our buddha has done something very difficult – he's managed to teach the Dharma to an "unreceptive world". "Unreceptive" is *vipratyayanīya* and the translator tells me that he could have used a stronger word, such as "hostile". Our lack of receptivity or our hostility to the Dharma is due to the fact that we live in a "degenerate age", which may be a reference to the three ages of the Dharma. The sutra was written about 600 years after the Buddha, and it's possible that the author believed that he or she was then living in the second age.

The sutra ends by returning to Prince Jeta's Grove in Anāthapiṇḍada's Park:

> This is what the Blessed One said. Their hearts filled with joy, the Venerable Śāriputra, the monks and bodhisattvas, along with the gods, human beings, titans, and gandharvas, rejoiced at what the Blessed One had said.

As Luis O. Gomez points out in his book *The Land of Bliss*, the scenario of the Buddha teaching his disciples in Anāthapiṇḍada's Park "frames" the description of Sukhāvatī – a scene within a scene, a story within a story.[57] At the end of Chapter 1 I suggested that the description of the Buddha and his assembly in Anāthapiṇḍada's Park represented a pure buddha-field within an impure buddha-field. Now, at the end of the sutra, everyone in Anāthapiṇḍada's Park rejoices, "their hearts filled with joy". The myth of Sukhāvatī – the Realm of Happiness – has become a reality in this world, or at least in a small part of it for a short while. Now, approximately 2,000 years after this sutra was written, this world is still an impure buddha-field and looks like continuing to be so for the foreseeable future. This chapter began with the Buddha recommending that living beings cultivate "a heartfelt desire for that buddha-field", which meant a desire to be reborn there after their death. This is the literal meaning – or the naive realist reading – of the sutra. Another way of reading that sentence is that we should cultivate a heartfelt desire for Sukhāvatī here, in this life, in this world. Read in this way, the purpose of the sutra and its myth of Sukhāvatī is to offer not an escape from this world but a way to bring at least some of its pure qualities – happiness, wisdom, beauty, faith, imagination – into our impure world. Our task then is to co-create pure buddha-fields within this world of suffering.

Part Two

The Longer Sūtra on the Abundance of Wonderful Qualities Which Adorn Sukhāvatī

Chapter Three

The mythic history of Sukhāvatī

A few weeks after his Awakening, the Buddha began to consider teaching the Dharma he had discovered. He knew that it would be difficult for most people to understand and he wondered where to start. This is an impure buddha-field after all, in which people are generally unreceptive to the Dharma, as we saw at the end of the last chapter. Initially he thought of his two former teachers, Āḷāra Kālāma and Uddaka Rāmaputta, for whom he still had a great deal of respect, but he discovered that they had both died. He then thought of his five former companions, who had accompanied him in the extreme ascetic practices. They had lived and practised together for six years but the five ascetics had left Śākyamuni in disgust when he gave up on these practices, thinking that by so doing he'd given up the quest for Awakening. They might be difficult to convince but he knew that they were sincere and dedicated practitioners, so they might listen, and, if they did, perhaps they'd understand. He made some enquiries and discovered that they were now at Isipatana, a deer park near Varanasi. This was about 150 miles from Uruvelā, where the Buddha was, so he walked there in search of them.

It's interesting that the first people the Buddha wanted to teach were those he knew and who had taught him or practised with him previously. In the last chapter I made the point that the teaching and learning of the Dharma is essentially a personal exchange. One of the characteristics of the Dharma, according to the Buddha, is that it's "of the nature of a personal invitation". This is especially so, of course, in an oral society. When the five saw the Buddha approaching they were still contemptuous of him – perhaps resentful too – and unwilling to speak to him, but he managed to win them round and before long they were deep in discussion. They talked for days, perhaps weeks, taking it in turns to go into Varanasi to beg for food, two at a time, which they brought back to share. One by one, they understood what the Buddha was trying to explain to them, and in a few weeks all five had awakened. They were the first arhats in the world. In Mahāyāna terms, the purification of the buddha-field had begun, for the world is purified through the purification of minds, and now there existed six purified, awakened minds.

Soon afterwards a young man named Yaśas stumbled upon the Buddha in the deer park and they began to talk. Amazingly, Yaśas awakened there and then. Later Yaśas' father also awakened, as did four of Yaśas' close friends. Word spread, more people sought out the Buddha, and in a short while sixty people had awakened to the truth of things. The Buddha then told them to go off in different directions and teach the Dharma, "that will be of benefit to many people, that will bring happiness to many people, out of empathy for the world". Now the purification of this world began in earnest, for a Buddha cannot purify an impure buddha-field on his own, but does so in co-operation with others.

After this the Buddha returned to Uruvelā because he wanted to repay the generosity of the local people who had supported him before his Awakening. He couldn't repay them in kind, of course, but he could give them the gift of the Dharma. There he encountered three brothers – the Kāśyapa brothers – all of whom were spiritual practitioners from another tradition. They too were deeply impressed by the Buddha and they too awakened as a result of his teaching. He then set out for the great city of Rājagṛha, the capital of Magadha, which was the kingdom of King Bimbisāra. He wanted to make good a promise he'd made to the king that when he had awoken he'd share what he'd learnt with the king and his subjects. So this is what he did, spending a few days in a bamboo grove on the outskirts of the city teaching them the Dharma. At the end of that visit the king donated the bamboo grove to the Buddha and his sangha – his community.

Not far from there is the Vultures' Peak, which became a favourite retreat for the Buddha, and this is where the *Longer Sukhāvatīvyūhaḥ Sūtra* begins. Actually, it's really called simply the *Sukhāvatīvyūhaḥ Sūtra*, but it's referred to as the *Longer Sūtra* to distinguish it from the other sutra of that name, the one we explored in the previous two chapters. I'll refer to them as the *Longer* and *Shorter Sūtras* for this and the following chapters until Chapter 7. The *Longer Sūtra* is classed as a *vaipulya* sutra, *vaipulya* meaning "broad, vast, extensive". *Vaipulya* sutras are all of these things, not only in their vision of the universe and the breadth of their teachings, but also in their length. The translation from Sanskrit into English is about fifty pages long and the translation from the Chinese almost seventy, whereas the

Shorter Sūtra is a mere six pages. It's therefore not going to be possible to comment in detail on every paragraph of the text as I did with the *Shorter Sūtra* – that would make for a very long book. Instead I'm going to explore some of its main themes. Before I do that though, it may be helpful to give you a summary of the whole sutra so that you know roughly where we are as we explore these themes.

The structure of the sutra is quite simple:

1. Introduction. The Buddha and his disciples are on Vultures' Peak, just outside the city of Rājagṛha. Ānanda notices that the Buddha's complexion is brighter than usual.
2. The Buddha recounts to Ānanda the mythical history of Amitābha and his buddha-field Sukhāvatī.
3. He describes Amitābha and Sukhāvatī in detail.
4. He then tells the Bodhisattva Ajita (Maitreya) about the different kinds of rebirth experienced by the beings living in Sukhāvatī, depending on their degree of faith.
5. Conclusion. Millions of beings attain various levels of Awakening on hearing the sutra, and all of the Buddha's disciples on Vultures' Peak are delighted.

So let's join the Buddha now as he sits on the top of the Vultures' Peak, along with 32,000 monks (or a mere 12,000 in the Chinese version of the sutra), as well as "a great many bodhisattvas". That's a lot of people, isn't it? I wonder who counted them? And how did they all fit onto the Vultures' Peak? These are literal-minded questions, of course, and literal-mindedness won't do when reading Mahāyāna sutras, in which time and space are elastic to say the least. The sutra begins its account of those present by mentioning by name the five former ascetics (the first ones to awaken after the Buddha), Yaśodeva[58] and his four friends, and the three Kāśyapa brothers. Also present are the Buddha's two chief disciples, Śāriputra and Mahāmaudgalyāyana, and his cousin and close friend Ānanda.

> All of these monks, and the others who were with him, were distinguished elders, great śrāvakas ... with the exception of one person – the Venerable Ānanda, who had not yet completed his training.

This is Ānanda with the amazing memory, who had listened to so many of the Buddha's teachings, and who is therefore considered to be the narrator of most sutras. But, strange to say, after twenty or so years of close companionship with the Buddha, after listening to and memorizing so many of his teachings, after serving him selflessly for so long, when the Buddha died Ānanda had still not awakened. Why was he so slow? After all, Yaśas awakened at his first meeting with the Buddha. Behind this question lies an assumption, of course: that people are pretty much the same when they encounter the Dharma, and that if they all make the same amount of effort they'll progress at pretty much the same speed. But people are different from each other, with different backgrounds, different temperaments, and different abilities. According to Buddhism, much of what makes us who we are is conditioned not only by events and our actions in this life, but also by our previous lives. Still, it does seem strange that someone so close to the Buddha took so long to wake up.

Soon after the Buddha's death his most senior disciples met to recite all of the teachings they'd heard, collect them all together and agree on their authenticity and accuracy. Ānanda would obviously have been indispensable in that task, but one of the other senior disciples said that Ānanda shouldn't be allowed at the meeting because he was not an arhat. This apparently stung him into action, and he went off into the forest to meditate until he awoke fully to the truth of things. When, later, he took his place in the assembly, the other arhats were delighted to discover that he was at last liberated. One possible reason for Ānanda's relative tardiness might have been that he spent the whole of his life serving the Buddha. Perhaps while the Buddha was alive Ānanda considered the Buddha's needs to be more important than his own spiritual development. However, once the Buddha had died, and it became important that he awoke, he did so. My teacher therefore once said that Ānanda was rather like a bodhisattva, "putting off" his own Awakening for the sake of others. He wasn't technically a bodhisattva – he hadn't taken the bodhisattva vow, he hadn't eschewed Awakening in this life so that he could become a buddha in the distant future – but he did embody the selfless spirit of the bodhisattva.

In the *Shorter Sūtra* the Buddha addresses Śāriputra, who doesn't say a word throughout; the whole text is a monologue. But here, in the *Longer Sūtra*, the Buddha speaks to Ānanda in response to something that Ānanda says to him:

> Your faculties, Blessed One, are bright and tranquil. Your skin is perfectly pure in colour, and your face shines with the colour of unadulterated gold ... I cannot remember ever having seen

> the Blessed One like this before, with his tathāgatha faculties so bright and tranquil, his face perfectly pure in colour, and his skin shining with the colour of pure gold. The thought occurs to me, Blessed One, "Today the Tathāgata truly dwells in the abode of the buddhas, the abode of the victorious ones, the abode of the all-knowing ones. Today the Tathāgata truly dwells in the abode of the great nāgas. He brings to mind the tathāgatas, the arhats, the perfectly awakened buddhas of the past, the present, and the future."

"Bright and tranquil" translates *viprasanna*, a very rich word with many connotations. *Prasanna* is the Sanskrit equivalent of the Pali *pasanna*, which we encountered in the Introduction, as the fourth dimension of a mind ready to know and see things as they really are. *Vi-* is an emphatic prefix, meaning "very". *Prasanna* then is a characteristic not only of a mind prepared but also of a mind that actually knows and sees things as they are. And it's interesting that the Buddha's state of mind is expressed in his body, especially his face. Returning for a moment to the Buddha's "graduated discourse" that we explored in the Introduction, you may have wondered how the Buddha knew that his listener was prepared to receive wisdom. The ancient texts tell us that the Buddha possessed extrasensory perception; while this may be true, I don't think we need to assume any magical powers in this instance. The state of mind of his listener was expressed in their body and face, and no doubt their eyes.

Coming back to the *Longer Sūtra*, Ānanda notices that the Buddha's skin is "shining with the colour of pure gold". This echoes an episode in the Pali text the *Mahā-Parinibbāna Sutta*, which recounts the last days of the Buddha's life. On the final day of his life someone gave the Buddha and Ānanda each a set of golden robes, and after Ānanda had helped the Buddha put his on, he said:

> Marvellous it is, O Lord, most wonderful indeed it is, how clear and radiant the skin of the Tathāgata appears! This set of golden-hued robes, burnished and ready for wear, Lord, now that it is arranged upon the body of the Blessed One, seems to have become faded, its splendour dimmed.[59]

The Buddha then explains that there are only two occasions when a Buddha's skin appears extremely clear and radiant: the night of his Awakening and the night of his passing away into parinibbāna. And tonight, he tells Ānanda, he will pass away. Here though, in the Longer Sūtra, Ānanda supposes another reason for this radiance, which the Buddha confirms, contradicting what he said in the earlier text. It's possible that the author of the *Longer Sūtra* didn't know this passage from the *Mahā-Parinibbāna Sutta*, and that he or she came up with his or her own reason for the Buddha's golden appearance, ignorant of the "real" reason. But I think the two passages are too similar for this to be the case. I think it's more likely that the author did know it, assumed that readers/hearers knew it too, and gave another reason for the Buddha's appearance consciously, as a response to the earlier text. In the *Mahā-Parinibbāna Sutta* passage, the reason given for the Buddha's golden appearance is that he is just about to die, or, to put it in the words of the text, pass away into parinibbāna. What does this mean? Unawakened beings are reborn in accordance with their karma into one of the six realms of existence. A buddha, by contrast, is not reborn. This doesn't mean that a buddha ceases to exist though. In one of the early Pali texts the Buddha is asked what happens to an awakened being after death: are they reborn or do they cease to exist? The Buddha replies that neither of these options applies, because "when all categories have been removed, then all ways of speaking are also removed."[60] In other words, it's not possible to say what happens to a buddha after death because none of the ways we can think about it are adequate. To quote a well-known formula: enlightened beings are not reborn; nor are they reborn; nor are they both reborn and not reborn; nor are they neither reborn nor not reborn! That just about covers every possibility, doesn't it? At the death of the physical body a buddha enters parinibbāna, which is nibbāna (Awakening) without remainder or residue – that is, without the residue of karma-vipāka – the results of previous skilful or unskilful action. You may remember that we are reborn into one of the six realms of existence in accordance with how we've lived in this life. A fully awakened person is not reborn in any of those realms because they have gone beyond the law of karma.

This is all very well, but it's very metaphysical and paradoxical. For all practical purposes the Buddha has simply died. This wasn't a problem for the Buddha, nor was it a problem for his fully awakened disciples. It was a problem for others who were left behind though, none more so than Ānanda, who loved the Buddha deeply. A few hours after the incident of the Buddha's golden appearance, Ānanda was found leaning against a doorpost, weeping, and saying:

> I am still but a learner, and still have to strive for my own perfection. But, alas, my Master, who was so compassionate towards me, is about to pass away!

The Buddha hears about this and asks someone to bring his faithful old friend to him, and he says:

> Enough, Ānanda! Do not grieve, do not lament! For have I not taught from the very beginning that with all that is dear and beloved there must be change, separation, and severance? Of that which is born, come into being, compounded, and subject to decay, how can one say: "May it not come to dissolution!"? There can be no such state of things. Now for a long time, Ānanda, you have served the Tathāgata with loving-kindness in deed, word, and thought, graciously, pleasantly, with a whole heart and beyond measure. Great good have you gathered, Ānanda! Now you should put forth energy, and soon you too will be free from the taints.[61]

For the not-yet awakened, the Buddha's death means that he is now effectively absent from the world, and it's this absence that the author of the *Longer Sūtra* addresses when he or she gives an alternative reason for the Buddha's golden appearance: he dwells in the abode of the buddhas of the past, present, and future. They are all, in some sense, present at every moment, just as the Buddha will be after he dies. Present in some sense. The Buddha taught a middle way between the philosophical extremes of eternalism and annihilationism. Eternalism is the view that there is a self or soul that continues unchanged throughout time without end. Annihilationism is the view that when we die nothing of us continues. On one level the doctrine of rebirth or, more correctly, rebecoming, represents the middle way between these extremes: there is no enduring self that continues unchanged throughout those lives, yet there is continuity. On a higher level, the doctrine that a buddha is neither reborn nor not reborn represents that middle way: he is neither present nor absent, and nor is he both present and absent.

Up until this point, as far as his disciples know, the Buddha is simply a human being who has, by his own efforts, awakened. From this point of view the Buddha is *the* Buddha – alone, unique, a one-off. Now though, as he dwells with, or brings to mind, all the buddhas of the past, the present, and the future, it becomes clear that he is *a* buddha, part of a lineage and cosmic community of buddhas.

As we'll see, the incident of the Buddha's golden appearance in the *Longer Sūtra* also acts as a trigger for the Buddha to tell the mythic history of the Buddha Amitāyus. Amitāyus – "Infinite Life" – symbolizes the continuing presence of the Buddha. Philosophically this falls into the error of eternalism, but the *Sukhāvatīvyūhaḥ* sutras are not philosophical texts, they are imaginative. I stated in the previous chapter that the *Sukhāvatīvyūhaḥ* sutras take the *via positiva* approach to Awakening, and they extend this to the person of the Buddha too, emphasizing his presence rather than his absence. The philosophical explanation is correct on the conceptual level but, in that we are embodied creatures, who encounter other people through the five physical senses, we feel the *absence* of the Buddha more naturally than we do his presence. If we feel the Buddha's presence at all it's likely to be through the sixth sense, the mind, which is not tied to its local environment in the way that the other senses are, allowing it the freedom to roam wherever it will and embrace whatever it wishes. However, the mind sense is always susceptible to being overwhelmed by the immediacy of the other senses.

The philosopher of religion John Hick makes an interesting point in this regard. Because we have a physical body our experience of the world through the five senses is, as it were, compulsory; cold air feels cold, water feels wet, bright light is dazzling, and so on. Of course there are times when we "escape" the physical world, when we're asleep for example, or under anaesthetic, but we can also leave the world of the physical senses while fully awake, in meditation. In the second of the dhyānas our awareness withdraws from the five senses, leaving only the mind sense. This experience is not compulsory; we have to choose to have it, and we have to make special efforts to enter that state. As I wrote in Chapter 1, according to Buddhism, mind states and the world we inhabit are intimately connected, and, while we can speak of the dhyānas psychologically as mental states, we can also talk of them cosmologically as worlds or spheres of existence. Ānanda gives expression to this idea when, after noticing the Buddha's glowing golden skin, he surmises that it's because the Buddha "dwells in the abode of the buddhas", but also because he "brings to mind the tathāgatas, the arhats, the perfectly awakened buddhas of the past, the present, and the future." These are two different ways of saying the same thing. To be in contact with the Buddha then is an act of choice in which we go beyond the physical world with its immediate demands on our attention to what we might call the imaginal world.

In response to Ānanda's supposition that the Buddha's tranquil and bright appearance is a result of his dwelling in the abode of the buddhas, the Buddha asks him whether devas, or perhaps buddhas, had told him that this was the case, or whether he had come to this conclusion through his own reflection and intelligence. Ānanda replies that it was the latter, at which the Buddha warmly congratulates him:

> "Excellent, Ānanda, excellent. You choose the best possible starting-point, and go on to reflect in just the right way, with great presence of mind. By thinking to ask the Tathāgata about this matter, Ānanda, you have acted in a way that will be of benefit to many people. It will bring happiness to many people. You have acted out of empathy for the world, for the sake of a great many people, in a way that will be of benefit to gods and human beings, and that will bring them happiness.

The Buddha says that Ānanda's asking him about his radiant appearance and so on "will be of benefit to many people. It will bring happiness to many people." He has "acted out of empathy for the world". These are the same words he used when he told his first sixty disciples to go off in different directions and teach the Dharma. Ānanda's purpose – his life's work – was to enable the Buddha to teach, and to make sure that whatever he taught was passed on to others, and on this occasion he gives the Buddha the opportunity to speak about Amitāyus and the mythic history of Sukhāvatī, which will be of great benefit to the world. The implication is that, if Ānanda hadn't mentioned the Buddha's golden appearance, the Buddha would not have taught this sutra. Incidentally, the word translated as "empathy" is *anukampā*, which literally means "to tremble with". This reminds me of the phenomenon of sympathetic resonance. When a string of a musical instrument, say a guitar or piano, is struck, other strings sound "sympathetically", so that we hear not just the note of the string that has been struck, but others too – we hear a chord. Indian and Western baroque instruments make use of this phenomenon by having extra strings that are not actually struck, but sound sympathetically, giving the instrument a fuller and richer resonance. Ānanda is rather like a sympathetic string to the Buddha, sounding in response to his words, although on this occasion the Buddha responds to Ānanda.

The theme of the Buddha's death is continued in the next section of the sutra, when the Buddha says:

> Even if the Tathāgata were to cause knowledge and vision to arise in innumerable, uncountable blessed ones, tathāgatas, arhats, perfectly awakened buddhas, Ānanda, his own knowledge would not be diminished. Why is this? Ānanda, it is because the causes of the knowledge and vision of the Tathāgata are indestructible.

He goes on to say that, if he wanted to, he could live on one bowl of food

> for a whole aeon, for a hundred aeons, a hundred thousand aeons, a great many countless hundreds of thousands of aeons, or even longer, and the Tathāgata's faculties would not fade away. The colour of his face would be unaffected, and the colour of his skin would be undiminished. Why is this the case? Ānanda, it is because the perfection that the Tathāgata has attained is dependent on his samādhi.

The Buddha died of food poisoning, and this passage seems to be a reference to that: whereas in the *Mahā-Parinibbāna Sutta* one bowl of food killed the Buddha, in the *Longer Sutra* one bowl of food would enable him to live forever. Not that the bowl of food in itself would be the cause of his longevity; the cause would be his *samādhi*, or meditative concentration. According to the *Mahā-Parinibbāna Sutta*, the Buddha had the power to overcome his fatal illness but didn't use it. A few days before his death he told Ānanda that he could, if he wished, live on for an aeon.[62] This was possible, he said, because he had perfected the four supernormal abilities (*iddhipāda*), which are the concentrations (*samādhi*) of desire (for Awakening), energy, consciousness, and discernment. Ānanda didn't take him up on this suggestion, even though the Buddha mentioned it three times – it seems his sympathetic resonance failed him at this crucial moment – so the Buddha didn't use this power, and instead renounced the life principle. In other words, he chose to die when he did.

Now the Buddha begins telling the mythic history of Amitāyus and Sukhāvatī:

> In the past, Ānanda, long ago, inconceivably many, innumerable, countless aeons upon countless aeons ago, a tathāgata, an arhat, a perfectly awakened buddha by the name of Dīpaṃkara ... arose in the world.

He goes on to say that before Dīpaṃkara there existed another buddha called Pratāpavat, and before him another, naming altogether eighty-one buddhas, each one no doubt living "inconceivably many, innumerable, countless aeons upon countless aeons" before the subsequent buddha. An aeon is a kalpa, which is a very long time indeed. To get some idea of its duration we're asked to imagine a rock, one mile square. Now imagine a goddess floating down from the heavens every hundred years and brushing the rock, just once, with a piece of Benares silk. The amount of time it would take for the rock to be worn away by the silk would be a kalpa. This is typical of Mahāyāna sutras' fondness for extremely large numbers, long tracts of time, and vast regions of space. For Mahāyāna Buddhists the spiritual life is lived not only in the quotidian world of people, houses, trees, rivers, days, weeks, months, and years, but also the cosmic, imaginal world of inconceivably vast space and time. Listened to in a ritual context, perhaps after meditating, such passages can have the effect of opening our minds to the wonder and mystery of the universe, an awareness of how relatively small we are, and how short our lives.

However, it can be difficult to read or listen to passages like this one, in which all eighty-one buddhas are named, and we may find ourselves wanting to skip onto the next part, in which hopefully something will actually happen. Because they are proper names, translators usually leave them in their original language, in this case Sanskrit. If we don't know Sanskrit, reading all these names is a meaningless exercise, and therefore rather tedious, which is a pity because each name has a meaning, and often a poetic one. Happily, as well as giving the original Sanskrit names, Śraddhāpa has translated them into English, so we're able to enjoy the exuberant imagination of the abode of the buddhas, or at least of whoever thought these names up! Here are some of my favourites in their English translation: "He Who Is Like the Rising Sun", "Fragrance of Sandalwood", "He Who Is Like Lapis Lazuli in Appearance", "Moonbeam", "He Whose Voice Is Like a Musical Instrument", "He Whose Radiance Is Adorned with Falling Blossoms", "Glorious Mountain Peak", "He Who Playfully Attains the Higher Forms of Knowledge with an Intellect Greater Than the Ocean", "Thunderbolt", "He Who Has Abandoned the Delights of the Senses", "Golden", "King of Flower Gardens in Whom the Higher Forms of Knowledge Have Fully Blossomed", "He Who Is Like an Open Parasol in the Wind", and "Mind of a Lion".

These are all names of buddhas, so they all, in some mysterious way, evoke qualities of the awakened mind. Awakening is in some sense like an open parasol in the wind! If we read or listen to these names in an open, receptive state, our imagination can be stimulated and this is tantamount to stimulating the faculty of faith. Interestingly, one of the Pali words translated into English as "faith" is *pasāda,* whose primary meaning, according to the Pali–English dictionary, is "clearness, brightness, purity; referring to the colours (visibility) of the eye". Faith in this sense is different from belief. To have faith in this sense is not to believe certain propositions, it's to imagine greatly, so this long list of buddhas' names should be seen not as a rather long-winded preamble to the story of Amitāyus – a preamble that we might feel would best be omitted – but as an integral and important part of the sutra. It's a signal that to really understand the story that follows, we need to awaken our faith/imagination.

The final buddha mentioned in this list, and therefore the furthest back in time (eighty-one times measureless, countless, inconceivable aeons ago, in fact!) is Lokeśvararāja, or "Sovereign King of the World". The Buddha continues the story by telling Ānanda that, at that time

> there was a monk called Dharmākara who was supremely mindful, intelligent, knowledgeable, wise, supremely energetic, and totally committed.

Dharmākara prostrates himself at Lokeśvararāja's feet and praises him:

> Your radiance is infinite, your intellect limitless and incomparable.
> There is no other radiance which can illuminate this world.
> Nothing in the whole world shines like you do.
> Neither the sun, jewels, a great snowy peak, nor the light of the moon can compare.

He continues in this vein for two more verses and then makes the bodhisattva vow – the *praṇidhāna*:

> The King of Kings, with all the powers of a buddha,
> whose splendour is boundless, sheds his light in all directions.
> May I become a buddha like him, a lord of the Dharma,
> and bring emancipation from old age, death, and birth. ...
> I now undertake this commitment:
> I will become a buddha, and protect all living beings. ...
> My radiance will shine throughout as many world systems as there are
> grains of sand in the River Ganges, and throughout the buddha-fields they contain,
> which are even more numerous, without end.
> This is how I will apply my energy.
> My buddha-field will be exalted, unsurpassed, supreme.
> In that perfectly formed world, everything will be superior.

> The happiness of the realm of nirvana is beyond compare.
> I will cleanse that buddha-field of impurity.
> Living beings will gather there from all of the ten directions of space,
> and when they come they will soon achieve happiness.
> With the Buddha as the witness to my practice,
> I will cultivate an aspiration which is filled with the power of truth and energy.

Some time after making this vow Dharmākara makes a number of very specific vows, but before we explore these I want to dwell for a while on this more general vow, which is the kernel of all the vows that follow. In the previous two chapters I've touched upon the bodhisattva vow in relation to both Śākyamuni (the buddha of this world system) and Amitābha. The Sanskrit word translated as "vow" is *praṇidhāna*, which the translator has rendered as "heartfelt desire". Dharmākara's heartfelt desire is to benefit all beings, and to benefit them in the highest sense possible – to guide them to Awakening – and he vows to practise over countless lifetimes to bring this about. Desires are usually selfish – things, people, or experiences that I want for myself. The bodhisattva vow is a completely different order of desire. It's completely, radically unselfish. It's the expression of a mind – a heart – that has seen through the delusion of a fixed and separate self and wants the best for everyone. In fact, only someone who was quite selfless would be capable of this desire.

Desire and imagination are closely connected. Our desires are activated and sustained by our imagination: we imagine our future life once we've secured a career, we imagine having a loving relationship with a person we find attractive, we imagine having certain experiences on a holiday we've booked. The novelist and art critic Siri Hustvedt makes the point that desires are different from needs:

> While a need is urgent for bodily comfort or even survival, a desire exists at another level of experience ... The difference between need and desire may be behind the fact that I've never heard anyone talk of a rat's "desire" – instincts, drives, behaviours, yes, but never desires. The word seems to imply an imaginative subject, someone who thinks and speaks.[63]

What Hustvedt calls an imaginative subject is what I have called reflexive awareness in Chapter 1. Because we are aware of ourselves as subjects, we can imagine ourselves in the future, in another place, doing different things with different people. A young, single woman, studying medicine, can imagine herself in the future as a successful doctor, married to a loving husband, and having glamorous holidays in far-flung parts of the world. This ability to imagine ourselves in the future has a downside of course; we can waste a lot of time fantasizing about impossible futures or catastrophizing over unlikely scenarios. There is a difference between fantasy and imagination. A fantasy is the imaginative faculty used in the service of selfhood: we fantasize about having sex with someone, about winning a competitive sport, about being famous, about getting a great job. Even fantasies about saving someone from danger, at the risk of one's own life, are really about the agrandizement of the self. Imagination – in the sense that I've been using it – doesn't fixate on the self, and in fact has the potential to go far beyond the self, as in Dharmākara's vow.

In his paper "A defence of poetry" the poet Shelley writes:

> The great secret of morals is love; or a going out of our nature, and an identification of ourselves with the beautiful which exists in thought, action, or person, not our own. A man, to be greatly good, must imagine intensely and comprehensively; he must put himself in the place of another and of many others; the pains and pleasure of his species must become his own. The great instrument of moral good is the imagination.[64]

We've seen that, according to Buddhism, unethical actions lead to suffering. Shelley tells us something more about this: that much of our suffering comes about because our desires lack imagination. We desire pleasure when we could desire happiness, we desire worldly happiness when we could desire the happiness of Awakening, we desire the love of another person when we could desire to love everyone and everything that lives, we desire our own small happiness when we could desire the highest happiness for all beings.

Faith is a kind of desire: the desire for Awakening and the desire for the happiness of all beings are expressions of faith. Of course, some forms of faith are merely selfish desires: a fantasy born of fear, an escape from reality, or a desire for the self to live eternally (in heaven). From the Buddhist point of view, that kind of faith is unskilful, and this includes the desire to be reborn into Sukhāvatī if conceived of as a heaven. In that case the devotee merely desires the continuation of the self, in an environment of great pleasure, happiness, and beauty. The heartfelt desire required to be reborn in Amitābha's pure land is the desire to let go of such self-clinging. Sukhāvatī is an imaginative depiction of non-selfhood, or at least a state of mind close to non-selfhood, not a fantasy of a pleasurable eternal life for the self.

The seed of Dharmākara's exalted imaginative desire can be found in a short sutta from the early teachings in the Pali canon. In the first chapter of the *Sutta Nipāta* is the *Mettā Sutta*, or *Discourse on Loving Kindness* (Skt *maitrī*), in which the Buddha says:

> *Let all creatures indeed be happy and at peace;*
> *May they all have deep-welling happiness.*
> *May all living beings, weak or strong, omitting none ...*
> *Those dwelling near or far away,*
> *Born or unborn – may every living being abound in bliss ...*
> *Just as a mother protects with her life her child, her only child,*
> *Bring forth an all-embracing (loving) mind.*
> *Bring forth unbounded love for all the world:*
> *Above, below, across, in every way,*
> *Love unobstructed; without any enmity ...*
> *Wield this blessing power of mindfulness of boundless love:*
> *For this is what men call: "Abiding in the Divine".*[65]

There are two specific aspects of Dharmākara's vow: his light and his "field", that is, his world system. He begins by praising the Buddha Lokeśvararāja's light, which he says is infinite and boundless, and then he vows that once he is a buddha his light will shine throughout the universe. The image of light radiating in all directions of the universe is very similar to the Buddha's teaching from the *Mettā Sutta*, in which he asks his listeners to cultivate an unbounded mind of loving-kindness "above, below, across, in every way". Here though he teaches the development of loving-kindness only "for all the world", whereas Dharmākara vows that his light will radiate not only throughout his world, but "throughout as many world systems as there are grains of sand in the River Ganges". This difference of scope highlights one of the main differences between the early teachings of the Buddha and the teachings of the Mahāyāna sutras. On the whole the early discourses are on a human scale, set within the parameters of this world. The context in which Mahāyāna sutras are set is the whole cosmos, in which this world is seen to exist within a world system (roughly equivalent to a galaxy), which is itself merely one world system in a universe of countless world systems. Dharmākara's vow then is akin to the Buddha's teaching of loving-kindness, but taken out of its human, historical context and expanded into a cosmic panorama.

Dharmākara vows that his field or world system will be "exalted, unsurpassed, supreme ... Living beings will gather there from all of the ten directions of space, and when they come they will soon achieve happiness." While his light represents his desire to liberate all beings from suffering, his wish to purify a world system represents the practical manifestation of this desire in the concrete world. Dharmākara wants to create an environment that is conducive to happiness, ultimately the happiness of Awakening. Whereas his light is boundless, reaching all parts of the cosmos, his land exists in a particular location, and all locations are limited in size – they have boundaries.

The difference between Dharmākara's light and his field is similar to the difference between *mettā* – loving-kindness towards all beings – and *mitratā* – friendship. With practice it's possible to feel a strong and deep desire for the welfare of all beings, as strong a love as a mother has for her child, but it's not possible to know all these beings personally, let alone develop friendships with them. Given the limitations of time and space we can only develop friendships with a few people in our short lifetimes. This is so even for a buddha. After his Awakening the Buddha spent most of his life wandering, meeting people, teaching them, extending the hand of friendship towards everyone he met. How many was that, I wonder? Is the figure in the hundreds or the thousands? However many, it would have been very few compared to the number of people living at that time. Although buddhas wish to help everyone, there is only so much they can do. Their minds are unlimited but their bodies are constrained by the limitations of time and space.

I expect we've all experienced similar limitations in our own lives, albeit on a more modest scale. There are certain things over which we have some degree of control, while there are countless other things that are completely outside our influence. We can, of course, allow ourselves to feel frustrated by our inability to change things, but the trick seems to be to work in those areas in which we can have some influence and not worry unduly about those areas – the rest of the vast universe! – in which we can't. The Buddha was well aware of the suffering of humanity and no doubt knew that he was only able to help a very small percentage of the population, but he didn't seem to fret unnecessarily over this. For what would be the point? Someone once told me that she'd worked for a while as a cashier in a supermarket, and as part of her training she was told that at busy periods, when a long queue had formed at her check-out desk, she needed to pay full attention to the customer she was serving and not worry about all the others in the queue – because while she was able to serve the customer in front of her, she could do nothing in that moment for those waiting to be served. This is sound advice for life generally, isn't it? All we can do is pay full attention to whatever it is we're doing or whoever it is we're with, letting go of all the other things we could be doing and all the other people we could be helping.

After making this vow Dharmākara asks the Buddha Lokeśvararāja to teach him the Dharma, so that he – Dharmākara – may himself become a buddha in a future age. He also asks him to describe in detail all the excellent qualities of all the buddha-fields in the universe. The Buddha grants his request and proceeds to tell him of the eighty-one million trillion buddhas and their buddha-fields. Eighty-one is very specific, isn't it? You may remember that earlier in the sutra eighty-one buddhas of the past are mentioned. Perhaps that's got something to do with it – a symmetry of time and space.

The Buddha tells Ānanda that it takes ten million years for Lokeśvararāja to describe all these buddha-fields. Dharmākara then concentrates all of the qualities of these buddha-fields into one buddha-field and, after paying homage to the Buddha Lokeśvararāja, spends the next five aeons meditating on this vision. He then "brought into being a buddha-field which was eighty-one times more supreme, unparalleled, and immeasurable" than all the other buddha-fields Lokeśvararāja had revealed to him. Now if we assume that Dharmākara lived for a similar length of time as Lokeśvararāja, five aeons would be one eighth of his life. In human terms, say ten years, which is quite a large proportion of a life, isn't it? And all the time that Dharmākara is sitting meditating – whether it's five aeons or ten years – he's not actively helping anyone, not alleviating the suffering of living beings one jot. We could say that he's on retreat.

Buddhists are sometimes criticized for spending time on retreat, meditating – "gazing at their navels" – when they could be out helping people, feeding the hungry, providing shelter to the homeless, giving to the poor. Even teaching the Dharma would be better, these critics think, than sitting there doing nothing. This argument is quite weak though. In the safety instructions on an aeroplane, we're told that "in the unlikely event" that we have to use the oxygen masks provided, we're to put them on ourselves before helping others with theirs. This is sensible advice. You can't help others if you've passed out. We can go out and start helping others right now and we may be of some use, but we also need to work on ourselves – especially on our mental states – otherwise we may make things worse.

I've made light of the enormous numbers used in the sutra, and I think the author was aware of the potential humour inherent in them, but they do have a serious purpose. Imagine meditating and focusing the mind on an object – say the breath – and becoming absorbed in that experience to the exclusion of all else. With that absorption comes a deep stillness and serenity. Your mind now withdraws from the physical senses and you experience no sounds, no bodily sensations, no thoughts. There is just the mind, fully concentrated, tranquil, quiet, alert. Into this blessed state come the words of the sutra, telling of vast tracts of time and enormous areas of space, so big as to be beyond comprehension – infinite buddhas in world systems the size of galaxies, buddhas going way back into the inconceivable past, meditations lasting five aeons. What kind of effect is such imagery going to have? Surely it will open our mind, take us out of the quotidian, parochial world we usually occupy – of tasks done and not done, worries, fears and anxieties, self-preoccupation. You may remember that in Chapter 1 I listed the four dhyānas – states of meditative absorption – of the formless world. The first is the sphere of infinite space and the second the sphere of infinite consciousness. After contemplating the infinity of space the meditator then turns inwards and realizes that a mind that can contemplate infinite space must itself be infinite. Mind, like space and time, is ultimately *amita* – limitless, without borders, immeasurable.

At the end of his five aeons of contemplation, Dharmākara makes his celebrated vows. For the Chinese and Japanese Pure Land traditions these vows are of supreme importance, and much Pure Land doctrine and practice is based on them. There are actually seven surviving versions of the sutra – one Sanskrit, one Tibetan, and five Chinese – and each version has a different set of vows: one version has eighteen, another has twenty-four, another thirty-six, one has forty-six, another forty-seven, and two have forty-eight. The Pure Land traditions base their interpretations on one of the Chinese versions of the sutra, which has forty-eight vows. If there are different sets of vows, there must have been different authors, or perhaps one original author and a few "editors". Each of the vows – from whichever set – stems from what I've called the kernel vow that Dharmākara makes earlier in the sutra. The developed sets of vows are simply specific applications or ramifications of that earlier general vow, limited only by the ingenuity of each different author or editor. I'll explore these more specific vows in the next three chapters.

After recounting Dharmākara's vows the Buddha then describes his subsequent lives as a bodhisattva. This period lasted, as you can probably guess, for an unimaginably long time, over countless lives. One of the interesting features of this section is that Dharmākara's practice as a bodhisattva is largely defined by the vows he has made. He "fulfilled the vows he had set forth" and "stood firmly in his resolution to do as he had promised". In Chapter 1 I briefly related how bodhisattvas become buddhas: first they make a vow to become a buddha; then they practise for innumerable lives until they are reborn into a world system that has no buddha. There, they awaken to Buddhahood, introduce the beings living there to the Dharma, and transform that world system into a buddha-field, either a pure or an impure one. In the *Longer Sūtra* though, this sequence is significantly different from that. As we've seen, Dharmākara's practice is largely a practice of the specific vows he has made, and this involves creating a buddha-field over the long course of his career as a bodhisattva:

> Whilst he was perfecting the complete purity, the greatness, and the excellence of his buddha-field, and whilst he was practising the bodhisattva path, for innumerably, inestimably, inconceivably, incomparably, immeasurably, incalculably, indescribably many countless hundreds of thousands of millions of years, he did not waver towards sensual desire, ill-will, or cruelty. No notion of sensual desire, ill-will, or cruelty arose in him, nor any notion of forms, sounds, smells, tastes, or physical objects ... He was unwaveringly committed to striving to develop positive qualities ... He dwelt in the state of emptiness, the state of freedom from characteristics, the state of freedom from desire, the state of freedom from accumulation, and the state of non-arising ... By practising the path of the bodhisattva, he led immeasurably many, innumerable, countless hundreds of thousands of millions of living beings to unsurpassed perfect Awakening, so many that it is not easy to express their numbers in words.

Dharmākara didn't simply practise in a general way and then, in his final life when he became a buddha, establish a buddha-field. Rather, he spent all of his lives as a bodhisattva creating his buddha-field. Notice that there are two great dimensions of his bodhisattva practice, two areas that he transforms: his mind – "he did not waver towards sensual desire, ill-will, or cruelty" – and the world – "he led immeasurably many innumerable countless hundreds of thousands of millions of living beings to unsurpassed perfect Awakening". The bodhisattva doesn't just practise the Dharma with the motivation to help others once he or she is a buddha; helping others is an integral part of his or her practice on the way to Buddhahood. Creating a buddha-field, an environment conducive to the practice of the Dharma, is an important aspect of that help. It's not enough just to teach people the Dharma; bodhisattvas also create the conditions that help them to practise. As I wrote at the end of Chapter 1, going to a class at a local Buddhist centre, meditating with others, going on a retreat, meeting up with friends who are also trying to practise – all these activities are like small pure buddha-fields in the midst of our impure buddha-field. And at the end of Chapter 2 I made the point that part of Buddhist practice is to co-create pure buddha-fields within this world of suffering.

An interesting aspect of this is that even before Dharmākara became a Buddha – before he had fully awakened – he was able to help others to awaken. This implies that it's possible to help others to achieve what we haven't yet achieved, to understand what we haven't yet understood. So, although we undoubtedly need to work on ourselves, we can also help others before we're fully awake.

This description of Dharmākara's bodhisattva practice also includes another interesting feature:

> The roots of virtue that he had perfected were such that, wherever he was born, a great multitude of countless hundreds of thousands of millions of precious things appeared out of the earth ... He produced all kinds of ornaments made of precious jewels; all kinds of clothes and robes; all kinds of flowers, incense, perfumes, garlands, ointments, parasols, banners, and flags; and all kinds of music and song. These things arose from the palms of his hands, and from every pore on his body. He produced all kinds of food and drink which were delicious to eat and exquisite to imbibe, as well as all kinds of other enjoyable, delightful things which flowed forth from the palms of his hands as he manifested them.

In the *Shorter Sūtra* we encountered "roots of virtue" – *kuśalamūla* – which constitute one of the conditions for rebirth into Sukhāvatī. They are ethical or skilful actions – those based on positive mental states such as contentment, generosity, goodwill, and awareness – and they result in happiness, both in this and in our next life. They also result in the development of positive qualities and traits. Just as drops of water eventually fill a large pot, so numerous acts of kindness, for instance, result in a kind person, and it's similar with other skilful actions such as generosity, helpfulness, or reflection. These positive qualities and traits, cultivated through skilful actions, are known collectively as merit (*puṇya*), and as we practise the spiritual life our "roots" of merit – *puṇyamūla* – grow. They grow into positive qualities that benefit not only the individual who possesses the merit, but also everyone with whom he or she comes into contact. In this section on Dharmākara's bodhisattva practice, they are depicted as treasures, jewel ornaments, flowers, incense, flags, music, food, and drink – all expressions of wealth, pleasure, and beauty. The Sukhāvatī sutras thus describe the fruits of the spiritual life in terms of beauty. The bodhisattva's merit is manifested as beauty, and the world he or she creates is beautiful. This gives us an important clue as to the nature of the features of Sukhāvatī, such as the golden ground, jewel trees, and lotuses. The environments that Buddhists create – the temples, teaching centres, retreat centres, shrine rooms, gardens – should be as beautiful as we can make them, because beauty has a positive effect on people. It opens and lifts the heart. It also purifies the mind, making us less selfish, and more generous and kind. Beauty helps us to live the spiritual life, because the spiritual life is beautiful.

Returning to the sutra, Ānanda then asks the Buddha whether Dharmākara has yet become a buddha, and, if so, whether he has passed away or is still living and teaching the Dharma. The Buddha replies that he is in fact now a buddha, that his name is Amitābha, and that he lives in his pure buddha-field in the west. This is the first mention of Amitābha in the sutra, and from now on the Buddha speaks not of the past – the history of the Bodhisattva Dharmākara – but of the present Buddha Amitābha. For most of the rest of the sutra, the Buddha describes Amitābha, his pure buddha-field Sukhāvatī and the beings living there, as well as the effect Amitābha has on beings in other world systems. This section – which takes up over half of the sutra – is a description of the fulfilment of Dharmākara's vows, and goes into more detail than do the vows themselves.

In the following three chapters I'm going to explore Dharmākara's vows and their fulfilment. The vows fall into four main categories:

those concerned with the attributes of the buddha that Dharmākara will become; those concerned with the effects that that buddha – Amitābha – will have on beings in world systems other than Sukhāvatī; those concerned with the land and the various elements in it; and those concerned with the beings living there (some of these also concern the land, in that they are to do with the way those beings perceive or interact with the land). Not that they are neatly ordered in the way this might suggest. Although there are clusters of vows pertaining to one or another subject, they don't seem to be in any particular order, and it's likely that they were added to as time went by.

However, as well as exploring the text on its own terms we also need to ask what significance, if any, the story of Dharmākara/Amitābha has for our own lives: what can it mean to us? In the following chapter I'll try to answer this question, and in doing so I'll consider Amitābha's influence – through his light and his name – on beings who live in world systems other than his own, specifically ours. In Chapter 5 I'll revisit the land of Sukhāvatī, noting especially the differences between the way it's depicted in the *Longer* and the *Shorter Sūtras*; and in Chapter 6 I'll look in some detail at the nature of the beings who live there.

Chapter Four

The buddha beyond the Buddha

In the previous chapter I explored the mythic history of Amitābha and his pure buddha-field, Sukhāvatī. In doing that I commented on the story on its own terms, that is, as a story. I didn't question the veracity of that story. If you've read the first two chapters of this book, though, you won't be surprised to learn that I don't take it literally. I do believe, however, that the story is true in a different sense. I think it tells us something important about the spiritual life, about the way it works, about a deeper spiritual or transcendent truth that is usually hidden from us by our habitual ways of seeing and being. It tells us this not in conceptual or philosophical terms, but in a fantastical story. You might wonder why the author or authors decided to offer us this truth in a story rather than in a philosophical treatise. We'll never know the answer to that question, but one possible reason might be that he, or she, or they were simply more inclined to tell stories than to write conceptual discourses. Or it could be that the story expresses their message better than a more philosophical work could. The Buddha once said that the Dharma he'd awakened to was beyond the sphere of reason. Conceptual, analytical, philosophical discourse takes us only so far – as far as reason can go in fact – while stories, myths, metaphors, similes, and poems have the potential to suggest a truth that lies beyond reason's grasp. The Buddha often used similes or stories to illustrate something that he'd just taught in conceptual terms, and occasionally he would break out into verse.

In this chapter I'm going to attempt to put in abstract conceptual terms what I think the sutra expresses through the story. Some people would consider this to be an invalid undertaking. They would say that trying to express the "meaning" of a story in conceptual terms inevitably diminishes it. This is no doubt true, partly for the reasons I've already stated, but also because a story can be interpreted in more than one way, and in offering one interpretation others may be missed. But for those of us who have been brought up in a rationalist, scientific culture, trying to "understand" what the story expresses – that is, to put it into conceptual terms – helps us to give ourselves fully to it. Once we've satisfied our rational mind then perhaps we can go back to the story *as* story, and allow it to speak to us on its own terms. When we do this – when we read or listen to the story as story, rather than "translating" it into conceptual terms – its other meanings may reveal themselves to us.

In most presentations of the bodhisattva career – from the vow to full Awakening – the expectation or hope is that the reader/listener will be inspired to emulate that career. The author wants to inspire us to eschew the "smaller" Awakening of the arhat for the vast Awakening of a buddha. However, the writers of the Sukhāvatī sutras don't appear to be doing that. Their purpose doesn't seem to be to encourage us to do what Dharmākara did, but rather to be the recipients of his vows and practice. Put simply, they don't ask us to *create* buddha-fields, but to aspire to be born in Amitābha's. Of course, as we've seen, there are bodhisattvas as well as śrāvakas in Sukhāvatī, and what makes a bodhisattva a bodhisattva is the taking of the bodhisattva vow, which includes creating a buddha-field. Nevertheless, we as readers are encouraged to cultivate the heartfelt desire to be born in Sukhāvatī, not to create our own buddha-field. So in a way we are back to the position of Śākyamuni's immediate disciples: Amitābha is the Buddha and we are his disciples, trying to awaken under his influence and within his orbit.

But, in that case, why posit another Buddha, distinct from Śākyamuni? More particularly, why have a sutra in which the Buddha Śākyamuni talks exclusively about, and extols the virtues of, the Buddha Amitābha and his buddha-field? A clue to this puzzle may be found in an early Pali text. According to this text, in the first few weeks after his Awakening, the Buddha had the following thought:

> One suffers if dwelling without reverence or deference. Now on what brahman or contemplative can I dwell in dependence, honouring and respecting him?[66]

This statement contains two ideas that surprised me when I first read it. The first one tells us that reverence and deference are natural human emotions, the lack of which causes us to suffer. I wouldn't have been surprised if the Buddha had said "One suffers if dwelling without kindness and compassion", or "without awareness and mindfulness", but that an absence of reverence is a cause of suffering did surprise me. Also, I wouldn't have been surprised if the Buddha had said, "If you encounter someone more spiritually developed, who is altogether wiser and kinder than you are, it's good to feel reverence and deference towards them, and you'll be happier if you do so." What surprised me was the idea that our happiness and well-being depend on our having someone or something to revere, the inference being that, if you don't revere anyone, you'd better find someone you can revere. I suspect that this statement surprised me because of my societal conditioning. I've been brought up in a largely rational, scientific era, in which religion – and therefore faith – has been, and continues to be, discredited. Added to that is the pervasive notion of egalitarianism – the belief that everyone is equal. This is a good and necessary idea if understood as the principle that everyone should have equal opportunities, but it tends to veer into the view that no one is any better than anyone else: no one is wiser, kinder, more intelligent, more generous than me, and therefore there is no one worth revering. This view leads to a kind of flat universe, in which there is no recognition of others' more developed qualities, and therefore no incentive to cultivate our own qualities, to become better than we currently are. This is, I think, the kind of suffering the Buddha had in mind. It's the suffering of stasis, in which the kind of world and mind we currently inhabit is all there is – there's nowhere better to go, no development of mind. For some people this simply means a life of low-level suffering – work, weekends, supermarkets, utility bills, Internet surfing, the daily commute, housework, leisure time. For many others it's a life of intense and deep suffering – civil war, the destruction of their home, the murder of loved ones, poverty, famine, drought. Reverence is the recognition of transcendence, which the Cambridge online dictionary defines as "greater, better, more important, or going past or above all others".

The second part of the Buddha's statement – which is actually a question – surprised me because even he, who was fully awake, felt the need to honour and respect someone. This surprised me because I didn't expect the Buddha to feel this need. I assumed that faith, which I defined in the previous chapter as the desire for Awakening, ended with Awakening. The fact that the Buddha looked for someone he could honour and respect suggests that faith is *more* than simply the desire for Awakening. It continues even after one is fully awake. In his book *Faith and Belief: The Difference Between Them,* Wilfred Cantwell-Smith states that belief, in the modern sense of the word, denotes assent to certain conceptual propositions, whereas faith is

> a quality of human living. At its best it has taken the form of serenity and courage and loyalty and service: a quiet confidence and joy which enable one to feel at home in the universe, and to find meaning in the world and in one's own life, a meaning that is profound and ultimate, and is stable no matter what may happen to oneself at the level of immediate event. Men and women of this kind of faith face catastrophe and confusion, affluence and sorrow, unperturbed; face opportunity with conviction and drive; and face others with a cheerful charity.[67]

The serenity, courage, loyalty, and service come from faith in someone – or something – that transcends us and our immediate situation. This description allows Cantwell-Smith to write that "the Buddha certainly had faith: a religious faith mighty, contagious, creative." The Buddha asks himself the question: "Now on what brahman or contemplative can I dwell in dependence, honouring and respecting him?" Brahmans (*brāhmaṇas*) and contemplatives (*śramaṇas*) were the two principal strands of spiritual seekers in India at the time of the Buddha. The Buddha's two teachers before his Awakening – Uddaka Rāmaputta and Ārāḷa Kālāma – were *śramaṇas*. Asking himself whether there is anyone he can honour and respect, and surveying the whole universe, he finds no one. This is bad news as far as he's concerned, and he doesn't leave it there.

> What if I were to dwell in dependence on this very Dhamma to which I have fully awakened, honouring and respecting it?[68]

There being no person he can revere, he wonders whether he could instead revere the Dharma. Dharma can be understood in two ways: as the truth that the Buddha discovered on awakening, and as the corpus of his teachings and practices that enable others to also realize that truth. Obviously he is referring to the former in this passage. At this point in the text, the god Brahma Sahampati appears and answers the Buddha's question, declaring that all buddhas of the past "dwelled in dependence on the very Dhamma itself, honouring and respecting it", and that all future buddhas will do the same. (As I pointed out in my book *The Art of Reflection*, Brahma Sahampati can be seen as the personification of the Buddha's faculty of reason.[69])

So the Buddha decides to honour and respect the Dharma, the truth he has awoken to. This is of very great significance, because it suggests that the Dharma is greater than the Buddha. Yet we are told in other texts that the Buddha had fully realized the Dharma, had, in a sense, *become* the Dharma, so that there was no difference between them: "He who sees me, sees the Dharma, and he who sees the Dharma, sees me." Let's investigate this, first by asking once again what the Dharma is. The essence of the Dharma – we could say its philosophical basis – is the law of conditioned co-production or dependent co-arising, which states that everything exists in dependence on other existents, which in turn depend on yet other existents, and so on, ad infinitum. The universe is thus a concatenation of events, each of which is linked to – dependent on – other events, and provides the conditions for further events. There are three ways in which this concatenation occurs – things come into existence (in traditional terms, they arise), they exist for a while (they abide), and they die, or break down, or otherwise go out of existence (they cease). Each of these categories is in fact a process: the first a process of generation, growth, development; the second a process of maintenance, preservation, repair; and the third a process of decay, deterioration, decomposition. In the realm of the mind, these processes occur when a thought, emotion, image, memory, or idea arises, then abides for a while, and then ceases. These processes can be unconscious and automatic or conscious and chosen. By unconscious I mean unselfconscious – that is, a thought occurs to you but you are not aware that you are having that thought; you are, as it were, "lost" in it. Because you're not aware of having that thought, the process that follows is unconscious and therefore automatic. For instance, you might see an advert for something that causes craving to arise in your mind. Because you're not aware of this happening – that is, you haven't recognized or identified the craving – your mind dwells on it, and so the craving grows and intensifies. Alternatively, with the help of the practice of mindfulness, we can choose what we dwell on. In this case, we see the advert and a feeling of craving may arise in the mind, but because we are *conscious of* – aware of – that feeling, we now have some *choice* as to whether to dwell on the object and develop that craving, or to let go of it and allow it to cease.

In this way we can learn to eradicate unskilful states from our mind – unawareness, craving, anger, animosity – and generate skilful states of mind – awareness, contentment, friendliness, generosity. The spiritual life consists in the eradication of unskilful and the development of skilful mental states, which form the basis for Awakening. Most of us probably do a bit of both: we are sometimes unaware, unselfconscious, and at those moments we inadvertently allow unskilful states to arise and grow.

At other times, when we are aware, we notice the unskilful state arising and allow it to fall away, replacing it with a more skilful state. Whichever we do tends to lead into more of the same – either a vicious or a virtuous cycle. Actually either can become a spiral, as one state can lead to an intensification of that state, perhaps leading to a physical action, which can also intensify that state. A skilful action (thought, word, or deed) tends to lead to greater happiness and freedom, and that encourages us to continue to act skilfully, leading to yet greater happiness and freedom.

The Buddha talked about this virtuous spiral a number of times. On one of these occasions he said that virtue – ethical action – leads to freedom from remorse, or a clear conscience as we would say.[70] He went on to say that freedom from remorse leads to joy, and joy leads to greater joy – rapture or ecstasy. If we continue to act skilfully the rapture quietens to become serenity, which in turn leads to an even deeper happiness, which allows our mind to become absorbed. "A happy mind is an absorbed mind." "Absorption" is a translation of *samādhi*, which indicates a deeply meditative state, a mind so absorbed in the object of meditation that there is no distraction whatsoever. Such a state enables us to see clearly, to gain insight, to see things as they are, which in turn leads to disenchantment – a state in which we are no longer enchanted, fooled, by the appearance of things. This leads to dispassion, that is, freedom from the passions or cravings and their inevitable results in suffering, leading, eventually, to knowledge and vision of liberation, or full Awakening.

The final experience in the sequence is usually understood as the end of the process, the stopping point, and therefore permanent. Nirvana then is seen as different in kind from everything else in the universe, all other things being impermanent. But in what sense is nirvana permanent? Is it permanent in the sense of being static and unchanging, or is it permanent in the sense of being a continuous flow of awakened states? The author of this sutra seems to consider it to be the latter, for near the beginning of the text Ānanda notices that the Buddha's appearance is more than usually bright, this radiance coming from his dwelling in the abode of the buddhas, implying that at other times he doesn't dwell in that abode.

So now another question arises: what kind of change is it? Is it cyclic or progressive? That is, does the process of Awakening cycle around a number of equally awakened states, such as sometimes dwelling in the sphere of the buddhas and at other times not, or sometimes wishing to dwell in solitude and other times wishing to teach others, or does it progress from one awakened state to another *more* awakened state, and so on indefinitely? If the process is of the second type, then Awakening is not really the end point of the spiritual life but the beginning of a new process. The sutta from which I quoted above – the one in which the Buddha looks for someone he can revere, and, not finding anyone, decides to revere the Dharma – suggests that Awakening is a progressive process. If it were not progressive, and the Buddha had realized it fully, he would be equal to it, and therefore would be unable to revere it. So let me now return to the question that began this discussion: why posit another Buddha apart from Śākyamuni? Why did the authors of these sutras write in such detail about Amitābha and his pure buddha-field Sukhāvatī ? Perhaps they intuited that Awakening is not a fixed point, from which no further progress was possible. Perhaps Amitābha symbolized for them the progressive nature of Awakening, and as such the personification of the Dharma that the Buddha Śākyamuni decided to revere. Perhaps he is, as my teacher once put it, "the buddha beyond the Buddha". The Buddha Śākyamuni narrates all three sutras (that is, the authors have him narrate them), which at least *suggests* that Amitābha is the greater buddha. Therefore, in the Pure Land traditions of China and Japan, Śākyamuni's significance is that he is the messenger of Amitābha.

As we've seen, this interpretation is implicitly denied in both the *Shorter* and the *Longer Sūtras*. In the *Shorter Sūtra*, after listing all the buddhas and their pure buddha-fields in the ten directions, and anticipating that the reader may assume that Śākyamuni is an inferior buddha because of the impurity of his buddha-field, the Buddha tells Śāriputra that all those other buddhas consider him to have done something very difficult in teaching the Dharma in a world in which beings are hostile and unreceptive. In the *Longer Sūtra* the Buddha says that, although he dwells in the sphere of the buddhas, his Awakening is not diminished thereby. However, the fact that the Buddha narrates all three sutras, and encourages the reader to cultivate a heartfelt desire to be born into Sukhāvatī, strongly suggests symbolically that Amitābha is the greater buddha – more fully awakened than Śākyamuni. In fact, when we take into account the myth expounded in the *Longer Sūtra*, that Dharmākara

> brought into being a buddha-field which was eighty-one times more supreme, unparalleled, and immeasurable than the eighty-one quadrillion buddha-fields the Blessed One, the Tathāgata Lokeśvararāja, had described to him

then it appears that Amitābha is the Buddha beyond not only Śākyamuni, but all buddhas. He is the buddha principle par excellence. He personifies, and his pure buddha-field embodies, the dynamic, progressive, never-ending nature of Awakening.

This, I think, is what the myth implies about the goal of the spiritual life. It also says something about the path. I want to return now to what I called the virtuous spiral – the sequence of skilful states leading from virtue to Awakening – because the Buddha said something important about how we move through that sequence, which also has a bearing on the "meaning" of the Amitābha story. He said that:

> For a person endowed with virtue, consummate in virtue, there is no need for an act of will, "May freedom from remorse arise in me." It is in the nature of things that freedom from remorse arises in a person endowed with virtue, consummate in virtue.[71]

He continues in this way through the whole sequence, that is, "For a person free from remorse, there is no need for an act of will: 'May joy arise in me' ... " and so on. No "act of will" is needed to rise from one stage to the next; we don't need to try to make it happen, it's natural. But this doesn't mean that no effort is involved. Notice that the practitioner moves from one state to the next only when the preceding state is fully developed: it is in the nature of things that freedom from remorse arises in a person endowed with virtue, consummate in virtue, and so forth. Developing and consolidating one particular stage of the path takes great effort, and only then does the next stage naturally arise.

It may not arise immediately though, or even any time soon. If we take the example of the second stage in the series we can see why this is so. "Freedom from remorse arises in a person endowed with virtue, consummate in virtue." The word translated here as "consummate" is *sampanna*, which means "successful, complete, or perfect", and obviously it will take some time and a lot of effort to get our ethical practice to this level. However, once we've done this, freedom from remorse arises naturally, without our having to do anything more, and the same goes for all of the succeeding stages.

In a way the Buddha isn't saying anything remarkable here. After all, the same principle works in many ordinary, everyday situations. For instance, if we eat a lot of the wrong kind of food, it's in the nature of things that we'll put on weight, and there's no need for an act of will: "May I put on weight." We just eat those unhealthy foods and it happens, without us having to do any more about it. Similarly, if we plant a seed in good soil, and make sure it gets enough water and sunlight, it's in the nature of things that it will grow into a plant. There's no need for an act of will: "May a plant grow." We just plant the seed and nature does the rest. What *is* remarkable about the Buddha's observation is that he noticed this natural process occurring in the mind, specifically with regard to positive mental states. He noticed that if we develop a positive state of mind fully it *becomes* something else: freedom from remorse *becomes* joy, joy *becomes* rapture, and so on. And each positive mental state transforms into the next one without our having to do anything to make that happen. It's *involuntary*. It happens *to* us.

Now why should it be "in the nature of things" that the succeeding stage in the Buddha's sequence arises from the preceding one? Why should serenity, for example, arise from the state of rapture, or happiness arise from the state of serenity? Why does the mind work in this particular way? As I pointed out in Chapter 2, the Buddha didn't concern himself with questions about *why* things happen the way they do. He simply observed that certain things arise in dependence on certain conditions, and didn't offer any explanations as to why they behave that way. They just do, and that's all we need to know. How do we know that the Buddha was right, though? There's only one way to verify this: by testing it against your own experience. And you can only do that by retracing the Buddha's steps, by practising the Dharma, and noticing what happens.

So it seems that the spiritual life is a process of skilful effort followed by (involuntary) positive effect. More specifically, skilful effort leads to positive effect, and then more skilful effort is needed to intensify and deepen that positive effect, leading to a new positive effect, and so on. At a certain point in that virtuous spiral there is a qualitative difference in positive effect, and that occurs when absorption becomes knowing and seeing things as they really are. At this point the spiral becomes more than merely virtuous; it becomes an Awakening spiral, and all of the stages from this point are deepening stages of that first Awakening. Up until this point the practitioner has been on the "mundane" path, but now he or she is on the "transcendental" – *lokottara* – path.

This transition from the mundane to the transcendental is crucial and decisive. Up to the stage of absorption we are always liable to fall back; up to this point our spiritual development is *reversible*. We can in fact fall right back to the state we were in before we began to live the spiritual life. In traditional terms, we can fall into any one of the realms of suffering: the realms of the hungry ghosts, the animals, the hells, or the jealous gods. But from the stage of knowing and seeing things as they really are we can no longer fall back from Awakening – our development is now *irreversible*. The reason for this is that we've now caught a direct glimpse of the Dharma, we have awoken to the truth of things, which means that we'll never be fooled by the lure of worldly happiness again. This is why the stage following knowing and seeing things as they are is disenchantment – we are no longer enchanted by the things of the world.

But the stage of irreversibility doesn't denote *only* the impossibility of falling back. In Chapter 1 I mentioned the four stages of Awakening in the early, Pali texts: stream-entry, once-returning, non-returning, and full Awakening. It's at the stage of knowing and seeing things as they are that one becomes a stream-entrant, which means that one enters the stream that flows inevitably to full Awakening. The metaphor is given conceptual expression in the doctrine that the stream-entrant is assured of full Awakening within seven lives. This means that it's not only the stage at which we can't fall back, but also the stage at which we can't help but move forward. My teacher uses the analogy of a spacecraft on its way to the moon to illustrate this: for the first stage of the journey the rockets strain against the gravitational pull of the earth, but at a certain point the craft escapes the earth's pull and enters the gravitational pull of the moon. Similarly, while we are on the "mundane" path – the virtuous spiral up to and including the stage of absorption – we are attracted to the goal of Awakening, but we are also subject to the "gravitational pull" of the world. The attraction to the goal of Awakening is faith. Sometimes our faith is stronger than the pull of the world and we make some progress, but at other times it is overwhelmed by unskilful mental states and we find ourselves falling back into painful realms once again. This push–pull dynamic continues until we have a decisive insight into the Dharma, at which point we enter the gravitational pull of Awakening. Awakening is now more attractive to us than anything the world has to offer and we are drawn irresistibly towards it.

As we've seen, all this happens naturally – as the Buddha said, "it's in the nature of things." It's one way in which conditioned co-production or dependent co-arising works. Early Buddhist scholars identified five strands or orders of conditionality, which they called *niyamas*. *Niyama* means "restraint, limitation, necessity", which refers to the fact that things don't happen randomly – an acorn doesn't grow into a holly bush, water doesn't become ice on a hot summer's day – but are restrained, limited by certain laws. The first of these is called the *utu-niyama*, which is the physical inorganic strand of conditionality: when I throw something up in the air it falls back down; when I put a flame underneath a pot of water it heats up. All the laws of physics and chemistry are involved here. Then there is the *bīja-niyama*, which pertains to the physical organic area of life, represented by the study of biology, botany, and physiology. I've already given two examples of this *niyama* – eating too much of certain kinds of food results in us putting on weight, and a seed becomes a plant. The third strand of conditionality, *mano-niyama*, pertains to the instinctual ways the mind works. No doubt we've all had the unpleasant experience of being in a car when a vehicle coming in the opposite direction swerves to avoid something and heads towards us. The fear we feel at this moment is due to this level of conditionality. This *niyama* works in other ways as well. I'm writing this part of the book away from home, in a house in the English countryside, and the first morning I woke here I experienced one of those moments in which I didn't know where I was. For a few seconds my mind grasped after some kind of recognition. These instinctive impulses are common to all animals, but the fourth strand – *karma-niyama* – only operates in those who possess self-awareness and who can therefore see the effects their actions have on their mind and on others. The *karma-niyama* is what I've previously called the law of karma: skilful, ethical actions result in happiness and unskilful actions bring about suffering. Returning to the virtuous spiral, the stages from virtue to absorption exemplify the positive aspect of the *karma-niyama* order of conditionality. With the next stage in that sequence – knowing and seeing things as they are – we leave the mundane and enter the transcendental path, and with that we also leave the *karma-niyama* and enter the *dharma-niyama*, the strand of conditionality that pertains to the mind of the person who realizes that there is no enduring self: from knowing and seeing things as they are all the way to complete Awakening.[72] As we've seen, the stage of knowing and seeing things as they are is also the stage of irreversibility. Just as time moves in only one direction, so the *dharma-niyama* moves in only one direction – towards Awakening.

In the *Shorter Sūtra*, Amitāyus and his pure buddha-field Sukhāvatī are symbols of the *dharma-niyama* order of conditionality, which takes over from the *karma-niyama* at the point of insight. We can see this dynamic in the path outlined in the sutra:

1. "Heartfelt desire" to be born in Sukhāvatī
2. "Roots of virtue" – ethical action
3. "Absorbing the mind undistractedly" in the name of Amitāyus
4. At the moment of death, being met by Amitāyus and his retinue
5. Dying with an "undistorted mind"
6. Birth in Sukhāvatī.

The first three of these correspond to the first half of the spiral path, from virtue to absorption, while four to six correspond to the second half of the spiral, from knowing and seeing things as they really are. The first three are expressions of the *karma-niyama* order of conditionality – they are things that the practitioner has to do in order to be born in Sukhāvatī. And the second three constitute the *dharma-niyama* – they happen to the practitioner; they are the involuntary positive effect of skilful effort. In the symbolic terms of the sutra, at the moment of death Amitāyus comes to meet the deceased person.

Towards the end of the *Shorter Sūtra* the Buddha broadens his theme from Amitāyus to other buddhas residing in the ten directions of space and gives the sutra a subtitle: "Embraced by all the buddhas". These buddhas are personifications of the awakened mind and to be embraced by them suggests something more than just their presence – it suggests that they are active, that they are acting on us, just as Amitāyus actively meets the practitioner at the moment of death. I wrote above that at the stage of irreversibility the practitioner is more attracted to the goal of Awakening than he or she is to the pleasures of the world, but that is to see the process as entirely self-directed. The metaphor of entering the stream, by contrast, suggests an outside force acting on the practitioner, as does my teacher's simile of the moon's gravitational pull. Amitāyus and the other buddhas symbolize this "outside" force – they symbolize other-power.

We need to be careful here though, as we are perilously close to theism. We should remember that other-power is not other as opposed to self, but other as opposed to the unawakened mode of perception, which operates within the self/other duality.

The mythic history of Amitāyus and Sukhāvatī as told in the *Longer Sūtra* – Dharmākara's making of the vows and his subsequent practice as a bodhisattva over innumerable lifetimes, resulting in his full Awakening as Amitāyus and creation of Sukhāvatī – gives an explanation as to why other-power, or the *dharma-niyama* strand of conditionality, is effective. To see how let's look at two of Amitāyus' most important symbols – his light and his name. There are two vows concerning his light:

> Blessed One, may I not attain unsurpassed, perfect Awakening if, when I have attained Awakening, it is possible to measure the extent of my radiance as it shines forth from my buddha-field, even by saying that it extends throughout countless hundreds of thousands of millions of buddha-fields. ...
>
> Blessed One, may I not attain unsurpassed, perfect Awakening unless, when I have attained Awakening, all of the living beings in innumerable, uncountable, inconceivable, incomparable buddha-fields who are touched by my radiance are filled with a happiness which surpasses that of gods and men.

Each vow begins with the words "Blessed One", which is a translation of *bhagavat*, an epithet of the Buddha. This is because Dharmākara makes these vows before the Buddha Lokeśvararāja, and is addressing him. The grammatical structure of the vows is strange and rather awkward, expressed as a paradoxical double negative. Put more simply, in the first of these vows Dharmākara states that when he becomes a buddha his light will be immeasurable, and in the second he vows that, when he is a buddha, anyone who is filled with his light will attain a happiness beyond both men and gods. This is the happiness of Awakening – the third principal level of happiness that we explored in the first chapter: the "still greater unworldly happiness". In terms of the spiral path, it's the happiness experienced from the stage of knowing and seeing things as they really are to realization of knowledge and vision of release or Awakening.

The strange grammatical structure of the vows is, I think, significant. In effect Dharmākara says, "*May I not awaken* if such and such does not come about *when I'm awakened*." This is like saying, "May I not go to Italy if, when I get there, the sun isn't shining" or "May I not graduate as a doctor if I don't cure people of diseases when I've qualified." Why are they phrased in this way? Later in the sutra, after the Buddha has told Ānanda the story of Dharmākara's vows and his subsequent lives as a bodhisattva, Ānanda asks about Dharmākara's current status – did he eventually become a buddha or not? The Buddha replies that he did indeed become a buddha and that he now lives in his pure buddha-field, Sukhāvatī. The implication of this is that all of his vows have been fulfilled – if they weren't, he couldn't now be a buddha. The vows and their fulfilment are therefore "guarantees" that, for instance, Amitābha's light is immeasurable, and that anyone filled with that light will experience the happiness of Awakening. In non-mythical terms, they tell us that "it's in the nature of things" that skilful effort results in positive effects, especially the positive effect of insight and Awakening.

Immediately after answering Ānanda's question the Buddha proceeds to tell him about Amitābha's light. First he confirms the fulfilment of the first of the two vows, saying that his light is immeasurable, pervading "many countless hundreds of thousands of buddha-fields". However, although immeasurable, his light *doesn't* fill every buddha-field:

> The only exception to this is those worlds which are filled with the light of other buddhas, other blessed ones who, because of the power of the vows they have taken, extend their radiance for one, two, three, four, five, ten, twenty, thirty, forty, or fifty yojanas, a hundred yojanas, a thousand yojanas, a hundred thousand yojanas, or for a very great many countless hundreds of thousands of yojanas.

This sentence does two things: it maintains a reverence for all buddhas and simultaneously makes Amitābha the pre-eminent buddha. All buddhas radiate light, but, whereas their light, extensive as it might be, is finite, Amitābha's radiance is infinite. In that "our" buddha, Śākyamuni, is one of these other buddhas, this is further confirmation that the author of the sutra considers Amitābha to be beyond him.

The next part of the description of his light is celebrated by the Pure Land schools and I'm going to quote most of it, because I've been "translating" the message of the sutra into conceptual terms and I'd like to allow it to speak in its own terms of exuberant imagery, wealth, and beauty:[73]

> Ānanda, there is no comparison one could make and no example one could give that would be sufficient to express the immeasurable extent of the light of this tathāgata, Amitābha. This, Ānanda, is why he is called "Infinite Light". This is why he is called "Infinite Radiance", "Infinite Splendour", "Unending Radiance", "Unobstructed Radiance", "Radiant Flame", "Outpouring of Radiance", "The Radiance of Heavenly Jewels", "The Radiance of Unobstructed Rays of Coloured Light", "Delightful Radiance", "Enchanting Radiance", "Exhilarating Radiance", "Harmonizing Radiance", "Pleasant Radiance", "Friendly Radiance", "Radiance Filled with Great Energy", "Incomparable Radiance", "The Radiance of Mighty Kings and Lords", "The Radiance Which Outshines the Sun and the Moon",

> "Supreme", and "The Radiance Which Outshines the Protectors of the World, Śakra, Brahmā, the Gods of the Pure Abodes, Maheśvara, and All the Other Gods".
>
> His noble, pure, vast radiance brings happiness to the body and thrills the mind. It brings joy, gladness, and happiness to gods, titans, nāgas, yakṣas, gandharvas, garuḍas, mahoragas, kinnaras, human beings and non-human beings. It encourages goodness, skilfulness, and gladness in those living beings who base themselves on what is skilful in limitless, unbounded buddha-fields.

The light that radiates from buddhas symbolizes their wisdom and compassion, specifically their particular expression of the Dharma. In the case of "our" buddha, for instance, it includes conditioned co-production, the four noble truths, the threefold way, the five spiritual faculties, the three marks of existence, and so on. Buddhas in other world systems may teach differently according to the dispositions of the beings in those world systems. In the Vimalakīrti Nirdeśa, for instance, there is said to exist a pure buddha-field consisting entirely of perfumes, and the buddha there teaches through aromas. As we've seen, most buddhas' light extends a finite distance, while Amitābha's light is infinite. His sphere of influence is boundless. An interesting feature of the three sutras we're exploring is that Amitābha says hardly anything throughout. He says just one thing, in fact, in the *Longer Sūtra*, in which he responds to a question about his smile, which he says is due to the fact that his vows have been fulfilled. All "teachings" in the sutras come from the land – the birds, the sound of the wind in the jewel trees, and, as we'll see in the next chapter, the sound of the rivers. Amitābha doesn't teach, so he has no particular teachings. His light doesn't symbolize any particular conceptual formulations of the Dharma, but is instead the buddha principle pervading those areas of the universe that are not filled with the light from other buddhas. The Buddha Śākyamuni once said that the Dharma exists "whether or not tathāgatas arise in the world" – it exists even in those world systems that don't have buddhas. Buddhas don't create the Dharma, they discover it. Amitābha's light symbolizes that universal Dharma. It is reality, it is the way things are, which is ever-present, always there to be discovered. Put like that it sounds passive, but Amitābha's light is active; it is other-power, the *dharma-niyama*, radiating outwards in all directions of the universe. The Dharma – reality – is impinging on us all the time, but we, for the most part, do our best to ignore it.

In Chapter 1 I recounted the story of Anāthapiṇḍada's first hearing the word "Buddha" and the effect it had on him. Hearing and meditating on the name of the Buddha Amitābha / Amitāyus is of great importance in both the *Shorter* and the *Longer Sūtras*. Just as his light pervades the whole universe, so does his name, and like his light it stands for the buddha principle, the eternal Dharma. There are thirteen vows concerning his name, twelve of which relate to beings in world systems other than Sukhāvatī. Great spiritual benefits are promised for anyone who hears his name. For instance, the eighteenth vow in the Sanskrit version states that, if anyone who conceives the aspiration to awaken hears Amitābha's name and remembers it with faith, Amitābha will meet him or her at the moment of their death surrounded by his retinue of śrāvakas and bodhisattvas, and he or she – the practitioner – will die without anxiety. This of course relates to the section in the *Shorter Sūtra* that we explored in Chapter 2 and above.

The vow that follows this one, the nineteenth in the Sanskrit version, eighteenth in the Chinese, is considered by many Pure Land teachers to be the most important of all of the vows. The twelfth- / thirteenth-century Japanese master Shinran – the "founder" and inspiration of the Shinshū school – called it the primal vow, sometimes simply referring to it as *the* vow, as if all the other vows were contained in this one.

> Blessed One, may I not attain unsurpassed, perfect Awakening unless, when I have attained Awakening, living beings in innumerable, uncountable buddha-fields who have heard my name, who are intent on my buddha-field, and who dedicate their roots of virtue to being born there – even those who have only cultivated this thought ten times – are reborn there. This is with the exception of those who have committed the five acts which have immediate consequences, or whose opposition to the true Dharma obstructs them from being born there.

If we take it out of its awkward grammatical structure, this vow states that anyone who hears Amitābha's name, is intent on beings born in Sukhavati, and dedicates his or her roots of virtue to rebirth there will be reborn there. This includes those who have only cultivated the thought (the intention) ten times, but excludes those who have committed the "five acts which have immediate consequences", and those who oppose the Dharma. The "five acts" are the weighty karmas that I mentioned in Chapter 2, which result in rebirth in one of the hell realms: murdering an arhat, killing your mother and / or your father, wounding a buddha, and causing a division in the sangha. The second part of this vow makes rebirth in Sukhāvatī seem very easy: one only needs to make the resolution ten times and, as for ethical practice, it's enough not to have committed the five weighty karmas or have opposed the Dharma in some way. Even more radical than this is a passage that occurs later in the sutra, where the Buddha says that,

> if a single mental state of determination and serene faith arises in the living beings who hear the name of the Blessed One Amitābha, their progress towards unsurpassed, perfect Awakening will become irreversible.

Not even as many as ten thoughts are necessary. A single thought (mental state) can catapult us to the stage of irreversibility. These passages contradict the message of the Buddha's teaching of the Awakening spiral, in which the practitioner moves incrementally from one stage to the next, bringing each stage to perfection before being able to move to the next. The *Longer Sūtra* says that it's possible to circumvent this process and leap over the first half of the path – from virtue to absorption – and land somewhere in the second half – from knowing and seeing things as they are to full Awakening. It suggests that we can dispense with the *karma-niyama* and go straight to the *dharma-niyama*, straight from self-power to other-power.

The early Chinese Pure Land teachers would have interpreted these passages in the light of the doctrine of the three ages of the Dharma, as would their later Japanese heirs. For those living in the third age of the Dharma, when it's no longer possible to achieve Awakening by one's own efforts, the cultivation of ten thoughts – no, even just one moment of serene faith – is sufficient because Dharmākara's vow does the rest. As I don't regard the doctrine of the three ages of the Dharma as really Buddhist, I can't accept this interpretation at face value, but it still has a lot to tell us. Before we look at what that is though, I want to consider another Pure Land interpretation.

One of the main concerns of the seventh-century Chinese teacher Shandao was the spiritual plight of the common man and woman, that is, the materially poor lay follower. The path as set out by the Buddha, in the teaching of the Awakening spiral, for example, but also in the *Shorter Sūtra* with its cultivation of many roots of virtue and meditative absorption, demands a certain amount of time devoted to spiritual practice. Monks and nuns may well have had that amount of time, but lay followers didn't. They had to earn their living and bring up their children, so they had very little – if any – time for formal spiritual practice. Not only that; many of them had occupations, such as farming, fishing, or hunting, which meant that they broke the first precept – to abstain from harming living beings – every day of their lives. How could these people cultivate the necessary roots of virtue and meditative absorption to be born in Sukhāvatī? Shandao's answer was that the monastics gained access to Sukhāvatī through their practice of ethical purity and meditation, while the laity did so through faith alone. Looking at the nineteenth vow again, it's possible to interpret the first part of the vow as pertaining to the monastics and the second part as concerning the laity.

What both of these interpretations have in common is the important truth that, although there is a path to Awakening, in principle it's possible to awaken at any time, in any place, and in almost any mental state, excepting only those that result in murdering an arhat and so forth. Reality is all around us, there to be seen by anyone. As the *Zenrinkushu* tells us:

> *Nothing whatever is hidden;*
> *From of old, all is clear as daylight.*

All we have to do is look with open eyes. In principle that's true, but in practice it doesn't happen very often, because most of us have our eyes very firmly closed, or, to put it another way, we are fast asleep and very hard to wake. The spiritual path helps us to open our eyes; it prepares us, and most of us need that preparation. So we do need to practise, but at the same time we need to bear in mind that Awakening can happen at any time, in almost any circumstances. We could practise for many years and fail to gain insight because we assume that we are not yet ready – that our desire to see things as they are is not strong enough, or our ethical practice has not matured sufficiently, or our meditation practice is too distracted – and these thoughts can become a self-fulfilling prophecy: because we think we're not ready, we close ourselves to the possibility of insight occurring right now. This is a form of doubt. Faith, we could say, is open-mindedness. It is the state of mind in which we are open to the possibility of seeing things as they are at any moment. So we could understand the nineteenth vow as saying that, although we need to devote ourselves to spiritual practice to prepare our minds for Awakening, with enough faith we can break through our delusions right now. What the nineteenth vow tells us is that faith ultimately trumps practice.

The "single mental state" that has the power to catapult us straight to the irreversible stage is not just an ordinary thought; it is a moment of great faith – faith that is tantamount to wisdom. For the Pure Land teacher Shinran, this was the central and defining experience of the spiritual life. Faith was the act of *entrusting oneself* to Dharmākara's vows in the belief that they had made it possible for ordinary people to reach the stage of irreversibility through faith alone. Having reached that stage, birth in Sukhāvatī is assured. In fact, one has already been reborn there; the stage of irreversibility *is* Sukhāvatī. Shinran wrote that faith in other-power acted in a "crosswise" manner, as opposed to the "vertical" way of self-power practice – crosswise in that faith cuts across the idea of a path leading upwards, as it were, to Awakening.

Pure Land Buddhists like to cite the great Mahāyāna philosopher Nāgārjuna to give some authority to their claims for faith over practice. In a text attributed to him called the *Discourse on the Ten Stages* (to Buddhahood) he apparently writes:

> To the practisers of Mahāyāna, the Buddha said: "To make vows and seek the path to buddhahood is a task harder than lifting the whole universe".
>
> You say that the stage of irreversibility is extremely difficult to enter, requiring a long period of practice, and ask me if there is a path of easy practice whereby you can attain this stage quickly. These are words of a cowardly and contemptible man, and not those of a brave man with a strong aspiration. If, however, you insist on hearing from me about this method of practice, I will explain it to you.
>
> There are innumerable modes of entry into the Buddha's teaching. Just as there are in the world difficult and easy paths – travelling on foot by land is full of hardship and travelling in a boat by sea is pleasant – so it is among the paths of the Bodhisattvas. Some exert themselves diligently, while others quickly enter irreversibility by the easy practice based on faith.[74]

Despite Nāgārjuna's disparagement of the idea of an easy path and his reluctance to tell his interlocutor about it, what he actually says about it seems to me to be wholly positive and very attractive. I'm left wondering why, if both paths lead to the same place, anyone would choose the hard path. If there is an easy path, why wouldn't you take it? However, this is not as simple as it may seem. We need to ask what makes the path of faith easy. It's easy not because it requires little effort, but because the effort made by someone of great faith seems effortless. The easy path is not the lazy path! I'm sure you've noticed how easy it is to do something that you want to do, and how much easier it is than doing what you think you ought to do. Faith, as I pointed out in Chapter 3, is a form of desire, and when you desire something you are motivated to do something to get it. Faith simply makes you want to practise, and it makes the experience of practice enjoyable. When you have faith, practising the Dharma is easy because there is nothing else you'd rather do. In the state of faith you long for Awakening – or Sukhāvatī – as a lover longs for their beloved, and the lover is happy to endure any hardship to be with their beloved. Or think of the music lover who will travel for miles and queue for hours to listen to her favourite musician, or the footballer who happily trains for hours every day because he loves playing. The trick is to love the Buddha, Dharma, and Sangha. Then the path is easy. And enjoyable.

This prompts another question though: how do we learn the "trick" of loving the Three Jewels? How do we develop that kind of faith? We can't just decide to have it, and, if we don't have it, we have no choice but to follow the "hard" path of effort. Of course any kind of Dharma practice requires *some* faith – if we had no faith at all we simply wouldn't practise. Returning again to the Awakening spiral path, as we've seen, this tells us that skilful effort results in positive effect, and the experience of that positive effect strengthens our faith. This motivates us to make more effort, resulting in yet more positive effect, which in turn strengthens our faith further. So faith develops as we practise; it grows with experience, which means that we enter the "easy path" only after treading the "hard path" for some time. The easy path then is the advanced path!

One of the characteristics of the stream-entrant – the person who has reached the stage of irreversibility – is unshakeable faith in the Three Jewels. It's unshakeable because he or she has now experienced the positive effect of insight into the true nature of things. The easy path then begins with insight. The hard path is the *karma-niyama* and the easy path is the *dharma-niyama*. The hard path is self-power practice and the easy path is other-power embracing us.

Of course "path" is a metaphor, and we have a tendency to take metaphors literally. It's easy to envision a path leading from where we are now to Awakening, and so we tend to think of the spiritual life as a linear progression, rather like the path the Buddha sets out in the Awakening spiral. However, for many people their spiritual life doesn't follow such a neat, straight, linear progression. It seems to be more untidy than that, and more problematic. For many of us, our "path" – if we can call it that – is winding, meandering, sometimes leading us into jungle thickets where the path disappears completely, or it is blocked by great obstacles – fallen trees, overturned articulated lorries, piles of rubble – and liberally strewn with holes down which it's easy to fall. We make effort, and nothing happens. We redouble our efforts and – nothing happens. At least, that's the way it seems. Actually something *is* happening, but it's happening outside of our conscious, willing mind. Juan Ramon Jimenez expresses this experience beautifully in his poem "Oceans":

> *I have a feeling that my boat*
> *has struck, down there in the depths,*
> *against a great thing.*
> *And nothing*
> *happens! Nothing ... Silence ... Waves...*
> *– Nothing happens? Or has everything happened,*
> *and are we standing now, quietly, in the new life?*[75]

In his book *The Varieties of Religious Experience*, William James compares this phenomenon with another experience with which we're all familiar: that of being unable to remember a person's name. As hard as we try, the elusive name just won't come, "as though the name were jammed, and pressure in its direction only kept it all the more from rising".[76] It's only when we've given up the effort to remember, when we're doing something else, thinking of something completely different, or of nothing at all, that the name comes to us spontaneously, seemingly unbidden. James thinks that a similar process occurs in the spiritual life – we practise, make effort over and over, but with no positive effect, until we give up. Only then does the positive result come. He quotes a Dr Starbuck, who identifies two kinds of spiritual aspirant: the "volitional type" and the "type by self-surrender", but his explanation suggests not so much two types of people as two parts of a single process, beginning with volitional effort – what we could call self-power – followed by self-surrender – other-power. Self-effort can only take us so far – as far as the stage of absorption in the spiral path. To reach the next stage – knowing and seeing things as they are, the stage of irreversibility – we have to let go of the self, let go of self-willing, and allow the path to unfold before us.

If there are two religious "types", I would say that one is the kind of person who makes this transition smoothly, without any difficulty, while the other has a spiritual crisis: they feel they are getting nowhere, as if all their efforts have come to nothing, and they give up in despair. Only then does the insight come, and because the experience is not willed – because they don't seem to have brought it about – it seems to come from somewhere else, even from another person or presence. H.G. Wells describes such an experience in his novel *Mr Britling Sees It Through*. This is a description of an actual experience Wells had towards the end of the First World War, at a time when he was very low, utterly demoralized by the war:

> And for the first time clearly he felt a Presence, of which he had thought very many times in the last few weeks. A Presence so close to him that it was behind his eyes and in his brain and hands. It was no trick of his vision; it was a feeling of immediate reality ... It was as if he had been groping all this time in the darkness, thinking himself alone amidst rocks and pitfalls and pitiless things, and suddenly a hand, a firm, strong hand had touched his own. And a voice within him bade him be of good courage ... It was the crucial moment of Mr Britling's life ... "I have thought too much of myself", said Mr Britling, "and of what I would do by myself. I have forgotten that which was with me."[77]

As a result of this experience Wells wrote a booklet called *God the Invisible King*. There he makes it clear that what he calls "God" is not the creator of the universe, but a kind of spiritual force or presence, which he also called "the Captain of Mankind". Amazingly, his description of this presence is very similar to the traditional Indo-Tibetan paintings of the celestial Bodhisattva Mañjuśrī, the crown prince of wisdom:

> if a figure may represent him it must be the figure of a beautiful youth, already brave and wise, but hardly come to his strength. He should stand lightly on his feet in the morning time, eager to go forward, as though he had but newly arisen to a day that was still but a promise; he should bear a sword, that clean, discriminating wisdom, his eyes should be as bright as swords; his lips should fall apart with eagerness for the great adventure before him, and he should be in very fresh and golden harness, reflecting the rising sun. Death should still hang like mists and cloud banks and shadows in the valleys of the wide landscape about him. There should be dew upon the threads of gossamer and little leaves and blades of turf at his feet.[78]

One of the interesting things about these two quotes is that, although in the second one Wells describes the Presence as another being, in the first one, writing in the fictional mode of Mr Britling, he refers to it as being "so close to him that it was behind his eyes and in his brain and hands". The Presence is neither the self nor other, or it's both self and other.

In this chapter I've tried to put into conceptual terms what I think the sutra expresses through the mythic history of Amitābha and Sukhāvatī. Firstly, the Dharma is natural. If we practise the Dharma, "it's in the nature of things" that we will grow towards Awakening: positive (involuntary) effect naturally follows skilful effort. Secondly, at its higher levels this positive involuntary effect can be experienced as an outside force acting on us. Not that a real, eternal, enduring being comes into contact with oneself, but that, as we progress on the path to Awakening, as our consciousness outgrows the smaller confines of the self, a sense of otherness begins to be felt. This otherness is consciousness-without-self-or-other. Thirdly, this experience can break through our deluded, limited mind at any moment. Ultimately this experience is not dependent on any particular set of conditions. Amitābha's light and his name stand for this ever-present possibility.

Having conceptualized the story, though, I'm aware of a kind of flattening of its meaning, a loss of depth, a reduction of resonance. Take the story away and the meaning is diminished. Take the story away and you also take the imagination away. It's rather like a description of a piece of music:

> After two introductory chords, the violoncellos state the principal theme. It is simply the notes of a common chord, swinging backwards and forwards in a quietly energetic rhythm. Then, as the violins enter with a palpitating high note, the harmony becomes clouded, soon, however, to resolve in sunshine.[79]

That sounds very nice, doesn't it? But we have no idea what it actually sounds like. Reading or hearing a description of a piece of music is not to actually hear it. Once we've heard it we might be able to recognize it from the description, but not before. Just after writing the above I happened to turn on the radio. Rufus Wainwright was singing "Somewhere over the rainbow" – a recording of an encore from a concert the previous evening – and I was arrested, moved, my heart was touched, my body suffused with pleasure. I had to stop what I was doing and listen, give my whole attention to it. Reading a description of it wouldn't have had that effect on me, as I'm sure it hasn't on you.

We also lose something else when we conceptualize the meaning of the sutras – the personal. After his Awakening the Buddha looked for some*body* to revere. A person. Only after coming to the conclusion that there was no one in the universe more awakened than himself did he decide to revere the Dharma. Consciousness-without-self-or-other is a nice phrase but it's abstract, and it's harder to feel for abstractions than it is for people. Being embraced by all the Buddhas, or being met by Amitābha and his retinue of śrāvakas and bodhisattvas, are *personal* experiences. They are *felt*. Consciousness-without-self-or-other is impersonal, and appeals more to our intellect than it does to our emotions.

At the beginning of this chapter I said that once we've satisfied our rational mind then perhaps we can go back to the story as story, and allow it to speak to us on its own terms. I hope you'll do that now.

Chapter Five

Awakening in beauty

In Chapter 1 I suggested that the imagery of Sukhāvatī may have developed from *kasiṇa* meditation, that is, meditation on earth, water, fire, air, blue, yellow, red, white, space, and consciousness (or light). The Buddha taught these meditations to help his disciples leave the world of sense desire (*kāma loka*), at least temporarily, and enter the world of form (*rūpa loka*) or, to put it another way, move from worldly to unworldly happiness. There are of course differences between the *kasiṇas* and the objects in Sukhāvatī. The *kasiṇas* are simple sense objects found in this world whereas the objects in Sukhāvatī are imaginary – golden ground, trees made of precious substances, lotuses the size of cartwheels, and so on. There is another difference too: the *kasiṇas* are spiritually neutral, in that they are not symbols – they don't point to anything other than themselves. The earth *kasiṇa* is just earth, the water *kasiṇa* is just water, and so forth. The objects in Sukhāvatī, by contrast, have been created by Dharmākara – they are all manifestations of his merit – so that the practice of meditating on them, imagining them, is not only an exercise in concentration, it's also a practice of faith and devotion. To imagine being in Sukhāvatī is to be in Amitābha's field of influence, we could even say to be in his mind.

However, the *kasiṇa*s would not have been spiritually neutral for those who were taught by the Buddha. In Chapter 2 I made the point that the Dharma is essentially a personal communication, especially in a society based on the spoken rather than the written word. When one of the Buddha's disciples meditated on the water *kasiṇa*, for instance, they would have been conscious of the fact that the practice had been given to them by the Buddha, and they would have gazed at and imagined the water *in relation to* the Buddha. By doing those practices they were, in a sense, dwelling with him. Imagine that your friend has recommended a film to you, so you go to see it. You watch the film alone, but are very conscious of your friend's strong recommendation, their obvious love of the film, and their desire that you too enjoy it, so in a sense you are watching it *with*, or at least *in relation to*, your friend. Assuming that you *do* enjoy the film, your pleasure will be associated with your friend – each time you are surprised or amused or moved your friend will come to mind, and at the end of the film you will think of them. Perhaps you will phone or text them to tell them how much you enjoyed it, and to thank them for recommending it to you. The early Buddhists would, I think, have practised meditation in this relational way.

In the Sukhāvatī sutras that attitude is made explicit, in that everything seen, everything imagined, is an expression of Amitābha. We already looked around Sukhāvatī in Chapter 1, but the description in the *Shorter Sūtra* is a mere sketch compared to that in the *Longer Sūtra*, which is in comparison more like an elaborate painting in oils. There are also a number of differences between the two descriptions: in the *Longer Sūtra* the features are more fantastical and often bigger; more features are introduced; the teaching of the Dharma is more explicitly concerned with insight and its effects on the hearers; and, whereas in the *Shorter Sūtra* Sukhāvatī appears in splendid isolation, in the *Longer Sutra* we see it *in relation to* other world systems such as our own.

In the *Longer Sūtra*, Sukhāvatī is described in two ways: firstly in the vows, which state Dharmākara's intentions for how his pure land will be. As we've seen, these vows have all come to fruition so they are more than just wishes – they are descriptions. Secondly, later in the sutra the Buddha describes Sukhāvatī to Ānanda in greater detail. This section represents the fulfilment of the vows. The purpose of listening to or reading Dharmākara's long list of vows and their fulfilment is to help us to imagine Sukhāvatī in detail, to develop gratitude and faith in Amitābha, and to cultivate our own heartfelt desire to be born there. All of the elements of the land are to be imagined as vividly as possible. I would say visualized but, as I mentioned in Chapter 1, the descriptions are not only visual: they include the senses of smell, hearing, touch, and even, in one instance, taste. In imagining Sukhāvatī we're not just looking at it, we're immersed in it, being touched by it, smelling it, hearing the sounds all around us, tasting it. This is actually another way in which imagining Sukhāvatī is similar to *kasiṇa* meditation, which begins with simply looking at an object. However, when we come to the second stage of the practice, which consists in seeing the object in our mind's eye, the Buddha said that we should contemplate the *kasiṇa* "above, below, across, undivided and immeasurable".[80] When meditating on the colour blue, for example, we are to imagine blue all around us. This feels very different from looking *at* a blue object, which is finite and delimited. It feels more as if blueness were a medium like a gas or liquid in which we are *immersed*, so that blue is not just a visual experience but includes the whole body in a *feeling* of blueness.

Looking initially at the four vows pertaining to the land, three of them are more or less what we'd expect from our reading of the *Shorter Sūtra*: there will be no realms of suffering, that is, no hells, animals, hungry ghosts, or titans. There will be "hundreds of thousands of jars made of all kinds of jewels ... filling the air with various exquisite fragrances", the fragrances being beyond the range of divine or human senses. Sweet-smelling jewel flowers will constantly rain down, and clouds of enchanting music will play constantly. The fourth of the vows concerning the land is rather different, and intriguing. Dharmākara vows that his buddha-field will be:

> so clear that innumerable, uncountable, inconceivable, unequalled, immeasurable buddha-fields are visible all around, as clearly as looking at one's face in a highly polished mirror.

This is the first instance we've seen of Sukhāvatī's relationship with other world systems: it will be so luminous that all other buddha-fields will be seen in it. I'm reminded of William Blake's famous lines from "Auguries of innocence":

> *To see a World in a Grain of Sand*
> *And a Heaven in a Wild Flower,*
> *Hold Infinity in the palm of your hand*
> *And Eternity in an hour.*[81]

In principle everything we care to look at is clear, in that everything is real – Sukhāvatī, a grain of sand, a wild flower, even a crumpled sock or a dustbin! If we really look at one thing, with an open but concentrated mind, we can understand its nature, and if we understand the nature of one thing we understand the nature of everything. But, if that's the case, our own world is also clear and we should be able to see all buddha-fields in it too. So in what way is Sukhāvatī any clearer than our own world? It partly depends on who is looking at it. It's not clear from the text who the intended viewer is: did Dharmākara mean the beings living in Sukhāvatī or beings from other world systems like our own? If he meant the former, we return to the fact that we don't merely perceive the world, but create it. Sukhāvatī is populated by beings in various stages of Awakening and their world is partly an expression of their minds.

(Only partly an expression of their minds because of course Dharmākara created Sukhāvatī. However, in that they were born there as a result of their own Awakening, they participate in that creation. They, along with Amitābha, continually co-create Sukhāvatī, as we'll see at the end of this chapter and in the next.) Sukhāvatī is clear in the eyes of those who live there because their minds are clear. In principle, those of us who live in an impure buddha-field could see all buddha-fields in our own world, but in practice we have great difficulty in seeing things the way they are. We have great difficulty in seeing anything very clearly. An impure buddha-field like ours is a place of darkness, obscurity, and confusion because the minds of the beings who live here are dark, obscure, and confused so, although our world is clear, we don't see it as such. However, with training and practice it becomes possible to see it clearly. In one of the early Pali texts the Buddha says:

> The mind, O monks, is luminous, but it is defiled by adventitious defilements.
>
> The mind, O monks, is luminous, and it is freed from adventitious defilements.[82]

This implies that consciousness is intrinsically luminous, bright, or radiant, and that the "defilements" – all the unskilful states of mind that "darken" the mind – are foreign to its nature. They don't have to be present for consciousness to function, and indeed they aren't present in the states of meditative absorption (dhyāna). The Buddha's description or evocation of the fourth dhyāna ends with him saying that the meditator

> sits, permeating the body with a pure, bright awareness. Just as if a man were sitting covered from head to foot with a white cloth so that there would be no part of his body to which the white cloth did not extend; even so, the monk sits, permeating the body with a pure, bright awareness. There is nothing of his entire body unpervaded by pure, bright awareness.[83]

Even the fourth dhyāna is not a state of wisdom though. The mind of the meditator in the fourth dhyāna is pure and bright in that the unskilful states of greed, hatred, and delusion are not currently present, but they could return when he or she emerges from meditation. As the eleventh-/twelfth-century Tibetan yogi Milarepa sang:

When your body is rightly poised, and your
consciousness absorbed deep in meditation,
You may feel that thought and mind both disappear;
Yet this is but the surface experience of Dhyāna.
By constant practice and mindfulness thereon,
One feels radiant Self-awareness shining like a brilliant
lamp.
It is pure and bright as a flower,
It is like the feeling of staring
Into the vast and empty sky.
The Awareness of Voidness is limpid and transparent,
yet vivid.
This Non-thought, this radiant and transparent
experience
Is but the feeling of Dhyāna.[84]

But, in that case, we're back to the original question: what makes Sukhāvatī so clear? How is it clearer than our world? Let's remind ourselves that Sukhāvatī is a symbol, that is, an image freighted with meaning. Every feature in it – the trees, ponds, flowers, ground, birds, nets of bells – symbolizes aspects of the mind, either the exalted mind of meditative absorption or the awakened mind. As such, it is what my teacher has called an "illumined image" – an image that is more than the image, because it carries meanings, associations, allusions, feelings that are invested in it by the person imagining it. The crumpled sock lying on my bedroom floor is real – "clear" – and so I could use it as my object of contemplation and possibly awaken thereby. But my sock doesn't carry with it associations of the spiritual life and Awakening. The small statue of the Buddha that I own does carry those associations for me, so when I look at it I "see" much more than the eight-inch-high, deep-red resin form on the wooden box that is my shrine. Incidentally, I bought this buddha figure from a home-furnishings shop in Manchester over three decades ago. The shop was selling table lamps made from copies of a statue of a buddha, with the lamp holder protruding from the top of the buddha's head! Apart from this unfortunate fact they were very lovely. I'd noticed that the shop had been selling some without the lamp fitting, and I went in to buy one. When I asked, I was told that they'd sold out. However, they did have the original from which they'd taken the mould and they were willing to sell it to me. So the buddha figure in front of whom I meditate, to whom I bow down, who symbolizes for me the Buddha, that greatest of human beings – wise, compassionate, free – has been for someone else presumably nothing more than an attractive table lamp. For me he is an illumined image; for them he is illumined only by the light shining from the lamp on his head.

Let's move on to the section in which the Buddha describes Sukhāvatī to Ānanda, and which represents the fulfilment of Dharmākara's vows. The jewel trees are described in more detail than they were in the *Shorter Sūtra*. While some are made of just one precious substance – gold, silver, emerald, and so on – others consist of two:

> The trees made of gold, Ānanda, have roots, trunks, limbs, branches, leaves, and flowers made of gold, and fruit made of silver. The trees made of silver have roots, trunks, limbs, branches, leaves, and flowers made of silver, and fruit made of lapis lazuli. The trees made of lapis lazuli have roots, trunks, limbs, branches, leaves, and flowers made of lapis lazuli, and fruit made of quartz.

And so on through different combinations. Some are made of all seven precious substances:

> Some of the trees, Ānanda, have roots made of gold, trunks made of silver, limbs made of lapis lazuli, branches made of quartz, leaves made of sapphire, flowers made of ruby, and fruit made of emerald. Some of the trees, Ānanda, have roots made of silver, trunks made of lapis lazuli

and so on. These are not just pretty pictures but meditations, each tree to be visualized as clearly as possible, requiring and enabling a pure and bright awareness from which wisdom can arise.

Someone recently told me that one of the things she finds unattractive about the imagery of Sukhāvatī is that the trees and flowers are made of minerals, making the land seem dead and unnatural. However, the Buddha begins his description of Sukhāvatī by saying that it is "abundant, bountiful, comfortable, with plentiful supplies of food", suggesting growth and life, and the jewel trees, for instance, "are pleasant to the touch, and smell wonderful". We have to try to imagine things that we've never experienced in this world, or at least to imagine two types of things that we've experienced separately, but never before fused together: plants that are at the same time jewels, precious metals that are simultaneously trees.

Lotuses cover the ground in every direction and are, like the jewel trees, made of the seven precious substances. While in the *Shorter Sūtra* they are merely the size of cartwheels, in the *Longer Sūtra* they are anything from half a yojana to ten yojanas in circumference. A yojana is approximately nine miles, which means that some of the lotuses are ninety miles in circumference! In the three sutras we're exploring, size, or scale, has spiritual significance. In a conversation with the art critic Martin Gayford, David Hockney said this:

> We think that the photograph is the ultimate reality, but it isn't, because the camera sees geometrically. We don't. We see partly geometrically and partly psychologically. If I glance at the picture of Brahms on the wall over there, the moment I do he becomes larger than the door ... When I'm looking at your face now, it's rather big in my vision because I'm concentrating on you and not on other things. But if I just move for a moment to look over there, your face becomes small. Isn't that what is happening? Isn't the eye part of the mind? If you look at Egyptian pictures, the Pharaoh is three times bigger than anybody else. The archeologist measures the length of the Pharaoh's mummy and concludes that he wasn't any larger than the average citizen. But actually he was bigger – in the minds of the Egyptians. The Egyptian pictures are truthful in some way, but not geometrically.[85]

This is perhaps why the lotuses in the *Longer Sūtra* are anything from five to ninety miles in circumference – their size depends on the state of mind of the observer. Hockney distinguishes between geometrical and psychological vision, and we could add another category – spiritual vision, or the perception of someone in whom the divine eye has opened. Not only are the lotus flowers in the *Longer Sūtra* bigger than those in the *Shorter Sūtra*, but also:

> From each of these lotus flowers made of precious substances, thirty-six trillion rays of light shine forth, and from the tips of each of these rays of light, thirty-six trillion golden buddhas come forth, each possessing the thirty-two major physical characteristics of a great person. They travel to innumerable, uncountable world systems to the east, and teach the Dharma to the living beings who dwell there. In the same way, they travel to innumerable, uncountable world systems to the south,

> to the west, to the north, above, below, and in the intermediate directions, and teach the Dharma to the living beings who dwell there.

This is another instance of Sukhāvatī being in relationship with other world systems. The first instance – Sukhāvatī being so clear that one is able to see all other world systems in it – is a passive image. It's there for all to see, but we have to look. It's also an image of wisdom – in looking at it we understand the nature of all things. This second instance is active and expresses compassion – the buddhas go to other world systems to teach the Dharma to the beings there. Visualizing the lotuses in the *Shorter Sūtra* is simply an exercise in concentration, resulting in samādhi. Visualizing the lotuses in the *Longer Sūtra*, with their trillions of buddhas going out in all directions, is at once a meditation on the vastness of space, an act of devotion, and an expression of compassion for all beings everywhere. It's a psychedelic and cosmic version of the lines of the *Mettā Sutta* I quoted in Chapter 3:

> *Bring forth unbounded love for all the world:*
> *Above, below, across, in every way,*
> *Love unobstructed...*

There is one attribute of Sukhāvatī that I've found to be quite unpopular among my Western Buddhist friends: there are no hills or mountains there, instead it is "delightfully flat like the palm of one's hand". In the earlier Pali texts, the Buddha often talked approvingly of "a delightful stretch of level ground", and once used this as a simile for Awakening. Flat, level ground must have been highly valued in India at that time. However, there is a way of understanding this idea that goes beyond the merely cultural. Sukhāvatī is the "place" of Awakening, in which everything is clearly seen, nothing obscured. Beautiful as hills and mountains are, and enjoyable as it is to walk on them, they do stand in the way, and thereby block our view, of what lies beyond them. The flatness of Sukhāvatī represents wisdom, in which everything is clearly seen at all times. However, as we've seen, clarity of vision is not the only way we can understand wisdom. It can also be described in terms of the imagination, and the Buddha does this when he says that not only is the ground flat, but "every part of the ground is covered in various different kinds of precious substances and jewels".

Another feature of Sukhāvatī not mentioned in the *Shorter Sūtra* is the rivers, which are anything from 5 to 450 miles wide and 100 miles deep, and all "flow smoothly with sweet-smelling, fragrant waters". So far three senses are involved in imagining Sukhāvatī – sight, hearing, and smell – but the sense of touch is also included:

> The living beings who wish to enjoy the delights of heavenly games and pleasures on those riverbanks will find that, when they go down into the rivers, the water only comes up to their ankles, if that is what they wish. If they wish the water to come up to their knees, to their hips, or to their ears, then it will do so, and they will experience heavenly pleasures. If they wish the water to be cool, then it is cool for them. If they wish the water to be warm, then it is warm for them. It is just as cool or warm as they like.

At first sight the pleasure of bathing in the rivers seems to be purely sensual, but the pleasures are described as "heavenly", which suggests that immersion in the water of the rivers represents the experience of dhyāna. The fact that the beings in Sukhāvatī can choose the depth to which they immerse themselves, and the temperature, suggests that they have total control of their mental states. The rivers produce a delightful and melodic sound, which is

> profound, ungraspable, unfathomable, and pure. It is a delight to the ear, and it touches the heart. It is enchanting, delightful, and it soothes the mind. It is agreeable and appealing to listen to, murmuring "impermanence, peace, no self". It brings happiness to those who hear it, and it reaches the ears of all the living beings in that world system.

In the Introduction we saw that the Buddha would sometimes give a "graduated discourse", guiding his listener to a state of mind in which they are ready to see things as they are. The sound of the rivers in Sukhāvatī does the same thing, delighting the hearer, touching their heart, and soothing their mind. It then "murmurs" the words "impermanence, peace, no self" – traditional objects of insight practice.

I say that these are traditional objects of insight practice, but this is only half true, or, to be precise, two thirds true. In fact it's an unusual list, one that I can't remember encountering anywhere else. It's similar to the very well-known three characteristics of existence (*lakṣaṇas*) taught by the Buddha: impermanence, suffering, and no self (that is, devoid of a fixed and enduring self or essence), except that suffering is replaced by peace. The reason for this is indirectly made clear by the Buddha a few paragraphs later:

> Ānanda, the word "unskilful" is not heard anywhere in that world system, Sukhāvatī. Neither are the words "hindrance", "falling into a state of misfortune at death", or "suffering" heard there. Not even the words "feelings which are neither pleasant nor unpleasant" are heard there, Ānanda, so the word "suffering" is certainly not heard there.

The word "suffering" is not heard (i.e. doesn't exist) in Sukhāvatī because no one experiences it. Why would you need a word for something that doesn't exist?

The words "impermanence, peace, no self" are abbreviations of slightly longer formulations – another example of the author's expectation that the reader/listener is already familiar with the Buddha's teachings. The full formulations make it clear that each of these words has a different referent: all *conditioned things* are impermanent, *nirvana* is peace, and *all things whatsoever* are without self or essence. "Conditioned things" are things or events that depend for their existence on a number of other things or events. Their conditioned-ness and their impermanence are closely connected: it's because they are conditioned that they are impermanent. For instance, a plant is dependent for its existence on a number of conditions: earth, which contains the minerals it needs; water; light; a certain temperature; and so on. If any of these conditions ceases to be, then the plant will also cease to be. The fact that the rivers murmur "impermanence" suggests that Sukhāvatī and the beings who live there are subject to change, which in turn suggests that they are subject to conditionality. Which they are, although the only kind of change that they experience is irreversible spiritual development, the *dharma-niyama* strand of conditionality.

The Buddha also said – to beings in our impure buddha-field – that all conditioned things are suffering, or painful, meaning that if we rely on them to make us happy we will suffer, partly at least because they are impermanent: any kind of happiness that depends on something that will change is going to end in tears. This teaching is relevant for us – in our impure buddha-field – because we do suffer, but it's not relevant to the beings in Sukhāvatī because they don't. Instead, in Sukhāvatī the Buddha teaches that nirvana is peace. Rather than asking the beings there to reflect on the suffering inherent in conditioned existence – a suffering that they don't feel – he asks them to reflect on the deep and lasting tranquility of Awakening. It's interesting that, in the earliest of the Pali texts, before the Buddha had fully codified his teaching, he spoke of the goal of the Dharma life as the state of peace or calm. By this he didn't mean the temporary and relatively superficial kind of calm we might experience on a summer's day when we have nothing to do, or even the deeper kind that we might experience in meditative absorption, but the peace that comes with complete freedom from negative mental states. This kind of peace is the highest happiness, or perhaps a peace transcending both suffering and happiness.

When the Buddha said that *all things whatsoever* are without self, he was referring to both the conditioned and the unconditioned. The unconditioned is nirvana – Awakening or, in the language of the earliest suttas, peace. This can be somewhat confusing because in one sense nirvana *is* conditioned: to grow towards it requires that we put certain conditions in place – ethical conduct, meditation practice, and so on. However, once attained, nirvana is no longer dependent on those conditions for its continued existence.

I've discussed this teaching produced by the rivers in Sukhāvatī for a few paragraphs, yet it takes up just three words in the sutra. It comes and it goes – impermanence, peace, no self – like bubbles on the surface of the water. We have to bear in mind, of course, that the authors of Mahāyāna sutras assume that the reader or listener is familiar with the teachings of the Buddha as found in the earlier texts, so that they will understand the significance of these three words without needing a commentary. It's interesting nevertheless that this important wisdom teaching takes up such a small part of the text, especially if we compare it to the *Prajñāpāramitā* (*Perfection of Wisdom*) sutras, which are composed almost entirely – as their name suggests – of wisdom teachings. You might wonder whether, considering the shortness of life, you wouldn't be better off reading those texts. If wisdom were simply a matter of knowledge, the answer to this would be "yes". If it were simply a matter of knowledge though, now that you know that all conditioned things are impermanent, that nirvana is peace, and that all things whatsoever are without self or substance, you are presumably enlightened. If you're not it's because you're not ready. The whole of our being needs to be involved in our efforts, not just our intellects. We need to be emotionally, physically, and imaginatively engaged. That's why the *Longer Sūtra* is so long, including a list of the names of previous buddhas, a mythical story of a bodhisattva in the remote past who decides to become a buddha, and a detailed description of his buddha-field, full of imagery, not just visual but also audial, olfactory, and tactile. In the midst of all this superabundant, highly colourful, magical, playful, and sensuously pleasurable imagery, slipped into the text without fanfare appear these few words – "impermanence", "peace", "no self". The sutra, in other words, is a practice, not a textbook. Reading or listening to the sutra repeatedly guides us to the state of mind in which we are ready to receive wisdom.

The Buddha goes on to say that the beings living in Sukhāvatī hear – whenever they wish – words and phrases such as "Buddha", "Dharma", "Sangha", "emptiness", "freedom from desire", "freedom from accomplishment", and "freedom from birth", as well as "great loving-kindness", "great compassion", "great sympathetic joy", and "great equanimity". All of these words and phrases indicate highly positive spiritual experiences or aspects of Awakening. When they hear these words or phrases

> an exhilarating joy and gladness will arise in them, along with the inclination towards solitude, contentment, peace, cessation, the Dharma, and the perfect cultivation of roots of virtue, which results in Awakening.

On hearing these words and phrases they enter a state of mind in which they are ready to receive wisdom. "The inclination towards solitude" perhaps needs some explanation. Literally, the text says simply "solitude" – the translator has added "the inclination towards", to show that what is meant is a desire for solitude. But why should an inclination to solitude be part of a mind prepared for wisdom? The word translated as "solitude" is *viveka*, which the Buddha often used in reference to meditation, especially meditative absorption – dhyāna. In order to experience dhyāna, he said, one first needs solitude, and he would advise his disciples to leave the town or village and find a quiet place where they could meditate undisturbed. However, he also used *viveka* metaphorically, meaning "detached" or "secluded" from sense desires and unskilful states. *Viveka* is the same in both Sanskrit and Pali, and the Pali–English dictionary defines it not only as "secluded", "lonely", and so on, but also as "singleness (of heart)" and "discrimination of thought", both of which are necessary for insight to arise.

> Moreover, Ānanda, in the mornings, all four corners of that world system, Sukhāvatī, are filled with winds that blow through the multitude of different species of beautiful, multicoloured trees made of precious substances which give off sweet-smelling, divine fragrances. These winds make the trees sway, shake,

> bend, and wave, such that many hundreds of beautiful flowers – flowers which give off fragrances that soothe the mind – fall to the majestic ground made of precious substances. They cover the buddha-field in a carpet of flowers forty feet deep ... The flowers are delicate, and as pleasant to the touch as *kācilindika* cloth, although this is a poor comparison ... When the morning has passed these flowers disappear completely, and that buddha-field becomes clear, delightful, and beautiful, unmarked by the flowers that were there before. All four corners of that buddha-field are then once again filled with winds that scatter fresh flowers, just as before. This happens at midday, at sunset, and in the first, second, and third watches of the night, just like in the morning. Any living beings who are touched by the winds which are perfumed by these various different fragrances experience the happiness of a monk who has attained cessation.

In this passage sensuous pleasure involving sight, touch, and smell represents the happiness of Awakening, as expressed in the phrase "a monk who has attained cessation", which is synonymous with Enlightenment.

Immediately after this the Buddha says:

> Nowhere in that buddha-field, Ānanda, is there anything that resembles fire, a sun, a moon, planets, constellations, or stars; nor is there total darkness, or even a word to designate it. There are no words to designate night and day, except when the Tathāgata uses these words in a conventional sense.

This passage is reminiscent of the early Buddhist text that I quoted in Chapter 2 (the *Udāna*), in which the Buddha talks about a condition

> where there is no earth, no water, no fire, no air; ... There gleam no stars, no sun sheds light, there shines no moon, yet there no darkness reigns.[86]

The passage from the *Longer Sūtra* suggests that those living in Sukhāvatī live in that condition (just as there are no words for suffering in Sukhāvatī because there is no experience of suffering, so the words "fire", "sun", "moon", and so forth don't exist because the things they designate don't exist). Commenting on those passages from the *Udāna* in Chapter 2, I said that the Buddha was there taking the *via negativa* approach, emphasizing the discontinuity between the awakened and the unawakened state:

Awakening is like nothing we've ever experienced, like nothing in this world, so it can't be described by reference to anything in this world. All we can say is that it's not like this, or that, or anything at all. The Pure Land sutras, on the other hand, take the *via positiva* approach: Awakening is something like your current experience, but incomparably better; it's like this.

The notion of there being no fire, sun, moon, and so on would have had a much greater significance for the ancient Indians than it does for us. At the time when the *Longer Sūtra* was written there would have been no electrical or gas appliances, so fire and the sun would have been the only sources of heat and – along with the moon, constellations, and stars – light. Mechanical clocks hadn't been invented either so the sun, moon, planets, constellations, and stars would have been the instruments by which people measured time – the position of the sun in relation to the earth giving day and night, the moon marking the passing of months, the constellations times of the year. So, by saying that they don't exist in Sukhāvatī, the Buddha seems to be implying that there is not only no heat or light, but also no time. However, all three do exist in Sukhāvatī of course – how could a world and living beings exist without them? In any case we've just seen, in the passage immediately preceding this one, that time exists in Sukhāvatī – morning, midday, afternoon, and the three "watches" of the night.

The answer may be in the caveat at the end of the passage: "There are no words to designate night and day, except when the Tathāgata uses these words in a conventional sense." So, although the Buddha may speak of day and night – and therefore time – we aren't to take that as signifying that they really exist. Yet, clearly, time passes in Sukhāvatī. The word "existence" has a technical philosophical meaning in Buddhism. It refers to the (mistaken) belief that things exist independently (of conditions), and therefore eternally (if a thing isn't dependent on other things for its existence, then there is no reason why it should ever cease to exist). When Buddhist texts tell us that no thing exists, they are saying that nothing exists in this sense – independently and eternally.

Later Mahāyāna philosophers made the point that a "thing" is a mental construct, and therefore dependent for its existence not only on other things, but also on our mind's tendency to reify our experience ("reify" means to turn an abstract concept into a thing). They therefore spoke of two truths: conventional and ultimate. The conventional truth is that things exist (relatively, dependently); the ultimate truth is that no thing exists (absolutely, independently). So, returning to our conundrum of there being no words or designations for day and night in Sukhāvatī while clearly day and night do come and go: the beings who live there understand that day and night are mental constructs, and that really there are no such "things". This being the case they don't speak of them as such. The Buddha, however, has the prerogative of referring to them in conventional language in order to teach the Dharma.

All this gives us an important insight into Amitāyus' "eternal life". The name "Amitāyus" is explained in the *Longer Sūtra* as the infinite prolongation of life:

> Ānanda, the lifespan of the Blessed One, the Tathāgata Amitābha, is unlimited. It is not easy to get an idea of its length, even if one thinks in terms of hundreds of aeons, thousands of aeons, hundreds of thousands of aeons, countless aeons, countless hundreds of aeons, countless thousands of aeons, countless hundreds of thousands of aeons, a great many countless hundreds of thousands of aeons. The boundless lifespan of that blessed one, Ānanda, is truly unlimited. That is why that tathāgata is known as Amitāyus, "Infinite Life".

Taken literally this seems to express the wrong view of eternalism: that the goal of the Buddhist life – Awakening – results in eternal life. There is another way of understanding the name Amitāyus though, suggested by the translation "measureless" for *amita*. The sun, moon, planets, constellations, and stars are instruments by which the ancient Indians measured time in days and nights, months, years, and so on. If they don't exist then time – time that can be measured – doesn't exist in Sukhāvatī. Perhaps then the name Amitāyus doesn't imply the infinite prolongation of life, but means life that cannot be measured. There is some basis for interpreting it in this way in the early Buddhist texts. In Chapter 3 I quoted a text in which the Buddha is asked what happens to an awakened being after death. Are they reborn or do they cease to exist? The Buddha's answer is that neither of these options applies, because, "when all categories have been removed, then all ways of speaking are also removed." Just before this the Buddha says, "There is no measuring of him who has gone" (that is, who has died).[87] The Buddha cannot be categorized or measured.

This interpretation of the name "Amitābha" flies in the face of what the sutra actually says, of course, but we must remember that the Pure Land sutras take the *via positiva* approach to Awakening, and in doing so open themselves to the charge of philosophical naivety. They present the awakened state as a wonderful, rich, bountiful, beautiful land in which the inhabitants enjoy whatever pleasures they want at any time they want them, where the teaching of the Buddha is always available, and where they and the Buddha live eternally. However, passages like the one we've been considering imply that the sutras are philosophically more subtle than is often assumed.

Philosophical subtlety aside, what has all this got to do with us and the living of our lives? The meaning of Amitāyus is that life, any life, is measureless. Life can't be contained by units of measurement. In one sense it is, of course, contained by those measurements. After all, a life lasts only so many years; it's made up of successive days, and those days consist of hours, which are in turn divided into minutes and seconds – but those are only mental constructs. They are aspects of conventional truth. The ultimate truth is that time is measureless. Both kinds of truth are true: when we see the sun come up in the east we experience what we call daytime, and when we see it go down in the west we experience what we call night-time. I arrange to meet a friend at 2pm in a certain cafe and, when I arrive, there he is waiting for me. The mental constructs of conventional truth work for all practical purposes. We just need to be careful not to be misled by our mental constructs into thinking that time *is* the units of measurement we impose on it. When we do that we are trapped in our mental constructs rather than experiencing our direct experience. What *is* our direct experience of time? You can answer that question for yourself right now if you stop reading, put the book down for a few moments, and simply be aware. *Don't look at your watch!* Be aware of *time passing*, whatever that metaphor means. We might say "moment by moment", but moments are simply imprecise units of time too. Time isn't really divided into moments, is it? It doesn't have any natural divisions, does it? If you've joined me in this thought experiment you may have realized that time is something other than the units of measurement we use. You may have sensed that it's uncontainable, mysterious, inconceivable. The unimaginably long time units of the sutra, "inconceivably many, innumerable, countless aeons upon countless aeons", are the author's way of pointing to the strangeness, the mystery, the inconceivability of time. Our lives are more than the number of years we may live. At the time I'm writing this a young man named Stephen Sutton has just died of bowel cancer, aged 19. The reason I know about him is because his death was widely reported in the UK, and the reason for this was that from the time of his diagnosis at 15 he spent the rest of his life raising awareness of the disease in young people, and raised over 4 million pounds towards cancer research. Before his death he wrote, "I don't see the point in measuring life in terms of time anymore."[88]

In his book *Philosophy as a Way of Life*, the scholar of ancient Western philosophy Pierre Hadot distinguishes between what he calls finite time and infinite time. Finite time is measurable time; infinite time is immeasurable. He writes that the Epicurean and Stoic philosophies

> posit as an axiom that happiness can only be found in the present, that one instant of happiness is equivalent to an eternity of happiness, and that happiness can and must be found immediately, here and now. Both Epicureanism and Stoicism invite us to resituate the present instant within the perspective of the cosmos, and to accord infinite value to the slightest moment of existence.[89]

To accord infinite value to a moment of existence is to experience time outside of our units of measurement (conventional truth), and thus to live for a moment in eternity (ultimate truth).

In Chapter 3 I recounted the Buddha's movements soon after his Awakening: how he sought out his former companions in the austere practices and taught them the Dharma; how he encountered the Kāśyapa brothers, and then the layman Yaśas and his companions, teaching them all, enabling them to awake; and finally how he walked to Rājagṛha to fulfil a promise he'd made to King Bimbisāra to teach him if and when he awoke to the truth of things. He did all of this *soon* after his Awakening. *Immediately* after he awoke though, he stayed in and around the spot where he had been sitting, which was under the boughs of a tree – a banyan or peepul tree or, to give its Latin name, *Ficus religiosa*. Buddhists call it the bodhi tree, or tree of Awakening. Apparently he spent a number of weeks there. One tradition has it that he spent the first week rapt in meditative absorption, after which he reflected on his experience. Another tradition says that after that first week he spent another week in walking meditation and a third in contemplation. A third tradition maintains that he spent the first week after his Awakening simply gazing at the tree in gratitude – thankful to it for sheltering him from the intense rays of the sun or from the rain, and so enabling him to meditate undisturbed and thereby awaken.

The bodhi tree has naturally become an important aspect of Buddhist iconography. It has become an "illumined image", emblematic of Awakening. I want to end this chapter by exploring Amitābha's bodhi tree as described in the *Longer Sūtra*. As you have probably guessed, it is not at all like the humble tree that Śākyamuni sat beneath 2,500 years ago. Rather it is

> a thousand yojanas tall. Its branches and leaves spread out over eight hundred yojanas, and its roots extend over five hundred yojanas. It is always covered in leaves, always in flower, always bearing fruit. It is a variety of different colours, many hundreds of thousands of colours, and it has many different kinds of leaves, flowers, and fruit. It is beautified with a great multitude of many different kinds of adornments, and filled with jewels and precious stones that radiate moonlight. ... It surpasses even the trees of the gods. Golden threads hang from its branches ... ruby necklaces, sapphire necklaces ... strings of bells, strings of precious stones, and other objects made of precious substances, as well as nets of gold, nets of pearls, nets of all kinds of precious substances ... and beautified with small bells, with nets of jewels, with gold, and with all kinds of precious substances. It is adorned with whatever living beings request, according to their disposition.

There are three ways in which Amitābha's tree of Awakening differs from the tree under which Śākyamuni awakened: its size, its perpetual fertility, and its adornments. The tree of Awakening in Sukhāvatī is of vast dimensions. If we take the figures literally, it is 9,000 miles high, with a breadth of 7,200 miles, while its roots spread for 4,500 miles. It is therefore larger than the earth, whose polar diameter – the distance from the north to the south pole – is 7,899.99 miles. The massive dimensions of the tree symbolize the vast cosmic vision of the Mahāyāna, in which one's own spiritual development is conceived as taking place within a much greater context – that of delivering all beings whatsoever from suffering. The boughs and branches of Amitābha's tree spread over thousands of miles, sheltering hundreds of thousands of beings in its beneficent shade.

The tree isn't subject to the cycle of the seasons – the succession of growth and decay – but is "always covered in leaves, always in flower, always bearing fruit". This isn't a static image in which the leaves, flowers, and fruit remain in a state of suspended animation, but an image of perpetual springtime, life ever bursting forth, unstoppably, joyously, stupendously alive, never wilting, decaying, or dying, its leaves continuously sprouting in their pure light-green colours, flowers forever opening into beauty, fruit always ripening into perfection –

from joy
to joy to joy, from wing to wing,
from blossom to blossom to
impossible blossom, to sweet impossible blossom.[90]

This perpetual fertility symbolizes the second half of the spiral path, the irreversible series of Awakening states – from knowing and seeing things as they really are, through disenchantment, through dispassion, through knowing and seeing liberation, never falling back, never regressing to worldly states. And if Awakening is indeed a dynamic state, continually developing, growing, becoming more awakened, then the perpetual springtime of the tree of Awakening symbolizes that too.

Whereas the vast dimensions of the tree and its ever-renewing leaves, flowers, and fruits are attributes of the tree itself, the beautiful adornments are placed there by the beings in Sukhāvatī. This reminds me of something that one of my teacher's friends once said to him: "What you love, you adorn." Loving parents buy the nicest clothes they can afford for their children, lovers buy gifts of clothes and jewellery for each other, home lovers make their house and garden look as beautiful as their means allow, family members cut the grass around the graves of their deceased loved ones and place fresh flowers there, and religious devotees decorate their shrines with colourful silks and flowers. Love and beauty are closely intertwined.

However, there is perhaps another meaning to be found in the decoration of the tree. Skilful actions – those based on positive mental states such as contentment, generosity, goodwill, and awareness – result in the development of positive qualities and traits. Just as drops of water eventually fill a large pot, so numerous acts of kindness over a period of time result in a kind person. Similarly with other skilful actions such as generosity, helpfulness, or thinking clearly. These positive qualities and traits, cultivated through skilful actions, are known collectively as merit (*puṇya*), and as we practise the spiritual life our "store" of merit grows. From this came the further idea of the possibility of transferring one's merit – *pariṇāmanā* – to another person. This may have originated in a desire to help friends or relatives in illness or at death; people would transfer or dedicate their merit to the ill or deceased person in the belief that this would help them to recover from their illness or to have a better rebirth. From a strict doctrinal point of view it isn't possible to literally transfer one's merit to another: your acts of kindness, for instance, can only make *you* into a kind person. However, *pariṇāmanā* amounts to the *wish* to benefit another at your expense – if you *could* give the positive results of your practice to another, you would.

In Mahāyāna Buddhism this idea was extended to the transference of merit to one's own future Awakening. This may seem selfish compared to transferring merit to others' welfare, but we should remember that the Mahāyāna Buddhist's goal is to become a buddha so as to help vast numbers of people free themselves from suffering. Some scholars refer to this kind of *pariṇāmanā* as *transformation* of merit.[91] This is because merit is mundane; it is accumulated through the law of karma, which operates within the mundane world, whereas Awakening is beyond the world – *lokottara* – beyond the law of karma. So, in dedicating one's merit to Awakening, one is transforming positive, although mundane, qualities into supramundane wisdom. In terms of the *niyama*s – the five strands of conditionality that we looked at in the previous chapter – this represents a transformation of the *karma-niyama* into the *dharma-niyama*.

As we discovered when we explored the *Shorter Sūtra*, one of the conditions for rebirth in Sukhāvatī is the possession of many roots of virtue, or, we could say, much merit. Everyone in Sukhāvatī therefore has a great store of merit. One of Dharmākara's vows is that in Sukhāvatī the bodhisattvas will be able to "plant any kinds of roots of virtue they wish", which could be in the form of gold, silver, jewels, pearl, lapis lazuli, seashells, crystal, coral, quartz, sapphire, ruby, emerald, incense, flowers, garlands, ointments, perfumes, robes, parasols, banners, lamps, music, dance, or song. So, when the Buddha says that the tree of Awakening is "adorned with whatever living beings request, according to their disposition", he could mean that they are transferring or transforming their merit to their future Buddhahood. This is a beautiful way of saying that Buddhists dedicate all the qualities they've developed to the goal of Awakening, and it means that the tree of Awakening is not only a symbol of the awakened mind, it's also a symbol of sangha, spiritual community; members of the sangha adorn the path to Awakening with their beautiful qualities.

> Moreover, Ānanda, the sound that bodhi tree makes when the wind stirs it can be heard in immeasurably many world systems. The living beings in those world systems whose ears hear the sound of that bodhi tree will not have to fear diseases of the ear until they attain Awakening.

This is another instance of a feature of Sukhāvatī affecting beings in other world systems. When we hear the sound of the tree we will never suffer from a disease of the ear, and the text goes on to say that, when we see the tree, smell its perfume, or taste its fruits, we will never again have to fear any disease of the eye, nose, or mouth. Similarly, when the light of the tree shines on us, we will never again suffer any disease of the body, and, if we take up the practice of meditating on the tree, our minds will not become distracted until we have awakened. This is an example, quite common in Mahāyāna sutras, of the spiritual or transcendental affecting the physical. As such it represents a crossing over of levels of conditionality – the *dharma-niyama* affecting (in this particular case) the *bīja-niyama*, the organic level of conditionality. Although there is increasing evidence that our states of mind and emotions do have some effect on our physical health, we need to beware of assuming that living a spiritual life will result in freedom from illness. Although the *bīja-niyama* may be conditioned to a certain extent by the *karma-* and *dharma-niyama*s, it also works independently of them. This is important because the corollary of the belief that living the spiritual life will result in good health is the belief that all illnesses are due to unskilful states of mind. This belief is quite common in certain "spiritual" circles, but it has two very unfortunate consequences: firstly, a reluctance, even in some cases a refusal, to submit to medical procedures that can cure the illness; and secondly, the feeling that one has somehow caused the illness by one's unethical behaviour, either in this life or in a previous one. Although it may be possible that we have brought an illness upon ourselves, unless we have compelling evidence that this is the case, we should treat it as a physical illness, and therefore use physical remedies (as well as working on our states of mind).

The text now turns its attention once again to the beings who live in Sukhāvatī:

> The progress towards unsurpassed, perfect Awakening of all those living beings becomes irreversible because they have seen that bodhi tree.

They are, of course, already irreversibly on the way to Awakening by virtue of the fact that they have been born in Sukhāvatī. We could say that Sukhāvatī is the stage of irreversibility. Irreversible from what, though? Remember that there are two different kinds of disciples in Sukhāvatī – śrāvakas and bodhisattvas. Śrāvakas are those whose motivation in living the spiritual life is mainly for their own benefit. Their aim is to become arhats, and all of the śrāvakas in Sukhāvatī are assured of reaching that goal. The case of the bodhisattvas is a little more complicated. They are, as we've seen, motivated to become buddhas for the sake of all beings. However, they are susceptible to falling back from that aspiration until they reach a certain stage in their progress. If they do fall back they do so to the lesser goal of arhatship – Awakening for themselves alone. The text tells us that, on seeing the tree of Awakening, the beings who live in Sukhāvatī become irreversible from "unsurpassed, perfect Awakening", that is the Awakening of a buddha. Both the śrāvakas and the bodhisattvas become irreversible bodhisattvas on seeing the tree of Awakening.

I've been discussing this in traditional Mahāyāna terms, taking the doctrine of two different paths leading to two distinct kinds of Awakening as literal. However, as I wrote towards the end of Chapter 1, the idea of a "selfish" nirvana is a contradiction in terms, as Awakening consists in the realization that there is no enduring and separate self, and if there is no self there can be no selfishness. Thus there is really only one kind of Awakening and therefore only one kind of irreversibility, which leaves us with just one question: what is it that makes someone unable to fall back? The final clause of the next sentence gives us the answer. On seeing the tree of Awakening the beings there

> attain three kinds of patient acceptance: they practise what they hear, they conform to it, and they patiently accept the fact that all phenomena are unarisen.

"Patient acceptance" is a translation of *kṣānti*, which here may mean something more like willing acceptance or even liking. Some scholars are of the opinion that *kṣānti* in this context comes from the root *kam* ("to be willing to") rather than *kṣam* ("to bear", "to be able to").[92] The third kind of *kṣānti* – "the fact that all phenomena are unarisen" – is *anutpattika-dharma-kṣānti*, and it's this insight that makes a bodhisattva's progress towards Buddhahood irreversible. To understand what this insight is we have to go back to the Buddha's teaching that things don't exist as separate, independent, or enduring entities. When we examine this more closely we realize that "things" don't "arise" or "cease" – that is, come into or go out of existence. This is not to say that nothing exists, but that no (independent, enduring) thing exists.

There aren't many recorded writings of the ancient Greek philosopher Heraclitus, but if he hadn't written anything else he'd be immortal for this: "No man ever steps in the same river twice, for it's not the same river and he's not the same man." You can't step into the same river twice because a river is a body of moving water, so the second time you step into it you're stepping into a different body of water and therefore, in a sense, a different river. That's easy enough to understand, but Heraclitus goes on to say something really startling – and very Buddhist: not only is the river the man steps into now not the same river he stepped into a few moments ago, but he's not the same man now as he was then. The man is as fluid, as changing, as evanescent, as the river. Of course for all practical purposes it *is* the same river – the body of moving water continues to flow within the same banks from one year to the next, so you can agree to meet a friend at a specific spot on the bank of the river at a specific time, even though when you meet her it's a different river from the one it was when you arranged the meeting. Similarly, you and your friend can manage to meet even though you are both different people from the ones who arranged the meeting. From the point of view of conventional truth you and the river exist, but, from the point of view of the ultimate truth, neither of you does.

To "patiently accept the fact that all phenomena are unarisen" is to perceive everything from the point of view of ultimate truth. All dry land, as it were, has been left behind, and you are now coursing in the flow of reality. Not that there's a "you" – a kind of fixed point – which is coursing in the flow. "You" are part of that flow, as are others. Hence *kṣānti* as "patient acceptance", because we now realize that ultimately there is nothing to hold on to – no *thing* to hold on to – and no *one* who can do the holding, which at first is deeply threatening to our sense of security. Yet *kṣānti* in its more positive sense of willing or liking makes sense too, because seeing through the delusion of fixed and enduring things and selves is joyfully liberating. To continue the analogy of being in water: when we are learning to swim we feel very insecure, we don't "trust" the water to hold us up, we fear drowning and so we tend to hold on (tense up), which unfortunately makes it more likely that we'll sink. Therefore we have to exercise *patient acceptance* (of the fear of drowning). However, once we've learnt to swim we have the confidence that comes from knowing in experience that we will float, which allows us to "let go" (relax), and *enjoy* the sense of freedom that swimming gives us.

Before they saw the tree of Awakening the śrāvakas in Sukhāvatī had been toiling under the delusion that they were trying to awaken for their own benefit, while the bodhisattvas thought they were striving to awaken for the benefit of others. On seeing the tree they all realize that Awakening is neither for self nor for others because ultimately there *is* no self and no other. It's this insight that prevents bodhisattvas from falling back from their progress to the full Awakening of a buddha, because, once you've seen through the delusion of fixed and separate things and beings, you can't go back to seeing them in this way again. It's similar to the moment when a child realizes that there is no Santa Claus. They can't revert to this belief once they've seen through it.

This insight also applies to the tree of Awakening and everything else in Sukhāvatī, where nothing arises and nothing ceases, yet everything vividly exists. The following verses from a Tibetan text put this very well. The opening line of each stanza – "Eh Ma Oh!" – is an expression of wonder.

Eh Ma Oh!
Dharma Wondrous Strange!
Profoundest Mystery of the Perfect Ones.
Within the Birthless, all things take their birth,
Yet in that birth, nothing is born.

Eh Ma Oh!
Dharma Wondrous Strange!
Profoundest Mystery of the Perfect Ones.
Within the Ceaseless, all things cease to be
Yet in that ceasing, nothing ceases.

Eh Ma Oh!
Dharma Wondrous Strange!
Profoundest Mystery of the Perfect Ones.
Within the Non-abiding, all abides,
Yet thus abiding, there abideth naught.

Eh Ma Oh!
Dharma Wondrous Strange!
Profoundest Mystery of the Perfect Ones.
In Non-perception, everything is perceived,
Yet this perceiving is quite perceptionless.

Eh Ma Oh!
Dharma Wondrous Strange!
Profoundest Mystery of the Perfect Ones.
In the Unmoving, all things come and go,
Yet in that movement, nothing ever moves.[93]

Chapter Six

Transcendent community

I have on a wall in my flat a reproduction of the Taima mandala, a Japanese painting of the third of the three Sukhāvatī sutras, the *Guān Jīng*. At the centre sits Amitāyus, with his two chief bodhisattvas on either side – Avalokiteśvara and Mahāsthāmaprāpta. These are Sukhāvatī's equivalents of the Buddha Śākyamuni's two chief disciples, Śāriputra and Mahāmaudgalyāyana. Surrounding them are other bodhisattvas, thirty-four in all. Amitāyus is larger than the two chief bodhisattvas, and all three are about three times bigger than the surrounding bodhisattvas, illustrating David Hockney's comments that we see psychologically as well as geometrically; the more important something or someone is to us, the bigger they seem. Amitāyus and the bodhisattvas all sit on a raised dais. The bodhisattvas have long blue-black hair, over which they wear crowns or diadems, and cloth of blue, red, green, pink, white, turquoise, and lilac drapes their bodies. Their hands are in various gestures and some are holding objects: lotuses, a book, a fly-whisk, a conch shell. They each look in a different direction – some look straight at the viewer; others look towards Amitāyus; some are looking down, as if in thought; others look outward. Some are smiling, others look serious. They are all graceful, gentle, serene, and lovely.

Stepping back from the picture and widening my gaze, I see many other beings, some sitting on lotuses in a pond, others in pavilions and small palaces, some walking over arched bridges between one palace and another, others flying through the air on clouds, their colourful robes streaming behind them like banners, and, at the bottom of the painting, a few dancing to the accompaniment of eight musicians. The painting is teeming with living beings. In previous chapters I've described the features of the land and discussed Amitābha and his attributes. In this chapter I will describe the beings who live there and in doing so we'll be reflecting on Sukhāvatī as a symbol of sangha – spiritual community. As the Buddha says in another Mahāyāna text, the *Vimalakīrti Nirdeśa*, "a buddha-field of bodhisattvas is a field of living beings."[94]

Of the forty-six vows in the Sanskrit version of the sutra that we're looking at, twenty-eight – over half – concern the beings in Sukhāvatī, which gives us some idea of how important they are in the symbolism of the sutra. As I pointed out in Chapter 2, in the *Shorter Sūtra* the Buddha says that living beings should cultivate a heartfelt desire to be born in Sukhāvatī, and he gives only one reason for this:

> They should do this because, in that buddha-field, they will be in the company of good people such as these bodhisattvas.

The reason why it's good to be in their company is not simply because it's very pleasant, but because living with such beings, seeing them, conversing with them, helps us to grow spiritually. Being with them is itself a spiritual practice.

I've been referring to the "beings" or "living beings" in Sukhāvatī – awkward nouns – rather than people, because they're not all humans; there are gods too. At least that's what the *Shorter Sūtra* says. In the *Longer Sūtra* it seems truer to say that they are human-gods or god-humans. That is,

> In that world system, there is no difference between gods and human beings, except that one might use the words "god" or "human being" as a linguistic convention when counting them.

The translation says "gods and human beings", but strictly speaking Sukhāvatī is peopled with only gods and men. This is due to the thirty-fourth vow, which states that, when women in buddha-fields other than Sukhāvatī hear Amitābha's name, they will "become disgusted by their femininity, and are never again born as women". This seems to be an expression of ancient Indian social conditioning rather than an awakened point of view. In his book *The Land of Bliss*, Luis Gomez writes that this vow is a cause of some concern and embarrassment in contemporary Pure Land Buddhist circles, and

> [s]ome modern Japanese commentators interpret the passage as meaning that women will be free of the social constraints that maintain them in an inferior status in the human world.[95]

This is a nice way of interpreting the vow, although almost definitely not what the author had in mind – if it were, why would women need to cultivate disgust of their femininity?

Another argument I've heard used to excuse the vow is that gods are androgynous, that is, neither clearly male nor clearly female. In that the humans in Sukhāvatī are indistinguishable from gods, then they too must be androgynous; they have transcended differences of gender. Looking again at the reproduction of the Taima mandala on my wall, in many ways this seems to be true. It's difficult to tell at first glance whether the bodhisattvas are men or women – they have long black hair, some of it swept up into a bun while the rest hangs down onto their shoulders. They are adorned with jewelled tiaras and diadems, necklaces, armlets, bracelets, and anklets. They wear colourful clothes – what we would call robes – and their faces could be those of either men or women. The only indication that they are men is that they don't have breasts (which we can clearly see because their torsos are partly naked). Attractive as this interpretation is, it's not completely convincing because, like the previous one, it doesn't explain why women need to become disgusted by their femininity to prevent their rebirth as women, whereas there is no mention of any need for men to become disgusted by their masculinity to prevent them being reborn as men. I think we have to accept that the author was conditioned by the cultural mores of the society he (or she?) lived in, and that the thirty-fourth vow is an expression of that conditioning. This means that we don't have to interpret the vow in ways that merely explain it away. Instead we can simply reject it and imagine the beings in Sukhāvatī as men and women, or as neither men nor women but god-like beings.

They're not merely gods of course; they have deep insight, and this is expressed visually by everyone there being the colour of gold, gold symbolizing Awakening. All the buddhas described in the Mahāyāna sutras are golden, even Amitābha. I say even Amitābha because in the Indo-Tibetan system of the five buddhas he is red in colour. You may remember that the sutra began with Ānanda noticing that the Buddha's skin was "radiating with a golden colour", and that the reason for this was that he was dwelling in the abode of the buddhas. The golden colour of the inhabitants of Sukhāvatī reflects that idea and suggests that they constantly dwell in that abode. One of the interesting things about gold is that it's literally an other-worldly element. Because of its high density most of it sank to the earth's core billions of years ago. Virtually all discovered gold – all the gold that we have seen – is thought to have been deposited later by meteorites.

The description of the beings in Sukhāvatī then is of an ideal sangha, a spiritual community par excellence. In Chapter 1 I quoted the scholar Paul Harrison, who thinks that the detailed descriptions of Sukhāvatī are not "something already existing, but ... blueprints for something which is to be constructed in the mind".[96] Similarly, the descriptions of the beings who inhabit Sukhāvatī can be considered to be a blueprint, not to be constructed only in the mind, but to be lived, here in our world. Not that we'll ever finally achieve this level of community, not in this impure world of ours at least, although we can experience it fleetingly whenever we, or someone near us, act completely unselfishly, generously, kindly, wisely. At moments like that we see flashes of the brilliance of the ideal, transcendent community, the measureless community of Sukhāvatī.

I've referred to the beings living there as the ideal or transcendent sangha because everyone there is on the transcendental path – they are all irreversible from Awakening. (In traditional Mahāyāna terms, some are irreversible from arhatship and others from Buddhahood, but, as I've made clear in previous chapters, I don't accept this distinction as a real one.) In terms of the spiral path that we explored in Chapter 4, they are all somewhere along the continuum of knowing and seeing things as they really are: disenchantment, dispassion, and knowledge and vision of release. So in exploring the sutra's description of them we're trying to imagine what it might be like to live in a community of such beings. A community consists of individuals, and, although the sutra refers to the beings in Sukhāvatī in the collective – they are like this or like that – it's really each person who is "like this" or "like that", and it's only because of each person's individual practice and attainment that the community as a whole can be said to be like this or that. However, they are also in contact with one another, and the description of them is at least as much about the way they relate to one another as it is about the way they are in themselves, alone as it were. So we're studying them as individuals and also as a community.

The first thing to say is that there are very many of them. In fact, the Buddha tells Ānanda that:

> it is not easy to grasp the size of the Tathāgata Amitābha's sangha of śrāvakas, even if one thinks in terms of countless śrāvakas, countless hundreds of śrāvakas, countless thousands of śrāvakas, countless hundreds of thousands of śrāvakas, a profusion of śrāvakas, myriads of śrāvakas, great hosts of śrāvakas, untold śrāvakas, an abundance of śrāvakas, great multitudes of śrāvakas, numberless śrāvakas, multitudinous

> śrāvakas, immeasurably many, innumerable, incalculably many, incomparably many, inconceivably many śrāvakas.

The Buddha then goes on to give two similes to help us to get an idea of just how vast the assembly is. In the first he says that the monk Mahāmaudgalyāyana, who has supernormal powers, could, if he wished, count in one day and night all the many stars in the universe. Suppose that a "great many countless hundreds of thousands of monks" also possessed the same supernormal powers as Mahāmaudgalyāyana, and that these monks spend "a great many countless hundreds of thousands of years" counting the beings in Sukhāvatī. At the end of that period they would not have managed to count even the "tiniest minuscule fraction of them". In the second simile we are to imagine a single hair split into a hundred slivers. If we were to dip one sliver of this hair into the ocean, the tiny drop of water adhering to it would of course be negligible compared to the rest of the mighty ocean. Now the number of beings that those billions of monks would have counted by the end of those billions of years is as small in relation to the whole community as this tiny drop of water compared to the ocean.

What does this mean and why does the sutra insist on this point? Let me remind you that the sutra is a practice, not a textbook, so the question we need to ask is not why there are an infinite number of beings in Sukhāvatī, but what spiritual benefit there might be in imagining such a limitless sangha. Being in the midst of this community would not be at all like being in a large crowd of ordinary people. We have to imagine being surrounded by beings with deep insight, pure ethics, and no sense of self or, to put it more simply, beings who are completely unselfish and therefore compassionate, gentle, and kind, no matter where you were and whoever you happened to be among. There would be no need to be on guard against any insensitivity, unkindness, thoughtlessness, or malice, no need to be fearful or anxious, and this would enable you to relax and be emotionally open to those around you. In a word, it would allow you to trust them. Trust is the belief that someone is good and honest, and will not harm you. We tend to flourish in these circumstances.

Trust is connected to faith. Many years ago, on a seminar with my teacher, we asked how we could develop a stronger sense of faith in the Buddha, Dharma, and Sangha. He replied that the issue was a wider one than simply that of faith. It was, he said, really a question of trust. If you lack faith, then you need to examine the extent to which you are able, or unable, to trust other people. Of course it would be naive to trust everyone. Not everyone is good and honest, and some will try to harm you – so it's reasonable to be wary of those you don't know, and to be distrustful of those who have shown that they are bad, dishonest, and harmful. However, if a person has shown themselves to be trustworthy yet you continue to distrust them, that is unreasonable of you, and unfair to them. This is not the place to enquire into the reasons for this unreasonable lack of trust, nor, in extreme cases, how it might be treated. The important point here is that a sangha – a spiritual community of people who are doing their best to be good, honest, and harmless – is the best context for faith to grow. The reason for this is that faith is a form of trust. To have faith in the Buddha and his teaching is to trust that he has your best interests at heart and that he knows the way to complete happiness. If you find it difficult to trust people generally, then you'll find it difficult to have faith in the Buddha.

I've said that sangha is the best context for faith to grow, but we need to distinguish between different kinds – or levels – of sangha. Sangha as the third of the Three Jewels is the transcendent sangha, consisting of those who have deep insight into the Dharma and are as a consequence irreversible from Awakening. Such people are, and always will be, trustworthy. It's to this level of sangha that Buddhists go for refuge. Not all spiritual communities are transcendent sanghas though. People involved in a Buddhist community will be at different stages on the path. Some will be beginners, practising the path of ethics as best they are able but at times falling short of even the most basic precepts. (I say beginners, but some people remain at this stage for a long time.) Others will be more established in ethical practice and will live for the most part in very skilful states of mind. However, even such people, until they've reached the stage of irreversibility, are liable to fall back into unskilful states, leading to unethical behaviour. Some will have had deep insight into the true nature of things and have become irreversible from Awakening. Even these may be unethical at times – they are not yet fully awake after all – although any breach of ethics they commit will be minor and they will soon confess their fault and do their best to make amends. In any spiritual community it's wise to be selective in how much trust we place in the individual members of that community, but, if it really is a spiritual community – if those involved in it are sincerely trying to practise the Dharma – then a certain level of basic trust would seem to be reasonable. We can at least trust that they are doing their best to be ethical even if there are times when they fail. However, there may be those in the community whom we've seen being consistently kind, gentle, straightforward, and ethically sensitive over a long period of time. These we can reasonably trust. The beings who live in Sukhāvatī are of this kind. Imagining them is a practice in trust.

As I wrote above though, imagining living among such wonderful beings is only the first part of the practice. The point is to try to bring about something of that community – a reflection or an echo – into this world, into our daily experience. Buddhist practice doesn't consist only in transforming oneself; it also includes changing the world. In Mahāyāna terms, it means creating a buddha-field – or co-creating one. A few pages back I quoted the Buddha, who said that a buddha-field consists of living beings. He said this in reply to a question about how a bodhisattva purifies (or creates) a buddha-field. His answer is very long, but I'll just give you the first few lines:

> the buddha-field of a bodhisattva is a field of living beings. Why is this? It is because a bodhisattva obtains a buddha-field to the extent that he helps living beings. A bodhisattva obtains a buddha-field as living beings develop discipline. A bodhisattva obtains a buddha-field as living beings enter into buddha-knowledge through entering his buddha-field. A bodhisattva obtains a buddha-field as living beings cultivate noble spiritual faculties through entering his buddha-field. Why is this? Son of good family, it is because the buddha-fields of bodhisattvas are created for the sake of living beings.[97]

We saw in Chapter 3 that after Dharmākara had made his momentous vows he spent innumerable lives practising as a bodhisattva, and that there were two dimensions to his practice: transformation of himself and transformation of the world. The picture of Sukhāvatī, with its many living beings, is a "blueprint" for our world, a kind of utopia. Not that we will be able to completely transform our world into Sukhāvatī, at least not in this life, but we can at least make it a little more like it.

The first thing we must do is work on ourselves because we can't change the world without changing ourselves. Dharmākara, remember, spent five aeons in contemplation before setting out to create his pure buddha-field. If we want to live in a community of people anything like those who live in Sukhāvatī, we have to become something like them ourselves. When the Buddha said in the *Shorter Sūtra* that we should cultivate a heartfelt desire to be born in Sukhāvatī so that we can live with such beings, he didn't mean that we should wish to passively receive all the benefits of living with them, but that we should strive to become like them. We'll only be able to fully participate in a spiritual community when we practise the spiritual life and give to others what we'd like to receive from them. To live with them means becoming like them.

The descriptions of the beings in Sukhāvatī are quite long and I don't have the space to comment on all of them. This means that I've had to be selective. I've done this with no particular criteria in mind apart from what strikes me as interesting or useful, and I hope that what I include here will interest you sufficiently to encourage you to read these parts of the sutra yourself. Before we start though, a word of warning is necessary. In contemplating such beings there is a tendency, at least within some people – myself included – to compare ourselves unfavourably with them. If we're not careful we can use the descriptions as a stick to beat ourselves with. I don't believe the author or authors of the sutra intended that. I think they wrote the text to cheer people up, not to depress them! The sutra is a celebration of the beauty of the spiritual life, and the description of the beings living there is a celebration of the beauty of those living the spiritual life. Quoting from the *Vimalakīrti Nirdeśa* again, this time Vimalakīrti himself, in a long paeon of praise of bodhisattvas, says this:

Though they worship buddhas by the millions,
With every inconceivable offering,
They never dwell upon the least difference
Between the buddhas and themselves.[98]

As we reflect on the qualities of the beings who live in Sukhāvatī, it's best not to "dwell upon the least difference between" them and ourselves, but instead to allow them to inspire us without thinking too much about our own failings. Of course if we compare ourselves with them we are going to find ourselves wanting – they are ideal beings, the personification of everything good and kind and wise, living in an ideal world. We are imperfect human beings living in an impure world and, no matter how hard we try, how dedicated we might be to the spiritual life, we are all no doubt very far from the ideals we aspire to. The point is not to compare ourselves with these beings, but to rejoice in them, and in rejoicing let some of their qualities become ours. Perhaps we can drop the very idea of their qualities, and our failings, as if they were possessions. Perhaps we can just see them as qualities, which belong to no one. This is in fact how the beings in Sukhāvatī see it, so if we can do this we'll already be approaching something of their state of being.

Let's begin with the tenth vow, which states that the beings who live in Sukhāvatī will not

> conceive any notion of ownership, even of their own bodies.

The reason they don't conceive of the idea of ownership is because they have no conception of the idea of a self to whom things could belong. When there's no sense of self, there's no idea of property. Without a "me" there's no "mine". This even extends to their own bodies – they don't have any sense that their bodies "belong" to them. This may seem very strange: surely their bodies are theirs? It depends on what we mean by "theirs". To simplify this discussion I'll transpose it to the first person and talk about me and my body. What would it mean for me not to regard my body as mine? Here we have to distinguish between different senses of the word "mine". In the first sense my body is mine in that only I can feel the warmth of the sun on my cheek and the coolness of the tiles on the soles of my feet. You are also able to have these experiences, but your experiences aren't my experiences. I might be in a place where the sun is shining onto my cheek while my bare feet touch cool tiles, while you may be in a place where there is dense cloud cover and your feet are clothed in thick woollen socks, in which case right now the experiences of warm cheeks and cool soles of feet are mine, while the experiences of cool cheeks and warm feet are yours. But, even if we happened to be in the same place at the same time, both feeling the warmth of the sun on our cheeks and the coolness of the tiles on our feet, I'd still be experiencing those sensations in my body and you'd be feeling them in yours. The sensations of warmth and coolness are relatively simple, but the same principle applies when it comes to emotions: when I feel saddened by something that's happened to a friend, only I feel that sadness. You may feel sad too, but I don't feel your sadness.

Another sense in which I might regard my body as mine lies in the fact that I am able to move it – I can walk, sit, lie down, run, lift a cup of coffee to my mouth and sip it, and so on. Assuming that you have a similar state of health to me, you can do the same with your body. I can't do any of that with your body, just as you can't do any of that with mine. These two aspects of my body are linked, of course: when I move my arms and legs I also experience them moving, and when I sip the coffee from the cup I've brought to my lips I experience the hot liquid and the taste of the coffee on my tongue. So my body is mine in that I experience sensations and emotions through and in it, and am able to move it.

All this is so of awakened beings too – that is, for those who have realized that they have no enduring self. They too will feel the sun warming their cheeks and the cool tiles on the soles of their feet if the sun is shining and they are standing on cool tiles. They too can move their bodies at will, and they are unable to move others' bodies. The realization that there is no enduring self doesn't mean that we lose all sense of ourself as a person and merge into an undifferentiated mass. Some people say that nirvana is just that – the self merges with the universe in the same way as a drop of water merges with the ocean. Awakening is definitely not like that though; awakened beings feel physical sensations and experience emotions, and they have volition. The Buddha used to rest in the afternoon, for instance, because it was too hot to do anything else; that is, he felt the heat in his body and he decided to rest in a shaded area. Realizing that you don't have a self doesn't mean that you don't exist as a person; it's to realize that your self isn't a fixed thing and doesn't endure, unchanged, over years or lifetimes. Therefore each being in Sukhāvatī enjoys the pleasure and beauty of the land in their own body; when one of them decides to wade into a river to feel the warmth or cool of the water – whichever they desire – it is only that being who wades into the water and experiences that pleasure. The other beings there don't experience that pleasure unless they too step into the river.

The fact that only I feel sensations in my body makes the experience of living in this particular body very compelling. My pleasures and pains seem to me to be more important than yours because I feel them, whereas I don't feel yours. I infer that you also feel pleasure and pain in your body but I don't literally feel them. Similarly, the fact that I can move my body at will but am unable to move yours gives me a compelling sense that my body is mine, and not yours. This means that I instinctively give priority to my body over yours. No doubt our brains have evolved in this way to ensure that we act in the best interests of our own survival. The challenge of the spiritual life is to go beyond the survival instinct, so that I would give as much value to your experiences as I do to mine, in spite of the fact that I don't experience your experience. Awakened beings do this, even though they too only experience their experience and don't experience others' experience. What makes this possible is the imagination. In Chapter 3 I quoted a part of Shelley's paper "A defence of poetry":

> A man, to be greatly good, must imagine intensely and comprehensively; he must put himself in the place of another and of many others; the pains and pleasure of his species must become his own.[99]

The pains and pleasures of others can't literally become our own in the sense of our actually experiencing them, but they can become our own metaphorically, in the sense that we can imagine experiencing them. Knowing what physical pain feels like in my own experience, when I see you stubbing your toe, or hear you telling me that you've stubbed it, or crying out in pain as a result of stubbing it, your pain can become mine in that I can imagine what it feels like to be you experiencing the pain of a stubbed toe. Similarly, knowing what it feels like to succeed in something, when I see you succeed, or when you tell me about your success, I'm able to imagine what it feels like to be you experiencing success. How vividly I imagine your pain or success depends on my ability to suspend the compulsion to focus on my immediate experience and focus instead on the experience you seem to be having. To love another, or feel compassion for their suffering, or feel glad for their good fortune, is to refrain from prioritizing one's own experience over theirs. This is what awakened beings naturally do.

The third sense in which I might regard my body as mine is to regard it as my possession. Not only do I experience bodily sensations, not only am I able to move the body – it also belongs to me. I feel that it's mine, not yours. The beings who live in Sukhāvatī, however, don't regard their own bodies as their property. We could understand this in a philosophical way, in that nothing exists as a discrete "thing"; every thing is dependent on other "things" for its relative and impermanent existence, so it doesn't really make sense to say that we own anything. It would be like saying that we own a cloud or a wave on the ocean or a drop of dew on a blade of grass. Our bodies are just like everything else that exists in that they are not independent, discrete entities, so it doesn't really make sense to regard them as our possessions.

This is all very intellectual though, and perhaps it would be more useful to look at this in a more social or ethical way. The beings in Sukhāvatī don't conceive of their bodies as objects to use for their own personal benefit. Among the monks mentioned by name at the beginning of the *Longer Sūtra* – that is, the monks who are present when the Buddha teaches the sutra – are three close friends: Aniruddha, Nandika, and Kampila. One of the Pali suttas tells of an occasion when the Buddha visited them when they were living together in the Park of the Gosinga Sāla-Tree Wood. (In the following passages I will refer to them in the Pali spellings of their names: Anuruddha, Nandiya, and Kimbila.) The Buddha asked them how they were getting on with each other:

> I hope ... that you are all living in concord, with mutual appreciation, without disputing, blending like milk and water, viewing each other with kindly eyes.

They reply that they are indeed living in that way, and the Buddha then asks them to be specific: "How do you live thus?" Anuruddha replies:

> Venerable sir, as to that, I think thus: "It is a gain for me, it is a great gain for me, that I am living with such companions in the holy life". I maintain bodily acts of loving-kindness towards those venerable ones both openly and privately; I maintain verbal acts of loving-kindness towards those venerable ones both openly and privately; I maintain mental acts of loving-kindness towards those venerable ones both openly and privately. I consider: "Why should I not set aside what I wish to do and do what these venerable ones wish to do?" Then I set aside what I wish to do and do what these venerable ones wish to do. We are different in body, venerable sir, but one in mind.

Nandiya and Kimbila then echo Anuruddha's words, but the Buddha asks them to be even more specific. He wants to know how they live like this in practice. Anuruddha replies again:

> Venerable sir, as to that, whichever of us returns first from the village with almsfood prepares the seats, sets out the water for drinking and for washing, and puts the refuse bucket in its place. Whichever of us returns last eats any food left over, if he wishes; otherwise he throws it away where there is no greenery or drops it into water where there is no life. He puts away the seats and the water for drinking and for washing. He puts away the refuse bucket after washing it and he sweeps out the refectory. Whoever notices that the pots of water for drinking, washing, or the latrine are low or empty takes care of them. If they are too heavy for him, he calls someone else by a signal of the hand and they move it by joining hands, but because of this we do not break out into speech. But every five days we sit together all night discussing the Dhamma. That is how we abide.[100]

What's interesting about these passages is the way the three relate to one another, with such a high degree of mutual kindness that they have become "different in body ... but one in mind". This is not to be confused with group consciousness, in which there is very little – if any – self-awareness. A "group" in this context is some kind of power structure in which the needs of the individual members of that group are subordinated to the needs of the group as a whole. Most groupings of people – national, religious, ethnic, familial, corporate – are groups in this sense. To practise the spiritual life we have to emancipate ourselves from the group – which means that we have to free ourselves of our emotional dependence on it – and become autonomous individuals: able to think for ourselves, take individual responsibility, and make our own decisions on the basis of the skilful mental states and insights that we have individually cultivated. I may be reading too much into this, but it seems to me that that individuality is expressed in the Taima mandala by the fact that the thirty-four bodhisattvas surrounding Amitābha are all different from one another, making different gestures with their hands, and all looking in different directions. It would have been easy for the artist to have painted them all alike, in the same "uniform", all looking towards Amitābha, but instead they are depicted as unique individuals.

But there is another level of consciousness, beyond reflexive self-awareness. The three companions living together in the Park of the Gosinga Sāla-Tree Wood are autonomous individuals, and their "blending like milk and water" constitutes not a loss of individuality but a transcendence of it. My teacher speaks of three levels of human consciousness: group consciousness, in which there is no reflexive self-awareness; individual consciousness, in which reflexive awareness has been developed to a very high degree; and what he's called the "third order of consciousness", or the "collective consciousness of the spiritual community", in which autonomous individuals relate freely and spontaneously with other autonomous individuals. It's this level of consciousness that Anuruddha, Nandiya, and Kimbila exemplify, and this is what it means for the beings in Sukhāvatī to not regard their bodies as their property. Their bodies are different from each other, but their minds are "one" in that they "set aside" their own wishes and place their bodies at the service of others.

The beings in Sukhāvatī of course don't need to do any of the practical work of setting out water to drink and so on; that's all magically done for them by the land. At least that's what the sutra says, but perhaps what that really means is that everyone in Sukhāvatī lives as Anuruddha and his two friends do, viewing each other with kindly eyes and setting aside what they wish for in order to give others what they wish for, so that it seems as if the land is magically giving them everything they need. Last year I was on a three-month retreat in the Spanish mountains. There were fifteen of us in the first month and then eleven for the last two months. Most of the time we were in silence, just like Anuruddha, Nandiya, and Kimbila. We ate together three times a day and in the first week, while we were still speaking, we were able to ask for what we needed – the salt and pepper, the margarine and peanut butter, tea or coffee. When we entered the silent period though, we had to find other ways of communicating our needs. At first we used an improvised and rather clumsy sign language – pointing to the jam, making a shape of a T with our index fingers to indicate that we wanted a cup of tea, first three fingers pointing downwards to form the letter M for marmalade, or was that marmite? and so on. A little later, once we'd got to know each other's preferences better, simply catching another's eye and looking at something on the table was enough to have it sent our way. Later still, we didn't need to communicate our needs at all; they were met spontaneously. As soon as I sat down with my bowl of porridge, milk and honey would appear in front of me, and then when I'd finished the porridge a slice of toast would be passed to me, followed by margarine, peanut butter, and marmalade. A steaming cup of coffee would also be placed beside my plate, followed soon after by the milk. None of this was magic, of course. It was all due to my companions noticing what I needed and giving it to me, and while this was happening I would also be passing various things to the others on my table. It was all quite effortless and was perhaps a glimpse – a taste! – of what it might be like to live in Sukhāvatī, in the "collective consciousness of the spiritual community".

This experience was not merely very positive, but closer to reality than those experiences which are characterized by separation, estrangement, misunderstanding, and hostility. In his book *The Courage to Teach*, Parker J. Palmer makes the startling statement that reality is communal. That is:

> Reality is a web of communal relationships, and we can know reality only by being in community with it.[101]

He takes as the theoretical basis for his claim the findings of modern science, particularly biology and physics, which, he says, have in the past fifty years moved from an understanding of nature as one of "fragmentation and competition to [one of] community and collaboration". In particular, he refers to the American scholar of science and religion Ian Barbour, who considered nature to be essentially relational and interdependent. This of course is now a commonplace, but Barbour's understanding of this was penetrating – reality is not made up of separate substances or particles, but of events and relationships.

This is very close to the Buddha's insight of *anattā* or no self – that there are no enduring and discrete things, but only processes, always in relationship with – affecting and being affected by – other processes. Reality therefore is profoundly relational – everything exists in relationship to, and dependent on, other things (or, more accurately, events or processes). For this reason Palmer writes that "we can know reality only by being in community with it" or, to put it the other way round, we can't understand reality by looking at it as separate and unrelated observers. To understand reality we have to be a part of it, in a way we have to be friends with it. Friendship, compassion, generosity, empathy, and a sense of community with other human beings help us to awaken because they are the emotional and social expressions of reality. This is why the Buddha told Ānanda that spiritual friendship is the whole of the spiritual life, and why the *Shorter Sūtra* says that we should cultivate a heartfelt desire to be born in Sukhāvatī so that we will be in the company of the bodhisattvas who live there.

Later in the text, when the Buddha is telling Ānanda about the fulfilment of Dharmākara's vows, he elaborates on the theme of ownership:

> The living beings in that buddha-field have no notion of ownership. As they walk about, wander around in that buddha-field, neither delight nor discontent arises in them. As they stroll across that buddha-field, they have no particular expectations. They are free of expectations. Those living beings simply do not think in that way.

The Sanskrit word translated as "delight" is *rati*, which can also be translated as "love, attachment, pleasure, liking for, fondness". *Rati* can be skilful or unskilful, depending on what one is delighting in. "Discontent" is *arati*, which can also be translated as "dislike" or "aversion". Given that Sukhāvatī is the land of utmost happiness, where even the word "suffering" doesn't exist, it's easy to understand why the beings there would feel no discontent, but perhaps difficult to understand why they would feel no delight. However, this line comes immediately after the sentence about ownership, suggesting that what is meant is a possessive delight, or an attachment to pleasure. The non-arising of delight and discontent seems to be expressed in the idea that the beings there "wander around" and "stroll across" Sukhāvatī, both phrases suggesting a relaxed non-attachment to things or experiences. In one of the *Perfection of Wisdom* sutras, the Buddha says of bodhisattvas:

Without a home they wander, dharmas never hold them,
Nor do they grasp at them.[102]

"Home" in this quote can be understood both literally and metaphorically: in its metaphorical sense home represents an attachment to certain experiences and mental states. Because they are free of possessiveness or attachment, the beings in Sukhāvatī "have no particular expectations". "Expectation" is *apekṣā*, which also means "looking for, hope, need, requirement". You might think that it's easy for them to have no particular expectations, because every want and need is spontaneously fulfilled as soon as they think of it, but that is to look at it the wrong way round. The many sensuous pleasures that the beings in Sukhāvatī experience symbolize the happiness of non-attachment, non-grasping. When we stop looking for, hoping, needing, and requiring happiness and pleasure, then we are able to experience the greatest pleasure and happiness. I'm reminded once more of William Blake's poem:

He who binds to himself a joy
Doth the wingèd life destroy;
But he who kisses the joy as it flies
Lives in eternity's sunrise.[103]

Such a state of being is hard to imagine for those of us with a strong sense of self:

> The sphere in which they dwell is inconceivable. They own nothing, and grasp at nothing. They worry about nothing, and are bound to nothing. Free of grasping, they are completely liberated and unblemished.

The Buddha then elaborates further:

> Moreover, Ānanda, the living beings who have been born in that buddha-field, in Sukhāvatī, have no perception of anything as belonging to others, no perception of anything as belonging to themselves, no perception of inequality, no division, no conflict, and no hostility.

When he says that the beings in Sukhāvatī "have no perception of anything as belonging to others", he doesn't mean that they treat others' property with disrespect, he means that the very idea of property doesn't apply there. No one owns anything in Sukhāvatī, and this means that there is no conflict and no hostility, because conflict and hostility only arise among those who believe in their own selfhood and property. On the contrary,

> They are filled with patience and gentleness. ... They are free of hatred, and have calmed any harshness. ... They are free of greed, and delight in sharing what they have. They give freely, they are open-handed, and delight in the practice of generosity. They are not miserly in giving either physical gifts or the gift of the Dharma. ... They are ethically sensitive. ... They are gentle, and living with them brings happiness. They are helpful, rays of light in the world. ... They are straightforward and honest.

The realization that reality is relational or communal is not merely cognitive; it is affective too. Someone with deep insight will be kind, compassionate, patient, generous, sensitive; they will tremble with – *anukampā* – others in their joy and suffering. A well-known saying in Buddhist circles is that the path is the goal, meaning that the goal of the spiritual life is the full and spontaneous expression of all the practices we undertook to get there. If positive emotions such as kindness are the expressions of insight, then to reach that insight we need to practise kindness and so forth.

We should remember though that all the "objects" in Sukhāvatī are really symbols of spiritual and transcendental qualities. These are partly given by Amitābha – the result of his practice over innumerable lifetimes – and partly created by the beings who live there; as we've seen, their merits are manifested in jewels, banners, music, food, and so on. So the properties of Sukhāvatī are in fact the collective merits of Amitābha and everyone in his assembly. It is these merits – the qualities that have been developed through each individual's spiritual practice – that they regard as belonging to no one. When they see someone being generous, for example, they don't regard their generosity as their possession. To think of a positive quality as someone's property is to reify it (make it into a thing), and when we do that it's easy to slip into thinking that there is a limited supply of it. If we conceive of a positive quality in this way, then when we see others possessing it in an abundant degree we may unconsciously assume that there can't be much left for us, and this can lead to envy or resentment. This is irrational of course but we don't always think – or behave – rationally. In reality positive qualities are limitless, free, open to everyone who makes the effort to develop them, which means that we can all have as many and as much of them as we want. Perhaps this is another clue to the idea of the *amita* sangha – the limitless community: the qualities that they embody are limitless.

So far I've been exploring the qualities of the beings in Sukhāvatī as expressed in conceptual terms, but I wouldn't be doing justice to the text if I looked only at those. Many of their qualities are expressed in similes. For instance, they are compared to the five great elements:

> They are like the earth, because of their patience with both the purity and the impurity of all living beings. They are like water, because they wash away the roots of all defilements and carry them off. They are like fire, the king, because they burn up the defilement of pride in relation to any phenomenon whatsoever. They are like the wind, because there is nothing in the world they hold on to. They are like space, because they co-exist with all phenomena and they own nothing anywhere.

They are also compared to various animals:

> They are like bulls, because they are supreme amongst all the great herds of living beings. They are like great elephants, because they are in perfect control of their minds. They are like excellent, thoroughbred horses, because they are so well-trained. They are like lions, the kings of the animals, because they are courageous, self-confident, and unafraid. ... They are like birds, because they do not hoard any of the things that they come across.

In Chapter 1 I made the point that, at the time when these texts were written, India was a predominantly oral (rather than literate) society. Most people therefore would not have been able to read these sutras, but would have heard them recited, probably in a ritual context. Scholars of oral societies have pointed out that their inhabitants tend to think concretely rather than abstractly. For instance, in his book *Orality and Literacy*, Walter J. Ong writes:

> Oral cultures tend to use concepts in situational, operational frames of reference that are minimally abstract in the sense that they remain close to the living human lifeworld.

He refers to the pioneering work of Alexander Luria, who in 1931–2 interviewed people from the remoter areas of Uzbekistan and Kirghizia, some of whom were illiterate (or, to put it more positively, oral) and some of whom had learnt to read. When shown geometrical figures such as circles or squares, oral people identified them as representations of real things they knew:

> A circle would be called a plate, sieve, bucket, watch, or moon; a square would be called a mirror, door, house, apricot drying-board.[104]

On the other hand, school students, who were moderately literate, identified these shapes by their geometric names. Using the elements or animals to describe spiritual qualities and attainments – things that would have been part of the listener's "living human lifeworld" – would probably have had a greater effect on the listener than a more conceptual description. For instance, the first quality I explored – that the beings in Sukhāvatī have no conception of ownership – would have been immediately and more directly understood by the simile of birds, who "do not hoard any of the things that they come across".

At the end of the description of the beings who live in Sukhāvatī the Buddha tells Ānanda to turn to the west, scatter flowers, and prostrate himself in that direction. Ānanda does this and then requests to see Amitābha and his assembly of bodhisattvas. Amitābha responds to this by emitting a ray of light from the palm of his hand that fills "a great many countless hundreds of thousands of buddha-fields". Everyone then sees him

> rise over all buddha-fields like Mount Sumeru, the king of mountains, supreme in all the ten directions of space – bright, shining, brilliant, dazzling. They saw the great assembly of bodhisattvas, and the sangha of monks. They were able to see all this through the power of the Buddha, and because of the complete purity of his radiance.
>
> If the whole of the earth were to be turned into a single body of water, such that no trees, no mountains, no islands, no grass, bushes, plants, or great trees, no rivers, chasms, or cliffs could be discerned, then there would be nothing but the earth itself, transformed into a single ocean. In the same way, there were no distinguishing features or characteristics in that buddha-field, except for the śrāvakas whose radiance extended for six feet

> and the bodhisattvas whose radiance extended for countless hundreds of thousands of yojanas.

We've seen that in the *Shorter Sūtra* the Buddha gives only one reason for desiring rebirth in Sukhāvatī – to live in the company of the bodhisattvas there – and Ānanda demonstrates his wisdom by asking to see not the magnificent and beautiful objects in Sukhāvatī but Amitābha and his bodhisattvas. Amitābha reveals himself and all the beings who live there – the bodhisattvas and the śrāvakas – all the features of the land merging in the sangha, just as if the earth were submerged by the ocean. Not only that:

> At the same time, the bodhisattvas, śrāvakas, gods, and human beings in the world system of Sukhāvatī all saw the Tathāgata, the Arhat, the Perfectly Awakened Buddha Śākyamuni in this world system of Earth teaching the Dharma surrounded by a sangha of monks, all arhats.

The light that Amitābha radiates not only enables Ānanda and the rest of the Buddha's assembly to see him and his sangha but also enables the beings living in Sukhāvatī to see the Buddha Śākyamuni and his sangha. On one level this simply underlines a point made earlier in the *Shorter Sūtra*, that this world is also a buddha-field, albeit an impure one, and that "our" buddha is no less a buddha than Amitābha. Just as Ānanda and the other members of Śākyamuni's assembly revere Amitābha, so Amitābha's community reveres Śākyamuni.

But there seems to me to be another dimension to this miracle. It symbolizes Parker J. Palmer's insight that reality is communal. Amitābha's light illuminates the whole universe, enabling all beings in all world systems to see all other world systems, and therefore enabling all beings in all other world systems to see oneself. It's an image of unrestricted communication, of seeing and being seen. It's an image of the whole universe becoming awakened or, to use another metaphor, enlightened.

The Buddha then turns to the Bodhisattva Maitreya, also known as Ajita, and asks him if he too can see Sukhāvatī and the beings there, and he replies in the affirmative. The Buddha then asks him whether he can see that some beings there live inside closed "exquisite lotus flowers". He says that he can, and continues:

> I see that they are able to move around, play, and enjoy themselves in palaces fifty, a hundred, or five hundred yojanas

> in size, palaces like those of the gods of the thirty-three, or of the yāma gods.

He also notices that others sit cross-legged on open lotus flowers, and he asks the reason for this difference. The Buddha replies that it depends on the degree of their faith: prior to their birth in Sukhāvatī, those in the closed lotuses entertained doubts about the possibility of being born there. Despite their doubts they were reborn there due to the abundance of their roots of merit.

> However, they are not able to see the Buddha, hear the Dharma, see bodhisattvas, discuss the Dharma with others and have it explained to them, cultivate any roots of virtue, or practise the Dharma in any way. They do not enjoy themselves or find contentment there.

Although they live as gods their spiritual development is temporarily suspended: they are cut off from the Buddha and the bodhisattvas, unable to hear or talk about the Dharma, unable to practise the Dharma. In other words, for the first 500 years of their lives, Sukhāvatī is a heaven rather than an Awakening realm. Planting roots of merit – practising ethics – only results in skilful mental states, not in wisdom. The implication of this is that faith is tantamount to wisdom. This is made clear in the sentences that precede the above quotation:

> You see, Ajita, the wisdom of someone who has been deprived of the benefits of seeing buddhas and bodhisattvas, of hearing the Dharma, and of discussing it with others for five hundred years is ordinary, unexceptional, deficient, and limited. Someone like that has been deprived of the opportunity to practise and attain roots of virtue, all because they have fallen into doubt.

Not that they are completely devoid of wisdom. If this were the case they wouldn't have been born in Sukhāvatī – they would have been born into one of the heaven realms. However, their insight is weak and limited, so weak that they seem to have temporarily forgotten it, and it takes a long time for them to remember or rediscover it. Another way of putting this is that they have been temporarily distracted from the transcendental path – the path of wisdom – by the happiness, pleasure, and beauty of the dhyānas. You may remember that the stream-entrant is assured of Awakening in their next seven lives. It's possible for them to awaken fully in their present life, but they may also procrastinate for quite a long time. As the Buddha says: "You see, Ajita, what a great waste of time doubt is for bodhisattvas."

The Buddha then gives a simile to illustrate further the situation of the beings in the closed lotuses. He asks Ajita to imagine that there was a king, who had a prison

> covered in gold and lapis lazuli, with ropes made of strips of fine cloth and garlands of flowers hanging from the walls. Imagine that there were canopies everywhere, in a variety of different colours, and that the prison was covered in cotton and fine cloths. Imagine that there were flowers and blossoms scattered everywhere, and that the air was perfumed with the finest perfumes. Imagine that it had a great multitude of terraces, turrets, small windows, pavilions, and arched doorways, all made of the seven kinds of precious substances. Imagine that it was covered in nets of small bells. ... Imagine, then, that the king's son was thrown into this prison on account of some misdeed, and put into shackles made of gold from the Jambū River. Imagine that there was a couch prepared for him there with different kinds of woollen and cotton cloths spread over it, quilts from Kaliṅga thrown over it, a covering over the top, and a great multitude of beautiful red cushions at either end. He would either sit or lie on that couch, and different kinds of pure food and drink of the highest quality would be offered to him. Do you think, Ajita, that the pleasures available to this prince would be exquisite?

Ajita replies that they would indeed be exquisite. The Buddha then asks whether he thinks that the prince would enjoy the various pleasures of that luxurious prison, and whether he would experience satisfaction and contentment there, to which Ajita replies:

> No, Blessed One. If the king had him led away and thrown into the prison, his only wish would undoubtedly be to be set free. He would strive to find nobles, princes, ministers, ladies of the court, merchants, householders, or castellans who could free him from the prison. The prince, Blessed One, would experience no pleasure in that prison, and he would not be set free until the king showed him mercy.

The parable of the imprisoned prince is introduced here to make an important point. In terms of the three principal levels of happiness that we explored in Chapter 1, the prince in his luxurious prison symbolizes worldly happiness, that of sensual pleasure, and the beings in the closed lotuses symbolize unworldly happiness, the happiness of the dhyānas or the god realms. The prince is unable to enjoy the sensual pleasures of his prison because he yearns for freedom, and the same is true of the beings in the closed lotuses: although the pleasures of the gods may seem limitless and eternally satisfying, actually they are limited and impermanent, just as are sensual pleasures. The Buddha (or at least the author of the sutra) wants us to see that the god-like pleasures of the meditative absorptions are ultimately as unsatisfactory as sensual pleasure, and he wants us to aspire instead to the third principal level of happiness – still greater unworldly happiness – symbolized by the beings sitting in the open lotuses. Therefore, towards the end of the sutra the Buddha says:

> You must now engage in the kind of spiritual practice which is free from doubt. Have no uncertainty about the unobstructed knowledge of the buddhas, which is free from attachment. Do not enter the prison made of jewels possessing all of the finest qualities.

The sutra portrays the two lower levels of happiness – worldly and unworldly – as places of confinement. They may be luxurious, pleasant, and beautiful, but they are places of confinement nevertheless. The highest level of happiness – still greater unworldly happiness – by contrast is open, spacious, and free. You may remember that in Chapter 1 I quoted a verse from the *Dhammapada* in which the Buddha recommends that we renounce a limited happiness for an abundant happiness. What makes the latter kind of happiness abundant is freedom. Often we sacrifice our freedom for pleasure and a limited kind of happiness. We tie ourselves to a job, or a relationship, or a property, or a persona, which gives certain benefits – money, security, comfort, prestige – but which effectively closes down the possibility of a greater happiness.

Giving up a limited happiness for an abundant happiness entails a certain amount of discomfort, because you have to renounce your present level of happiness before you can enjoy the more abundant happiness you are hoping for, and there is usually a time lag. For instance, you might give up eating chocolate. In giving it up, you are deprived of the pleasant taste and the feeling of well-being that chocolate gives. (Chocolate apparently releases serotonin in the brain, producing feelings of pleasure, and as chocolate melts in your mouth it produces an increase in brain activity and heart rate that is more intense than that associated with passionate kissing, and lasts four times as long. No wonder chocolate is so popular![105]) And what do you get in return? Not much at first. Instead, your life probably seems a bit more impoverished than it was before. However, after a while your dependence on the pleasure you get from chocolate will wane and you will find that you no longer crave it. Only then do you start to experience the more abundant happiness, the happiness that comes with freedom from craving. In this respect there is an interesting passage in the description of the beings who live in Sukhāvatī:

> They have ascended to the entrance into the knowledge of a buddha, which is difficult to awaken to. They have found the narrow path. They are free of doubt. They no longer have any questions. Their understanding is not dependent on others.

The path to complete freedom is a narrow one. It's the path of discipline and restraint, which may seem to be the opposite of freedom. However, as any musician will tell you, in order to get to the point where they can express themselves freely, countless hours of disciplined study and practice are necessary. This is as true for jazz as it is for classical musicians. To be able to improvise you need to know the rules of harmony, you need to know all the keys, you need to be able to sight-read – that is, play what's on the page instantly – and you need to have honed your technique to the point where you can effortlessly play what you can read on the page or hear in your mind. This kind of disciplined study is needed for any skill that we might want to develop – that's why they are often called disciplines – and it's true of the spiritual life too. To gain the abundant happiness of complete freedom necessitates giving up the relative freedom of doing just what we want now.

Having a narrow practice shouldn't be confused with narrow-mindedness though. The Cambridge online dictionary defines "narrow" firstly in a purely factual sense: "having a small distance from one side to the other, especially in comparison with the length". Its secondary meaning, though, is "mainly disapproving. Limited to a small area of interest, activity or thought. As in the phrase 'They are unable to see beyond the narrow world of the theatre.'" My teacher once said that our interests should be very wide while our practice should be narrow. This is because a narrow practice goes deep. A wide practice – that is, a practice in which we do a little bit of this and a little bit of that, changing from one month to the next, from one week to the next – keeps us on the surface of things.

Of course there's a certain amount of risk involved in giving up a limited happiness for an abundant happiness. What if it doesn't work? What if you sacrifice a limited happiness only to get a more limited happiness, or even unhappiness? In many instances no great harm is done – if you find that giving up chocolate doesn't give you access to more abundant happiness you can always revert to eating it again. But what if you give up your well-paid job and your comfortable home to pursue the Buddhist path, only to find that you are now more unhappy than you were before, and poor and homeless too? Well, there's always a risk in anything worth doing. Just consider the risk the Buddha took when he left home to pursue his quest for Awakening. He came from a very well-off family (some say his father was a king but it seems more likely that he was one of the leaders of a republic), with a very attractive future, so he had a lot to lose. Later, when he was a *śrāmana*, a wanderer, he was twice the leading disciple of well-known spiritual teachers, and in both cases those teachers offered him the joint leadership of their community. But he turned both opportunities down because he knew that he had not yet realized full Awakening, and he left those teachers and their communities to search alone once again.

The sutra ends with the Buddha telling Ajita that hundreds of thousands of millions of trillions of bodhisattvas from numerous buddha-fields will be reborn in Sukhāvatī – "in order to see the Tathāgata Amitābha, to worship him, attend him, put their queries to him, and ask him questions" – another instance of the *Longer Sūtra*'s elevation of Amitābha and Sukhāvatī to the best of all buddhas and buddha-fields, as well as an explanation of why the number of beings in Sukhāvatī is limitless! Then follow a number of passages extolling the virtues of the sutra itself, for instance:

> one should be willing to plunge into threefold thousand great thousand world systems filled with fire without thinking of turning back even once – just to hear this discourse on the Dharma.

This is a typical example of Mahāyāna hyperbole, meaning simply that one should be prepared to undergo any hardship in order to hear the sutra. The next thing the Buddha says is much more down to earth, and is to be taken literally:

> Therefore, you should engage with this discourse on the Dharma with determination so that you can hear it, grasp it, and bear it in mind. You should engage with it with great energy so that you can master it, explain it in detail, and cultivate it in meditation. You should copy it carefully into a book so that you can remember it.

In an article on Mahāyāna Buddhism the scholar David Drewes reviews the various theories that Western scholars have proposed about the Mahāyāna and the practices that Mahāyānists have engaged in. He points out that, of the various practices the sutras recommend, "far and away more frequently than all the others" are what he calls sutra-oriented practices, such as the ones quoted here. Passages like this one have been largely ignored by scholars or considered to be simply devices to encourage people to preserve the sutras. A more straightforward explanation, he thinks, is that they were the main practices that Mahāyāna Buddhists engaged in:

> Part of the problem with imagining this to be so is that Westerners have long tended to ignore the importance of Buddhist textual practices, especially those connected with memorization, recitation, and preaching, imagining true Buddhism to be primarily a matter of meditation and philosophy. In fact, composing, memorizing, reciting, preaching, listening to, and copying texts – a vast labor of extending Buddhist narrative – seem always to have been significantly more important than philosophy and meditation in South and Southeast Asian Buddhism, in both theory and practice.[106]

The Buddha then entrusts Ajita with the sutra, so that it won't perish. Ajita is to be the future buddha (Maitreya) of this impure buddha-field and the Buddha gives the sutra to him "so that the Dharma of the buddhas is not lost, so that it does not disappear". Finally, while the sutra was being spoken by the Buddha, countless numbers of beings attained all sorts of advanced stages of Awakening, and when the Buddha has finished speaking "the threefold thousand great thousand world systems then [shake] in six different ways", various miracles occur, magical flowers rain down, human and heavenly musical instruments play, a great shout of joy can be heard (reaching as far as the highest of the pure abodes), everyone is filled with joy and they all rejoice at the Buddha's words.

I made the point in Chapter 1 that in Mahāyāna sutras the Buddha's teaching is a cosmic event that affects not only those he is speaking directly to – when the Buddha speaks the universe changes – and this is a lovely example of that idea. The joy that everyone feels on hearing the Buddha teach this sutra is felt throughout the whole of the universe.

Part Three

The Sūtra on the Visualization of the Buddha Amitāyus

Chapter Seven

Tears falling like rain

We now come to the third of the sutras, which purports to be a translation from Sanskrit into Chinese, although no Sanskrit original has been discovered. Its full Chinese title is *Fó shuō guān wúliàngshòu fó jīng*, but I'll refer to it by its common abbreviation, *Guān Jīng: the Vizualisation Sūtra*. It begins, like the *Longer Sukhāvatīvyūhaḥ Sūtra*, with the Buddha staying on Vultures' Peak in Rājagṛha, accompanied by 1,250 monks and 32,000 bodhisattvas, led by Mañjuśrī, the Dharma prince. However, after telling us this the sutra immediately switches to events happening nearby:

> At that time there was a prince in Rājagṛha called Ajātaśatru. Under the influence of his evil friend Devadatta he captured his father, King Bimbisāra, locked him in the seventh floor of the prison tower, and ordered his ministers to have no contact with him.

Bimbisāra was, as we saw in Chapter 3, a follower of the Buddha. Devadatta had previously been one of the Buddha's disciples too, but had turned against him. He was, like Ānanda, one of the Buddha's cousins, and, like Ānanda, had left home to become a monk, or śrāvaka. Tradition has it that Devadatta was ambitious, and that a few years before the Buddha's death, when he was visiting Rājagṛha, Devadatta addressed the Buddha at a large gathering, which included many monks as well as King Bimbisāra:

> My Lord, the Exalted One is now grown old, is aged, far gone in years, he has come to life's end. ... Let him hand over the care of the Order to me, and I will take care of it.[107]

The Buddha refuses Devadatta's request in the strongest terms, saying that he wouldn't even hand on his leadership to his two chief disciples, Maudgalyāyana or Śāriputra, and certainly won't hand it on to him. Devadatta reacts very angrily to this and secretly approaches Bimbisāra's son, Ajātaśatru, with a proposal that they plot together to seize temporal and spiritual power: Ajātaśatru is to kill his father and thus become king, while Devadatta will murder the Buddha and become the leader of his sangha. Ajātaśatru agrees to this proposal and one night attempts to creep into his father's bed chamber with a knife concealed in his clothing. However, he is apprehended by one of the king's guards, and the king wakes up. Bimbisāra asks his son why he wishes to kill him, and Ajātaśatru confesses that he wants to become king. Bimbisāra, remarkably, decides to abdicate and give his kingdom to his son. Devadatta, however, is not satisfied with this. Consumed by jealousy because Bimbisāra is such a loyal supporter of the Buddha, he again persuades Ajātaśatru to kill his father. Ajātaśatru therefore imprisons Bimbisāra with the intention to starve him to death.

Meanwhile, Devadatta attempts to kill the Buddha. First he hires some mercenaries – presumably using Ajātaśatru's money. This doesn't work because each time one of them approaches the Buddha, he teaches the would-be assassin the Dharma and the man becomes his disciple! Devadatta then tries to do the job himself, pushing a massive rock from Vultures' Peak down to where the Buddha is walking. However, the rock smashes into smithereens before it reaches the Buddha, and the worst that happens is that he is lightly wounded by a shard of rock. Finally Devadatta lets loose a crazed elephant to attack the Buddha, but the elephant is subdued by the waves of loving-kindness coming from him. As a result of these attempts on the Buddha's life, some of his disciples set a guard around him, but he orders them to disband, explaining that he doesn't need to be protected. Soon after this Devadatta gives up his attempts to murder the Buddha and instead sets up a rival spiritual community, thereby causing a schism in the sangha. Wounding a buddha and causing a schism in the sangha are two of the "five acts which have immediate consequences" that constitute unskilful weighty karma. According to Buddhist doctrine it is not possible to kill a buddha.

Although Ajātaśatru didn't allow any court officials to visit Bimbisāra in his dungeon, he did let his mother, Queen Vaidehī, see her husband, and she visited him every day. Before each visit she would cover her whole body with honey and ghee (clarified butter) mixed with wheat flour, and fill her jewel ornaments with grape juice. Bimbisāra would lick Vaidehī's body and drink the juice from her jewellery, and this kept him alive. After three weeks Ajātaśatru began to wonder why his father had not died, and questioned the prison guard, who told him of Vaidehī's ruse. Reacting furiously, Ajātaśatru called for his mother to be brought to him and drew his sword to kill her. However, two members of his court, a minister named Candraprabha and the prince's physician, Jīvaka, stepped between Ajātaśatru and Vaidehī, pointing out that, although many a king had killed his father in order to usurp the throne, they had never heard of a king killing his mother. Grasping their swords, they told the king that if he committed this outrage they would both leave the court. It seems that in the royal court of Rājagṛha, killing one's father was acceptable but killing one's mother was not! Ajātaśatru was pacified and put away his sword, and, instead of killing Vaidehī, ordered that she should be thrown into the deepest dungeon and never released. Although her life had been spared, the situation was now hopeless for the queen and her beloved Bimbisāra, whose death she was now powerless to prevent.

The sutra tells us that Vaidehī grew "emaciated with worry" and that "her tears fell like rain." Facing the direction of Vultures' Peak, she worshipped the Buddha, and asked him to send his two disciples, Mahāmaudgalyāyana and Ānanda, to visit her. Not only did he send them to her, he miraculously appeared in her room himself, the colour of gold and seated on a magnificent lotus throne made of a hundred different kinds of precious substances.

On seeing him, Vaidehī took off her jewellery and prostrated on the ground before him, weeping bitterly. She asked the Buddha what evil she could have committed in previous lives to have borne such an evil son, and then asked the Buddha to show her "a place free of sorrow" where she could be reborn, and to teach her how to visualize "a place where the effects of all actions have been purified". In response to this, a ray of golden light shone from between the Buddha's eyebrows, illuminating innumerable world systems in all directions of space. This light then transformed into a golden platform, settling above the Buddha's head, and on that platform could be seen all the buddha-fields in the whole universe. Vaidehī said that, wonderful as all these were, she wished to be born in Amitābha's buddha-field, Sukhāvatī, and she asked the Buddha to teach her how to contemplate that land. Before teaching Vaidehī to visualize Sukhāvatī, the Buddha smiled and rays of light of five different colours shone from his mouth onto Bimbisāra's head as he sat in his dungeon. Bimbisāra, "in his mind's eye", saw the Buddha clearly, knelt down before him, and effortlessly made spiritual progress to the stage of a non-returner. Although Vaidehī hadn't explicitly asked the Buddha to help Bimbisāra, one of the reasons for her extreme distress was that she was no longer able to keep her husband alive, and of course the Buddha knew that. It's interesting that, although the Buddha was able to help them both spiritually, he seemed unable to help them materially. If he could magically appear in Vaidehī's dungeon, could he not also magically help them to escape? It seems not, and this expresses the fact that the Buddha's domain is spiritual and transcendental rather than material. The Buddha then turned to Vaidehī and said:

> You do not know it yet, but the Buddha Amitābha is not far away. You should concentrate your awareness on that buddha-field, and visualize it with great care. I will now reveal to you in comprehensive detail how you can purify the effects of your actions by doing so, so that in the future any ordinary person who wishes to purify the effects of their actions will be able to be reborn in the western buddha-field of Sukhāvatī.

For the rest of the sutra the Buddha speaks to Vaidehī. In fact, just as Ānanda instigates the Buddha's teaching in the *Longer Sukhāvatīvyūhaḥ Sūtra* with his remark about the Buddha's golden appearance, so Vaidehī instigates all of the Buddha's teaching in this sutra with her request to be shown Sukhāvatī. I think it's significant that, while in the two Sukhāvatī sutras the Buddha speaks to two of his most prominent monks, one of whom is fully awakened, in this sutra the Buddha addresses Vaidehī, who is a lay follower, a woman, and, according to the Buddha, "an ordinary person, with a weak and feeble mind". Be that as it may, Vaidehī is undoubtedly the heroine of the story, showing unswerving loyalty to her lord Bimbisāra and immense courage in risking her life and freedom to keep him alive.

This story is based on actual events, but why did the author decide to start the sutra with it? Possibly because the situation that Bimbisāra and Vaidehī find themselves in is about as far from Sukhāvatī as it's possible to be. Sukhāvatī is a land of utter happiness, where even the words for suffering and pain don't exist, where there is no conception of property, and where there is no conflict or dispute; on the contrary, those who live there "are filled with patience and gentleness ... free of hatred ... free of greed, and delight in sharing what they have". Vaidehī and Bimbisāra's situation, by contrast, is one of intense suffering, suffering that has been caused by greed, envy, and animosity, through actions instigated by Devadatta but then carried out by their own son, someone whom they would have expected to love and protect them. Perhaps the author wanted to illustrate the relevance of Amitābha and Sukhāvatī to us in our world of suffering.

My teacher makes a useful distinction between what he calls the power mode and the love mode. When we act in the power mode we treat people as objects – objects that we use and sometimes abuse for our own ends. When we act in the love mode we treat people as people, who think, feel, desire, suffer, just as we do. When we act in the love mode, therefore, we don't – we *can't* – treat people as objects. We don't use people. Another way of putting this is that, when we act in the power mode, other people don't matter. They are seen merely as objects to be used for the furtherance of our own aims. When we act in the love mode, people do matter. The spiritual life consists in the gradual shift from the power mode to the love mode. That's why the Buddhist path begins with ethics, which is the practice of treating others as if they were subjects. Which they are, of course.

In the previous chapter I made a distinction between the group and the spiritual community. The group is a social structure in which the needs of the individual are subordinated to the needs of the group, whereas a spiritual community is a free association of individuals, in which each person takes responsibility for himself or herself, and in which there therefore exist no sanctions, no rewards for being "good", and no punishments for being "bad". The members of a spiritual community act in accordance with natural morality, which is based on the law of karma: ethical actions result in happiness and unethical actions in suffering. This occurs naturally – no one does it to us. "It is in the nature of things that joy arises in a person free from remorse", as the Buddha says in the *Cetanā Sutta*. The group has at its basis conventional morality, which is the sum total of the mores and laws of that particular society, and these are enforced by rewards for "good" behaviour – that is, behaviour that is in accordance with the group's conventions and laws – and punishment for bad behaviour. These rewards and punishments are not all officially determined by the authorities. Often they are enforced by the members of the group through the display of approval for "good" behaviour – smiles, congratulations, entry into elite social groupings – and disapproval for "bad" behaviour: dirty looks, shunning, refusal of entry into certain social groupings.

Not all groups are the same, of course. Some are more positive than others. A positive group is one that reflects the law of karma, or natural morality. That is, its laws and conventions encourage its members to treat others as subjects, not objects. A positive group rewards actions that are kind, generous, and compassionate, and punishes those that are unkind, cruel, or selfish. A positive group therefore is closer to the spiritual community than is a negative group. *Closer* to the spiritual community, but still a group, in that it uses rewards and punishments, encouraging its members to behave ethically, but ultimately, when necessary, punishing bad behaviour. A positive group uses the power mode then, but in the service of the love mode. That is, the use of the power mode in a positive group is benign. A spiritual community eschews the use of the power mode altogether.

However, because the positive group encourages its members to act in accordance with the love mode, members of a positive group can more easily make the transition to the spiritual community. In the *Shorter Sukhāvatīvyūhaḥ Sūtra*, you may remember, the Buddha says that we should cultivate a heartfelt desire to be born in Sukhāvatī so that we can live with the beings there – in other words, so that we can enjoy living in a spiritual community. He goes on to say that we won't be born there "with only a few roots of virtue". The practice of ethics is a necessary prerequisite for joining the spiritual community. In this context he uses the phrase "a child of good family". This is a phrase often used by the Buddha, and it's obvious from things that he said elsewhere that he didn't mean good family in the conventional sense of a family that upholds the conventions of the group. A good family is one that practises and encourages its members to practise natural morality, to act in accordance with the love mode, to treat others as subjects, not as objects. If we've been taught to be ethical, it will be easier for us to take up the spiritual life.

Our family is of course the first group that we know. King Bimbisāra and Queen Vaidehī were disciples of the Buddha, so presumably their family was a positive group, and Ajātaśatru was therefore "a son of good family", and yet he acted abominably towards his parents. There were other forces working on him though. He was dazzled and impressed by Devadatta's magical powers, and Devadatta had poisoned his mind, tempting him with the power of the throne. In Chapter 4 I wrote about the "gravitational pull" of the world – the tendency for us to fall back into old unskilful ways until we've reached the stage of irreversibility, from which point the gravitational pull of Awakening is stronger than that of the world. I was writing there about the individual practitioner, but the spiritual community as a collective is also susceptible to the gravitational pull. The spiritual community has a tendency to become a group, and the positive group has a tendency to become a negative group. Of course the idea of gravity in this instance is a metaphor; it's not really an external force, it's the effect of greed, hatred, and delusion acting on our minds. A negative group is one in which greed, hatred, and delusion are encouraged, even institutionalized.

It's interesting to compare the story of Bimbisāra and Ajātaśatru with the confinement of the prince in the *Longer Sukhāvatīvyūhaḥ Sūtra*. There, a king incarcerates his son for a misdeed of some kind, but in a palace

> covered in gold and lapis lazuli, with ropes made of strips of fine cloth and garlands of flowers hanging from the walls ... and different kinds of pure food and drink of the highest quality would be offered to him.

In this case, the incarceration is benign – the only suffering that the prince experiences is that of not being free to go wherever he wishes. And his punishment is just – he is confined to the palace for a misdeed he has committed. It is the benign punishment of the positive group, the power mode in the service of the love mode, the king punishing his son to discourage him from misbehaving in the future. Bimbisāra's imprisonment, however, is unjust: he has done nothing unethical for which he should be punished. His imprisonment is therefore not a reflection of natural morality but an expression of the power mode pure and simple. To Ajātaśatru his father is simply an object standing in the way of his becoming king.

I think the reversal of roles in the two stories is also significant. The confinement of the prince by his father for a misdeed is not only just but also reflects how power should be used in a group if it is to reflect natural morality: the king represents the authority of the group, and therefore the power mode, but in the service of the love mode. Ajātaśatru's imprisonment of Bimbisāra is not only unjust, but indicates something going badly wrong in the structure of the positive group. The son exerting negative power over the father symbolizes irrational, negative forces overcoming the reasonable and benign power of the ethically skilful. Interestingly, Bimbisāra freely *gives* his power to Ajātaśatru. Although at first sight this may seem to be an incredibly positive act, expressive of love, generosity, and a renunciation of power, in fact it leads to great suffering, not only for Bimbisāra and Vaidehī, but also – in the long term – for Ajātaśatru. Bimbisāra's abdication of the throne was an expression of love for his son, a desire to give him what he wanted to make him happy, but it was unwise – it would have been better for everyone if he hadn't done it. Bimbisāra *rewarded* Ajātaśatru for his misdeed, when he should have punished him. Symbolically, when he did this the positive group allowed greed, envy, and animosity to have power. It thus became a negative group. Love is helpless in the face of power. Vaidehī succeeded for a while in keeping her husband alive through subterfuge, but this didn't last long. When she was found out she was rendered powerless.

I should point out that my interpretation of the prince's confinement from the *Longer Sukhāvatīvyūhaḥ Sūtra* here is not what the author of the text had in mind. The imprisoned prince is introduced in the sutra to illustrate the plight of the beings born within closed lotuses in Sukhāvatī, which symbolize the confinement of the mental state of doubt or ignorance. In that case their confinement is not a punishment given by an external force but the natural result of a limited mind. However, stories, myths, and legends admit of multiple interpretations.

There is a Pali text that recounts how Ajātaśatru visited the Buddha years after he had murdered his father.[108] The Buddha gives him a comprehensive teaching, after which Ajātaśatru confesses his crime. When Ajātaśatru leaves, the Buddha remarks to the monks present that, had he not killed his father, he would have gained insight strong enough to become irreversible on the path to Awakening. Some time after that meeting, Ajātaśatru is murdered by his own son and is reborn in one of the hell realms.

Let's return to the *Guān Jīng*, and to Vaidehī, who is now locked in a dungeon, unable to see her beloved husband, and therefore unable to keep him alive. She is now utterly helpless and, in her great distress, she calls on the Buddha. She reminds him that he used to send Ānanda to "comfort" her, and requests that he send Ānanda and Maudgalyāyana to her now. He does more than that. Not only does he send the two monks, but he magically appears in her room too, and not in his usual human appearance, but as he appears when he dwells in the abode of all the buddhas:

> His body was the colour of pure gold, and he was seated on a lotus flower made of a hundred different kinds of precious substances. Maudgalyāyana stood to his left, and Ānanda to his right. Śakra, Brahmā, the protectors of the world, and all the other gods surrounded him in the air, showering him with heavenly flowers.

I wrote above that love is helpless in the face of power, and so it is, on its own level. That is, love has no weapons to prevent power from doing whatever it wants to do. Vaidehī now accepts defeat and asks only for comfort and consolation in her distress.

My teacher has made a useful distinction between what he calls a difficulty and a problem. A difficulty can be solved, given sufficient effort and intelligence, whereas a problem cannot be solved on its own level. Yet at the same time we feel that it *has* to be solved, because it's painful, and we therefore can't leave it alone. At first Vaidehī treats the imprisonment of Bimbisāra as a difficulty, to which she applies effort and intelligence. To a certain extent she is successful – she at least keeps him alive for a little while, when without her help he would have died. Now that she too is imprisoned, though, there is nothing she can do. The difficulty has become a problem, or perhaps it would be more accurate to say that what she thought was a difficulty is actually a problem (in that nothing she could have done would have made any difference ultimately). So she gives up trying to solve the problem and at that moment the Buddha appears in her chamber. Rather than give her comfort and consolation, the Buddha offers her a different perspective. It is the perspective of one who dwells in the abode of all the buddhas, which is the abode of the deathless. Not the literal deathlessness of immortality, but a state of mind that has gone beyond the duality of life and death, freedom and imprisonment, love and hate.

Vaidehī hasn't fully understood this yet, and she asks the Buddha to tell her what evil she committed in previous lives to have borne such an evil son. She also wonders how the Buddha could have such an evil cousin as Devadatta. These questions could be indicative of a common misunderstanding of the law of karma, the notion that everything that happens to us is a result of our previous actions, from this and former lives. This is not what the Buddha taught. While our past actions (in the sense of volitional actions – karma) will definitely have consequences, they are not the only factors that determine our present experience. As I explained in Chapter 4, the law of karma is just one strand of conditionality; there are other strands, such as the physical inorganic and the organic, operating independently of our karmic actions. One could be practising pure ethics, cultivating higher states of consciousness and seeing into the nature of things while at the same time a cancerous growth may be developing in one's body; or tectonic plates deep in the earth may be about to move, causing a massive earthquake where we live; or someone half-crazy with resentment may be plotting to harm us. None of these things would be caused by our karmic actions; none of them are our "fault".

What Vaidehī is expressing, I think, is the natural human tendency to ask, when bad things happen, "Why is this happening to me?" What we are really asking is, "What have I done to deserve this?" Sometimes bad things happen to good people and we struggle to make sense of it. It's as if, somewhere deep inside us, we feel that life should be fair, and when bad things happen to good people we feel a sense of injustice. Part of growing up perhaps is the realization that life *isn't* fair. Bad things do happen to good people sometimes and there's no redress, no cosmic judge to put things right. It's not that life is unfair; it's just life, the various strands of conditionality going on inexorably without any particular reference to me or you. You might think that this contradicts the law of karma, which states that skilful actions result in happiness and unskilful actions in suffering, but the fact is that many other conditions also affect our welfare.

The Buddha doesn't answer Vaidehī's questions about karma, perhaps because it would have served no purpose to do so. Of what use would that knowledge have been to her? She then says:

> Blessed One, it is my heartfelt desire that you would reveal to me a place free of sorrow, free of the defilements. ... My only heartfelt desire is that the Buddha, who is like the sun, might teach me how to visualize a place where the effects of all actions have been purified.

This request expresses the objective and the subjective poles of the Sukhāvatī myth: it is a land, an objective realm that we can see and be born into, and it's a visualization practice, something that we imagine, that we create in our own minds.

In response to these questions the Buddha reveals all the pure buddha-fields in all the directions of space:

> Some were made of the seven kinds of precious substances, some of nothing but lotus flowers. Some resembled the palaces of gods who have power over the creations of others, and some were like crystal mirrors in which all the other buddha-fields in the ten directions of space appeared. In this way, Vaidehī was able to see an infinite number of buddha-fields, in all their majesty.

Vaidehī, however, is not satisfied with these. She tells the Buddha that she wishes to be born in Amitāyus' buddha-field Sukhāvatī and asks him to teach her "how to contemplate that buddha-field and attain meditative concentration". This is another echo or reflection of Dharmākara's request to the Buddha Lokeśvararāja that he reveal to him all the buddha-fields that exist in the whole universe. He (Dharmākara) then concentrated all of the most wonderful qualities of these into one buddha-field, thereby imagining a buddha-field better than all others in the cosmos, which he contemplated for five aeons.

Vaidehī's desire to be born into Sukhāvatī may seem like escapism, and I want to address that issue before going any further. Non-religious people, especially anti-religious people, often accuse the religious of indulging in escapism. Escapism is defined as "the avoidance of reality by absorption of the mind in entertainment or in an imaginative situation, activity, etc."[109] There are three possible courses of action open to us when we are trapped in a painful situation. The first is to escape, or try to. The second is to distract ourselves. The third is to transcend the situation. I've listed escape as the first option because, if it's possible, that's obviously the best thing to do. To distract ourselves is escapism. The definition of escapism I've quoted is what we might call secular escapism, but there's also religious escapism, which consists in reading about, thinking about, and discussing religious matters, but not practising. A religious escapist spends their time imagining freedom but not doing anything to free themselves. You may be indulging in this form of escapism as you're reading this book, just as I may be indulging in it as I write it. The third option usually only comes into play when the first has proven impossible: transcend the situation. We transcend a situation by changing. If the terms of the situation won't change, then there is only one thing we can change – ourselves. When we're trapped in a painful situation, which by definition means that we don't have the freedom to change it or leave it, we can only find freedom elsewhere. We can cultivate a mind of freedom – freedom within confinement. The first step is acceptance. We have to accept the situation we're in, accept that we can't, at the moment anyway, escape it. This means being willing to be with it and feel it: the suffering, the frustration, the sense of being trapped, the awfulness of it. It means not distracting ourselves from the pain of it. This takes courage and faith. Courage because it's painful and faith because we need the confidence to feel that by being with the pain we'll find the inner resources to find freedom in the confinement.

Last year a loved member of the sangha in which I practise died suddenly, under tragic circumstances. His wife has been writing regularly about her process of grieving in a blog called *Widow's Voice*. In one of her blog entries she has written eloquently and movingly about the moments of acceptance, the quiet moments when she allows herself to feel her grief fully, and the context of faith and sangha in which these moments are held.

> I sit in meditation most days, but some days, I am afraid to make space for what will come, afraid that whatever it is underneath all my busyness and chatter might overwhelm me, if I allow it to surface. I sit at home, on my own, or meditate with friends at the [Buddhist] Centre.
>
> When I make time and space to sit in silence, not planning or doing or thinking, the sadness inevitably erupts, from a place deep within, from the pit of my stomach, and, most often, I cry. It is not something I can control, and I think it is best that I don't try to control it. It feels healing to sit quietly, before the shrine, with all that I am, at that moment, and to let the tears come. I breathe with the tears, and let them fall onto my cushion, not moving to quell them or rub them away.
>
> Particularly during our ritual pujas, in which we chant and recite ancient sutras and sacred texts, I am moved to tears. The aroma of incense, the trail of smoke rising to the ceiling, the glow of candlelight, the harmonies of chanting, the people in my sangha bowing in humble reverence before the shrine – all of these elements combine to move me beyond my thinking head and toward my heart. It is then, when I allow the controls I place upon myself to slip away, that my sorrow arises. I remember Stan and feel his absence from our sangha. I feel the emptiness he left behind.[110]

Vaidehī is engaged in an inner struggle. She is suffering terribly, with no hope of escape or respite, and she feels unable to bear it on her own, so she calls on the Buddha. She asks him to show her Sukhāvatī and to teach her how to meditate on it. Is the vision of Sukhāvatī that the Buddha reveals to Vaidehī a distraction from her suffering? Does it amount to religious escapism? If that *were* the case, what would be wrong with that? The problem with escapism is that the escapist refuses to look at reality and attempt to find real solutions to their problems. But Vaidehī can't be accused of that. She's done all she can practically do but now finds herself in a situation in which she is helpless. So why *shouldn't* she escape into fantasy as a way of coping with incredible suffering? But I don't believe she is doing that. The vision of Sukhāvatī doesn't distract her from her suffering but allows her to bear it fully by giving her a bigger context in which to hold it. In fact, as we'll see, it does even more than that. It enables a deep transformation of consciousness to unfold, in which she finds limitless freedom in her confinement.

Actually Vaidehī's situation is just an intense and urgent version of the one we're all in. We are trapped in a physical body that will only last a short while, we don't know how long, and we are unable to prevent our loved ones from getting ill, growing old, and dying. We may do our best for them, just as Vaidehī did for Bimbisāra, but in the end we are powerless. For this reason the Buddha said that everyone – "whether one is a woman or a man, lay or ordained" – should frequently reflect on the following five facts:

1. I am of the nature to grow old. There is no way to escape growing old.
2. I am of the nature to become ill. There is no way to escape illness.
3. I am of the nature to die. There is no way to escape death.
4. All that is dear to me, and everyone I love are of the nature to change. There is no way to escape being separated from them.
5. I am the owner of my actions; I am born of my actions; I am related to my actions; I am supported by my actions; any thoughts, words or deeds I do, good or evil, those I will inherit.[111]

The first four of these are simply statements of the way things are – we are growing old, we'll get ill, we'll die, and the things that are dear to us will change, break, or be taken away from us, if not in life, then in death. You may think this rather depressing, but the Buddha didn't ask his followers to reflect on these facts to make them depressed. He wanted them to see very clearly the actual situation they were in. He wanted them to stop distracting themselves, to stop indulging in escapism. Actually I have found that reflecting on these facts doesn't make me depressed or sad. I know deep down that they are true, and to dwell on them for a while – to come a little closer to accepting my situation – comes as a relief.

The fifth reflection is different from the first four in that it's a reflection on karma – our actions. The purpose of reflecting on the first four facts is to learn to accept them, but the fifth reminds us that the kind of life and death we experience is up to us. Yes, we are growing old and we are going to die, we can't do anything about that, but the way we grow old and the state we're in when we die matters, and we *can* do something about that.

Once we've reflected on these five facts as they apply to ourselves, the Buddha said we should reflect on them as they apply to everyone. For instance, for the first fact we reflect like this:

> I am not the only one of the nature to grow old, who cannot escape growing old. To the extent that there are beings – past and future, passing away and re-arising – all beings are of the nature to grow old, no one can escape growing old.

Having reflected on our own predicament, we widen our gaze and reflect that everyone else is in the same situation. Reflecting on these five facts as they apply to ourselves engenders wisdom; reflecting on them as regards others brings about compassion.

Returning to the sutra, when Vaidehī asked the Buddha to teach her how to contemplate Sukhāvatī the Buddha smiled, and five-coloured rays of light shone from his mouth onto Bimbisāra's head. Bimbisāra clearly saw the Buddha in the distance – through the walls of his cell – and knelt down before him. As he did so he "attained the state of a non-returner naturally and spontaneously". Bimbisāra found freedom within the confinement of his dungeon. Although the walls imprisoned his body, they were unable to imprison his mind and heart. The state of a non-returner is the third of four stages of awakening, which I briefly explained in Chapter 1. Interestingly, from the point of view of freedom, the Buddha spoke about ten fetters or shackles that keep us firmly trapped in delusion, and the non-returner has broken the first five of these:

1. Self-view: the mistaken notion that there is an enduring self
2. Dependence on rites and rituals (as ends in themselves): the idea that simply going through the motions of spiritual practice is enough to awaken
3. Doubt: not honest questioning of the doctrine, but the unwillingness to really commit oneself to the spiritual life, and rationalizing that unwillingness with spurious "doubts"
4. Sensuous desire: craving for experience in the world of the senses; attachment to the first principal level of happiness – worldly happiness
5. Hatred or aversion.

The five-coloured rays of light that shine from the Buddha's mouth onto Bimbisāra's head may symbolize the breaking of these five fetters. The fact that the light comes from the Buddha's mouth suggests his (oral) teaching, and the head signifies, in Buddhist symbolism, not the mind but the body, perhaps illustrating that Bimbisāra has understood the Dharma not just intellectually but with the whole of his being. And he makes spiritual progress effortlessly – spontaneously and naturally. All this happens without him doing anything at all: the Buddha directs the five-coloured light onto Bimbisāra's head as a result of Vaidehī's request to teach her how to visualize Sukhāvatī. The king, devoted as he was to the Buddha, was simply sitting in his cell, waiting for death. Perhaps what this suggests is that Bimbisāra had fully accepted his situation, and in accepting it has transcended it. He had been a disciple of the Buddha for a long time – even from before the Buddha became the Buddha, when he was a bodhisattva searching for the truth. He was familiar with the Buddha's teaching and had, up to a point, been practising it. I say "up to a point" because he was a king, and so he would have had many other calls on his time, many other matters to occupy his mind. Now though, as he sits in his prison, knowing that he will soon die, he can reflect on his situation, on the Dharma, to the exclusion of all else. His spiritual progress is effortless because in his acceptance of his situation he has realized that there is nothing he can now do: he has given up reliance on the self – self-power – and given himself to other-power. And there we will leave him, in his dungeon, starving to death at the order of his son, separated from his beloved and loyal consort Vaidehī, alone, and freer than he's ever been.

In his poem "Sweet Darkness", David Whyte says

You must learn one thing.
The world was made to be free in.

Give up all the other worlds
except the one to which you belong.

Sometimes it takes darkness and the sweet
confinement of your aloneness
to learn

anything or anyone
that does not bring you alive

is too small for you.[112]

The world had become too small for Bimbisāra. When they die, non-returners are born in one of the pure abodes and gain Enlightenment there. Used as many of us are to the idea of heaven as a reward for good behaviour, we may see it in that way: Bimbisāra was a good man who was treated badly, but that's OK, because he went to heaven. He got his just reward just as Ajātaśatru later got his in going to hell. But we need to be careful that we don't project that kind of idea onto Buddhist texts. You may remember from Chapter 1 that, according to Buddhism, the world is to a large extent an objectification of our mental state. We're not born into a particular kind of world because we deserve it, but because that is the world we're already occupying mentally. Bimbisāra was already dwelling in the pure abodes while he was sitting in his cell; his body just took a little longer to catch up.

The Buddha now turns his attention to Vaidehī and tells her to concentrate her mind and visualize Sukhāvatī:

> I will now reveal to you in comprehensive detail how you can purify the effects of your actions by doing so, so that in the future any ordinary person who wishes to purify the effects of their actions will be able to be reborn in the western buddha-field of Sukhāvatī.

Before he tells her how to do that though, he says that whoever wishes to be born in Sukhāvatī should first cultivate merit in three ways. While both of the Sukhāvatī sutras emphasize the importance of growing roots of merit, they are not specific about what these are or the means to grow them. The Buddha now spells it out to Vaidehī:

> Firstly, one should respect and support one's parents, honour and serve one's teachers, cultivate a mind filled with compassion and refrain from taking life, and practise the ten kinds of skilful action. Secondly, one should hold fast to the Three Refuges, observe all the precepts, and conduct oneself properly. Thirdly, one should cultivate a mind set on Awakening, and a deep faith in cause and effect. One should read and recite the Mahāyāna sutras, and encourage others in their practice.

I read these as a progressive sequence: the first way of cultivating merit consists solely in the practice of ethics; the second in going for refuge to the Three Jewels and the ethical practice that streams from that; and the third in the arising of the Bodhicitta – the desire to awaken for the sake of all beings – and the practices that follow from that. The first way of cultivating merit consists of practices that engender an ethically skilful person, but not necessarily one trying to awaken; with the second, one becomes a Buddhist, that is, one makes a commitment to practise the Dharma in order to awaken; and with the third, one enters the Mahāyāna, the Great Way – that is, one doesn't conceive of the spiritual life as being about awakening for oneself only, but for the sake of all beings. Let's look at these a little more closely.

The first way of cultivating merit has four aspects:

a. Respecting and supporting one's parents
b. Honouring and serving one's teachers and elders
c. Cultivating a mind filled with compassion and refraining from taking life
d. Practising the ten kinds of skilful action.

Respecting and supporting one's parents
The Buddha made it clear that he regarded love and respect for one's parents to be important. He once told a young layman that he should care for his parents by supporting them, doing their duties, keeping the family tradition, making himself worthy of his inheritance, and offering alms in honour of his departed relatives. However, it's unusual for the Buddha to begin his teaching with a precept to respect and support one's parents. Of course it has a direct connection with the story, but it doesn't seem likely that Vaidehī will need this precept at this particular point in time. It's a bit like telling someone who has just been robbed that they shouldn't rob people – why would you say that? I think there may be a Confucian influence here. One of Confucius' principal values was filial piety, that is, a love and respect for one's parents, elders, and ancestors, which was considered to be the prime virtue and the basis of all right human relations. For instance, the classic Confucian treatise on filial piety, the Xiào Jīng, states: "Now filial piety is the root of (all) virtue, and (the stem) out of which grows (all moral) teaching."[113] In that the remaining three elements of the first act of merit are also ethical precepts, it would be in keeping with Confucianism to begin this section with caring for one's parents as the root from which the others grow.

But how could Confucianism have influenced a Sanskrit text? There are two ways in which this could have occurred. Firstly, the translation could have been altered to suit Chinese moral sensibilities. It's common for there to exist different versions of a Mahāyāna sutra – we've seen, for instance, that there are seven different versions of the *Longer Sukhāvatīvyūhaḥ Sūtra* in existence – which means that Buddhists considered it acceptable to change them. Secondly, the sutra could be a Chinese composition. Although the sutra is purported to be a translation from the Sanskrit, the Sanskrit original has never been found, leading many scholars to believe that there never was one. The reason it would claim to be a translation is to give it authority: Buddhism had come from India and so to be taken seriously the sutra had to seem to be of Indian origin. In addition, it purports to be a *sutra,* and sutras are by definition the word of the Buddha, which would mean it *had* to have come from India. This is not an uncommon occurrence; such texts are known in China as pseudo-sutras (*wěi-jīng*).

One of the problems the ancient Chinese had with the Indian Buddhist texts was their lack of emphasis on filial piety. In fact, in some ways they seemed to the Chinese not only lacking but positively opposed to this most treasured of Chinese virtues. They tell approvingly the story of Śākyamuni leaving home – leaving his parents – to become a homeless wanderer, and describe how many of his disciples did the same, with his encouragement. In Buddhist texts sangha – spiritual community – is a higher value than family, and spiritual friendship is more important than parental ties. For instance, in an early text the Buddha says:

> Leaving behind son and wife, and father and mother, and wealth and grain, and relatives, and sensual pleasures to the full extent, one should wander solitary as a rhinoceros horn.

In another verse from the same text he states that:

> If one can obtain a zealous companion, an associate of good disposition, who is resolute, overcoming all dangers, one should wander with him, elated, mindful.[114]

That this was problematic for the Chinese is illustrated in a number of texts, some strongly criticizing Buddhism for its lack of filial piety and others attempting to defend it. Obviously the Buddha's leaving home was a problem for the Chinese, and some apologists made the point that ultimately the best way to serve one's parents was to awaken and then lead them on the path to Awakening, as the Buddha did with his parents – so the Buddha was actually practising filial piety when he left his parents! Some went further and wrote "Buddhist" texts that extolled filial piety, such as the *Sūtra of Filial Piety*. We have our own cultural conditioning of course, through which we view – and distort – the Buddha's teaching. If any contemporary Westerner were to write a pseudo-sutra it would probably be called something like the *Sutra of Romantic Love*, or perhaps the *Sutra of the Happy Family*.

If the *Guān Jīng is* a Chinese composition, that throws some more light on the question of why the sutra begins with the story of Ajātaśatru et al. From the Chinese point of view Ajātaśatru commits the worst possible crime, and commencing the sutra with this story would engage the reader's sympathy for Bimbisāra and Vaidehī very strongly. But, although there may be some Confucian influence, overall the message of the sutra is definitely Buddhist. Bimbisāra and Vaidehī are both Buddhists, and they turn in their suffering to Buddhist monks – Maudgalyāyana, Pūrṇa, Ānanda, and of course the Buddha – all of whom had left home and therefore their parents in order to become wanderers. Overall, the message is that, while filial piety is a good thing, the transcendent values of Buddhism are higher.

Honouring and serving one's teachers and elders

Like our parents, our teachers have given us an immeasurable amount, and it is only natural that we should be grateful to them and treat them with consideration. I mentioned above that the Buddha told a young householder of five ways in which he should care for his parents, and in the same text he says that he should also attend to his teachers in five ways: by rising from his seat when greeting them, by attending on them, by being eager to learn, by personal service, and by paying respectful attention while receiving instructions. In traditional societies, the elders of the family, tribe, or village would have been the repositories of the family's and tribe's collective wisdom, so they would naturally have been teachers too.

Cultivating a mind filled with compassion and refraining from taking life

In a Pali text called the *Sallekha Sutta* the Buddha says that the practice of ethics – in fact the whole of the Buddhist path – starts with *ahiṃsā*, non-violence or non-harm. The traditional commentary on this text explains why this is so:

> But why is non-harm mentioned at the very beginning? Because it is the root of all virtues; non-harm, namely, is a synonym of compassion. Especially, it is the root-cause of morality because it makes one refrain from immorality which has as its characteristic mark the harming of others. ... Hence non-harm is an especially strong productive cause of morality; and morality, again, is the basis for concentration of mind, while concentration is the basis for wisdom. In that way non-harm is the root of all virtues.[115]

Non-harm or compassion then, rather than filial piety, is for Buddhism the root of all virtue.

Practising the ten kinds of skilful action

The ten kinds of skilful action are listed immediately after non-harm in the *Sallekha Sutta* – they are its practical working out in specific areas of life. The first three are actions of the body: to refrain from killing, from taking what is not given, and from sexual misconduct. The next four are actions of speech: refraining from untruthful, harsh, unhelpful, and divisive speech. The last three are actions of mind: refraining from covetousness, hostility, and wrong views about the nature of reality. I've listed the ten kinds of skilful action here in their negative form, which is how they are traditionally expressed – but, just as non-harm can also be expressed positively as compassion, we can also put them in a positive form, as the doing of skilful actions rather than the not-doing of unskilful ones. In their positive form they are: to act with loving-kindness, to be generous, to cultivate bodily contentment, to speak truthfully, affectionately, helpfully, and harmoniously, and to cultivate the mental states of contentment, compassion, and wisdom.

The second way of cultivating merit has three components:

a. Holding fast to the Three Refuges
b. Observing all the precepts
c. Conducting oneself properly.

To be a Buddhist is to go for refuge to the Three Jewels. Sometimes the Three Jewels are known as the Three Refuges, as here, and "holding fast" to them suggests a deep ongoing commitment. The second two components of this set are to do with ethics once again but, as I've written above, here they are the expressions of going for refuge to the Three Jewels. The purpose of the ethical practices described in the first act of merit is to gain merit only, whereas their purpose here is to lead to Awakening. The ethical practices themselves don't necessarily differ – it's the intention that makes the difference, and that's why they are not specified here in the second act of merit.

The third way of cultivating merit has four elements:

a. Cultivating a mind set on Awakening
b. A deep faith in cause and effect
c. Reading and reciting the Mahāyāna sutras
d. Encouraging people in their practice.

Cultivating a mind set on Awakening
A mind set on Awakening is the Bodhicitta, which as we've seen comes about as a result of making the bodhisattva vow – *praṇidhāna* – to awaken for the sake of all beings. Whereas with the second way of cultivating merit one becomes a Buddhist, now one becomes a specifically Mahāyāna Buddhist aspiring to become a bodhisattva.

A deep faith in cause and effect
"Cause and effect" is the law of conditioned co-production or dependent co-arising, which, as I explained in Chapter 4, is the philosophical basis of the Dharma. In that going for refuge to the Three Jewels presupposes faith in conditioned co-production – to go for refuge to the Dharma Jewel is to go for refuge to the law of conditioned co-production – it seems to me that this should really be included in the second way of cultivating merit.

Reading and reciting the Mahāyāna sutras
As we saw at the end of Chapter 6, reading and reciting as well as listening to, copying, and worshipping Mahāyāna sutras is a spiritual practice, perhaps the most common one among Mahāyāna Buddhists.

Encouraging people in their practice
Earlier in this chapter I introduced the five things the Buddha said everyone should frequently reflect on, and we saw that there are two dimensions to these reflections: oneself and others. Reflecting on the fact that we are subject to ageing, illness, death, loss, and the law of karma motivates us to practise the Dharma. Reflecting on the fact that everyone else is also subject to these things motivates us to help them; specifically, it motivates us to encourage them to practise the Dharma, because only the Dharma can ultimately help people to transcend the human condition. The *Longer Sukhāvatīvyūhaḥ Sūtra* says of the Bodhisattva Dharmākara:

> In his practice of the path of the bodhisattva, he encouraged others to practise the perfection of generosity just as he did himself. He encouraged others to practise the perfections of ethical conduct, patient acceptance, energy, meditation, and wisdom just as he did himself.

This means that Dharma practice is not just a personal self-improvement programme but has a social aspect. If we practise and encourage others to do so, we are creating a spiritual community. Encouraging people in their practice is not an exclusively Mahāyāna virtue – it also features in early Buddhism. Mahānāma was a prominent lay disciple of the Buddha. One day he asked the Buddha what it was that defined a lay follower, and the Buddha replied, "Going for refuge to the Three Jewels". Mahānāma then asked the Buddha what it was that made a lay follower virtuous, to which the Buddha answered, "Practising the five precepts". (The first four of these are identical to the first four of the ten virtuous acts. The fifth is to refrain from taking intoxicants, and, more positively, to cultivate mindfulness.) Mahānāma then asked another question: how does a lay follower engage in his own welfare, but not in the welfare of others? The Buddha answered:

> Mahānāma, inasmuch as a lay follower is possessed of faith himself, but rouses not others to possess faith; is possessed of virtue himself, but rouses not others to possess virtue; is possessed of liberality himself, but rouses not others to possess liberality ... is himself committed to the practice according to the Dhamma, but rouses not others to be committed to the practice according to the Dhamma; in that way, Mahānāma, a lay follower is engaged in his own welfare, but not in others' welfare.[116]

Finally Mahānāma asked how a lay follower engages in his own welfare and in the welfare of others, and the Buddha answers:

> inasmuch as a lay follower is possessed of faith himself, and rouses others to possess faith; is possessed of virtue himself, and rouses others to possess virtue; is possessed of generosity himself, and rouses others to possess generosity ... is himself committed to the practice according to the Dhamma, and rouses others to be committed to the practice according to the Dhamma; in that way, Mahānāma, a lay follower is engaged in his own welfare and in others' welfare.

There are many ways of encouraging others to practise the Dharma. We could divide them into direct and indirect ways. Direct ways include teaching; giving talks; leading study groups; asking people about their practice; writing articles, books, and blogs; and so on. Indirect ways include setting up and running Buddhist centres; organizing teachers to give talks and seminars; organizing retreats; designing websites and uploading inspiring material onto them; publishing books, magazines, and journals; and so forth. Notice though that Dharmākara encouraged others to practise "just as he did himself", and that Mahānāma asks the Buddha to tell him how a lay follower is engaged in his own as well as others' welfare. We can only effectively encourage others to practise if we ourselves are practising.

None of these ways of cultivating merit has any direct relation to being born in Sukhāvatī. As the Buddha says in the *Shorter Sukhāvatīvyūhaḥ Sūtra*, we need not only many roots of merit but also the heartfelt desire to be born there. As a result of the catastrophe that has engulfed Vaidehī, she now feels this heartfelt desire, and the Buddha tells her to

> Listen closely. Listen closely, and reflect carefully on what I am about to tell you. The Tathāgata will now explain how to purify the effects of one's actions, for the sake of all of the living beings in the future who will be tormented by the defilements. It is good, Vaidehī, it is excellent that you have asked me about this.

It's good not only for Vaidehī but also for everyone else, because Ānanda is present, and he, as you may recall, had the ability to remember everything the Buddha said. The Buddha now turns to him and says:

> Ānanda, you should bear what I am about to say in mind, and spread these words of the Buddha widely, sharing them with a great many living beings.

Staying within the mythic context of the sutra, Ānanda did repeat the Buddha's teaching to others, it was eventually written down, and was some time later translated into Chinese. Very recently – and here we move from the realm of myth to that of history – the Chinese was translated into English. From here on, everything the Buddha says to Vaidehī is meant not just for her, but for anyone who cares to read the sutra. Including you and me.

Chapter Eight

Opening the mind's eye

I began Chapter 6 with a description of the Taima mandala – the painting of Sukhāvatī as described in this sutra – and I want to return to it now, because I want to draw your attention to a curious figure in it. In the foreground, in front of the dais on which Amitāyus and the bodhisattvas sit, is a lotus pond. On each of the lotuses sits a being, and although they are in the foreground they are very small. One of these beings, so small that it's very easy to miss him, has his back to us. Who is he, and why is he looking away from the viewer? A clue to the answer is given in what the Buddha next says to Vaidehī (and, via Ānanda, to us):

> The Tathāgata will now explain how to visualize Sukhāvatī, for the benefit of Vaidehī and all living beings in the future.

The *Shorter* and *Longer Sukhāvatīvyūhaḥ Sūtras* describe Sukhāvatī but they don't give specific instructions on how to go about visualizing it. The *Guān Jīng* does, though, and from this point on the sutra is a visualization manual. Here then is the solution as to the identity of that small being in the foreground of the picture. He is the meditator. He is you or me, looking at – visualizing – Amitāyus, his bodhisattvas, and all the splendours of Sukhāvatī. It's significant that he is depicted as being in the picture, in Sukhāvatī, rather than looking at it from the outside. To visualize Sukhāvatī is to imagine being in it, being immersed in that world, not only looking but hearing and feeling it all around you.

> Through the power of the Buddha, they will all be able to see this pure buddha-field as clearly as looking at their own face in a mirror.

Throughout the sutra the Buddha makes it clear that the meditator has to work hard to visualize what he is describing, which suggests that any clarity achieved is due to the effort made by the meditator. Yet here the Buddha says that we'll be able to see Sukhāvatī clearly through the power of the Buddha. Both are true. In Chapter 4 I discussed the process described by the Buddha in the *Cetanā Sutta*, in which skilful effort is followed by (involuntary) positive effect. There, we saw that the succeeding stage of the path unfolds naturally before us when we have made the requisite effort in the preceding stage. In this case, the effort required is that we visualize each aspect of Sukhāvatī as clearly as we can, and the positive effect is that we'll eventually see everything as clearly as our own reflection in a bright mirror. The three stages of *kasiṇa* meditation make this process clear. Firstly we look at the *kasiṇa* and try to concentrate our mind on it. This is known as the preparatory image. Then we close our eyes and try to "see" the *kasiṇa* in our mind's eye. This is the acquired image. The acquired image is unstable and unclear, but with continued practice it becomes as vivid and steady as the physical object itself. This is the counterpart image. The first and second stages represent the application of willed effort, but the third stage occurs spontaneously; the acquired image becomes the counterpart image as a result of our practice of the first two stages. You may also remember that, according to Buddhaghosa,

> the counterpart image appears as if breaking out from the acquired image, and a hundred times, a thousand times more purified ... like the moon's disc coming out from behind a cloud, like cranes against a thunder cloud.[117]

So the appearance of the counterpart image happens to us, as it were – we don't control it. Whereas the Buddha described the sequence of involuntary effect following skilful effort as "natural" in the *Cetanā Sutta*, here he describes it in mythic terms, as occurring "through the power of the Buddha".

The Buddha then says:

> They will see the extraordinary, exquisite happiness that is to be found in that buddha-field, and because of the joy that will fill their hearts thereby, they will attain patient acceptance of the fact that all phenomena are unarisen.

I explained the deep insight known as the "patient acceptance of the fact that all phenomena are unarisen" at the end of Chapter 5, where I also mentioned that this is what makes one an irreversible bodhisattva. The Buddha says that we will attain this insight because of the joy that will fill our hearts as a result of seeing the "extraordinary, exquisite happiness" of Sukhāvatī. This is not worldly happiness, of course, it's unworldly and still greater unworldly happiness – the happiness of meditative absorption and insight. Seeing the happiness of Sukhāvatī, we become happy. Seeing the wisdom of Sukhāvatī, we become wise. To imagine is to become. This passage also tells us, incidentally, that the point of visualizing Sukhāvatī is at least as much to do with awakening in this life as it is to do with being born into Sukhāvatī in the next.

We can thus see in this sutra the unfolding of the threefold path of ethics, meditation, and wisdom. The Buddha has just taught Vaidehī the three ways of cultivating merit, which constitute mainly ethical practice; the visualization of Sukhāvatī that he is about to teach her corresponds to meditation; and the patient acceptance of the fact that all phenomena are unarisen pertains to wisdom.

The Buddha teaches Vaidehī how to visualize Sukhāvatī in a series of sixteen meditations:

1. The setting sun
2. Water flooding the area beneath the sun, which becomes ice and then the lapis lazuli ground of Sukhāvatī
3. Consolidation of visualization of the ground
4. The jewel trees
5. The ponds and streams
6. Pavilions, music, and consolidation of the visualization of the jewel trees, ponds, and streams
7. Amitāyus' lotus throne
8. Amitāyus and his two principal bodhisattvas
9. The body and light of Amitāyus
10. The Bodhisattva Avalokiteśvara
11. The Bodhisattva Mahāsthāmaprāpta
12. Oneself being born in Sukhāvatī
13. The simple image of Amitāyus
14. The three highest categories of beings born in Sukhāvatī
15. The three middle categories of beings
16. The three lowest categories of beings.

These fall naturally into three divisions, the first set (1–6) consisting of visualizations of the objects or ornaments in the land; the second (7–13) of Amitāyus and his two chief bodhisattvas; and the third (14–16) of the nine categories of beings born in Sukhāvatī. I'm going to focus mainly on the second set, and in particular on the visualization of Amitāyus. This is partly because we've already looked in some detail at the descriptions of the land in the two *Sukhāvatīvyūhaḥ Sūtras* and, although the descriptions in this sutra differ from those in many ways, I suspect it would be stretching your interest a little too far to explore Sukhāvatī once more. However, because one of the defining features of the *Guān Jīng* is that it tells us how to visualize Sukhāvatī, I will pay special attention to those instructions as they appear in the first three meditations.

There is another, more important reason for concentrating on the visualizations of Amitāyus. Returning to the figure in the painting, he – the meditator – is sitting directly in front of, and looking towards, Amitāyus. This is emblematic of a significant difference between the two Sukhāvatī sutras and the *Guān Jīng*. The Sukhāvatī sutras, true to their name, mainly describe Sukhāvatī, confining themselves to general descriptions of Amitāyus' measureless life and light, whereas the *Guān Jīng* describes Amitāyus in some detail. Not that it neglects the beautiful ornaments of Sukhāvatī – they too are described in great detail – but it does so as a precursor to and preparation for the visualization of Amitāyus. The oldest extant commentary on the *Guān Jīng* was written by Hui-Yuan, who lived in the sixth century. He was of the opinion that the "main import" of the sutra was the visualization of Amitāyus, which is reflected in its title.[118] In his commentary he asks the question:

> Since this sutra is concerned not only with visualizing the Buddha but also with visualizing the land, [the Bodhisattvas] Avalokiteśvara and Mahāstāmaprāpta, the nine grades of rebirth and so forth, why limit the title to The Visualisation of the Buddha Amitāyus?

To which he answers:

> The Buddha was singled out because the primary [concern of the sutra] is that of visualizing him.[119]

Hui-Yuan doesn't say why he holds this view, but I think there are good reasons for agreeing with him, reasons that will become clear as we explore the visualizations. As we'll see, visualizing Amitāyus has the potential to take the meditator further in their spiritual progress than do the visualizations of Sukhāvatī.

Let's begin our exploration of the sutra though with the first meditation, which is a description not of anything in Sukhāvatī but of a very familiar object from our own world – the setting sun. This and the next meditation act as a bridge from this world to Sukhāvatī. They are also very simple, enabling the meditator to practise the methods that he or she will be using in the later, extremely detailed, and elaborate visualizations, but with simple objects.

> The Buddha said to Vaidehī, "You, and all other living beings, should concentrate your mind, and gather your attention in one place. You should then focus your mind on the west. How should you focus your mind? All living beings, except those who were born blind or whose vision is impaired, should look at the setting sun. Gather your attention, sit upright, and gaze unwaveringly at the sun. Do not let your mind wander. Concentrate your mind without getting distracted, and look at the setting sun, which is like a drum suspended in the air. When you have looked at the sun in this way, you should be able to see it clearly, whether your eyes are open or closed. This is the first visualization, where the mind is focused on the sun.

We should begin our visualization of Sukhāvatī, the Buddha says, by concentrating our mind and gathering our attention in one place. No matter what meditation practice we take up, we need to be able to do this. If we are unable to concentrate our mind we won't be able to do anything else. As I've pointed out in a previous chapter, Mahāyāna sutras assume knowledge of the early texts, and in this case, the sutra assumes that we're familiar with meditation texts and that we know how to practise at least basic *śamatha* (concentration) meditations. For instance, when the text says "sit upright", it is referring to the correct meditation posture, and it assumes that we know what this posture is. Likewise, the phrases "concentrate your mind", "focus your mind", and "gather your attention" assume that we are adept at doing this, which means that we must have some experience of practices such as the Mindfulness of Breathing and the ten *kasiṇa* meditations.

Next, *after* we have concentrated our mind, the Buddha says that we should look at the setting sun, and again he emphasizes the importance of concentration with the phrases "gaze unwaveringly", "do not let your mind wander", "concentrate your mind without getting distracted". We should look at the sun in this way until we're able to see it clearly, whether we have our eyes open or closed. This description is very similar to the three stages of *kasiṇa* meditation.

> The Buddha then said to Ānanda and Vaidehī, "When you have completed the first visualization, you should focus your mind on water. Focus your mind and picture everything to the west as being covered by a great body of water. See the water as clear and pure. You should be able to picture it clearly, with undivided attention."

It seems that in practising this meditation we are not actually to look at water but to visualize – "picture" – it. We are now using only the imagination and, although on one level this is a visualization of a simple sense object, anyone who is familiar with the *Longer Sukhāvatīvyūhaḥ Sūtra* will sense a deeper symbolic resonance in it. In Chapter 6 I described a miraculous event that occurs towards the end of the sutra. In response to the request from Ānanda to see Amitābha and the bodhisattvas who live in Sukhāvatī, Amitābha fills all of the buddha-fields in the universe with light, and everyone is able to see him above those buddha-fields, his brilliant light erasing all the distinguishing features of Sukhāvatī. The text then uses an analogy to describe this: it's as if the whole of the earth were to turn into "a single body of water", submerging everything, so that there would be "nothing but the earth itself, transformed into a single ocean". In the same way, all the distinguishing characteristics of Sukhāvatī disappear, except for the bodhisattvas and śrāvakas who live there. The ocean in this analogy represents the transcendent spiritual community of Sukhāvatī. The description of the water in the second visualization doesn't mention any of this, but it suggests – illumines – it for those familiar with the *Longer Sukhāvatīvyūhaḥ Sūtra*.

> When you can see the water in your mind, imagine it freezing and turning to ice, brilliant and shining to its very depths. Then picture the ice turning into lapis lazuli. When you have completed this visualization, picture the lapis lazuli ground as being brilliant and shining to its very depths, both on the inside and on the surface.

This is the beginning of the transition from our world – the setting sun, water, and ice – to Sukhāvatī, with its ground of lapis lazuli. Lapis lazuli is a semi-precious stone of an intensely deep blue, with golden pyrites running through it. Of course lapis lazuli exists in this world, but here, in the second meditation, the whole ground is made of it. This is the beginning of the description of the purely imagined ornaments of Sukhāvatī, and from here on the descriptions become extremely detailed, very elaborate, and so bright that we cannot look at them:

> The lapis lazuli ground is supported from below by golden pillars inlaid with diamonds and the seven kinds of precious substances. These pillars have eight sides and eight corners, and each side is adorned with a hundred different kinds of precious substances. Each precious stone gives off a thousand rays of light, and each ray of light shines forth in eighty-four thousand different colours. When this light is reflected by the lapis lazuli ground, it becomes as brilliant as a hundred thousand million suns, so that it is impossible to look at it.

This reminds me of the composer Olivier Messiaen, who had chromesthesia – that is, he saw sounds as colours so that, for him, music was as much a visual experience as it was an aural one. One of his compositions is called *Couleurs de la Cité Céleste* (*The Colours of the Celestial City*), which he compared to the "rose window of a cathedral in flaming and invisible colors":

> His color-sounds (les sons-couleurs) were of utmost importance to him: Based upon his deep religious belief, Messiaen was of the opinion that color music – similarly to church windows of the Middle Ages – helped to overcome conventional perception to bring about a state of being blinded that ultimately led to faith.[120]

Just as the descriptions of Sukhāvatī in the *Longer Sukhāvatīvyūhaḥ Sūtra* differ in various ways from those of the *Shorter Sūtra*, so the descriptions in this sutra are different again. This needn't concern us unduly. They are not meant to be accurate descriptions of an actually existing world, but are three different meditators' visions of Sukhāvatī, three different imaginings, or reimaginings. Although the Buddha is very precise and specific about each of the things he describes in this sutra, telling us to visualize them just as he describes them (at the conclusion of each meditation he says "This is the correct way to perform the visualization. Doing it in any other way is not correct"), in the process of visualizing them we can't help but imagine them anew. Returning to the *kasiṇa* meditations, it's as if the counterpart image has a life of its own, so that, although we may begin by trying to visualize the object just as we see it, or a description just as described, the counterpart image springs out at us, as it were, overwhelming whatever it was that we'd been trying to "see". This means that there are as many Sukhāvatīs as there are people who imagine Sukhāvatī.

Paintings of Sukhāvatī, such as the one I have at home, are aids to visualization – in the terms of the *kasiṇa* mediations, they are preparatory images. In meditation I first look at the painting, or a part of it, for a while, and then I close my eyes and try to visualize it. Actually I'm not very good at visualizing, in the sense of seeing something clearly in my imagination. It's more that I feel its presence – and it has a strong presence, as strong as that of a person. So my acquired image is not so much an image as a feeling, and the clarity I sometimes experience is not so much a visual clarity as a concentration of mind and a purity of feeling. At those times the presence of the painting becomes more vivid, more alive and soft and yielding, as if it's not so much the physical painting I sense as the living thing of which the painting is an expression. At those times I couldn't say that the Sukhāvatī I'm imagining *looks* different from the painting; it's more that it *feels* different. The feeling comes out of the painting. I suppose what I'm saying is that, for me, Sukhāvatī is largely felt rather than seen, and that the painting on my wall, beautiful as it is and love it though I do, is only an approximation of the Sukhāvatī I imagine.

The second meditation is not just a visualization but includes

> innumerable musical instruments. The light also emits eight kinds of pure breezes which make the musical instruments sound. They play songs of suffering, of emptiness, of impermanence, and of no self.

Again it's clear that senses other than the visual are used in these meditations, so that the word "visualization" is not really adequate. Up until this point the meditation has been a *śamatha* practice – a way to concentrate the mind and enter dhyāna – but now, with the musical instruments singing of suffering, emptiness, impermanence, and no self, the meditation becomes a *vipassanā* practice. We've seen that *guān* means "to see", and therefore "to visualize", but in Buddhist Chinese it also connotes *vipassanā*, seeing things as they really are.

If you've read the fifth chapter of this book you may have noticed an inconsistency here. In the *Longer Sukhāvatīvyūhaḥ Sūtra* the Buddha says that the words "suffering" and "pain" don't exist in Sukhāvatī (because suffering and pain don't exist there). It therefore can't be possible for the musical instruments to sing of suffering, or at least it can't be possible for the beings in Sukhāvatī to hear that truth in the music. Music of course is unable to express conceptual content, and this allows us to project our own meaning onto it. We, living as we do in an impure buddha-field, do suffer, and so *we* hear the music singing of suffering because *we* are doing the practice; *we are creating Sukhāvatī*. This underlines the fact that the visualizations in this sutra are not so much *des*criptions as *pres*criptions. That is, they don't tell us what Sukhāvatī actually looks and sounds like, as if it were an objectively existing place, but tell us how *we* should try to see and hear it, how we should create it.

The third meditation consists in simply consolidating the practice of the second:

> When you have successfully focused your mind in this way, make sure you visualize everything completely clearly, so that whether your eyes are open or closed, the image does not fade. Break off the practice only when it is time to eat. Keep the image constantly in your awareness.

Presumably not only should we visualize everything completely clearly; we should also feel the breezes palpably and hear the musical instruments distinctly. The instruction to "break off the practice only when it is time to eat" could mean that the practitioner is expected to meditate all the time, in which case these instructions must be meant for monastics, who have the time to devote to meditation practice. Alternatively, it could mean that the practitioner should visualize Sukhāvatī while going about his or her daily business. In the previous chapter we encountered the lay disciple Mahānāma, who asked the Buddha some questions about the practice of lay followers. On another occasion the Buddha told him that he should take up the practice of the six *anussatis* – recollections or remembrances. They are the recollection of the Buddha, the Dharma, the Sangha, one's own virtues, one's practice of generosity, and the devas (gods). Although the *anussatis* are meditation practices, after describing each of them the Buddha says this:

> Mahānāma, you should develop this recollection [of the Buddha etc.] while you are walking, while you are standing, while you are sitting, while you are lying down, while you are busy at work, while you are resting in your home crowded with children.[121]

It could be that the visualizations described in the *Guān Jīng* are also to be practised in this way. If so, the sutra would seem to require that we live in two worlds simultaneously – that of the five senses and that of the imagination. This may seem to imply a divided mind, half in the world and half in imagined scenes, but I think it would be truer to say that our sensory perception of the world would be informed by – the world would be perceived through – our imagination. This is surely the point of Mahāyāna sutras like the ones we're exploring in this book. The visionary poet and painter William Blake seemed to live in this way:

> "What!" it will be questioned, "when the sun rises, do you not see a round disk of fire somewhat like a guinea?" "O! no, no! I see an innumerable company of the heavenly host crying, "Holy, holy, holy, is the Lord God Almighty!"[122]

The Buddha then says:

> If you attain a state of samādhi in the course of this practice, you will see the ground of that buddha-field so clearly and in such detail that you will not be able to fully describe it.

"The ground" of Sukhāvatī is the name of the second visualization but, as we've seen, it includes much more than just the ground. To "attain the state of samādhi" is to ascend from the stage of the acquired image to the counterpart image and beyond, in which the images that appear before us are no longer the products of our normal waking consciousness, constructed from memory, but are produced by the imagination, or the imaginal faculty.

> Those who visualize the ground of Sukhāvatī will free themselves of the effects of previous unskilful actions that would have kept them in samsara for eight billion aeons, and when they pass away they will certainly be born in that pure buddha-field. Have no doubt about this.

Meditative absorption – dhyāna – is skilful weighty karma, so heavy that it outweighs the effects of previous unskilful actions. Skilful weighty karma would normally result in rebirth in one of the god realms but, as we know, Sukhāvatī is not just a god realm but also an Awakening realm. This means that to be born there we need more than just the weighty karma of dhyāna; we also need insight, which is why the "visualization" of the ground includes the sounds of the musical instruments playing the songs of suffering, of emptiness, of impermanence, and of no self. The implication of this is that, if all we wish for is to be born in Sukhāvatī, these three meditations are sufficient. Why, then, the subsequent meditations? Because there is a further goal, and this is realized as a result of visualizing Amitāyus. So let's move on to those meditations now. Amitāyus first appears to Vaidehī in a spontaneous vision at the beginning of the seventh meditation:

> the Buddha Amitāyus appeared in the air above him, with the two great beings Avalokiteśvara and Mahāsthāmaprāpta on either side. They were blazing with light so brilliant that it was impossible to see them properly. Even the radiance of gold from the Jambū River multiplied a hundred thousand times could not compare with it.

In Chapter 6 I said that the two bodhisattvas are Amitāyus' equivalent of the Buddha's two chief disciples, Śāriputra and Mahāmaudgalyāyana. However, this vision seems to be a reflection of the episode in the story when the Buddha miraculously arrives in Vaidehī's room with Maudgalyāyana and Ānanda to each side of him. In Vaidehī's vision, Amitāyus appears above Śākyamuni, epitomizing their relationship in the Pure Land sutras: Śākyamuni is the messenger, telling Vaidehī and us about – revealing to us – the eternal Buddha Amitāyus. The description of Vaidehī's vision of Amitāyus, rather like the descriptions of him in the Sukhāvatī sutras, is quite unspecific. All we are told at this point is that he and his two bodhisattvas shine with brilliant light. Vaidehī falls to her knees and exclaims that it is due to the Buddha's power that she is able to see Amitāyus and the two bodhisattvas. She then asks how beings in the future – without the advantage of having the Buddha beside them – will be able to visualize him. The Buddha replies:

> Those who wish to visualize this Buddha should gather their attention, and focus their minds on a lotus flower made of seven kinds of precious substances growing from the earth. They should picture each petal of this lotus flower as being the colours of a hundred different kinds of precious substances, with eighty-four thousand veins running through it. Light shines forth from each vein in eighty-four thousand colours, like a heavenly painting. They should be able to see all of this clearly. The smaller petals of the lotus are two hundred and fifty yojanas long, and two hundred and fifty yojanas wide. The lotus flower has eighty-

> four thousand large petals and it is adorned with jewels, kings among gems, which shine between each of its petals. Each of these jewels radiates a thousand rays of light. This light is like a canopy made of precious substances which covers the whole of the earth.

The Buddha continues in this vein for some time and ends by saying:

> When you focus your mind in this way, do not visualize all the different elements at the same time, but visualize each element in turn. Visualize each petal, each jewel, each ray of light, the platform, and each banner, so that you can see them as clearly as if you were looking at your own face in a mirror.

Only when each individual part of the lotus has been visualized clearly and distinctly should one move on to the visualization of Amitāyus. Why is this so? For that matter, why do we need to visualize all the previous elements of Sukhāvatī in such detail? Why not go straight to Amitāyus? Vaidehī's vision of Amitāyus occurred after she had listened to and, we may assume, visualized the Buddha's very detailed descriptions of Sukhāvatī that came before. These visualizations enabled her to enter into the imaginal realm or, to put it another way, enabled her to develop the imaginal faculty – the faculty that apprehends beauty and truth. Amitāyus and the two bodhisattvas dwell constantly in the imaginal realm, so to see them we too have to enter that realm, otherwise the Buddha that we see will be a mere stereotype. The visualizations of Sukhāvatī give us access to that realm.

The visualization of the lotus on which Amitāyus sits is, like the setting sun and the water of the first two visualizations, a transitional meditation. The lotus is an aspect of the land but is also the first in the series of visualizations of Amitāyus. Before telling us how to visualize Amitāyus, the Buddha gives us a reason for doing so:

> When you have obtained a vision of these things, you should then focus your mind on the Buddha. Why should you do this? The body of all the buddhas, all the tathāgatas, is the realm of reality, and they enter into the focused minds of all living beings. Therefore, when you focus your mind on the Buddha, your mind takes on the thirty-two major physical characteristics, and the eighty minor physical characteristics of the Buddha. When your mind creates the Buddha, your mind becomes the Buddha. The

> ocean of all the perfectly awakened buddhas arises from the focused mind. Therefore, you should concentrate your attention with an integrated mind and visualize the Buddha, the Tathāgata, the Arhat, the Perfectly Awakened Buddha with great care.

The "realm of reality" is a translation of *fǎjiè*, which is the Chinese equivalent of the Sanskrit *dharmadhātu*. It expresses the truth that everything is real. The Buddha didn't teach that the world is illusory; he said that we are deluded, and that the purpose of spiritual practice is ultimately to know and see things as they are. Everything is real; we just don't see its reality. You might argue that our deluded minds must then be unreal, but deluded minds are as real as awakened minds. To be more specific, in Buddhist doctrine "real" means without an enduring self, substance, or essence, and the Buddha said that all things whatsoever are without a self, or essence. All things whatsoever includes even unskilful states of mind such as confusion, greed, and anger because they too are without self or essence. They are therefore as real as skilful states of mind, as real, in fact, as awakened states of mind. The dharmadhātu embraces both nirvana and samsara, wisdom and ignorance, the awakened mind and the unawakened mind. That is not to say that unskilful states are awakened – they are definitely not – but that, being without essence or enduring selfhood, they are of the same nature as awakening. The difference between an awakened and an unawakened mind is that the former knows and sees that all things are without selfhood, while the latter doesn't.

The Buddha says that the *body* – the physical form – of every Buddha contains or expresses the whole of reality. This is important because it's his body that we'll be visualizing. The second part of that sentence – "and they enter into the focused minds of all living beings" – means that, when we focus our mind on the body of a Buddha, that Buddha, who is the realm of reality, enters our mind. The text goes on to say that, when you focus your mind on the Buddha, your mind "takes on the thirty-two major physical characteristics, and the eighty minor physical characteristics of the Buddha". These are the traditional Indian symbolic marks of an awakened being, which we need not go into here. In his next sentence the Buddha puts this in non-technical language: "When your mind creates the Buddha, your mind becomes the Buddha."

How does this work? In Chapter 5 I wrote about the "illumined image", which I said is more than the physical form, because it carries meanings, associations, allusions, and feelings that are invested in it by the person imagining it. The figure of the Buddha is for Buddhists an illumined image, so when they regard an image of a buddha they "see" more than the mere physical form: they see an image that means Awakening, the complete absence of greed, hatred, and delusion, freedom from the suffering of the false idea of enduring selfhood, unbounded love for all the world, complete happiness and an unlimited mind; and they feel the potential for their own Awakening, they feel faith. The practice of creating the Buddha's form in meditation uses the practitioner's faith in the Buddha – we could even say their love of the Buddha – as the catalyst for their growth towards Awakening. Imagination/faith becomes Awakening/wisdom.

This may seem to contradict what the Buddha said to Vakkali. You may remember that Vakkali kept gazing at the Buddha until one day the Buddha told him to stop – "Enough, Vakkali! What is there to see in this vile body?" – and advised him that, if he really wanted to see the Buddha, he should try to see, that is, understand, the Dharma. However, we need to take care when reading something that the Buddha said to one person. We should always bear in mind that he was talking directly *to* that person, knowing what he or she needed at that moment. What he said to one individual at a particular time is not necessarily something that we should take as a general teaching, suitable for everyone at all times. In fact, we've already encountered another disciple of the Buddha who constantly looked at the Buddha – at least in his mind's eye. This was Piṅgiya, who told his teacher Bavari that he saw the Buddha with his mind as if with his eyes, that he couldn't stay away from him for even a moment, and that he spent the whole night revering him. And as we've seen, the Buddha praised Piṅgiya for this, encouraging him to continue with this practice, telling him that by so doing he would definitely awaken. It seems then that for Vakkali the Buddha's form was not an illumined image whereas for Piṅgiya it was.

Now the Buddha begins to explain how to visualize Amitāyus:

> When you focus your mind on the Buddha, you should begin by focusing on his image. Whether your eyes are open or closed, you should be able to see his image sitting atop the lotus like a jewel, the colour of gold from the Jambū River. When you can see the image of the Buddha sitting there, your mind's eye will open, and you will be able to see him completely clearly. You will also see the adornments of Sukhāvatī, which are made of the seven kinds of precious substances, the ground made of precious substances, the ponds made of precious substances, the rows of trees made of precious substances, the heavenly cloth made of precious

> substances draped over the trees, and the abundant nets made of precious substances which fill the sky.

Once we see the Buddha our "mind's eye will open" – our imagination will be awakened – and we will be able to see everything in Sukhāvatī clearly. One of the Sanskrit terms for "wisdom" is *vidyā*, which the German scholar and translator Herbert V. Guenther translated as "analytical aesthetic appreciation". The point he was making was that wisdom is not just an accurate perception of the world, it is also an appreciation of the beautiful in it. When we really see things as they are, we see them as beautiful. Everything in Sukhāvatī is unutterably beautiful, and immersing our minds in that beauty enables us to realize the truth. But it works the other way round too: when we see the Buddha – when our mind becomes the Buddha – we perceive the beauty of everything.

Next we are to imagine a lotus on either side of the Buddha, on which stand the two great bodhisattvas, Avalokiteśvara and Mahāsthāmaprāpta. Rays of golden light shine from them, illuminating all the jewel trees, and the three are seen sitting on lotuses at the foot of each tree, so that Sukhāvatī "is filled with such images".

> When you have successfully focused your mind in this way, you will hear the streams of water, the rays of light, all of the trees made of precious substances, the cranes, the *haṃsa*-geese, and the ducks, all proclaiming the wondrous Dharma. Whether you are absorbed in samādhi or not, you will always hear the wondrous Dharma. When you come out of samādhi, you should remember what you have heard, bear it in mind, and not forget it. Check whether what you have heard accords with the sutras. If it does not, you should regard it as a false mental construction. If it does accord with the sutras, you should regard it as a general perception of Sukhāvatī.

In the midst of all this imagery we hear the Dharma. As in the Sukhāvatī sutras, the Dharma is heard rather than seen, and we are told not only to remember it but also to check that it accords with the sutras. We heard the Dharma in meditation and we now have to check that it really was the Dharma and not a delusion – to check that we heard it in the imaginal realm and not the realm of fantasy. The implication of this is that spiritual experiences are not to be trusted absolutely. They have to be checked against the Dharma as written in the sutras – the word of the Buddha. This goes against the grain for those who believe that experience can't be questioned or doubted. The problem with relying on experience absolutely is that we don't just have experiences, we interpret them, and our interpretation may be a deluded one, a misinterpretation.

Say I have an experience in meditation, of light and bliss and joy and spaciousness and beauty. In the midst of this experience I then have another experience, a deeper one it seems to me. I experience, in or around me, some kind of force, a totally benign one, and this force seems to be inviting me to surrender to it. Although "it" isn't the right way of expressing it, because it seems somehow to be a personal force, it seems to be a being. It feels utterly brilliant, and I do surrender to it, and as I do I feel the whole weight of the burden of selfhood fall from me, and it's such a blessed relief. Quite wonderful, and quite beyond the power of language to express.

Say I then go on to interpret that experience, and I interpret it this way: that wonderful, totally benign force that I experienced was a real being, a sort of person, who was trying to communicate with me. This being is in some way always present, permanently existing. In fact it or he or she – I now realize – has always been present, is the Ground of Being, Godhead, and is responsible for everything that exists.

I then remember to check that interpretation against the Buddha's teaching as recorded in the sutras, and in doing that I realize that I've fallen into the wrong view of eternalism. I am reminded that, according to the Buddha's insight, the being that I experienced may or may not exist in some way, but if he or she or it does exist, they are not a real self in the way that I had interpreted them to be. Such a being, were they to exist at all, exists only in the way that I exist, that is, without an enduring selfhood, and is certainly not responsible for everything that exists.

Up until now the Buddha still hasn't told us what Amitāyus actually looks like, apart from his being radiantly golden. He now begins to get more specific, beginning with his light and his size:

> When you have successfully focused your mind in this way, you should then visualize the body, the major physical characteristics, and the radiance of the Buddha Amitāyus. Understand, Ānanda, that the colour of the body of the Buddha Amitāyus is a hundred quadrillion times more brilliant than gold from the Jambū River in the heaven of the yāma gods. The height of the Buddha's body is a number of yojanas equal to the number of grains of sand in the River Ganges multiplied by sixty quintillion.

In Chapter 7 I said that the sutra could be a Chinese composition rather than a translation from an Indian language. There is also a theory that it was written in central Asia. One of the reasons for this theory is that the descriptions of Amitāyus and the bodhisattvas are similar to actual images existing in Central Asia. For instance, the description of Amitāyus here may be based on the larger of the two colossal Buddhas that were built in the cliff face in Bamiyan, Afghanistan, and which the Taliban dynamited in 2001. The larger of the two Buddhas destroyed was 53 metres tall – nothing like as big as Amitāyus in this sutra of course, but the statue must have been very impressive all the same. There is a photograph on the Internet of the smaller of the two Buddhas – 35 metres high – with a man leaning against the foot, his head reaching only the top of the Buddha's ankle.

I suppose it's also possible that, rather than the description of Amitāyus in this sutra having been influenced by those images, those images were made in response to this sutra. We've seen that, in the imagery of Sukhāvatī, size denotes spiritual significance, and what the sutra is telling us here is that the awakened mind is so vast that it cannot be measured. It is, on the contrary, boundless, limitless. In visualizing Amitāyus we are to imagine him as being immense, larger than our galaxy, which means that we can't really sit back and look at him as an object. Instead, we should imagine him as being all around us, our limited mind existing within the limitless mind – or body – of the Buddha. We saw that earlier in the sutra the Buddha says that the reason for visualizing the Buddha is because "the body of all the buddhas, all the tathāgatas, is the realm of reality", which is an abstract way of speaking. The sheer size of Amitāyus as described in the visualization makes this point visually: the realm of reality (*dharmadhātu*) is the Buddha, or the body of the Buddha is the realm of reality.

The sutra then becomes more specific about some of the details of Amitāyus' appearance:

> Between his eyes there is a tuft of white hair that curls to the right, five times as big as Mount Sumeru. The Buddha's eyes are as clear as the pure, limpid waters of the four oceans. Light as magnificent as Mount Sumeru radiates from every pore on his body. The sphere of the Buddha's radiance envelops a billion world systems, each containing a billion worlds. Within the sphere of his radiance there are a number of emanation buddhas equal to the number of grains of sand in the River Ganges multiplied by a hundred trillion. Each of these emanation

> buddhas in turn is attended by an assembly of emanation bodhisattvas.

Mount Sumeru is a mythical mountain; in ancient Indian cosmology, it is the centre of our world system. Not only are we to visualize Amitāyus and his two bodhisattvas as unimaginably vast; we are also to see trillions of "emanation" buddhas and bodhisattvas everywhere. It's not necessary to trouble ourselves about their ontological status because, as I've pointed out previously, the sutra is not a textbook containing facts about existence, but a visualization manual. Multiplicity is another way in which the sutra expresses the dharmadhātu.

> Those who see these things in their mind in this way will see all of the buddhas in the ten directions of space, and this is therefore known as the Samādhi of the Recollection of the Buddhas. Those who perform this visualization will attain a vision of the bodies of all the buddhas.

These buddhas are not emanations of Amitāyus but separate, individual buddhas, existing in their own right, as it were. In Chapter 2 we saw that, although the *Shorter Sukhāvatīvyūhaḥ Sūtra* focuses on Amitāyus' buddha-field and encourages the reader to aspire to be born there, he is considered to be just one among many buddhas. This is evident in the last part of the sutra, which mentions thirty-nine buddhas (Amitāyus being just one of them), after which the Buddha tells Ānanda that an alternative title for the sutra could be "Embraced by all the buddhas". In the *Longer Sukhāvatīvyūhaḥ Sūtra*, however, Amitāyus is the pre-eminent Buddha, whose light radiates further than that of all other buddhas and whose buddha-field is superior to all others. The *Guān Jīng* returns to the standpoint of the *Shorter Sūtra*: the reason for focusing attention on Amitāyus is not because he is considered to be the best of all buddhas, but because he is the paradigm of all buddhas.

The sixth-century Chinese scholar and meditation master Zhiyi discusses this in a text called *Ten Doubts About Pure Land*. One of the "doubts" he addresses is the question of why we should "specifically seek rebirth in the Pure Land of one particular Buddha". Why aren't we encouraged instead to visualize all the buddhas and their buddha-fields? In answering this question Zhiyi quotes from a sutra called *Rebirth According to One's Vows*, in which the Buddha says this:

> Sentient beings in this Sahā World generally have polluted, scattered minds. Therefore, I only extol one Pure Land in the

> West, focussing their minds on a single realm. If they meditate on all Buddhas, the scope of attention will be too broad, their minds will be lost and scattered and they will find samādhi difficult to attain. Thus, they will fail to achieve rebirth in the Pure Land. Furthermore, seeking the virtues of one Buddha is the same as seeking the virtues of all Buddhas – as all Buddhas have one common Dharma Nature. That is why to focus on Amitābha Buddha is to focus on all Buddhas, to be born in the Western Pure Land is to be born in all pure lands.[123]

The text then continues:

> By attaining a vision of the bodies of the buddhas, they will perceive the mind of the buddhas.

In Chapter 4 I wrote that, although Sukhāvatī is peopled by bodhisattvas as well as śrāvakas, the real message of the Sukhāvatī sutras is to encourage their readers/listeners to be the recipients of Amitāyus' great compassion and to aspire to be born into his buddha-field. This message is continued in the *Guān Jīng*, with Vaidehī entreating the Buddha "to reveal to me a place free of sorrow". Even when she asks the Buddha to teach her how to visualize Sukhāvatī it is to enable her to be born there. However, in these passages about the visualization of Amitāyus there emerges another message. The purpose of visualizing Amitāyus is not to be born in Sukhāvatī but to "perceive the mind of the buddhas", which is to become a buddha. As the Buddha says in the *Longer Sukhāvatīvyūhaḥ Sūtra*: "Only a buddha can understand the good qualities of a buddha." Not that one becomes a buddha immediately. As we'll see, there are a few intermediate stages to traverse before one reaches full Buddhahood. However, to perceive the mind of the buddhas at least means to gain insight into the Dharma. The Buddha goes on to say:

> The mind of the buddhas is great compassion, an unconditioned compassion that embraces all living beings. Those who perform this visualization will be born in the presence of all the buddhas when they die, and attain patient acceptance of the fact that all phenomena are unarisen. Therefore, those who are wise should concentrate their minds and perform the visualization of the Buddha Amitāyus with great care.

The aspiration to be born in Sukhāvatī seems now to have been completely superseded by the aspiration to be born in the presence of all the buddhas and to become an irreversible bodhisattva. Earlier in the sutra the Buddha tells Vaidehī that through visualizing Sukhāvatī she will attain patient acceptance of the fact that all phenomena are unarisen, but now we learn that it is specifically the visualization of Amitāyus that results in this deep insight, while the visualization of Sukhāvatī (only) results in the assurance of birth there. The sutra's centre of gravity has shifted from birth in Sukhāvatī to the attainment of irreversible bodhisattvahood.

> Those who visualize the Buddha Amitāyus should begin by becoming absorbed by one of his physical characteristics. They should begin by visualizing the tuft of white hair between his eyebrows clearly. Those who visualize the tuft of white hair between his eyebrows will naturally and spontaneously be able to see his eighty-four thousand other physical characteristics.

The visualization of Amitāyus is, like all the visualizations in this series, extremely detailed and complex. However, we don't have to try to see every feature through our own conscious and willed effort, which would probably be impossible. All we have to do is visualize the tuft of hair between Amitāyus' eyebrows until it becomes very clear and distinct, and then everything follows "naturally and spontaneously". This translates the Chinese *ziran*, the same word the sutra uses when King Bimbisāra progresses "naturally and spontaneously" to the stage of non-returning as a result of the Buddha's light shining on his head. *Ziran* evokes a similar idea to the Pali *dhammatā*, which we've seen means "naturalness", specifically the naturalness of involuntary positive effect following skilful effort.

> Those who see the Buddha Amitāyus will be able to see all of the innumerable buddhas in the ten directions of space. When they see all of the innumerable buddhas, they will receive their prediction to Awakening in their presence.

According to Mahāyāna doctrine, to become a bodhisattva one first makes the bodhisattva vow (*praṇidhāna*). This vow cannot be made alone; it has to be witnessed by a buddha, who then predicts (*vyākaraṇa*) that in the far distant future one will become a buddha. This is problematic for those who wish to become bodhisattvas but who have never met a buddha in the flesh and are unlikely to do so. How are they to realize their ambition? In this passage, as a result of visualizing Amitāyus, the practitioner makes the bodhisattva vow before all the buddhas in the universe and receives from each one of them the prediction of his or her own future buddhahood. This is obviously a very exalted experience, but it expresses a simple but important aspect of Buddhist meditation. At the beginning of Chapter 5 I made the point that, when the Buddha's immediate disciples meditated, they would have been conscious of the fact that the practice they were doing had been given to them by the Buddha, and they would have therefore practised it in relation to, or in relationship with, him. This is in fact what makes a meditation practice a Buddhist practice. It's not necessarily the method or technique that makes it Buddhist – the Mindfulness of Breathing, for instance, can be practised by both Buddhists and non-Buddhists – it's the sense of meditating in relationship with, under the tutelage of, the Buddha. At first perhaps, the relationship is experienced as one way – the Buddha is present to the meditator, but the meditator doesn't feel that they are present to the Buddha. However, as we continue to practise in this relational way, we may begin to feel that we do become present to the Buddha, and that he is witnessing our spiritual life, our spiritual progress. Here, in this passage from the Guān Jīng, all the infinite buddhas in the universe witness our making of the bodhisattva vow and assure us that our efforts will result in success.

Visualizing Amitāyus then leads to two crucial experiences, the first in this life, the second in the next. In this life the practitioner sees all the buddhas and receives from them the prediction to buddhahood, thereby becoming a bodhisattva; in the next life they're born in the presence of all the buddhas, where they attain the patient acceptance of the fact that all phenomena are unarisen, thereby becoming an irreversible bodhisattva. Having said that, we'll see that Vaidehī becomes an irreversible bodhisattva in her present life, at the conclusion of the Buddha's teaching. She dies to her old self and is reborn as an irreversible bodhisattva in just a few hours. This is the spiritual climax of the sutra. The meditations that follow yield no further results, no deeper insights. In his book *Visions of Sukhāvatī*, Julian Pas makes a persuasive case for an early version of the sutra, with only ten or twelve meditations, the first half of which would have been visualizations of the land, and the second half of Amitāyus and the two bodhisattvas.[124] If he's right, the sutra would be neater and more symmetrical, and would also make sense from the point of view of consequent attainments – the visualizations of Sukhāvatī resulting in assurance of birth there, the visualizations of Amitāyus resulting in the arising of the Bodhicitta. However, unless someone discovers an earlier version of the sutra, there isn't a way to prove or disprove this theory and, in any case, even if an earlier version of the sutra were found that proved the theory, it wouldn't necessarily be better than the one we have.

The next two visualizations are of the two bodhisattvas, Avalokiteśvara and Mahāsthāmaprāpta, who are described in even more detail than is Amitāyus. Although the sutra is called the *Visualization of the Buddha Amitāyus*, at its conclusion the Buddha gives an alternative title: "The Visualization of Sukhāvatī, the Buddha Amitāyus, the Bodhisattva Avalokiteśvara, and the Bodhisattva Mahāsthāmaprāpta". We might ask, why visualize the two bodhisattvas, and why at this particular point? One reason may be that, as a result of visualizing Amitāyus, the Bodhicitta arises in the meditator – he or she becomes a bodhisattva, which entails practising for countless lives as a bodhisattva until finally attaining buddhahood. Whereas Amitāyus symbolizes the goal of the bodhisattva's life, Avalokiteśvara and Mahāsthāmaprāpta symbolize the path.

In the next meditation we shift our attention from Amitāyus and his bodhisattvas to ourselves, and we imagine being born in Sukhāvatī:

> When you have visualized these things, you should focus your mind and imagine yourself being born in Sukhāvatī, sitting cross-legged on a lotus flower. Imagine that the lotus flower is closed, and then that it opens. When the lotus flower opens, imagine five hundred rays of coloured light shining forth from your body. Imagine your eyes opening, so that you can see the buddhas and bodhisattvas filling the sky. Imagine hearing the sounds of the birds, the trees, and all the buddhas, every sound proclaiming the wondrous Dharma in accordance with the twelve divisions of the sacred scriptures. When you come out of samadhi, remember the things you have seen – do not forget them.

Up until now we have been working hard, and in this meditation we begin to experience the fruit of all our hard work. It's a receptive rather than an active meditation, in which we allow ourselves to experience the beauty, happiness, and wisdom of Sukhāvatī. We let it in. I enjoy doing this meditation very much. Imagining myself sitting within a closed lotus flower – shut off from the beauty and happiness of Sukhāvatī, unable to hear the songs of the magical birds and the sound of the rivers teaching the Dharma, closed off from Amitābha's brilliant light – symbolizes my actual situation beautifully. The closed lotus is my sheath of selfhood, which safeguards me – or so I believe – but at the same time effectively inhibits real spiritual growth. Imagining the lotus gradually opening brings a wonderful sense of expansion, openness, and freedom, a natural and effortless release from the limiting confines of selfhood.

As we've seen, the visualizations of Sukhāvatī and Amitāyus described in this sutra are highly demanding in their detail and elaboration. The thirteenth visualization offers a much simpler and easier option:

> Those who sincerely wish to be born in Sukhāvatī should visualize an image sixteen feet tall, seated on the surface of a pond. As I have already said, the size of the body of the Buddha Amitāyus is beyond measure, beyond the grasp of ordinary immature beings. However, because of the power of the vows that that Tathāgata took in the past, those who focus their minds on him will nonetheless be able to perform the practice. The merit gained by focusing the mind on the Buddha in this way is immeasurable, and the merit gained by visualizing all of his physical characteristics is even greater.

The last three meditations describe the nine "categories" of beings born in Sukhāvatī – three levels for each meditation. The three highest levels are Buddhists with a very high degree of ethical practice, who follow the Mahāyāna, and in whom the Bodhicitta has arisen. The three middle levels are people who practise ethics and care for their parents, and the lowest levels are those who have performed many unethical actions and feel no remorse. Some of these actions are extremely unethical:

> The lowest level of the lowest category is comprised of those living beings who act unskilfully, performing the five acts which have immediate consequences and the ten kinds of unskilful action, indulging in every possible kind of unskilful behaviour. Because of their unskilful actions, these foolish people are destined to be born in the three states of misfortune and experience immeasurable suffering for a great many aeons.

The "five acts which have immediate consequences" are the weighty karmas that result in rebirth in one of the hell realms: intentionally killing an arhat, killing your mother and/or your father, wounding a buddha, and causing a division in the sangha. The ten kinds of unskilful action are the opposite of the ten kinds of skilful action that I described at the end of the previous chapter. As the Buddha says, as a result of such behaviour these beings will be reborn into one of the hell realms. However, the Buddha continues:

> When the life of a foolish person like this is at an end, they may encounter a spiritual friend who is able to comfort them in many ways, explain the wondrous Dharma to them, and teach them how to recollect the Buddha. This good friend will say, "If you are not able to recollect the Buddha, you should recite the name of the Buddha Amitāyus with devotion." If the practitioner then recites "Namo Amitābhāya Buddhāya" with sincerity ten times in a row, then with each repetition they will free themselves of the effects of previous unskilful actions that would have kept them in samsara for eight billion aeons.

This contradicts the *Longer Sukhāvatīvyūhaḥ Sūtra*, whose nineteenth vow states that those who have committed the five acts which have immediate consequences are unable to be born in Sukhavatı. This doctrinal inconsistency is problematic for those who believe the sutras to be the word of the Buddha in the literal sense, as the ancient Chinese Pure Land masters did. Tanluan, for instance, spends a few pages explaining that the Buddha only appears to contradict himself, and it has to be said that, from a rational point of view, his arguments are not very convincing. If we don't believe that the sutras were literally spoken by the Buddha, there isn't really a problem – merely a difference of opinion between authors. Still, it's hard to believe that ten recitations of the Buddha's name, even if accompanied by a sincere mind, can cancel out the evil karma of eight billion aeons. Tan L'uan makes use of an interesting simile to illustrate how it's possible. A room, he says, may have been dark for a thousand years but, as soon as a light is brought in, the room immediately becomes bright; the length of time that it has been dark is of no consequence. It's an invalid simile, of course. Darkness is not the same as the karmic effects of unskilful actions, and light is not the same as Enlightenment. However, I don't think we need to worry too much about the truth or falsity of this. Just as the descriptions of Sukhāvatī in the sutras are not factual descriptions but spiritual practices, similarly, the position put forward in the sixteenth meditation of the *Guān Jīng* is not necessarily a truth statement. As I've repeatedly stated, the question we need to ask of these texts is not whether they are true, but what spiritual benefit we might derive from reading or practising them. Immediately before the fourteenth meditation begins, the Buddha refers once again to the two bodhisattvas, Avalokiteśvara and Mahāsthāmaprāpta, and he says:

> These two bodhisattvas help the Buddha Amitābha in the task of transforming all living beings.

In the meditations that follow we imagine this transformation. We imagine all living beings – at least all human beings – being reborn in Sukhāvatī, no matter who they are, no matter what they've done or not done, no matter whether or not they "deserve" it, and as such it's an expression of the bodhisattva vow – the heartfelt desire to deliver all beings from the suffering inherent in samsara.

In Chapter 3 I suggested that the seed of the bodhisattva vow could be found in the Buddha's teaching on *mettā* (Skt *maitri*) – loving-kindness. The last three meditations are rather like a very imaginative form of the Metta Bhavana meditation practice, in which the meditator develops *mettā* towards all beings whatsoever – *all* beings, not just the "good" ones. One of the traditional methods of cultivating *mettā* is to use phrases such as "May all beings be well, may they be happy, may they be free from suffering." To visualize people being born in Sukhāvatī is an imaginative way of wishing them the highest possible happiness. According to most accounts of Buddhist doctrine, the people described in the final meditation – the lowest of the lowest grade – cannot possibly be born in Sukhāvatī. That doesn't mean that we can't *wish* that they could be born there. Those who commit any of the five grave offences will suffer naturally as a result of those actions, in accordance with the law of karma, but there is no reason why we should wish them to suffer or rejoice in their suffering. Their suffering is not a *punishment*, it's the natural consequence of unskilful action. We should, on the contrary, wish them happiness and freedom from suffering. The Buddha once said:

> Monks, even if bandits were to carve you up savagely, limb by limb, with a two-handled saw, he among you who let his heart get angered even at that would not be doing my bidding. Even then you should train yourselves: "Our minds will be unaffected and we will say no evil words. We will remain sympathetic, with a mind of good will, and with no inner hate. We will keep pervading these people with an awareness imbued with good will and, beginning with them, we will keep pervading the all-

> encompassing world with an awareness imbued with good will – abundant, expansive, immeasurable, free from hostility, free from ill will." That's how you should train yourselves.[125]

Although I think it probable that originally the sutra didn't include the last few meditations, nevertheless the sequence as a whole does seem to form a cogent spiritual progression. The visualizations of Sukhāvatī bring about mental absorption and insight strong and deep enough to ensure rebirth in Sukhāvatī; those of Amitāyus result in the making of the bodhisattva vow and thus becoming a bodhisattva; and with the last three meditations the practitioner turns his or her attention away from concern with his or her own birth in Sukhāvatī and eventual Awakening, to "the task of transforming all living beings".

> Whilst the Buddha was speaking these words, Vaidehī and her five hundred ladies in waiting listened to what he was saying. They were immediately able to see Sukhāvatī, with all of its many different features, and they attained a vision of the body of the Buddha and the two bodhisattvas. Vaidehī exclaimed, "I have never experienced anything like this before!" Her mind became clear, and she attained great realization, and patient acceptance of the fact that all phenomena are unarisen.

Five hundred ladies in waiting? Where have they come from? This is the first mention of them in the sutra, yet they've apparently been present throughout the whole of the Buddha's teaching to Vaidehī. I can't help wondering how they all fitted into Vaidehī's dungeon! Once again I have to remind myself that this is a Mahāyāna sutra, and that my question is born of literal-mindedness. A more pertinent question is why the author suddenly decides to introduce them here. Perhaps he or she felt that the Buddha's teaching to Vaidehī is too precious for just one person, as if it deserves a bigger audience, even though Ānanda is present and will share it with others later.

Returning to Vaidehī, it's significant that the Buddha gave her much more than she asked for: "Blessed One, it is my heartfelt desire that you would reveal to me a place free of sorrow, free of the defilements", and more than he promised: "The Tathāgata will now explain how to visualize Sukhāvatī, for the benefit of Vaidehī and all living beings in the future." If he had only taught her the visualizations of Sukhāvatī he would have given her all that she asked for and fulfilled his promise. However, he went on to teach her how to visualize Amitāyus, and in so doing she became an irreversible bodhisattva. He took Vaidehī's heartfelt request for a refuge from suffering and helped her to transform that into the bodhisattva vow – the heartfelt desire to become a Buddha, and so to alleviate the suffering of all beings.

This reminds me of the famous parable in the *Saddharma Puṇḍarīka Sūtra*, which tells the story of a rich man who owns a large and rambling house that catches fire. There is only one way out of the house, through a gate that is itself in flames, and, although the man knows that he can easily escape through that gate, he is worried about his sons – twenty or thirty of them – who are inside the house, engrossed in their games, unaware of the danger they are in. He shouts to them, telling them of the danger, but they take no notice of him and continue to play their games. The father therefore thinks of a skilful means to tempt them out of the house. He tells them that he has brought for them some wonderful goat-carts, deer-carts, and ox-carts – they are just outside the gate, and if they come out immediately the boys can choose whichever ones they want for themselves. Accordingly they run out of the house in their eagerness to play with and possess these carts, but when they get there they find that there are in fact no carts. Instead, the man gives to each of his sons a marvellous carriage "tall, spacious, and adorned with numerous jewels", each drawn by a pure white ox, accompanied by many grooms and servants.

> At that time each of the sons mounted his large carriage, gaining something he had never had before, something he had originally never expected.[126]

The parable is told by the Buddha to illustrate that he originally only taught the Hīnayāna – the Small Vehicle – whose goal is that of the arhat – Awakening for oneself alone – as a skilful means, but that really what he wanted was for everyone to mount the Mahāyāna – the Great Vehicle – and aspire to the full and complete Awakening of a buddha. The goat-, deer-, and ox-carts that the rich man promised his sons represent the Hīnayāna, while the magnificent carriages that they actually received represent the Mahāyāna. Leaving aside the sectarian bias of this parable, what it illustrates is that when we first encounter the Dharma we can't help but conceive of Awakening in terms of that which we already know. Vaidehī asked for a vision of a pure buddha-field as a refuge from her suffering. The Buddha gave her that but then took her beyond it, as the sutra tells us, to the patient acceptance of the fact that all phenomena are unarisen, at which point she realized that there was actually nothing she could hold on to, no place outside of herself in which she could rest. She realized that Sukhāvatī was not a final resting place, free from the suffering from which she was so desperate to escape, but a mind perfectly in tune with the changing and insubstantial nature of reality.

> Her five hundred ladies in waiting developed minds set on unsurpassed perfect Awakening and a heartfelt desire to be born in that buddha-field arose in them. The Blessed One gave each of them a prediction that they would undoubtedly be born there and that, when they were, they would attain the Samādhi of Being in the Presence of All the Buddhas. Innumerable gods also developed minds set on unsurpassed Awakening.

Vaidehī's attendants, then, all become bodhisattvas and are assured of birth in Sukhāvatī. They won't reach final Awakening in Sukhāvatī though, because bodhisattvas vow to spend innumerable lifetimes creating their own buddha-fields. The twentieth vow of the *Longer Sukhāvatīvyūhaḥ Sūtra* states that the beings in Sukhāvatī will

> only experience one more birth before attaining unsurpassed, perfect Awakening. This is with the exception of those bodhisattvas, those great beings, who have taken the supreme vow, who clad themselves in mighty armour, who are awake to the needs of the whole world, who are devoted to the whole world, who are devoted to the attainment of complete nirvana by the whole world, who long to practise the path of the bodhisattva in all world systems, who long to meet all the buddhas, who establish as many living beings as there are grains of sand in the River Ganges in unsurpassed, perfect Awakening, who are committed to the highest practice, and who have perfected the practice of bringing benefit to all.

For bodhisattvas, Sukhāvatī is a transitional state, a long "retreat" in which they are able to cultivate qualities and attainments that will equip them for the extremely long and arduous path to Buddhahood.

In Chapter 6 we saw that Sukhāvatī is inhabited only by men and gods. We also saw that, according to the *Longer Sukhāvatīvyūhaḥ Sūtra*, women are advised to cultivate disgust at their womanhood so as to be reborn in Sukhāvatī as men. Yet, by the time the Buddha concludes his teaching in the *Guān Jīng*, Vaidehī and her five hundred ladies in waiting are all bodhisattvas, assured of birth in Sukhāvatī, and nothing is said of any need to cultivate disgust at their female nature. Perhaps the author of the *Guān Jīng* held a different view of women than did the author of the *Longer Sukhāvatīvyūhaḥ Sūtra*. Perhaps this is why he – or she – suddenly introduces the five hundred ladies in waiting at the end. If we take into account that countless heavenly beings – gods – also become bodhisattvas, the scene at the close of the *Guān Jīng* is the converse of that in Sukhāvatī: only women and gods are the immediate beneficiaries of the Buddha's teaching, the only beings who are seen to make spiritual progress through hearing them.

The sutra doesn't tell us what happened to Vaidehī immediately after this. Did she die in her dungeon or did Ajātaśatru eventually free her? Perhaps, once she had become an irreversible bodhisattva, the author of the sutra didn't consider what happened to her earthly body of very great consequence. So let's leave her now in her dungeon, the woman who at the beginning of this sutra was an "ordinary person, with a weak and feeble mind", but who at the end is an irreversible bodhisattva, and one of the greatest characters in Buddhist mythology.

We must also leave the Buddha, Amitāyus, and Sukhāvatī, for we have arrived at the end of the sutra, and the end of this commentary on the three sutras. Hopefully you will now read the sutras themselves, if you haven't already done so. And perhaps this is just the beginning of a further, deeper exploration of the sutras, a further opening of the mind's eye, an awakening of the imagination. Perhaps even of rebirth in Sukhāvatī.

> The Blessed One then returned to Vultures' Peak by walking through the air. Ānanda told the great assembly gathered there what had happened. Countless human beings, gods, nāgas, and yakṣas rejoiced when they heard what the Buddha had said. They venerated the Buddha, and left.

Part Four

The Pure Land Sutras, translated by Śraddhāpa

Introduction to the translations

Faith is the root of all attainments in this world,
so listen, and drive out your doubts.

In their own language

The art of translation has been interwoven with the Buddhist tradition since its very earliest days. As Buddhism spread from India to cover a third of the globe, translators played a key role in ensuring that the Dharma was able to take root and flourish in new cultures and societies, and thus helped to open the door to the deathless for millions. The names of the greatest translators – Marpa, Xuánzàng, Kumārajīva, and others – still ring through the centuries to inspire and challenge their spiritual descendents. To translate the teachings of the Buddha is to be part of one of the most ancient strands of the Buddhist tradition, and to take upon oneself an awesome responsibility.

This tradition of translation goes back to the Buddha himself. In the Pali canon we find the following conversation taking place between the Buddha and two of his disciples:

> There were two monks called Yameḷu and Tekulā, brothers who had been born as brahmins, and who were both eloquent and well-spoken. They went to see the Blessed One, and when they had greeted him respectfully and sat down to one side they said to him, "Bhante, there are monks with all kinds of different names, who have gone forth from all kinds of different clans, social positions, and families. They corrupt the teachings of the Buddha by speaking them in their own languages. Bhante, let us render the teachings of the Buddha into Vedic metre."
>
> The Buddha, the Blessed One, rebuked them, saying "You witless fools, how can you say such a thing? That would not inspire faith in those who have no faith, nor would it strengthen

> the faith of those who already possess it. Indeed, it would do just the opposite."
>
> When he had rebuked them, and explained the Dhamma to them, he said, "Monks, you are not to render the teachings of the Buddha into Vedic metre. If you do so, you will be guilty of transgressing the monastic code. People are to learn the teachings of the Buddha in their own language."[127]

In this story, the Buddha is crystal clear in his intentions. In contrast to the Vedic tradition which Yameḷu and Tekulā wished to emulate, Buddhism is to have no sacred language, no esoteric, impenetrable texts comprehensible only to an elite of linguistic specialists. The language of the Dharma is whatever language people speak, the language of the marketplace, the language that touches people's hearts.

But what does this mean for us, as English speakers in the twenty-first century? How are the teachings of a man who lived in India millennia ago to be translated into our language? Indeed, is it even possible for a translator to bridge such vast expanses of time, space, culture, and language in such a way that the teachings of the Buddha can speak to our existential situation, and lead us to liberation?

The art of betrayal

The old Italian saying "traduttore, traditore" means "to translate is to betray". I have always loved this phrase, as it is itself such an apt illustration of the point being made. While it is of course perfectly possible to render the meaning of the words into English, the subtle beauty of the play on words, the near-homophony of the two Italian verbs, and the balance of the phrase as a whole are lost, and the text itself, in a sense, betrayed. Indeed, in a very real sense, true translation is a hopeless endeavour. No matter how skilled the translator, something of the original text will always be lost, and something that was not present in the original text will always find its way into the translation. Bhikkhu Bodhi, undoubtedly one of the most accomplished translators of Buddhist texts in the modern world, put it most eloquently when he said:

> Any language, I have found, has an underlying conceptual scheme built into it by the metaphors that govern its vocabulary and by the connotations and nuances of its words. Thus in translating from one language into another, one is always faced

> with the problem of dissonance between their two underlying conceptual schemes. This leads to conflicts that often can only be resolved by sacrificing important conceptual connections in the original language for the sake of elegance or intelligibility in the target language. This problem becomes all the more acute when one is translating from an ancient language utilizing a somewhat archaic set of conceptual metaphors into a modern language pertaining to a very different culture.[128]

The translator of a Buddhist text, therefore, and perhaps especially the translator of a sutra, finds themselves in an impossible position. To translate the text is, in one way or another, to betray it, but to fail to translate it – as the Buddha made clear to his wayward disciples – is a betrayal of an even more serious kind. So how is the translator to proceed?

Those with no experience of translation (especially those who, like the majority of native English speakers, only know one language well) often think of fidelity as the sole criterion by which a translation is to be judged. A good translation is a faithful, even literal, one. The reality, though, is that any translation has to take into account the text's purpose. If you're translating a joke, the translation has to be funny in the language and culture it's being translated into. An instruction manual for a washing machine has to enable the reader to actually operate the washing machine. If the translated text does not fulfil its function, if the reader does not laugh or end up with clean clothes, the translation is a poor one, no matter how "faithful" it might be to the original in purely linguistic terms. Translation, in truth, is not a straightforward matter of fidelity to the original text, but of choosing the appropriate *kind* of fidelity – and, one might say, the appropriate kind of betrayal.

So what is the purpose of a sutra? From a Buddhist perspective the answer is clear: it is to enable the reader to attain Awakening, and this is the only criterion by which the translation of a sutra should be judged. Ultimately, the only person who is really able to make such a judgement, and therefore the only truly qualified translator of a Buddhist text, is one who themselves has attained Awakening, or at the very least a degree of transcendental insight. Indeed, the translators of old were renowned not simply as accomplished linguists but as practitioners possessed of deep wisdom and compassion. Alas, there are few, perhaps none, today who possess both the linguistic skill and the depth of insight to be considered truly equal to the task – and yet the Buddha's injunction, and therefore the imperative to translate, remains.

It is worth noting here that, historically, the majority of translators of Buddhist texts into English have neither possessed such a qualification nor even aspired to it or recognized its validity. They have mostly not been Buddhist practitioners at all, but scholars, translating for other scholars, and treating the texts as interesting objects of literary, cultural, and anthropological study rather than as aids to actually practising the Dharma. This has resulted in many translations which stick very closely to the syntax and idioms of the original languages and which often use obscure, technical terminology. Such translations are well suited to the purposes for which they were created, but the average Buddhist practitioner who picks up such a text will often find the language so dense and inelegant that after wading thorough a few pages they will look elsewhere for inspiration.

My approach to producing these new translations of the Pure Land sutras has been to regard this betrayal as the greater. I have therefore endeavoured to render the texts into English which is clear, elegant, and idiomatic, and which will speak to the heart as well as the head. In order to do this, I have avoided the more literal word-for-word approach which has characterized many previous translations of Buddhist texts, and instead focused on conveying the meaning of each sentence – or even in places each paragraph – as a coherent whole. A couple of examples will serve to illustrate what I mean by this.

Probably the first thing the reader will notice about these translations is that the famous opening words *evaṃ mayā śrūtam* are rendered not as "Thus have I heard" but as "This is what I have heard." A scholar of Sanskrit might object that as *evaṃ* means "in this way", and not "this", the traditional translation is more correct – and in one sense they are quite right. However, because I regard the texts I am translating not as cultural artefacts but as sacred Dharma texts, I do not regard it as important to convey the exact meaning of the Sanskrit word *evaṃ* in the original text. The meaning which is lost in my translation is not important. What is important is that the sentence have an emotional impact on the reader and draw them into the text. By using a sentence that an English speaker might actually use when they are about to relate something of great significance that they have witnessed, I hope to spark my reader's imagination. I hope to make it that little bit easier for you to picture yourself sitting at Ānanda's feet and listening to him relate the wonders he witnessed during the life of the Teacher.

Another representative example of this approach is the phrase *svārakṣitavākyaś cābhūt*, which appears at the beginning of section 34 in the *Longer Sutra*, and which I have translated as "He was careful about what he said." Max Müller's translation is "he was well guarded in his speech",[129] and many scholars would undoubtedly consider this more literal translation to be preferable to mine without so much as a second thought. After all, *ārakṣita* certainly does mean "protected" or "guarded", and not "careful", and the grammatical structure of Müller's translation is much closer to the grammatical structure of the original Sanskrit sentence. However, the problem with literal translations like Müller's is that they do not reflect the way people actually speak. Nobody would say something like "Oh, I need to guard my speech when he's around!" By asking oneself how the idea contained in the sentence taken as a coherent unit of meaning would most naturally be expressed in English, rather than focusing on the meanings of the individual words, one arrives at something more like the translation I have chosen.

Of course, such differences are subtle; nonetheless, I believe they are significant – especially when one takes into account the cumulative effect of hundreds of such decisions on the text as a whole. When we encounter an awkwardly phrased sentence in a text, we start analyzing it and trying to understand what it means, rather than allowing the meaning to touch our hearts and draw forth our inspiration. As the Buddha made clear to Yameḷu and Tekulā, he did not want his teachings transmitted in an elitist jargon that would put ordinary people off listening to them – or, in our day, reading them. People are to read the sutras in their own language, and to me that has to mean in the kind of English people actually use, and not a kind of hybrid translationese filled with the syntax and idioms of the source languages. In texts such as the Pure Land sutras the English will of course at times be heightened, poetic, formal, or dense. However, I have striven to ensure that, whatever the tone, the language feels elegant and natural, as well as conveying as much of the meaning of the original Sanskrit or Chinese as possible. It is my hope that this approach will enable more people to be inspired by these texts, and to use them to deepen their practice of the Dharma. To the extent I have been successful in this, which of course is for others to judge, the translations that follow can be considered, from a Buddhist point of view, to be truly faithful to the original texts.

Thick translation

However, no matter how they are translated the Pure Land sutras will never be easy or accessible texts for Western readers. They contain great spiritual truths, but these truths come to us not only in a foreign language but from a foreign time and a foreign culture. It is therefore quite appropriate, and indeed eminently traditional, that these texts are presented not on their own, but together with a commentary. While I have translated the language of these texts, the reader has in Ratnaguna's commentary a translation of their beating spiritual heart. As a supplement to this commentary, I have included a detailed glossary which includes all of the key terms used in the texts. The terms included in the glossary have been translated consistently except where otherwise noted. This will enable the reader to identify, for example, that wherever the word "faith" is used in the translation the original term used is *śraddhā* or 信 *xìn*.

This approach to translation – presenting the texts not simply on their own, but accompanied by a commentary, notes, and glossary – has been described as "thick translation".[130] The aim of this approach is to give the reader a more complex and multilayered impression of the original text and enable the more enthusiastic reader to delve more deeply into the meanings and nuances of individual terms, thus to some extent mitigating the fundamental problems of translation so eloquently summarized by Bhikkhu Bodhi. The apparatus presented alongside the texts themselves is therefore an integral part of the translation, and provides an important balance to the kind of loss involved in moving away from a more literal, scholarly style of translation.

Gender

One of the most significant aspects of the foreignness of the culture in which these texts originated is in terms of gender and in particular the use of gendered language. In Sanskrit and Chinese, male pronouns are sometimes used to refer to people in general, not simply to men. This is, of course, not the case in modern English and, if such usage is translated literally, the text becomes distorted – at least if one believes, as I do, that their intended audience is everyone and anyone who is able to hear and understand them, regardless of sex or gender identity.

Some English-language purists may object to my usage of the gender-neutral pronouns "they" and "them" to refer to a single person whose gender is unknown, claiming that these pronouns cannot be used in the singular. In fact, this usage of "they" and "them" goes back centuries – none other than William Shakespeare used them in this way[131] – and the attempt to restrict their usage to the plural only stems from the nineteenth century. Apart from the fact that "they" and "them" provide a more elegant and natural solution to the challenge of inclusiveness of language than the rather awkward "he or she" and "him or her", they extend that inclusiveness to embrace those whose gender identity is not adequately represented by the binary male/female divide.

Reading the translations

The translations, like any sacred text, should be read not once but multiple times, and are designed to be approached in different ways at different times. They are to be read, naturally, in conjuction with Ratnaguna's commentary. The reader may wish to read the commentary in its entirety, and then begin on the translations, or alternatively move back and forth, reading a chapter of the commentary, and then the part of the sutras being explored. At times, it will be useful to take a more intellectual, analytical approach to the texts, reading the notes, checking the glossary, and perhaps exploring what other Buddhist writers have had to say about some of the key terms. At other times it will be more appropriate to read the texts in a more emotive way, not getting too involved in the technicalities, but allowing the words to inspire the imagination and open the heart.

One practice that is thoroughly traditional and has much to recommend it is reading or reciting sutras aloud. Reading all three of the Pure Land sutras aloud at a measured pace will take something like six hours, and is a powerful way of engaging with them more deeply, say on a solitary retreat. If there is a particular section of the text that you find engages you, you might wish to read it aloud as a daily practice, immediately before or after meditating, for example. I have translated the sutras with this practice in mind, and have tried to ensure that the language is suited for this purpose.

Those who are inspired to take their study of these texts deeper may wish to look at other translations from the Sanskrit, Chinese, or Tibetan. This kind of comparative study will enable the more dedicated student to get a better and more rounded sense of the original than can be gained from any one translation in isolation. The other available translations of these texts into English are listed in the bibliography, but I would particularly recommend Luis Gomez' *The Land of Bliss*, which includes translations of the *Longer Sūtra* and *Shorter Sūtra* from both Sanskrit and Chinese. In my translations of these two sutras from Sanskrit, I have used the same division of the text into numbered sections as Gomez, in order to assist the reader who wishes to read the translations in parallel. Similarly, in my translation of the *Visualization Sūtra*, the divisions follow those of Inagaki's translation.

Finally, it must be said that no translation can ever be a fully adequate substitute for the original text and, as my own teacher Urgyen Sangharakshita has put it:

> The ideal method of studying Buddhism would be to read in the original language a number of carefully selected texts belonging to the Pāli, Sanskrit, Chinese, Tibetan, Mongolian, or Japanese canonical Buddhist literature.[132]

He does go on to comment that this will be impracticable "for all save the most diligent and earnest students",[133] but I expect that at least a few of my readers will fall into this category. For someone who is devoted to and inspired by the words of the Buddha and the ancient masters of our tradition, there is simply nothing to compare with the thrill of reading these texts in the original language. Mastering Sanskrit, or one of the other canonical languages, is undoubtedly an intellectual challenge, but as with all language learning the criterion for success is not so much talent or brilliance as the willingness to apply sustained effort and the patience to continue in the face of slow and incremental progress. My own experience has been that such effort and patience will be repaid many times over.

Thanks

On my journey to accumulate the necessary skills to study Buddhism according to the ideal method recommended by Sangharakshita, and to produce the translations which follow, I have received a great deal of help, advice, and encouragement. I would like to offer my profound thanks to all my teachers, secular and spiritual, in particular Ute Hüsken and Jens Braarvig at the University of Oslo, who taught me Sanskrit and other canonical languages; Marie Wells and Daniel Abondolo at University College London, where I studied translation; and Dharmacārīs Surata, Maitreyabandhu, Guṇaketu, and Śākyakumāra, who are my guides and my inspiration in the Dharma life. Guttorm Gunderson offered valuable advice and insights, particularly in relation to the *Visualization Sūtra*, and my fellow members of Maitrīkula Community, Dharmacārī Maitrīghoṣa and Jan Langhaug, have been unfailingly generous in their support and friendship throughout.

It has been a particular privilege to work with Dharmacārī Ratnaguna on this project, and to read the early drafts of his commentary while I was working on the translations. Although I was able to explain some of the words of the sutras to him, he explained their meaning to me, and that has been a most precious gift.

Lastly, I wish to thank Urgyen Sangharakshita, who founded the tradition to which I belong. His clarity and vision underpin whatever understanding of the Dharma I possess and have been able to bring to this sacred task – of enabling people to learn the teachings of the Buddha in their own language.

Dharmacārī Śraddhāpa
Maitrīkula Community, Oslo
September 2015

The Shorter Sūtra on the Abundance of Wonderful Qualities Which Adorn Sukhāvatī

Sukhāvatīvyūhaḥ (Saṃkṣiptamātṛkā)[134]
सुखावतीव्यूहः (संक्षिप्तमातृका)

Translated from Sanskrit by Dharmacārī Śraddhāpa

Homage to the All-Knowing One.

1. This is what I have heard. Once, the Blessed One was staying in Śrāvastī, in Jeta's Grove, in Anāthapiṇḍada's Park, with a great sangha of 1,250 monks who were known to have attained the higher forms of knowledge – elders, great śrāvakas who were all arhats. They included the elders Śāriputra, Mahāmaudgalyāyana, Mahākāśyapa, Mahākapphiṇa, Mahākātyāyana, Mahākauṣṭhila, Revata, Śuddhipanthaka, Nanda, Ānanda, Rāhula, Gavāṃpati, Bharadvāja, Kālodayin, Vakkula, Aniruddha, and many of the Blessed One's other great disciples. There were also many bodhisattvas there, great beings. They included Mañjuśrī, the youthful prince of the Dharma, the Bodhisattva Ajita,[135] the Bodhisattva Gandhahastin, the Bodhisattva Nityodyukta, the Bodhisattva Anikṣiptadhura, and many other bodhisattvas, great beings. Of the gods, the mighty Indra and Brahmā Sahāṃpati were present, along with a great many hundreds of thousands of other sons of the gods.

2. At that time, the Blessed One addressed the Venerable Śāriputra: "To the west, Śāriputra, there is a buddha-field, a world system, named Sukhāvatī which lies beyond countless hundreds of thousands of other buddha-fields. At the present time, a tathāgata, an arhat, a perfectly awakened buddha named Amitāyus dwells[136] there, teaching the Dharma. Why do you think, Śāriputra, that world system is called 'Sukhāvatī', the 'Realm of Happiness'? In that world system, Śāriputra,

in Sukhāvatī, living beings experience no physical or mental suffering, and there are endless causes of happiness. This is why that world system is called 'Sukhāvatī', the 'Realm of Happiness'.

3. "Moreover, Śāriputra, that world system of Sukhāvatī is adorned with seven railings, and seven rows of palm trees with nets of small bells. There are four kinds of beautiful, brightly coloured precious substances scattered all around: gold, silver, lapis lazuli, and quartz. That buddha-field, Śāriputra, is adorned with this abundance of wonderful qualities.

4. "Moreover, Śāriputra, in that world system of Sukhāvatī there are lotus ponds made of[137] seven kinds of precious substances: gold, silver, lapis lazuli, quartz, ruby, emerald, and coral. They are completely filled to the very brim with water which possesses eight good qualities, so full that a crow could drink from them, and the bottom of these ponds is evenly covered with golden sand.

"There are four beautiful, brightly coloured staircases leading down to each of these lotus ponds from the four cardinal directions. These staircases are made of four kinds of precious substances: gold, silver, lapis lazuli, and quartz. The lotus ponds are surrounded by beautiful, brightly coloured trees made of seven kinds of precious substances: gold, silver, lapis lazuli, quartz, ruby, emerald, and coral. Dark blue lotuses grow in these lotus ponds, lotuses dark blue in colour, of dark blue hue, dark blue in appearance. Yellow lotuses grow there, yellow in colour, of yellow hue, yellow in appearance. Red lotuses grow there, red in colour, of red hue, red in appearance. Pure white lotuses grow there, pure white in colour, of pure white hue, pure white in appearance. Many-coloured lotuses grow there, of many colours, of many hues, many-coloured in appearance. These lotuses are as big as cartwheels. That buddha-field, Śāriputra, is adorned with this abundance of wonderful qualities.

5. "Moreover, Śāriputra, in that buddha-field, there are divine musical instruments which are played constantly. The ground is a delightful golden colour. There, in that buddha-field, showers of divine māndārava flowers rain down three times each night and three times each day. In the time it takes to eat a single meal, the living beings who are born there travel to other world systems and honour countless hundreds of thousands of buddhas. When they have each showered a tathāgata with rains of countless hundreds of thousands of flowers, they return to their own world system to rest. That buddha-field, Śāriputra, is adorned with this abundance of wonderful qualities.

6. "Moreover, Śāriputra, in that buddha-field there are *haṃsa*-geese, curlews, and peacocks. Three times each night and three times each day, they fly down and sing together in harmony, each one with their own unique voice. When they sing, their voices proclaim the five spiritual faculties, the five spiritual powers, and the seven factors of Awakening. When they hear the song of the peacocks, the minds of the living beings who dwell there become absorbed by the Buddha, absorbed by the Dharma, absorbed by the Sangha. Do you think, Śāriputra, that there are living beings there who have come from the wombs of animals? You should not entertain such a thought. Why is this? It is because, Śāriputra, in a buddha-field, even the names of the hells, of animals, and of the world governed by Yama do not exist. The flocks of birds which sing songs of the Dharma are manifested by the Tathāgata Amitāyus. That buddha-field, Śāriputra, is adorned with this abundance of wonderful qualities.

7. "Moreover, Śariputra, in that buddha-field, when the wind stirs the rows of palm trees and the nets of small bells which adorn them, they make a delightful sound which soothes the mind. Śāriputra, the countless hundreds of thousands of divine musical instruments make a delightful sound which soothes the mind when they are played, and so too do the rows of palm trees and the nets of small bells when the wind stirs them. When the people there hear those sounds, they recollect the Buddha in their bodies, they recollect the Dharma in their bodies, they recollect the Sangha in their bodies. That buddha-field, Śāriputra, is adorned with this abundance of wonderful qualities.

8. "Śāriputra, why do you think that tathāgata is known as 'Amitāyus', 'Infinite Life'? Well, Śāriputra, the lifespan of that tathāgata and of the people who dwell in his buddha-field is unlimited. This is why that tathāgata is known as 'Amitāyus', 'Infinite Life'. That tathāgata attained unsurpassed perfect Awakening ten aeons ago.

9. "Śāriputra, why do you think that tathāgata is known as 'Amitābha', 'Infinite Light'? Well, Śāriputra, the light which radiates from that tathāgata shines unobstructed in all buddha-fields. This is why that tathāgata is known as 'Amitābha', 'Infinite Light'. That tathāgata has an immeasurably large sangha of śrāvakas who are pure arhats, whose numbers cannot easily be measured. That buddha-field, Śāriputra, is adorned with this abundance of wonderful qualities.

10. "Moreover, Śāriputra, the progress of those living beings who are born in the buddha-field of the Tathāgata Amitāyus as pure bodhisattvas will be irreversible, and they will only experience one more birth. The numbers of these bodhisattvas, Śāriputra, cannot easily be measured. It can only be said that there is an immeasurably large innumerable multitude of them. Living beings, Śāriputra, should cultivate a heartfelt desire for that buddha-field. Why should they do this? They should do this because, in that buddha-field, they will be in the company of good people such as these bodhisattvas.

"Śāriputra, living beings with only a few roots of virtue will not be born in the buddha-field of the Tathāgata Amitāyus. If a child of good family hears the name of the Blessed One, the Tathāgata Amitāyus, and if their minds become absorbed by it – for one night, two nights, three nights, four nights, five nights, six nights, or seven nights – if their minds become undistractedly absorbed by it, then when they die the Tathāgata Amitāyus, surrounded by his sangha of śrāvakas and accompanied by his assembly of bodhisattvas, will appear before them, and they will die with an undistorted mind. When they die, they will be born in the buddha-field of the Tathāgata Amitāyus, in the world system of Sukhāvatī. Therefore Śāriputra, it is with this purpose in view that I say that a child of good family should single-mindedly cultivate a heartfelt desire for that buddha-field in their minds.

11. "Just as I praise Sukhāvatī, Śāriputra, so too, to the east, as many buddhas, as many blessed ones as there are grains of sand in the River Ganges praise their buddha-fields. Led by the Tathāgata Akṣobhya, 'Unshakable', the Tathāgata Merudhvaja, 'He Whose Banner Is Like Mount Meru', the Tathāgata Mahāmeru, 'Great Mount Meru', the Tathāgata Meruprabhāsa, 'He Whose Splendour Is Like That of Mount Meru', and the Tathāgata Mañjudhvaja, 'He Whose Banner Is Gentleness', they each cover their own buddha-field with their tongue, and then describe it. You should trust in this discourse on the Dharma called 'Embraced by all the buddhas', which praises inconceivable good qualities.

12. "In the same way, to the south, as many buddhas, as many blessed ones as there are grains of sand in the River Ganges praise their buddha-fields. Led by the Tathāgata Candrasūryapradīpa, 'The Luminescence of the Sun and the Moon', the Tathāgata Yaśaḥprabha, 'Glorious Radiance', the Tathāgata Mahārciḥskandha, 'Great Mass of Flames', the Tathāgata Merupradīpa, 'The Luminescence of Mount Meru', and the Tathāgata

Anantavīrya, 'Limitless Energy', they each cover their own buddha-field with their tongue, and then describe it. You should trust in this discourse on the Dharma called 'Embraced by all the buddhas', which praises inconceivable good qualities.

13. "In the same way, to the west, as many buddhas, as many blessed ones as there are grains of sand in the River Ganges praise their buddha-fields. Led by the Tathāgata Amitāyus, 'Infinite Life', the Tathāgata Amitaskandha, 'Infinite Mass', the Tathāgata Amitadhvaja, 'Infinite Banner', the Tathāgata Mahāprabha, 'Great Radiance', the Tathāgata Mahāratnaketu, 'Great Brilliance Like That of Precious Substances', and the Tathāgata Śuddharaśmiprabha, 'Radiance of Pure Rays of Light', they each cover their own buddha-field with their tongue, and then describe it. You should trust in this discourse on the Dharma called 'Embraced by all the buddhas', which praises inconceivable good qualities.

14. "In the same way, to the north, as many buddhas, as many blessed ones as there are grains of sand in the River Ganges praise their buddha-fields. Led by the Tathāgata Mahārciḥskandha, 'Great Mass of Flames', the Tathāgata Vaiśvānaranirghoṣa, 'He Whose Voice Is Heard Everywhere', the Tathāgata Dundubhisvaranirghoṣa, 'He Whose Voice Is Like the Beating of a Drum', the Tathāgata Duṣpradharṣa, 'Unassailable', the Tathāgata Ādityasaṃbhava, 'Born of the Sun', the Tathāgata Jaleniprabha, 'He Whose Radiance Is Like the Ocean', and the Tathāgata Prabhākara, 'He Who Sheds His Radiance', they each cover their own buddha-field with their tongue, and then describe it. You should trust in this discourse on the Dharma called 'Embraced by all the buddhas', which praises inconceivable good qualities.

15. "In the same way, below, as many buddhas, as many blessed ones as there are grains of sand in the River Ganges praise their buddha-fields. Led by the Tathāgata Siṃha, 'Lion', the Tathāgata Yaśas, 'Glorious', the Tathāgata Yaśaḥprabhāsa, 'Glorious Splendour', the Tathāgata Dharma, the Tathāgata Dharmadhara, 'The Bearer of the Dharma', and the Tathāgata Dharmadhvaja, 'He Whose Banner Is the Dharma', they each cover their own buddha-field with their tongue, and then describe it. You should trust in this discourse on the Dharma called 'Embraced by all the buddhas', which praises inconceivable good qualities.

16. "In the same way, above, as many buddhas, as many blessed ones as there are grains of sand in the River Ganges praise their buddha-fields. Led by the Tathāgata Brahmaghoṣa, 'He Whose Voice Is Like

that of Brahmā', the Tathāgata Nakṣatrarāja, 'Star King', the Tathāgata Indraketudhvajarāja, 'The King Whose Banner Is Like the Brilliance of Indra', the Tathāgata Gandhottama, 'Supreme Fragrance', the Tathāgata Gandhaprabhāsa, 'Fragrant Splendour', the Tathāgata Mahārciskandha, 'Great Mass of Flames', the Tathāgata Ratnakusumasaṃpuṣpitagātra, 'He Whose Limbs Are Adorned with Blossoms Made of Precious Substances', the Tathāgata Ratnotpalaśrī, 'He Whose Glory Is Like That of Blue Lotuses Made of Precious Substances', the Tathāgata Sarvārthadarśī, 'He Who Sees All Goals', and the Tathāgata Sumerukalpa, 'He Who Resembles Mount Meru', they each cover their own buddha-field with their tongue, and then describe it. You should trust in this discourse on the Dharma called 'Embraced by all the buddhas', which praises inconceivable good qualities.

17. "Śāriputra, why do you think that this discourse on the Dharma is called 'Embraced by all the buddhas'? Those children of good family, Śāriputra, who hear the title of this discourse on the Dharma and who bear in mind the names of those buddhas, those blessed ones which it mentions, will all be embraced by the buddhas, and their progress towards unsurpassed, perfect Awakening will become irreversible. Therefore, Śāriputra, you should have faith in me and in these other buddhas, these other blessed ones. Trust in us. Do not doubt us. The progress towards unsurpassed, perfect Awakening of those children of good family who cultivate a heartfelt desire for the buddha-field of the Blessed One, the Tathāgata Amitāyus, in their minds, the progress of all of those who have done so, and the progress of all of those who will do so, will become irreversible. They either will be born, have been born, or are being born in that buddha-field. Therefore, Śāriputra, children of good family who possess faith should cultivate a heartfelt desire for that buddha-field.

18. "Śāriputra, just as I praise the inconceivable good qualities of those buddhas, those blessed ones, so too Śāriputra, those buddhas, those blessed ones praise my inconceivable good qualities. 'The Blessed One Śākyamuni, the king of the Śākyans, has done something which is very difficult to do. In the world system called Earth, he has attained unsurpassed perfect Awakening, and taught the Dharma to the whole of that unreceptive world, in a degenerate age, to degenerate beings with degenerate views, degenerate lifespans, and degenerate defilements.'

19. "I have done something which is extremely difficult to do, Śāriputra. In the world system called Earth, I have attained unsurpassed perfect

Awakening, and taught the Dharma to the whole of this unreceptive world, in a degenerate age, to degenerate beings with degenerate views, degenerate lifespans, and degenerate defilements."

20. This is what the Blessed One said. Their hearts filled with joy, the Venerable Śāriputra, the monks and bodhisattvas, along with the gods, human beings, titans, and gandharvas, rejoiced at what the Blessed One had said.

This is the Mahāyāna sūtra called *The Shorter Sūtra on the Abundance of Wonderful Qualities Which Adorn Sukhāvatī.*

The Longer Sūtra on the Abundance of Wonderful Qualities Which Adorn Sukhāvatī

Sukhāvatīvyūhaḥ (Vistaramātṛkā)
सुखावतीव्यूहः (वसि्तरमातृका)

Translated from Sanskrit by Dharmacārī Śraddhāpa

Oṃ. Homage to the Three Jewels.

Oṃ. Homage to all the glorious buddhas and bodhisattvas!

Homage to all the buddhas, bodhisattvas, noble ones, śrāvakas, and pratyekabuddhas who have dwelt, will dwell, or are currently dwelling in innumerable, countless world systems in the ten directions of space.

Homage to Amitābha. Homage to you, who possess inconceivable good qualities.

1. This is what I have heard. Once, the Blessed One was staying in Rājagṛha, on Vultures' Peak, with a great sangha of 32,000 monks.

2. These monks were all arhats who had rid themselves of the corruptions and who were free of the defilements. They had lived the Dharma life, and freed their minds by means of perfect understanding. They had thoroughly investigated their minds, and destroyed the bonds that tied them to cyclic existence. They had attained their goal, and emerged victorious. They had attained supreme self-mastery. Their minds were free, and they possessed the wisdom that comes with such freedom. They were like great elephants. They had attained the six higher forms of knowledge, and become powerful. They were absorbed in the eight kinds of liberation, and had attained the five spiritual powers. They were known to have attained the higher forms of knowledge, and they were all elders, great śrāvakas.

3. Among these monks were Ājñāta-Kauṇḍinya, Aśvajit, Bāṣpa, Mahānāman, Bhadrajit, Yaśodeva, Vimala, Subāhu, Pūrṇa son of Maitrāyaṇī, Urubilvā-Kāśyapa, Nadī-Kāśyapa, Gayā-Kāśyapa, Kumāra-Kāśyapa, Mahākāśyapa, Śāriputra, Mahāmaudgalyāyana, Mahākauṣṭhilya, Mahākaphila, Mahācunda, Aniruddha, Nandika, Kampila, Subhūti, Revata, Khadiravanika, Vakula, Svāgata, Amogharāja, Pārāyaṇika, Panthaka, Cullapanthaka, Nanda, Rāhula, and the Venerable Ānanda. All of these monks, and the others who were with him, were distinguished elders, great śrāvakas who were known to have attained the higher forms of knowledge, with the exception of one person – the Venerable Ānanda, who had not yet completed his training.

4. A great many bodhisattvas, great beings, led by the Bodhisattva Maitreya, were also there with the Blessed One.

5. The Venerable Ānanda rose from his seat, put his upper robe over one shoulder, placed his right knee on the ground, bowed to the Blessed One with folded hands, and said, "Your faculties, Blessed One, are bright and tranquil. Your skin is perfectly pure in colour, and your face shines with the colour of unadulterated gold. A cloud in the autumn sun shines a perfectly pure shade of yellow, the colour of unadulterated gold, and in the same way, Blessed One, your faculties are bright and tranquil, your face is perfectly pure in colour, and your skin shines with the colour of unadulterated gold. Blessed One, a flawless piece of jewellery made of gold from the Jambū River, and wrought in a furnace by a skilled craftsman or his apprentice, shines with the perfectly pure colour of unadulterated gold when it is placed upon a pale-coloured piece of cloth, and in the same way, Blessed One, your faculties are bright and tranquil, your face is perfectly pure in colour, and your skin shines with the colour of unadulterated gold.

6. "I cannot remember ever having seen the Blessed One like this before, with his tathāgatha faculties so bright and tranquil, his face perfectly pure in colour, and his skin shining with the colour of pure gold. The thought occurs to me, Blessed One, 'Today the Tathāgata truly dwells in the abode of the buddhas, the abode of the victorious ones, the abode of the all-knowing ones. Today the Tathāgata truly dwells in the abode of the great nāgas. He brings to mind the tathāgatas, the arhats, the perfectly awakened buddhas of the past, the present, and the future.'"

7. The Blessed One then said this to the Venerable Ānanda, "Excellent, Ānanda, excellent. Did the gods tell you the meaning of this, or was it

the buddhas, the blessed ones? Did you come to this understanding on the basis of your own reflections?"

8. The Venerable Ānanda replied, "The gods did not tell me the meaning of this, nor did the buddhas, the blessed ones. It was on the basis of my own reflections that the thought occured to me, 'Today the Tathāgata dwells in the abode of the buddhas. Today the Tathāgata truly dwells in the abode of the victorious ones, the abode of the all-knowing ones. He brings to mind the tathāgatas, the arhats, the perfectly awakened buddhas of the past, the present, and the future.'"

9. The Blessed One then said this to the Venerable Ānanda, "Excellent, Ānanda, excellent. You choose the best possible starting-point, and go on to reflect in just the right way, with great presence of mind. By thinking to ask the Tathāgata about this matter, Ānanda, you have acted in a way that will be of benefit to many people. It will bring happiness to many people. You have acted out of empathy for the world, for the sake of a great many people, in a way that will be of benefit to gods and human beings, and that will bring them happiness.

10. "Even if the Tathāgata were to cause knowledge and vision to arise in innumerable, uncountable blessed ones, tathāgatas, arhats, perfectly awakened buddhas, Ānanda, his own knowledge would not be diminished. Why is this? Ānanda, it is because the causes of the knowledge and vision of the Tathāgata are indestructible.

11. "Have no doubt, Ānanda, that the Tathāgata could live on a single bowl of alms for a whole aeon, for a hundred aeons, a hundred thousand aeons, a great many countless hundreds of thousands of aeons, or even longer, and the Tathāgata's faculties would not fade away. The colour of his face would be unaffected, and the colour of his skin would be undiminished. Why is this the case? Ānanda, it is because the perfection that the Tathāgata has attained is dependent on his samādhi.

12. "It is extremely rare, Ānanda, for a perfectly awakened buddha to appear in the world. Just as it is extremely rare for an udumbara flower to appear in the world, Ānanda, it is extremely rare for a tathāgata to appear in the world – a tathāgata who wants to help others and who strives to benefit others, one who is filled with empathy and who acts out of great compassion.

13. "Furthermore, Ānanda, it could only have been because of a tathāgata that you thought to ask the Tathāgata about this matter for the sake

of the bodhisattvas, the great beings, and in order that teachers might appear in the world for all of the living beings in it.

14. "So listen well, Ānanda. Listen carefully and allow your mind to become absorbed by what I am about to say to you." "Yes, Blessed One," replied Ānanda.

15. The Blessed One then said this to the Venerable Ānanda: "In the past, Ānanda, long ago, inconceivably many, innumerable, countless aeons upon countless aeons ago, a tathāgata, an arhat, a perfectly awakened buddha by the name of Dīpaṃkara, 'Bearer of Luminescence', arose in the world.

16. "Before Dīpaṃkara, Ānanda, long before, there was a tathāgata named Pratāpavat, 'Majestic'. Before him, long before, there was a tathāgata named Prabhākara, 'Bearer of Radiance'. Before him, long before, there was a tathāgata named Candanagandha, 'Fragrance of Sandalwood'. Before him, long before, there was a tathāgata named Sumerukalpa, 'He Who Is the Equal of Mount Sumeru'. Before him were Candana, 'Sandalwood';[138] Vimalānana, 'He Whose Face Is Pure'; Anupalipta, 'Undefiled'; Vimalaprabha, 'He Whose Radiance Is Pure'; Nāgābhibhū, 'He Who Is Supreme among the Nāgas'; Sūryodana, 'He Who Is Like the Rising Sun'; Girirājaghoṣa, 'He Whose Voice Is Like the King of Mountains'; Merukūṭa, 'He Who Is Like the Peak of Mount Meru'; Suvarṇaprabha, 'Golden Radiance'; Jyotiṣprabha, 'Brilliant Radiance'; Vaiḍūryanirbhāsa, 'He Who Is Like Lapis Lazuli in Appearance'; Brahmaghoṣa, 'He Whose Voice Is Like That of Brahmā'; Candrābhibhū, 'He Who Is Supreme Like the Moon'; Tūryaghoṣa, 'He Whose Voice Is Like a Musical Instrument'; Muktakusumapratimaṇḍitaprabha, 'He Whose Radiance Is Adorned with Falling Blossoms'; Śrīkūṭa, 'Glorious Mountain Peak'; Sāgaravarabuddhivikrīḍitābhijña, 'He Who Playfully Attains the Higher Forms of Knowledge with an Intellect Greater Than the Ocean'; Varaprabha, 'Peerless Radiance'; Mahāgandharājanirbhāsa, 'He Who Is Like the Great King of Fragrances'; Vyapagatakhilamalapratighoṣa, 'He Whose Speech is Free of the Impurity of Harshness'; Śūrakūṭa, 'Excellent Hero'; Raṇaṃjaha, 'He Who Has Abandoned the Delights of the Senses'; Mahāguṇadharabuddhiprāptābhijña, 'He Who by Means of the Higher Forms of Knowledge Has Attained an Intellect Endowed with Great Qualities'; Candrasūryajihmīkaraṇa, 'He Who Outshines the Sun and the Moon'; Uttaptavaiḍūryanirbhāsa, 'He Who Is Like Completely Pure Lapis Lazuli in Appearance'; Cittadhārābuddhisaṃkusumitābhyudgata, 'He Who Has Attained the Full Blossoming of the Flow of Thoughts

and of the Intellect'; Puṣpāvatīvanarājasaṃkusumitābhijña, 'King of Flower Gardens in Whom the Higher Forms of Knowledge Have Fully Blossomed'; Puṣpākara, 'Bearer of Flowers'; Udakacandra, 'He Who Is Like the Reflection of the Moon in Water'; Avidyāndhakāravidhvaṃsanakara, 'He Who Destroys the Darkness of Ignorance'; Lokendra, 'Lord of the World'; Muktacchatrapravātasadṛśa, 'He Who Is Like an Open Parasol in the Wind'; Tiṣya, 'Auspicious'; Dharmamativinanditarāja, 'King Who Takes Great Delight in Understanding the Dharma'; Siṃhasāgarakūṭavinanditarāja, 'King Who Takes Great Delight in the Most Excellent Lion of All'; Sāgaramerucandra, 'Moon of Mount Meru of the Ocean'; Brahmasvaranādābhinandita, 'He Who Takes Delight in the Sound of the Voice of Brahmā'; Kusumasaṃbhava, 'Blossom-Born'; Prāptasena, 'He Who Has Planted His Spear'; Candrabhānu, 'Moonbeam'; Merukūṭa, 'He Who Is Like the Peak of Mount Meru';[139] Candraprabha, 'Radiance of the Moon'; Vimalanetra, 'Guide Who Is Free of Impurities'; Girirājaghoṣeśvara,[140] 'The Lord Whose Voice Is Like the King of Mountains'; Kusumaprabha, 'Blossom-Radiance'; Kusumavṛṣṭyabhiprakīrṇa, 'He Who Scatters Showers of Blossoms'; Ratnacandra, 'Precious Moon'; Padmabimbyupaśobhita, 'He Who Is Adorned with the Golden Colour of Lotuses'; Candanagandha, 'Fragrance of Sandalwood';[141] Ratnanirbhāsa,[142] 'He Whose Appearance Is Like That of Precious Substances'; Nimi, 'Thunderbolt'; Mahāvyūha, 'Great Abundance'; Vyapagatakhiladoṣa, 'He Who Is Free of the Fault of Harshness'; Brahmaghoṣa, 'He Whose Voice Is Like That of Brahmā'; Saptaratnābhivṛṣṭa, 'He Who Is Covered in the Seven Kinds of Precious Substances'; Mahāguṇadhara, 'He Who Possesses Great Qualities'; Mahātamālapatracandanakardama, 'Great Fragrance of Sour Mangosteen Leaves, Sandalwood, and Jasmine';[143] Kusumābhijña,[144] 'He Whose Higher Forms of Knowledge Are Like Blossoms'; Ajñānavidhvaṃsana, 'He Who Destroys Lack of Knowledge'; Kesarin, 'Golden'; Muktacchatra, 'Open Parasol'; Suvarṇagarbha, 'He Whose Essence Is Gold'; Vaiḍūryagarbha, 'He Whose Essence Is Lapis Lazuli'; Mahāketu, 'Great Brilliance'; Dharmaketu, 'Brilliance of the Dharma'; Ratnaketu, 'Brilliance of Precious Substances'; Ratnaśrī, 'Glory of Precious Substances'; Lokendra,[145] 'Lord of the World'; Narendra, 'Lord of Men'; Kāruṇika, 'Compassionate One'; Lokasundara, 'He Who Is Thought Beautiful by All'; Brahmaketu, 'Brilliance of Brahmā'; Dharmamati,[146] 'He Who Understands the Dharma'; Siṃha, 'Lion'; and Siṃhamati, 'Mind of a Lion'.

17. "Before Siṃhamati, Ānanda, long before, a tathāgata, an arhat, a perfectly awakened buddha named Lokeśvararāja, 'Sovereign King

of the World', appeared in the world. He was perfect in wisdom and conduct, a sugata. He was a knower of the world, an unsurpassable guide for those who wished to train, a teacher of gods and human beings, awakened, and blessed.

18. "Moreover, Ānanda, at the time of the tathāgata, the arhat, the perfectly awakened buddha Lokeśvararāja, there was a monk called Dharmākara who was supremely mindful, intelligent, knowledgeable, wise, supremely energetic, and totally committed.

19. "Ānanda, that monk Dharmākara rose from his seat, put his upper robe over one shoulder, placed his right knee on the ground, and bowed to the Blessed One Lokeśvararāja with folded hands. When he had paid homage to the Blessed One, he stood facing him and spoke these verses:

(1) "'Your radiance is infinite, your intellect limitless and incomparable.
There is no other radiance which can illuminate this world.
Nothing in the whole world shines like you do.
Neither the sun, jewels, a great snowy peak, nor the light of the moon can compare.

(2) "'The body of the best of living beings is limitless,
just as the sound of the Buddha's voice is limitless.
There is no one in this world who can compare to you
in ethical conduct, samadhi, wisdom, or energy.

(3) "'The inconceivable, peerless Buddha is like the ocean.
He has attained the profound, vast, subtle Dharma.
The Teacher, though, does not let this make him arrogant.
He has left harshness and hatred behind him, from now until the end of time.

(4) "'The King of Kings, with all the powers of a buddha,
whose splendour is boundless, sheds his light in all directions.
May I become a buddha like him, a lord of the Dharma,
and bring emancipation from old age, death, and birth.

(5) "'May I possess supreme, excellent generosity, calm concentration,
ethical conduct, patient acceptance, energy, meditation, and samadhi.
I now undertake this commitment:
I will become a buddha, and protect all living beings.

(6) "'Striving for Awakening, which is the greatest blessing,
I will worship a great many countless hundreds of thousands of buddhas,
incomparable protectors as innumerable as the grains of sand in the River Ganges,
wherever they may be.

(7) "'My radiance will shine throughout as many world systems as there are
grains of sand in the River Ganges, and throughout the buddha-fields they contain,
which are even more numerous, without end.
This is how I will apply my energy.

(8) "'My buddha-field will be exalted, unsurpassed, supreme.
In that perfectly formed world, everything will be superior.
The happiness of the realm of nirvana is beyond compare.
I will cleanse that buddha-field of impurity.

(9) "'Living beings will gather there from all of the ten directions of space,
and when they come they will soon achieve happiness.
With the Buddha as the witness to my practice,
I will cultivate an aspiration which is filled with the power of truth and energy.

(10) "'May the knowers of the world in the ten directions of space,
whose knowledge is free from attachment, always cause this thought to arise in me.
Then, even if I end up in the Avīci Hell,
the power of my resolution will be unstoppable.'"

20. "Then, Ānanda, when that monk, Dharmākara, had stood facing the Blessed One, the Tathāgata Lokeśvararāja, and spoken these verses, he said this, 'Blessed One, I long to attain unsurpassed, perfect Awakening. Time and time again, I have cultivated and developed a mind set on unsurpassed, perfect Awakening. May the Blessed One, the Teacher, teach me the Dharma, so that I may soon attain unsurpassed, perfect Awakening and become a tathāgata in the world, an equal of the unequalled. May the Blessed One explain to me those features which are necessary for me to bring into being a buddha-field with an abundance of wonderful qualities.'

21. "The Blessed One, the Tathāgata Lokeśvararāja, then said to the monk, 'Then, monk, you should bring into being a buddha-field which is adorned with an abundance of wonderful qualities.'

"He replied, 'I am not capable of this, Blessed One. Only the Blessed One is capable of this. Tell me about the abundance of wonderful qualities which adorn the buddha-fields of other tathāgatas so that I can fill my own buddha-field with all of those features.'

22. "Then, Ānanda, when the Tathāgata, the Arhat, the Perfectly Awakened Buddha Lokeśvararāja had understood that monk's intentions, he spent ten million years giving explanations and descriptions of the features of the buddha-fields of eighty-one quadrillion buddhas, and the abundance of wonderful qualities which adorned them. He spoke out of a desire to help others, in an effort to benefit others, filled with empathy, in order to cultivate empathy, in order that buddha-fields might come into being, and out of great compassion for living beings.

23. "The lifespan of that blessed one, that tathāgata, was forty aeons.

24. "Then, Ānanda, that monk, Dharmākara, gathered all of the abundant wonderful qualities which adorned the buddha-fields of those eighty-one quadrillion buddhas into a single buddha-field. He touched his head to the feet of the Blessed One, the Tathāgata Lokeśvararāja, in worship, circumambulated him keeping him to his right, and then took his leave of him.

25. "For more than five aeons, he gathered a supreme, unparalleled abundance of wonderful qualities to adorn his buddha-field, an abundance of qualities such as had never before been brought together in one place anywhere in the ten directions of the universe. He then took the supreme vow.

26. "In this way, Ānanda, that monk brought into being a buddha-field which was eighty-one times more supreme, unparalleled, and immeasurable than the eighty-one quadrillion buddha-fields the Blessed One, the Tathāgata Lokeśvararāja, had described to him. He then approached the Tathāgata, touched his head to the feet of the Blessed One in worship, and said, 'Blessed One, I have managed to bring into being a buddha-field adorned with an abundance of wonderful qualities.'

27. "The Tathāgata Lokeśvararāja, Ānanda, replied, 'The Tathāgata would be glad to hear you speak, monk. Gladden those who are assembled

here. Inspire them. Roar a lion's roar which will lead bodhisattvas, great beings, now and in the future, to vow to create buddha-fields with qualities like yours when they hear it.'

28. "Then, Ānanda, the monk Dharmākara said to the Blessed One, 'Then hear me, Blessed One. When I attain unsurpassed, perfect Awakening, my buddha-field will be adorned with an abundance of wonderful qualities, just as I will describe it in my own unique vows.

(1) "'Blessed One, may I not attain unsurpassed, perfect Awakening if, when I have attained Awakening, there are any hells in my buddha-field, anyone is born there as an animal, there is a realm of hungry ghosts there, or anyone is born there as a titan.

(2) "'Blessed One, may I not attain unsurpassed, perfect Awakening if, when I have attained Awakening, any of the living beings who are born in my buddha-field die and are reborn in hell, as animals, in the realm of hungry ghosts, or as titans.

(3) "'Blessed One, may I not attain unsurpassed, perfect Awakening if, when I have attained Awakening, any of the living beings who are born in my buddha-field are not of a single colour, the colour of gold.

(4) "'Blessed One, may I not attain unsurpassed, perfect Awakening if, when I have attained Awakening, any distinction is made between gods and human beings in my buddha-field, other than for practical, conventional purposes such as saying, "These are gods, and these are human beings" in order to make a tally of their numbers.

(5) "'Blessed One, may I not attain unsurpassed, perfect Awakening unless, when I have attained Awakening, all of the living beings who are born in my buddha-field attain completely perfect mastery of supernormal abilities, such that they are able to traverse countless hundreds of thousands of millions of buddha-fields in a fraction of a second.

(6) "'Blessed One, may I not attain unsurpassed, perfect Awakening unless, when I have attained Awakening, all of the living beings who are born in my buddha-field are able to remember their previous lives, countless hundreds of thousands of millions of aeons into the past.

(7) "'Blessed One, may I not attain unsurpassed, perfect Awakening unless, when I have attained Awakening, all of the living beings who are born in my buddha-field acquire the divine eye, such that they are able to see countless hundreds of thousands of millions of world systems.

(8) "'Blessed One, may I not attain unsurpassed, perfect Awakening unless, when I have attained Awakening, all of the living beings who are born in my buddha-field acquire the divine ear, such that they are able to hear the true Dharma in countless hundreds of thousands of millions of buddha-fields simultaneously.

(9) "'Blessed One, may I not attain unsurpassed, perfect Awakening unless, when I have attained Awakening, all of the living beings who are born in my buddha-field have the ability to know the thoughts of others, such that they are able to know the mental activity of living beings dwelling in countless hundreds of thousands of millions of buddha-fields.

(10) "'Blessed One, may I not attain unsurpassed, perfect Awakening if, when I have attained Awakening, any of the living beings who are born in my buddha-field conceive any notion of ownership, even of their own bodies.

(11) "'Blessed One, may I not attain unsurpassed, perfect Awakening if, when I have attained Awakening, there are any living beings born in my buddha-field who are not firmly established in perfection, and remain so until they attain supreme, complete nirvana.

(12) "'Blessed One, may I not attain unsurpassed, perfect Awakening if, when I have attained Awakening, any living being is able to count the number of śrāvakas in my buddha-field who have attained unsurpassed, perfect Awakening. May this apply even if all the living beings dwelling in the threefold thousand great thousand worlds were to become pratyekabuddhas, and combine their efforts to count the number of such śrāvakas.

(13) "'Blessed One, may I not attain unsurpassed, perfect Awakening if, when I have attained Awakening, it is possible to measure the extent of my radiance as it shines forth from

my buddha-field, even by saying that it extends throughout countless hundreds of thousands of millions of buddha-fields.

(14) "'Blessed One, may I not attain unsurpassed, perfect Awakening if, when I have attained Awakening, it is possible to measure the extent of the lifespan of the living beings in my buddha-field, except in a case where a living being has chosen to shorten their lifespan as part of their vow.

(15) "'Blessed One, may I not attain unsurpassed, perfect Awakening if, when I have attained Awakening, there is any limit to the extent of my lifespan, even if it were to be limited to countless multitudes of hundreds of thousands of millions of aeons.

(16) "'Blessed One, may I not attain unsurpassed, perfect Awakening if, when I have attained Awakening, any of the living beings in my buddha-field even hear the word "unskilful".

(17) "'Blessed One, may I not attain unsurpassed, perfect Awakening unless, when I have attained Awakening, innumerable, uncountable buddhas, blessed ones, in uncountable buddha-fields praise my name, celebrate it, proclaim its glory, and exalt it.

(18) "'Blessed One, may I not attain unsurpassed, perfect Awakening unless, when I have attained Awakening, I appear at the moment of death to any living being in any world system who has set their mind on unsurpassed, perfect Awakening, who has heard my name, and who recollects me with a clear mind – appearing before them surrounded and accompanied by a sangha of monks, so that they can compose their minds.

(19) "'Blessed One, may I not attain unsurpassed, perfect Awakening unless, when I have attained Awakening, living beings in innumerable, uncountable buddha-fields who have heard my name, who are intent on my buddha-field, and who dedicate their roots of virtue to being born there – even those who have only cultivated this thought ten times – are reborn there. This is with the exception of those who have committed the five acts which have immediate consequences, or whose opposition to the true Dharma obstructs them from being born there.[147]

(20) "'Blessed One, may I not attain unsurpassed, perfect Awakening unless, when I have attained Awakening, those living beings who are reborn in my buddha-field only experience one more birth before attaining unsurpassed, perfect Awakening. This is with the exception of those bodhisattvas, those great beings, who have taken the supreme vow, who clad themselves in mighty armour, who are awake to the needs of the whole world, who are devoted to the whole world, who are devoted to the attainment of complete nirvana by the whole world, who long to practise the path of the bodhisattva in all world systems, who long to meet all the buddhas, who establish as many living beings as there are grains of sand in the River Ganges in unsurpassed, perfect Awakening, who are committed to the highest practice, and who have perfected the practice of bringing benefit to all.

(21) "'Blessed One, may I not attain unsurpassed, perfect Awakening unless, when I have attained Awakening, the bodhisattvas who are born in my buddha-field are all able to travel to other buddha-fields in the time it takes to eat a single meal and worship many hundreds of buddhas, many thousands of buddhas, many hundreds of thousands of buddhas, countless buddhas, a great many countless hundreds of thousands of buddhas, and experience their glory, which is the foundation of all happiness.

(22) "'Blessed One, may I not attain unsurpassed, perfect Awakening unless, when I have attained Awakening, the bodhisattvas in my buddha-field are able to plant any kinds of roots of virtue they wish, which come into being the moment the wish arises – roots of gold, silver, jewels, pearl, lapis lazuli, seashells, crystal, coral, quartz, sapphire, ruby, emerald, or any other kind of precious substance whatsoever, roots of any kinds of incense, flowers, garlands, ointments, perfumes, powdered sandalwood, robes, parasols, banners, flags, lamps, or any kind of music, dance, or song.

(23) "'Blessed One, may I not attain unsurpassed, perfect Awakening unless, when I have attained Awakening, all of the living beings who are born in my buddha-field are able to talk about the Dharma with complete understanding.

(24) "'Blessed One, may I not attain unsurpassed, perfect Awakening unless, when I have attained Awakening, the bodhisattvas in my buddha-field who think, "We should stay in this very world system and honour, revere, venerate, and worship the buddhas, the blessed ones, in innumerable, uncountable buddha-fields, making offerings of robes, almsfood, beds, seats, medicine, and utensils, as well as flowers, perfumes, lamps, incense, garlands, ointments, sandalwood powder, robes, parasols, banners, flags, all kinds of music, dance, and song, and showers of jewels" are immediately embraced by the buddhas, the blessed ones, out of empathy.

(25) "'Blessed One, may I not attain unsurpassed, perfect Awakening unless, when I have attained Awakening, the bodhisattvas who are born in my buddha-field attain the vajra-body and the vajra-strength of Nārāyaṇa.

(26) "'Blessed One, may I not attain unsurpassed, perfect Awakening if, when I have attained Awakening, any living being in my buddha-field is able to fully grasp the appearance of its adornments, even by means of the divine eye, such that they are able to perceive various different kinds of appearance and say, "This buddha-field has this kind of magnificent appearance."

(27) "'Blessed One, may I not attain unsurpassed, perfect Awakening unless, when I have attained Awakening, any bodhisattva in my buddha-field – even one who only possesses limited roots of virtue – is able to perceive the bodhi tree there rising a hundred yojanas into the air, unequalled in majesty.

(28) "'Blessed One, may I not attain unsurpassed, perfect Awakening unless, when I have attained Awakening, any living being in my buddha-field needs to study anything or have anything explained to them, or if their mastery of any of the four branches of learning is not perfect.

(29) "'Blessed One, may I not attain unsurpassed, perfect Awakening unless, when I have attained Awakening, my buddha-field is so clear that innumerable, uncountable, inconceivable, unequalled, immeasurable buddha-fields are visible all around, as clearly as looking at one's face in a highly polished mirror.

(30) "'Blessed One, may I not attain unsurpassed, perfect Awakening unless, when I have attained Awakening, there are hundreds of thousands of jars made of all kinds of jewels in my buddha-field constantly filling the air with various exquisite fragrances, noble fragrances which are beyond the scope of gods and men, perfumes worthy of being offered to tathāgatas and bodhisattvas in worship.

(31) "'Blessed One, may I not attain unsurpassed, perfect Awakening unless, when I have attained Awakening, sweet-smelling flowers made of various different kinds of jewels constantly rain down in my buddha-field, and clouds of musical instruments constantly play music which soothes the mind.

(32) "'Blessed One, may I not attain unsurpassed, perfect Awakening unless, when I have attained Awakening, all of the living beings in innumerable, uncountable, inconceivable, incomparable buddha-fields who are touched by my radiance are filled with a happiness which surpasses that of gods and men.

(33) "'Blessed One, may I not attain unsurpassed, perfect Awakening unless, when I have attained Awakening, bodhisattvas, great beings in uncountable, inconceivable, incomparable, immeasurable buddha-fields in all directions of space who hear my name escape birth and obtain the power of dhāraṇī because of the virtue of having heard it, and maintain this power until they sit on the seat of Awakening.

(34) "'Blessed One, may I not attain unsurpassed, perfect Awakening unless, when I have attained Awakening, women in innumerable, uncountable, inconceivable, incomparable, immeasurable buddha-fields in all directions of space who hear my name develop mindfulness, set their minds on Awakening, become disgusted by their femininity, and are never again born as women.

(35) "'Blessed One, may I not attain unsurpassed, perfect Awakening unless, when I have attained Awakening, all the world with its gods honours those bodhisattvas who practise the path of the bodhisattva in innumerable, uncountable, inconceivable, incomparable, immeasurable buddha-fields in the ten directions of space, who hear my name, and who bow to me with respect, making a full prostration.

(36) "'Blessed One, may I not attain unsurpassed, perfect Awakening if, when I have attained Awakening, any bodhisattva needs to wash, dry, sew, or dye his robes. May they receive exquisite new, fresh robes, robes that would meet with the approval of a tathāgata, as soon as the thought occurs to them that they might require them.

(37) "'Blessed One, may I not attain unsurpassed, perfect Awakening unless, when I have attained Awakening, living beings enjoy the happiness of an arhat free from craving, the happiness of a monk dwelling in the third dhyāna, the moment they are born in my buddha-field.

(38) "'Blessed One, may I not attain unsurpassed, perfect Awakening unless, when I have attained Awakening, the bodhisattvas who are born in my buddha-field are able to perceive whatever wonderful adornments they wish flowing in abundance from the different kinds of trees made of jewels.

(39) "'Blessed One, may I not attain unsurpassed, perfect Awakening if, when I have attained Awakening, bodhisattvas who have been born in other buddha-fields and who hear my name have any deficiency in their faculties or powers.

(40) "'Blessed One, may I not attain unsurpassed, perfect Awakening unless, when I have attained Awakening, bodhisattvas in those other buddha-fields who hear my name attain the samadhi called "Well-Balanced" as soon as they hear it, unless when those bodhisattvas have attained this samadhi, they are able to see innumerable, uncountable, inconceivable, unequalled, immeasurable buddhas, blessed ones instantaneously, and unless the extraordinary delight of this samadhi never fades.

(41) "'Blessed One, may I not attain unsurpassed, perfect Awakening unless, when I have attained Awakening, living beings in those other buddha-fields who hear my name are always born into noble families until they attain Awakening, because of the roots of virtue they acquire by hearing my name.

(42) "'Blessed One, may I not attain unsurpassed, perfect Awakening unless, when I have attained Awakening, living beings in those other buddha-fields who hear my name always

possess the roots of virtue which are the joy and gladness of the path of the bodhisattva until they attain Awakening, because of the roots of virtue they acquire by hearing my name.

(43) "'Blessed One, may I not attain unsurpassed, perfect Awakening unless, when I have attained Awakening, bodhisattvas in those other world systems who hear my name attain the samadhi called "The Attainment of Integration" as soon as they hear it, are able to honour innumerable, uncountable, inconceivable, unequalled, immeasurable buddhas, blessed ones, as soon as they have attained this state, and unless the extraordinary delight of this samadhi never fades until they sit on the seat of Awakening.

(44) "'Blessed One, may I not attain unsurpassed, perfect Awakening unless, when I have attained Awakening, the living beings born in my buddha-field are able to hear any Dharma-teaching they wish, the moment the thought occurs to them.

(45) "'Blessed One, may I not attain unsurpassed, perfect Awakening unless, when I have attained Awakening, the progress towards unsurpassed, perfect Awakening of the bodhisattvas in my buddha-field, or in any other buddha-field, becomes irreversible when they hear my name.

(46) "'Blessed One, Buddha, Teacher, may I not attain unsurpassed, perfect Awakening unless, when I have attained Awakening, the bodhisattvas in my buddha-field who hear my name attain the first, second, and third kinds of patient acceptance; and unless they become unable to fall away[148] from the Buddha, the Dharma, and the Sangha.'

29. "Then, Ānanda, when the monk Dharmākara had proclaimed these unique vows of his own, he spoke these verses, inspired by the glory of the Buddha:

(1) "'If I should attain Awakening, but not fulfil
the exceptional, supreme vows I have just made,
may I not become an excellent bull among living beings,
extraordinary, incomparable, and in possession of the ten
powers.

(2) "'If my buddha-field is not as I have described,
with a great profusion of different kinds of heavenly riches

to bring happiness to those who are suffering in hell,
may I not become a precious king of the world.

(3) "'If, when I sit on the seat of Awakening,
my name is not soon heard in a great limitless multitude
of buddha-fields in the ten directions of space,
may I not become a powerful protector of the world.

(4) "'If I should abandon my practice of mindfulness
and indulge in the delights of sense pleasures,
then even as I attain the unparalleled peace[149] of Awakening
may I not become a powerful teacher of the world.

(5) "'The Protector is limitless and incomparable, his vast radiance
shining forth in all buddha-fields, in every direction.
He has calmed all greed, hatred, and delusion.
He has calmed the fires of hell.

(6) "'When his brilliant, mighty eye appears,
the darkness which engulfs all people is chased away.
He leads them away from misfortune
towards heavenly states of limitless splendour.

(7) "'The light of the sun and the moon do not blaze in the sky,
nor does the fiery radiance of the hosts of bejewelled gods.
They are all outshone by the light of the Lord of All People
whose conduct in previous lives was perfectly pure.

(8) "'The best of human beings is a place of rest for those who are suffering.
There is no one like him anywhere at all.
He has performed hundreds of thousands of skilful actions,
and roars a lion's roar in the assembly.

(9) "'He naturally and spontaneously honoured the victorious ones of the past,
and practised countless, innumerable forms of spiritual discipline and austerities.
The best of living beings has fully come into the power of his vow,
the unparalleled accumulation of supreme understanding.

(10) "'May I become an extraordinary, unparalleled guide of human beings,
with knowledge supreme, free from attachment, with knowledge and vision,
and an understanding of the threefold nature of conditioned things,
just like the Blessed One, the Lord of All People.

(11) "'If I am to achieve Awakening
and fulfil the vows I have set forth,
may this thousandfold world system shake,
and the gods rain down blossoms from on high.'

(12) "The earth shook, and flowers rained down.
Hundreds of musical instruments sounded in the sky.
The most exquisite sandalwood powder poured from the shining heavens,
and a voice declared, 'You will be a buddha in this world.'

30. "Ānanda, the monk, the bodhisattva, the great being Dharmākara fulfilled the vows he had set forth. There are not many bodhisattvas, Ānanda, who have fulfilled vows like these. It does not often occur, Ānanda, that vows like these are made in this world. It is very rare, although not completely unheard of.

31. "Then, Ānanda, when the monk Dharmākara had proclaimed these unique vows of his own before the Blessed One, the Tathāgata Lokeśvararāja, before the world with its gods, its māras, its brahmā-gods, its renunciants and Brahmans, its living creatures, gods, human beings, and titans, he stood firmly in his resolution to do as he had promised.

32. "While he was perfecting the complete purity, the greatness, and the excellence of his buddha-field, and while he was practising the bodhisattva path for innumerably, inestimably, inconceivably, incomparably, immeasurably, incalculably, indescribably many countless hundreds of thousands of millions of years, he did not waver towards sensual desire, ill-will, or cruelty. No notion of sensual desire, ill-will, or cruelty arose in him, nor any notion of forms, sounds, smells, tastes, or physical objects.

33. "He was youthful, charming, gentle, happy, patient, and well-loved. He was easy to support, and didn't want much. He was easily satisfied, and fond of solitude. He was uncorrupted, clear-minded, reliable,

straightforward, honest, and not deceitful. He was open-hearted and spoke with affection. He was unwaveringly committed to striving to develop positive qualities. He had laid down his burden. He had fulfilled his great vow for the benefit of all living beings. He revered the Buddha, the Dharma, the Sangha, his teachers, his preceptors, and his spiritual friends. He was sincere in his practice of the bodhisattva path. He was kind, truthful, and humble, and possessed many other good qualities besides. He encouraged others to develop all kinds of positive qualities. He dwelt in the state of emptiness, the state of freedom from characteristics, the state of freedom from desire, the state of freedom from accumulation, and the state of non-arising.

34. "He was careful about what he said. In his practice of the path of the bodhisattva, he gave up speaking in ways which created ill-will in himself and others, and instead spoke in ways which brought benefit and happiness to himself and others.

35. "He practised awareness,[150] and when he entered a village, a city, a town, a country, a kingdom, or a royal palace, he remained composed, unaffected by forms, sounds, smells, tastes, physical objects, or mental objects.

36. "In his practice of the path of the bodhisattva, he encouraged others to practise the perfection of generosity just as he did himself. He encouraged others to practise the perfections of ethical conduct, patient acceptance, energy, meditation, and wisdom just as he did himself. The roots of virtue that he had perfected were such that, wherever he was born, a great multitude of countless hundreds of thousands of millions of precious things appeared out of the earth.

37. "By practising the path of the bodhisattva, he led immeasurably many, innumerable, countless hundreds of thousands of millions of living beings to unsurpassed perfect Awakening, so many that it is not easy to express their numbers in words. He honoured, revered, venerated, and worshipped innumerable, countless buddhas, blessed ones, making offerings of robes, almsfood, beds, seats, and medicine, and providing them with everything necessary to live comfortably and happily. He led so many living beings to Awakening – merchants, householders, ministers, and those from wealthy families – that it is not easy to express their numbers in words. He even led lords of the world to Awakening, as well as kings of the entire world, protectors of the world, Śakras, suyāma gods, gods of the Tuṣita Heaven, sunirmita

gods, gods who have power over the creations of others, kings of the gods, and even the Great Brahmā himself.

38. "He honoured, revered, venerated, and worshipped innumerable, countless buddhas, blessed ones, so many that it is not easy to express their numbers in words, and asked them to turn the wheel of the Dharma.

39. "He did so many skilful things like this while practising the path of the bodhisattva for innumerably, uncountably, inconceivably, incomparably, immeasurably, indescribably many countless hundreds of thousands of aeons that he breathed a heavenly scent of sandalwood when he exhaled, more exquisite than the perfumes of the gods. From his pores came the fragrance of blue lotuses. Because he was adorned with both the major and the minor physical characteristics of a great being, everyone found him to be handsome, gracious, and beautiful – exquisitely, supremely delightful in appearance. He produced all kinds of ornaments made of precious jewels; all kinds of clothes and robes; all kinds of flowers, incense, perfumes, garlands, ointments, parasols, banners, and flags; and all kinds of music and song. These things arose from the palms of his hands, and from every pore on his body. He produced all kinds of food and drink which were delicious to eat and exquisite to imbibe, as well as all kinds of other enjoyable, delightful things which flowed forth from the palms of his hands as he manifested them. In this way, Ānanda, the monk Dharmākara practised the path of the bodhisattva, in full possession of all the tools and all the forms of mastery of a bodhisattva."

40. The Venerable Ānanda then said to the Blessed One, "Blessed One, has this monk, this bodhisattva, this great being Dharmākara already attained unsurpassed, perfect Awakening? Has he attained complete nirvana? Has he not yet attained Awakening? Is he already awakened, and dwelling[151] somewhere right now, teaching the Dharma?"

The Blessed One said, "Ānanda, this tathāgata dwells neither in the past nor in the future. He has attained unsurpassed, perfect Awakening, and at this very moment he dwells teaching the Dharma in a world system called Sukhāvatī, which lies to the west, beyond a great many countless hundreds of thousands of other buddha-fields. This tathāgata, this arhat, this perfectly awakened buddha is named Amitābha. He is surrounded and accompanied by immeasurably many bodhisattvas and innumerable śrāvakas, and his fully perfected buddha-field is immeasurably vast.

41. "His radiance is infinite. It is not easy to measure its extent, even if you measure it in terms of hundreds of buddha-fields, thousands of buddha-fields, hundreds of thousands of buddha-fields, countless buddha-fields, countless hundreds of buddha-fields, countless thousands of buddha-fields, countless hundreds of thousands of buddha-fields, a great many countless hundreds of thousands of buddha-fields.

42. "Briefly though, Ānanda, one can say that the radiance of the Blessed One Amitābha shines forth to the east in a great many countless hundreds of thousands of buddha-fields, as many as there are grains of sand in the River Ganges. In the same way, the radiance of the Buddha, the Blessed One Amitābha shines forth to the north, the west, and the south, above and below, in all directions, in a great many countless hundreds of thousands of buddha-fields, as many as there are grains of sand in the River Ganges, in every direction. The only exception to this is those worlds which are filled with the light of other buddhas, other blessed ones who, because of the power[152] of the vows they have taken, extend their radiance for one, two, three, four, five, ten, twenty, thirty, forty, or fifty yojanas, a hundred yojanas, a thousand yojanas, a hundred thousand yojanas, or for a very great many countless hundreds of thousands of yojanas.

43. "Ānanda, there is no comparison one could make and no example one could give that would be sufficient to express the immeasurable extent of the light of this tathāgata, Amitābha. This, Ānanda, is why he is called Amitābha, 'Infinite Light'. This is why he is called Amitaprabha, 'Infinite Radiance'; Amitaprabhāsa, 'Infinite Splendour'; Asamāptaprabha, 'Unending Radiance'; Asaṃgataprabha, 'Unobstructed Radiance'; Prabhāśikha, 'Radiant Flame'; Utsṛṣṭaprabha, 'Outpouring of Radiance'; Sadivyamaṇiprabha, 'The Radiance of Heavenly Jewels'; Apratihataraśmirāgaprabha, 'The Radiance of Unobstructed Rays of Coloured Light'; Rājanīyaprabha, 'Delightful Radiance'; Premaṇīyaprabha, 'Enchanting Radiance'; Pramodanīyaprabha, 'Exhilarating Radiance'; Saṃgamanīyaprabha, 'Harmonizing Radiance'; Upoṣaṇīyaprabha, 'Pleasant Radiance'; Nibandhanīyaprabha, 'Friendly Radiance'; Ativīryaprabha, 'Radiance Filled with Great Energy'; Atulyaprabha, 'Incomparable Radiance'; Abhibhūyanarendrāmūnnayendraprabha, 'The Radiance of Mighty Kings and Lords'; Śrāntasaṃcayendusūryajihmīkaraṇaprabha, 'The Radiance Which Outshines the Sun and the Moon'; Abhibhūya, 'Supreme'; and Lokapālaśakrabrahmaśuddhāvāsamaheśvarasarva-

devajihmīkaraṇaprabha, 'The Radiance Which Outshines the Protectors of the World, Śakra, Brahmā, the Gods of the Pure Abodes, Maheśvara, and All the Other Gods'.

44. "His noble, pure, vast radiance brings happiness to the body and thrills the mind. It brings joy, gladness, and happiness to gods, titans, nāgas, yakṣas, gandharvas, garuḍas, mahoragas, kinnaras, human beings, and non-human beings. It encourages goodness, skilfulness, and gladness in those living beings who base themselves on what is skilful in limitless, unbounded buddha-fields.

45. "Ānanda, the Tathāgata could fill an aeon with discourses on the radiance of the Tathāgata Amitābha, which has come about as a result of his previous actions, and still not be able to put all of the good qualities of this radiance into words. This is beyond the skill of the Tathāgata. Why is this? Ānanda, it is because both the magnificent qualities of the radiance of the Blessed One, the Tathāgata Amitābha, and the wisdom and intelligence of the Tathāgata are immeasurable, inestimable, inconceivable, and boundless.

46. "Moreover, Ānanda, it is not easy to grasp the size of the Tathāgata Amitābha's sangha of śrāvakas, even if one thinks in terms of countless śrāvakas, countless hundreds of śrāvakas, countless thousands of śrāvakas, countless hundreds of thousands of śrāvakas, a profusion of śrāvakas, myriads of śrāvakas, great hosts of śrāvakas, untold śrāvakas, an abundance[153] of śrāvakas, great multitudes of śrāvakas, numberless śrāvakas, multitudinous śrāvakas, immeasurably many, innumerable, incalculably many, incomparably many, inconceivably many śrāvakas.

47. "Ānanda, the monk Maudgalyāyana has attained mastery of supernormal abilities. If he wanted to, he could count all of the stars in the threefold thousand great thousand world systems in the space of a night and a day. If there were a great many countless hundreds of thousands of monks with the same kind of supernormal abilities as Maudgalyāyana who did nothing but count the first assembly of śrāvakas of the Tathāgata Amitābha for a great many countless hundreds of thousands of years, they wouldn't even manage to count a hundredth of them, not even a thousandth, not the tiniest minuscule fraction of them.

48. "Ānanda, imagine that someone were to take a hair which had been split into a hundred slivers, and use one of those slivers to draw a single drop of water from the great ocean, which is eighty-four thousand yojanas deep and immeasurably broad. Which, Ānanda, do you think

would be greater in volume – the single drop of water drawn from the ocean by this sliver of hair, or all of the water remaining in the great ocean?"

Ānanda said, "Blessed One, even a thousand yojanas of the ocean would only be a very limited part of the entirety of the great ocean, so a single drop of water drawn from the ocean by a sliver of hair as you describe would be truly minuscule in comparison."

49. The Blessed One said, "The size of that single drop of water in comparison to all of the water remaining in the great ocean is just like the number of śrāvakas that all of those monks with supernormal abilities like those of Maudgalyāyana would be able to count if they spent a great many countless hundreds of thousands of years counting, in comparison to the entirety of the first assembly of śrāvakas of the Tathāgata Amitābha. There are so many that it is impossible to count them. The same can be said of the second and third assemblies. This Blessed One's sangha of śrāvakas is limitless and boundless, and can only be described as uncountable and innumerable.

50. "Ānanda, the lifespan of the Blessed One, the Tathāgata Amitābha, is unlimited. It is not easy to get an idea of its length, even if one thinks in terms of hundreds of aeons, thousands of aeons, hundreds of thousands of aeons, countless aeons, countless hundreds of aeons, countless thousands of aeons, countless hundreds of thousands of aeons, a great many countless hundreds of thousands of aeons. The boundless lifespan of that blessed one, Ānanda, is truly unlimited. That is why that tathāgata is known as Amitāyus, 'Infinite Life'.

51. "According to the standard way of calculating the length of aeons which is used in this world system, Ānanda, it is now ten aeons since the Blessed One, the Tathāgata Amitāyus, attained unsurpassed perfect Awakening.

52. "Sukhāvatī, Ānanda, the world system of the Tathāgata Amitābha, is abundant, bountiful, comfortable, with plentiful supplies of food, delightful, and filled with a great many gods and human beings. In that world system, Ānanda, no one is born into a state of misfortune – there are no hells, no animals, no realm of hungry ghosts, and no hosts of titans. The jewels of this world are as nothing compared to those which are found in Sukhāvatī.

53. "Ānanda, that world system, Sukhāvatī, releases various different kinds of sweet-smelling fragrances. Various different kinds of flowers

and fruit abound, and it is adorned with trees made of precious substances. It is inhabited by flocks of birds which are manifested by the Tathāgata, which sing various different kinds of melodies which soothe the mind.

54. "The trees made of precious substances are of various different colours, Ānanda, many different colours, many hundreds of thousands of different colours. There are golden-coloured trees made of gold, silver-coloured trees made of silver, lapis lazuli-coloured trees made of lapis lazuli, quartz-coloured trees made of quartz, sapphire-coloured trees made of sapphire, ruby-coloured trees made of ruby, and emerald-coloured trees made of emerald.

55. "Some trees are made of two kinds of precious substances: gold and silver. There are trees made of three kinds of precious substances: gold, silver, and lapis lazuli. There are trees made of four kinds of precious substances: gold, silver, lapis lazuli, and quartz. There are trees made of five kinds of precious substances: gold, silver, lapis lazuli, quartz, and sapphire. There are trees made of six kinds of precious substances: gold, silver, lapis lazuli, quartz, sapphire, and ruby. There are trees made of seven kinds of precious substances: gold, silver, lapis lazuli, quartz, sapphire, ruby, and seventhly emerald.

56. "The trees made of gold, Ānanda, have roots, trunks, limbs, branches, leaves, and flowers made of gold, and fruit made of silver. The trees made of silver have roots, trunks, limbs, branches, leaves, and flowers made of silver, and fruit made of lapis lazuli. The trees made of lapis lazuli have roots, trunks, limbs, branches, leaves, and flowers made of lapis lazuli, and fruit made of quartz. The trees made of quartz have roots, trunks, limbs, branches, leaves, and flowers made of quartz, and fruit made of sapphire. The trees made of sapphire have roots, trunks, limbs, branches, leaves, and flowers made of sapphire, and fruit made of ruby. The trees made of ruby have roots, trunks, limbs, branches, leaves, and flowers made of ruby, and fruit made of emerald. The trees made of emerald have roots, trunks, limbs, branches, leaves, and flowers made of emerald, and fruit made of gold.

57. "Some of the trees, Ānanda, have roots made of gold, trunks made of silver, limbs made of lapis lazuli, branches made of quartz, leaves made of sapphire, flowers made of ruby, and fruit made of emerald. Some of the trees, Ānanda, have roots made of silver, trunks made of lapis lazuli, limbs made of quartz, branches made of sapphire, leaves

made of ruby, flowers made of emerald, and fruit made of gold. Some of the trees, Ānanda, have roots made of lapis lazuli, trunks made of quartz, limbs made of sapphire, branches made of ruby, leaves made of emerald, flowers made of gold, and fruit made of silver. Some of the trees, Ānanda, have roots made of quartz, trunks made of sapphire, limbs made of ruby, branches made of emerald, leaves made of gold, flowers made of silver, and fruit made of lapis lazuli. Some of the trees, Ānanda, have roots made of sapphire, trunks made of ruby, limbs made of emerald, branches made of gold, leaves made of silver, flowers made of lapis lazuli, and fruit made of quartz. Some of the trees, Ānanda, have roots made of ruby, trunks made of emerald, limbs made of gold, branches made of silver, leaves made of lapis lazuli, flowers made of quartz, and fruit made of sapphire. Some of the trees, Ānanda, have roots made of emerald, trunks made of gold, limbs made of silver, branches made of lapis lazuli, leaves made of quartz, flowers made of sapphire, and fruit made of ruby. Some of the trees, Ānanda, have roots made of the seven kinds of precious substances, trunks made of the seven kinds of precious substances, limbs made of the seven kinds of precious substances, branches made of the seven kinds of precious substances, leaves made of the seven kinds of precious substances, flowers made of the seven kinds of precious substances, and fruit made of the seven kinds of precious substances.

58. "The roots, trunks, limbs, branches, leaves, flowers, and fruit of all of these trees, Ānanda, are pleasant to the touch, and smell wonderful. When the wind stirs them, they make a delightful sound which soothes the mind, and which is agreeable and appealing to listen to.

59. "That buddha-field, Ānanda, is filled with trees like this made of the seven kinds of precious substances. It is surrounded on all sides by clumps of banana trees made of the seven kinds of precious substances, and rows of palm trees made of precious substances. Golden nets hang everywhere.

60. "It is covered in lotus flowers made of the seven kinds of precious substances. Some of the lotus flowers are half a yojana across, some are a yojana across, some are two, three, four or five yojanas across, and some are even as much as ten yojanas across. From each of these lotus flowers made of precious substances, thirty-six trillion rays of light shine forth, and from the tips of each of these rays of light, thirty-six trillion golden buddhas come forth, each possessing the thirty-two major physical characteristics of a great person. They travel to innumerable,

uncountable world systems to the east, and teach the Dharma to the living beings who dwell there. In the same way, they travel to innumerable, uncountable world systems to the south, to the west, to the north, above, below, and in the intermediate directions, and teach the Dharma to the living beings who dwell there.

61. "Moreover, Ānanda, in that buddha-field, there are no Kāla Mountains, no Ratna Mountains, no Mount Sumeru, the king of mountains, no Cakravāla Mountains, and no Mahācakravāla Mountains, kings of mountains. Everywhere in that buddha-field it is delightfully flat like the palm of one's hand, and every part of the ground is covered in various different kinds of precious substances and jewels."

62. Ānanda then said to the Blessed One, "Blessed One, where in that buddha-field are the Four Great Kings to be found, who in this world dwell on the slopes of Mount Sumeru? Where are the gods of the thirty-three to be found, who in this world dwell on its summit?"

The Blessed One replied, "Ānanda, in this world, where on Mount Sumeru do you think Yāma dwells? Where do the gods of the Tuṣita Heaven dwell? What about the gods who delight in creation, the gods who have power over the creations of others, the brahmakāyika gods, the gods led by Brahmā, the Mahābrahmā gods, and so forth, all the way up to the *akaniṣṭha* gods?"

63. Ānanda replied, "Blessed One, it is impossible to fully comprehend the consequences of actions."

The Blessed One said, "Ānanda, you have understood that in this world it is impossible to fully comprehend the performance of actions and the consequences of actions, but you have not understood that it is impossible to fully comprehend the buddha-power of the buddhas, the blessed ones, and that it is impossible to fully comprehend the abundant merit accumulated by living beings who act in meritorious ways and cultivate roots of virtue."

64. Ānanda said, "I have no uncertainty, reservations, or doubts about this, Blessed One. I ask the Tathāgata about this issue in order to remove any uncertainty, reservations, or doubts that living beings may have in the future."

The Blessed One said, "Excellent, Ānanda, excellent. That is the right thing to do.

65. "Ānanda, there are also many different kinds of rivers that run through that world system, Sukhāvatī. There are great rivers a yojana

across. There are great rivers as much as twenty, thirty, forty, or fifty yojanas across, and twelve yojanas deep. All of these rivers flow smoothly with sweet-smelling, fragrant waters. As these waters flow forth, they carry within them great masses of flowers encrusted with different kinds of precious substances, and they fill the air with delightful, melodic sounds. Ānanda, imagine that there were a musical instrument composed of countless hundreds of thousands of parts, and that this musical instrument was played with great skill, and accompanied by heavenly choirs, such that it created a sound that soothed the mind. That is what the sound of these great rivers is like. It is profound, ungraspable, unfathomable, and pure. It is a delight to the ear, and it touches the heart. It is enchanting, delightful, and it soothes the mind. It is agreeable and appealing to listen to, murmuring 'impermanence, peace, no self'. It brings happiness to those who hear it, and it reaches the ears of all the living beings in that world system.

66. "Moreover, Ānanda, both banks of these great rivers are covered in various different kinds of fragrant trees made of precious substances, with clusters of flowers hanging from their branches. The living beings who wish to enjoy the delights of heavenly games and pleasures on those riverbanks will find that, when they go down into the rivers, the water only comes up to their ankles, if that is what they wish. If they wish the water to come up to their knees, to their hips, or to their ears, then it will do so, and they will experience heavenly pleasures. If they wish the water to be cool, then it is cool for them. If they wish the water to be warm, then it is warm for them. It is just as cool or warm as they like.

67. "The flowing waters that fill those great rivers are perfumed with the unsurpassable fragrances of sour mangosteen, agarwood, benzoin resin, and serpent-sandalwood. They are filled with fragrant flowers – heavenly blue lotuses, red lotuses, night lotuses, and white lotuses. By the banks of the river there are flocks of birds manifested by the Tathāgata, singing melodies which soothe the mind – birds such as *haṃsa*-geese, cranes, curlews, *cakravāka*-birds, ducks, parrots, mynas, cuckoos, kuṇāla-birds, sparrows, and peacocks. Black-billed geese beautify these rivers, and they are easy to ford. They are free of mud, and the bottom of these rivers is instead covered in golden sand. When the living beings there make any kind of wish, thinking, 'May our wishes come true', then whatever they wish for comes true.

68. "The sounds made by those waters, Ānanda, which soothe the mind, can be heard by everyone in that buddha-field. If any living

beings standing on the banks of the rivers, though, wish, 'May these sounds not reach my ears' then they will not reach their ears, even if they possess the divine ear. They will be able to hear whatever kinds of sounds they wish to hear, sounds that soothe the mind. They will be able to hear the words[154] 'Buddha', 'Dharma', 'Sangha', 'perfections',[155] 'stages', 'spiritual powers', 'self-confidence', 'the unique Dharma of the Buddha', 'the branches of learning', 'emptiness', 'freedom from characteristics', 'freedom from desire', 'freedom from accumulation', 'freedom from birth', 'non-arising', 'non-existence', 'cessation', 'peace', 'tranquillity', 'calm',[156] 'great loving-kindness', 'great compassion', 'great sympathetic joy', 'great equanimity', 'the patient acceptance of the fact that all phenomena are unarisen', and 'attaining the stage of initiation'. When they hear these words, an exhilirating joy and gladness will arise in them, along with the inclination towards solitude, contentment, peace, cessation, the Dharma, and the perfect cultivation of roots of virtue, which results in Awakening.

69. "Ānanda, the word 'unskilful' is not heard anywhere in that world system, Sukhāvatī. Neither are the words 'hindrance', 'falling into a state of misfortune at death', or 'suffering' heard there. Not even the words 'feelings which are neither pleasant nor unpleasant' are heard there, Ānanda, so the word 'suffering' is certainly not heard there.

70. "Ānanda, this is a short description of the world system of Sukhāvatī, not a detailed one. I could spend the rest of this aeon praising the sources of happiness in that world system, Sukhāvatī, and not be able to describe them all.

71. "The living beings who have been reborn in that world system, Sukhāvatī, and all those who will be reborn there in the future resemble the gods who have power over the creations of others. They have their form and appearance, and possess their powers and their strength. They are the same height as those gods, and possess their sovereignty, their accumulation of merit, and their position of superiority. They wear the same kinds of clothes, and enjoy the same kinds of gardens, palaces, and apartments. They enjoy the same kinds of sights, sounds, smells, tastes, and sensations of touch, and all of the other pleasures enjoyed by these gods.

72. "Moreover, Ānanda, in that world system, Sukhāvatī, living beings do not eat physical food such as soup or sugar-cane juice. Whatever kind of food they wish to eat, they form a perception in their minds[157]

of already having consumed it, and this satisfies both their bodies and their minds. They do not need to ingest it.

73. "Their bodies satisfied, if there is any kind of fragrance they wish to smell, the whole of that buddha-field becomes perfumed with that heavenly fragrance. If anyone there does not wish to smell that fragrance, though, not even a trace perception of it will appear in their minds.

74. "In the same way, whatever kinds of incense, garlands, ointments, powdered sandalwood, robes, parasols, banners, flags, and musical instruments they wish for fill the whole of that buddha-field.

75. "Whatever kinds of robes they wish for, in various different colours, in many hundreds of thousands of different colours, fill the whole of that buddha-field, and they see[158] themselves dressed in those robes.

76. "Whatever kind of jewellery they wish for, jewellery for the head, the ears, the neck, the hands, or the feet – diadems, rings, bracelets, arm-rings, necklaces, chokers, ear-rings, seal-rings, belts made of golden threads, golden nets,[159] pearl nets, nets made of all kinds of precious substances, or nets made of gold, precious substances, and small bells – all these different kinds of jewellery, studded with many hundreds of thousands of precious stones, can be seen to fill that buddha-field, hanging from the branches of the trees, and they see[160] themselves adorned with that jewellery.

77. "Whatever kinds of palaces they wish for, no matter what kind of appearance, features, construction, height, and width they wish them to have, with hundreds of thousands of turrets adorned with various different kinds of precious substances, with various different kinds of heavenly flowers strewn about, and couches covered with a multitude of cushions, those palaces appear before them. They live, play, and enjoy themselves[161] in those palaces, which spring forth from their own minds, surrounded, served, and attended by seven times seven thousand nymphs.

78. "In that world system, there is no difference between gods and human beings, except that one might use the words 'god' or 'human being' as a linguistic convention when counting them.

79. "Ānanda, if an inferior person or a eunuch were to stand in front of a king, a king of the entire world, they would not shine brightly and radiantly, nor would they be able to speak confidently and clearly. In just the same way, if Śakra, the Lord of the Gods, were to stand in front of the gods who have power over the creations of others, he would not

shine brightly and radiantly. Neither his gardens, his palaces, his clothes, his jewellery, his sovereignty, his supernormal abilities, his miraculous powers, nor his lordship, Ānanda, outshine theirs. His understanding of the Dharma and his enjoyment of the Dharma, though, do outshine theirs. The human beings in that world system of Sukhāvatī, Ānanda, should be seen as being just like those gods who have power over the creations of others.

80. "Moreover, Ānanda, in the mornings, all four corners of that world system, Sukhāvatī, are filled with winds that blow through the multitude of different species of beautiful, multicoloured trees made of precious substances which give off sweet-smelling, divine fragrances. These winds make the trees sway, shake, bend, and wave, such that many hundreds of beautiful flowers – flowers which give off fragrances that soothe the mind – fall to the majestic ground made of precious substances. They cover the buddha-field in a carpet of flowers forty feet deep. It is as if someone with great skill had covered the ground with flowers, using both hands to spread them out evenly to form a pleasing, beautiful arrangement. This is how the flowers, which are of various different colours and which give off various different fragrances, appear, covering the buddha-field in a carpet of flowers forty feet deep.

81. "The flowers are delicate, and as pleasant to the touch as *kācilindika* cloth, although this is a poor comparison. If you step on them, they sink down four inches, and when you step off them again, they rise up again exactly four inches.

82. "When the morning has passed these flowers disappear completely, and that buddha-field becomes clear, delightful, and beautiful, unmarked by the flowers that were there before. All four corners of that buddha-field are then once again filled with winds that scatter fresh flowers, just as before. This happens at midday, at sunset, and in the first, second, and third watches of the night, just like in the morning. Any living beings who are touched by the winds which are perfumed by these various different fragrances experience the happiness of a monk who has attained cessation.

83. "Nowhere in that buddha-field, Ānanda, is there anything that resembles fire, a sun, a moon, planets, constellations, or stars; nor is there total darkness, or even a word to designate it. There are no words to designate night and day, except when the Tathāgata uses these

words in a conventional sense. There is no notion of taking pleasure in ownership.

84. "Moreover, Ānanda, from time to time in that world system, Sukhāvatī, rain falls from rainclouds scented with heavenly fragrances. Multicoloured heavenly blossoms, heavenly precious stones, heavenly sandalwood powder, heavenly parasols, banners, and flags also fall from these rainclouds. The multicoloured heavenly blossoms remain suspended in the air in great heavenly multitudes, as do the heavenly precious stones and parasols, and all of the other adornments. Heavenly music plays, and heavenly nymphs dance.

85. "Moreover, Ānanda, all of the living beings who have been born, are being born, or will be born in that buddha-field are firmly established in perfection, and will remain so until they attain nirvana. Why is this the case? It is because no other category of living beings can be designated or defined as existing there – neither the category of living beings who are not firmly established in perfection, nor the category of living beings who are established on the wrong path.

86. "Ānanda, this is a short description of the world system of Sukhāvatī, not a detailed one. I could praise the sources of happiness in that world system, Sukhāvatī, until the end of this aeon and I would not be able to describe them all."

87. The Blessed One then spoke these verses:

(1) "If all living beings were to attain happiness,
purified understanding, and perfect skill,
and spend countless aeons or more
describing what Sukhāvatī looks like,

(2) "Then even when countless ages had come to an end
and the vajras of the gods had crumbled,
not even the most important features of Sukhāvatī
would have been explained, let alone the details.

(3) "If someone were to chop up as many world systems as there are atoms
in our world system, splitting and grinding them into tiny particles,
and then fill even more world systems than there were tiny particles
with precious substances, and make an offering of them,

(4) "The merit they would gain by doing so
would not amount to the tiniest fraction
of the merit they would gain
just from hearing the name of that world system, Sukhāvatī.

(5) "The merit gained by those who have faith in the words of the Victorious One,
and who possess wisdom, is even greater still.
Faith is the root of all attainments in this world,
so listen, and drive out your doubts.

88. "Ānanda, this is what the countless good qualities of that world system, Sukhāvatī, are like.

89. "Moreover, Ānanda, as many buddhas, as many blessed ones, as there are grains of sand in the River Ganges, dwelling in as many buddha-fields as there are grains of sand in the River Ganges in the ten directions of space, praise the name of the Tathāgata Amitābha. They celebrate it, describe its glory, and honour its good qualities.

90. "Why do they do this? They do it because if a single mental state of determination and serene faith arises in the living beings who hear the name of the Blessed One Amitābha, their progress towards unsurpassed, perfect Awakening will become irreversible.

91. "Ānanda, the living beings who honour that tathāgata, and whose minds become absorbed[162] by him, will plant a great many roots of virtue, an unlimited number of roots of virtue. If they dedicate their minds to Awakening and cultivate a heartfelt desire to be born in that world system,[163] then the Tahāgata, the Arhat, the Perfectly Awakened Buddha Amitābha will appear to them at the time of their death, standing before them surrounded by an assembly of monks. When they have seen that blessed one, they will die with clear minds, and be born in the world system of Sukhāvatī.

92. "Ānanda, children of good family who wonder, 'How can I see the Tathāgata Amitābha in this very life?' should cultivate a mind set on unsurpassed, perfect Awakening with the utmost unwavering determination, orient their minds towards that buddha-field, and dedicate their roots of virtue to being born there.

93. "If their minds do not become absorbed by that tathāgata, and they do not plant a great many roots of virtue, an unlimited number of roots

of virtue, again and again, an emanation of the Tathāgata, the Arhat, the Perfectly Awakened Buddha Amitābha – with exactly the same appearance, form, and dimensions – will appear at the time of their death, standing before them surrounded by a sangha of monks. If they die with unwavering mindfulness in a state of samadhi which is based on serene faith aroused by that vision of the Tathāgata, then they will be reborn in his buddha-field.

94. "Moreover, Ānanda, those living beings who recollect that tathāgata ten times, who long to be born in his buddha-field, who experience contentment when the profound Dharma is being spoken and do not feel conflicted or become dejected or depressed, whose minds become absorbed by that tathāgata even once, and who cultivate a longing to be born in his buddha-field, will see the Tathāgata Amitābha in their dreams. They will be born in the world system of Sukhāvatī, and their progress towards unsurpassed, perfect Awakening will become irreversible.

95. "The tathāgatas in uncountable, innumerable world systems in the ten directions of space see this purpose, Ānanda, and they praise and celebrate the name of the Tathāgata Amitābha, raising their voices in salutation. Moreover, Ānanda, bodhisattvas as numerous as the grains of sand in the River Ganges converge on that buddha-field from each of the ten directions of space. That assembly of bodhisattvas comes to see the Tathāgata Amitābha, worship him, attend him, ask him questions, and see the abundance of uniquely wonderful qualities which adorn his buddha-field."

96. Then, in order to further illuminate the issue, the Blessed One spoke these verses:

> (1) "Buddhas come from the east,
> from as many buddha-fields
> as there are grains of sand in the River Ganges,
> accompanied by bodhisattvas, to see the Guide Amitāyus.
>
> (2) "They bring with them handfuls of a great many different kinds
> of sweet-smelling flowers which delight the mind,
> with which they shower the Supreme Guide of Humanity,
> Amitāyus, who is worshipped by gods and human beings.
>
> (3) "In the same way, as many buddhas as come from the east
> come from buddha-fields to the west, the south, and the north,

from all the ten directions of space, accompanied by bodhisattvas,
to worship the Buddha, the Guide Amitāyus.

(4) "They bring with them a great many different kinds
of sweet-smelling incense which delights the mind,
and with which they shower the Supreme Guide of Humanity,
Amitāyus, who is worshipped by gods and human beings.

(5) "When these bodhisattvas have made their offerings,
worshipped the feet of Amitaprabha,
and circumambulated him clockwise, they say,
'Oh, how extrordinarily beautiful this buddha-field is!'

(6) "Their minds elevated, filled with incomparable joy,
they shower him with handfuls of flowers.
Before the Guide they declare their love and say,
'May our buddha-fields be like yours!'

(7) "The handfuls of flowers that they have thrown
then form a beautifully decorated parasol
a hundred yojanas across, with a brightly coloured pole,
that covers the whole of the Buddha's body.

(8) "When the bodhisattvas have honoured the Buddha in this way
they are contented, and they reflect,
'Living beings who hear the name of the supreme human being
gain a great attainment with ease.

(9) "'We ourselves gained the same great attainment with ease
when we came to this buddha-field.
Look at this buddha-field – like a dream –
which the Teacher has formed with loving kindness over
thousands of aeons.

(10) "'Look at this buddha, whose accumulation of merit is
unsurpassed.
Surrounded by bodhisattvas, he radiates beauty.
Amitābha's light is infinite and glorious.
His lifespan is infinite too, as is his sangha.'

(11) "The Protector Amitāyus smiled,
and three hundred and sixty trillion rays of light
shone from his face, bursting forth
to illuminate countless thousands of buddha-fields.

(12) "All of these beams of light returned to him,
and disappeared into the head of the Guide.
Joy arose in the gods and human beings
who saw those rays of light.

(13) "Then the Protector Avalokiteśvara,
that gloriously beautiful child of the buddhas,
stood up and said, 'Blessed One, Protector of the World,
what are the causes and conditions that have brought about this smile?

(14) "'You are skilled in what is meaningful, filled with affection and empathy,
the liberator of a great many living beings – please explain this to us.
When living beings hear your supreme voice,
which delights the mind, their minds become elevated.

(15) "'Bodhisattvas have come to Sukhāvatī
from a great many world systems to see the Buddha.
When they hear your voice a deep joy will arise in them
and they will immediately examine your buddha-field.

(16) "'As soon as they arrive in this unparalleled buddha-field
they attain supernormal abilities,
the divine eye, the divine ear,
and complete mastery in recollecting their previous births.'

(17) "The Buddha Amitāyus then explained,
'In the past, I vowed that living beings
who heard my name in any circumstances
would always end up in my buddha-field.

(18) "'The exquisite vow I made has now been fulfilled,
and living beings come to me from a great many world systems.
Their progress becomes irreversible,
and they will only be born once more.

(19) "'Any bodhisattva, therefore, who expresses the wish,
"May my buddha-field be like yours.
May I liberate a great many living beings
by means of my name, my voice, or my appearance,"

(20) "'Should not hesitate, but hasten
to the world system of Sukhāvatī.
When they arrive, they should make offerings
before Amitaprabha and countless thousands of other buddhas.

(21) "'They should make offerings to a great many countless buddhas,
using their supernormal abilities to visit a great many buddha-fields,
and make offerings to the sugatas there.
When they have expressed their devotion, they should return to Sukhāvatī.'

97. "Moreover, Ānanda, the bodhi tree of the Tathāgata, the Arhat, the Perfectly Awakened Buddha Amitāyus is a thousand yojanas tall. Its branches and leaves spread out over eight hundred yojanas, and its roots extend over five hundred yojanas. It is always covered in leaves, always in flower, always bearing fruit. It is a variety of different colours, many hundreds of thousands of colours, and it has many different kinds of leaves, flowers, and fruit. It is beautified with a great multitude of many different kinds of adornments, and filled with jewels and precious stones that radiate moonlight. It is filled with a multitude of jewels and precious substances the like of those worn by Śakra, as well as wish-fulfilling jewels and precious substances. It is decorated with a multitude of the best jewels and precious substances from the ocean. It surpasses even the trees of the gods. Golden threads hang from its branches, and it is overflowing with hundreds of chokers, jewelled chokers, necklaces, bracelets, ruby necklaces, sapphire necklaces, lion necklaces, belts, strings of bells, strings of precious stones, and other objects made of precious substances, as well as nets of gold, nets of pearls, nets of all kinds of precious substances, and nets of small bells. It is decorated with sea monsters, swastikas, shells, and moons, and beautified with small bells, with nets of jewels, with gold, and with all kinds of precious substances. It is adorned with whatever living beings request, according to their disposition.

98. "Moreover, Ānanda, the sound that bodhi tree makes when the wind stirs it can be heard in immeasurably many world systems. The living beings in those world systems whose ears hear the sound of that bodhi tree will not have to fear diseases of the ear until they attain Awakening. The uncountably, innumerably, inconceivably, incomparably, incalculably,

immeasurably, indescribably many living beings whose eyes see the light from that bodhi tree will not have to fear diseases of the eye until they attain Awakening. Moreover, Ānanda, the living beings who smell the fragrances emanating from that bodhi tree will not ever have to fear diseases of the nose until they attain Awakening. The living beings who taste the fruit of that bodhi tree will not ever have to fear diseases of the tongue until they attain Awakening. The living beings upon whom the light from that bodhi tree shines forth will not ever have to fear diseases of the body until they attain Awakening. Moreover, Ānanda, the living beings who take that bodhi tree as the object of their meditation will not have to fear that their minds might become distracted until they attain Awakening.

99. "The progress towards unsurpassed, perfect Awakening of all those living beings becomes irreversible because they have seen that bodhi tree. They attain three kinds of patient acceptance: they practise what they hear, they conform to it, and they patiently accept the fact that all phenomena are unarisen. They are able to do this through the power of the vows made by the Tathāgata Amitāyus, the service he offered to former victorious ones, and the fact that he completely fulfilled the vows and commitments he had made in an excellent, flawless, unblemished way.

100. "Moreover, Ānanda, the bodhisattvas who have been born, are being born, or will be born there only experience one more birth before attaining unsurpassed, perfect Awakening. This is with the exception of those bodhisattvas who, because of their vow, roar the great lion's roar, clad themselves in the supreme armour, and devote themselves to leading all living beings to complete nirvana.

101. "Moreover, Ānanda, the radiance of the śrāvakas in that buddha-field extends for six feet, and the radiance of the bodhisattvas extends for countless hundreds of thousands of yojanas. This is with the exception of two bodhisattvas, whose radiance shines forth constantly and uninterruptedly, filling the whole of that world system."

102. The Venerable Ānanda then asked the Blessed One, "Blessed One, what are the names of those two bodhisattvas?"

The Blessed One replied, "One of them, Ānanda, is the Bodhisattva, the Great Being Avalokiteśvara. The other is called Mahāsthāmaprāpta. They passed away from this buddha-field, Ānanda, and were born in Sukhāvatī.

103. "The bodhisattvas who have been born in that buddha-field, Ānanda, all possess the thirty-two major physical characteristics of a great person, and their bodies are perfect and complete. They are accomplished in meditation and the higher forms of knowledge, and skilled in analysis based on wisdom. Their faculties are sharp, and well-controlled. They have the faculties of one who possesses perfect knowledge, faculties which are neither too weak nor too powerful. They are patient in relation to attainments, and they possess limitless, boundless good qualities.

104. "Moreover, Ānanda, the bodhisattvas who have been born in that buddha-field will all be able to see the Buddha and hear the Dharma until they attain Awakening. They will all be able to recollect their previous births, with the exception of those who have previously resolved to appear in the midst of the five kinds of degeneration[164] in the period of the dissolution of an aeon, when buddhas, blessed ones, appear in the world – as I have appeared here.

105. "Moreover, Ānanda, through the power of the Buddha, in the time it takes to eat a single meal, the bodhisattvas who have been born in that buddha-field are all able to travel to other world systems and worship a very great many countless hundreds of thousands of buddhas for as long as they wish. If they think, 'I would like to make offerings of flowers, perfumes, lamps, incense, garlands, ointments, sandalwood powder, robes, parasols, banners, flags, standards, musical instruments, music, and song', all of these offerings will appear in their hands as soon as the thought occurs to them, and exactly as they have imagined them. When they offer all of these things to the buddhas, the blessed ones, they amass a great many, immeasurably many, innumerable roots of virtue.

106. "If they wish, 'May handfuls of flowers like these manifest in my hands', then handfuls of a great variety of different kinds of heavenly flowers with a variety of different fragrances will manifest in their hands as soon as the thought occurs to them. They scatter these flowers over the buddhas, the blessed ones, showering them and covering them with flowers.

107. "The handfuls of flowers which they scatter all around the buddhas manifest as floral parasols ten yojanas across in the air above. The first handful does not fall to the earth until the second has been scattered. Some of the handfuls of flowers manifest as floral parasols twenty yojanas across in the air above when they are scattered. Some manifest

as floral parasols thirty, forty, fifty, or even as much as a hundred or a thousand yojanas across in the air above when they are scattered.

108. "Those who experience unparalleled joy and gladness there, as well as a pleasurable excitement of the mind, plant a great many, unlimited, innumerable roots of virtue. After worshipping a very great many countless hundreds of thousands of buddhas in the course of a morning, they return to the world system of Sukhāvatī. They are able to do this because they are embraced by the power of the vows made by the Tathāgata Amitāyus, because they have listened to the Dharma that they have been taught, because of the roots of virtue they have planted with victorious ones of the past, and because they themselves have successfully fulfilled the vows they made, in a great variety of ways.

109. "Moreover, Ānanda, the living beings who have been born in that buddha-field all teach the Dharma with universal understanding.

110. "The living beings in that buddha-field have no notion of ownership. As they walk about, wander around in that buddha-field, neither delight nor discontent arises in them. As they stroll across that buddha-field, they have no particular expectations. They are free of expectations. Those living beings simply do not think in that way.

111. "Moreover, Ānanda, the living beings who have been born in that buddha-field, in Sukhāvatī, have no perception of anything as belonging to others, no perception of anything as belonging to themselves, no perception of inequality, no division, no conflict, and no hostility. They have minds of equality, minds of loving kindness, gentle minds, affectionate minds, diligent minds, clear minds, stable minds, unhindered minds, unshaken minds, unagitated minds, minds which practise the perfection of wisdom.[165] They have the kind of intellect that allows them to remember their thoughts. Because of their wisdom, they are like the ocean. Because of their intellect, they are like Mount Meru. They have accumulated many good qualities. Playfully they sing songs of the factors of Awakening. They are devoted to the songs of the buddhas.

112. "They examine their physical eye, develop the divine eye, attain the eye of wisdom, and cross over to the eye of the Dharma. They bring forth the eye of a buddha, reveal it, illuminate it, and describe it in detail.

113. "They develop knowledge that is free from attachment, and are well-versed in the sameness of the three worlds. Their minds are self-controlled and peaceful, and they have an understanding of the entirety

of the realm of reality. They are skilful in explaining the origins of things, they are able to explain phenomena. They are skilful in discerning what is to be accepted and what is not. They are skilful in discerning what is logical and what is not. They are skilled in remaining unmoved when surrounded by worldly conversations. They live with no expectations. They are able to recognize what is essential in conversations about the transcendental.

114. "They are skilful in investigating all phenomena. They dwell with an understanding that the fundamental nature of all phenomena is calm. The sphere in which they dwell is inconceivable. They own nothing, and grasp at nothing. They worry about nothing, and are bound to nothing. Free of grasping, they are completely liberated and unblemished. They dwell without restrictions and without roots in the higher forms of knowledge. They practise non-attachment, and do not become despondent. They are well-versed in the profound Dharma, and do not get discouraged by it. They have ascended to the entrance into the knowledge of a buddha, which is difficult to awaken to. They have found the narrow path. They are free of doubt. They no longer have any questions. Their understanding is not dependent on others. They are not arrogant.

115. "In their knowledge, they rise up like Mount Sumeru. In their intellect, they are unshakeable like the ocean. With their wisdom, and their completely pure, brilliantly radiant minds, they outshine even the sun and the moon. They shine forth with the colour of gold which has been purified by fire.

116. "They are like the earth, because of their patience with both the purity and the impurity of all living beings. They are like water, because they wash away the roots of all defilements and carry them off. They are like fire, the king, because they burn up the defilement of pride in relation to any phenomenon whatsoever. They are like the wind, because there is nothing in the world they hold on to. They are like space, because they co-exist with all phenomena and they own nothing anywhere.

117. "They are like lotus flowers, because nothing sticks to them. They are like great rainclouds, as dark as benzoin resin, because they rumble like thunder with the Dharma. They are like torrential rain, because they playfully rain down the waters of the Dharma. They are like bulls, because they are supreme among all the great herds of living beings. They are like great elephants, because they are in perfect control of their

minds. They are like excellent, thoroughbred horses, because they are so well trained. They are like lions, the kings of the animals, because they are courageous, self-confident, and unafraid. They are like banyan trees, the kings of the trees, because they shelter all living beings. They are like the king of mountains, because no matter what arguments anyone makes, they do not tremble. They are like the sky, because the extent of their loving-kindness cannot be measured. They are like the Great Brahmā, because they possess all roots of virtue, good qualities,[166] and sovereignty. They are like birds, because they do not hoard any of the things that they come across. They are like garuḍas, the kings of the birds, because they crush the arguments of others. They are like udumbara flowers, because they are hard to imitate.

118. "Like elephants, they remain composed and undistracted, their faculties never going astray. They are able to explain things in a skilful way, and they are filled with patience and gentleness. They are not envious, because they have no desire for the wealth of others. They discuss the Dharma with confidence, and they can never get enough of the Dharma. In their ethical conduct, they are like lapis lazuli. They are jewel mines, because of what they have heard. They are pleasant to listen to, because their voices are like great drums of the Dharma. They beat the great kettle-drum of the Dharma, sound the great conch shell of the Dharma, raise the great banner of the Dharma, light the torch of the Dharma.

119. "They see with wisdom, and are not bewildered. They are free of hatred, and have calmed any harshness. They are pure, and free of any vice. They are free of greed,[167] and delight in sharing what they have. They give freely, they are open-handed, and delight in the practice of generosity. They are not miserly in giving either physical gifts or the gift of the Dharma. They dwell in solitude, with no fear in their minds. They are dispassionate, reliable, robust, and steadfast. They are ethically sensitive. Free from the crowd, they are happy to live apart, and they have attained the higher forms of knowledge. They are gentle, and living with them brings happiness. They are helpful, rays of light in the world. They do not go astray. Their contentment is firmly established, and they are free from the darkness of delusion. They have left sorrow behind. They are free of impurities, abandoning them in an instant. They exercise the higher forms of knowledge effortlessly. Their reasoning is powerful, and their vows are powerful. They are straightforward and honest.

120. "They are characterized by the fact that they have planted a great many countless hundreds of thousands of roots of virtue. They have

pulled out the thorn of pride, and left greed, hatred, and delusion behind. They are pure, and committed to purity. They are praised by the victorious ones. They are learned in the affairs of the world. Their understanding has been completely purified. They are children of the victorious ones, and their minds are gripped by exhilaration. They are heroes, firm and selfless. They are free of any harshness. They are incomparable, untainted, integrated, unparalleled. They are bulls. They are ethically sensitive, steadfast, mindful, intelligent, and knowledgeable. They wield the sword of wisdom. They possess great merit. They are majestic. They have left harshness completely behind. They have abandoned impurity. They are absorbed in mindfulness, and they have seized hold of peaceful knowledge.

121. "This, Ānanda, is a brief explanation of what the living beings in that buddha-field are like. A tathāgata could spend their entire lifespan, lasting a great many hundreds of thousands of aeons, giving a detailed description of these good people, and still not be able to ennumerate all of their good qualities. However, such a tathāgata would not lose their self-confidence in this situation. Why is this? It is because, Ānanda, both the good qualities of those bodhisattvas and the unsurpassed wisdom and intelligence of a tathāgata are inconceivable and incomparable.

122. "Ānanda, stand up and face west. Scatter some flowers, and bow with folded hands. The Blessed One, the Tathāgata, the Arhat, the Perfectly Awakened Buddha Amitābha dwells[168] in that direction teaching the Dharma. He is untainted and pure, and his name is proclaimed without obstruction in the worlds in the ten directions of space. In every direction, as many buddhas, as many blessed ones as there are grains of sand in the River Ganges celebrate it, praise it, and glorify it, with unimpeded voices that echo again and again."

123. The Venerable Ānanda then said to the Blessed One, "Blessed One, I want to see the Tathāgata, the Arhat, the Perfectly Awakened Buddha Amitābha, Amitaprabha, Amitāyus, as well as the bodhisattvas, the great beings who have planted roots of virtue with a very great many countless hundreds of thousands of buddhas."

124. As soon as the Venerable Ānanda had spoken these words, the Tathāgata, the Arhat, the Perfectly Awakened Buddha Amitābha sent forth a ray of light from the palm of his hand, such that a great many countless hundreds of thousands of buddha-fields were filled with a great light. When that happened, all of the Kāla Mountains, the Ratna

Mountains, the Mount Merus, the Mount Mahāmerus, the Mucilinda Mountains, the Mahāmucilinda Mountains, the Cakravāla Mountains, and the Mahācakravāla Mountains, all of the walls, columns, trees, thickets, gardens, and palaces belonging to gods and human beings in those buddha-fields, were penetrated and suffused by the radiance of the Tathāgata.

125. Even if someone is standing only six feet away from another person, they can only see them once the sun has risen. In the same way, the monks, nuns, laymen, laywomen, gods, nāgas, yakṣas, rākṣasas, gandharvas, titans, garuḍas, kinnaras, mahoragas, human beings, and non-human beings in that buddha-field saw the Tathāgata, the Arhat, the Perfectly Awakened Buddha Amitābha rise over all buddha-fields like Mount Sumeru, the king of mountains, supreme in all the ten directions of space – bright, shining, brilliant, dazzling. They saw the great assembly of bodhisattvas, and the sangha of monks. They were able to see all this through the power of the Buddha, and because of the complete purity of his radiance.

126. If the whole of the earth were to be turned into a single body of water, such that no trees, no mountains, no islands, no grass, bushes, plants, or great trees, no rivers, chasms, or cliffs could be discerned, then there would be nothing but the earth itself, transformed into a single ocean. In the same way, there were no distinguishing features or characteristics in that buddha-field, except for the śrāvakas whose radiance extended for six feet and the bodhisattvas whose radiance extended for countless hundreds of thousands of yojanas.

127. The Blessed One, the Tathāgata, the Arhat, the Perfectly Awakened Buddha Amitābha, supreme among the assembly of śrāvakas and the assembly of bodhisattvas, could be seen shedding his radiance in all directions.

128. At the same time, the bodhisattvas, śrāvakas, gods, and human beings in the world system of Sukhāvatī all saw the Tathāgata, the Arhat, the Perfectly Awakened Buddha Śākyamuni in this world system of Earth teaching the Dharma surrounded by a sangha of monks, all arhats.

129. The Blessed One then addressed the Bodhisattva Ajita:[169] "Ajita, do you see the abundance of wonderful qualities which adorn that other buddha-field? Up in the sky there are delightful groves and delightful gardens, delightful rivers full of lotus flowers – strewn with red lotuses, blue lotuses, night lotuses, and white lotuses made of various different

kinds of precious substances. Below, from the ground up to the abode of the *akaniṣṭha* gods, the sky is strewn with flowers, beautified with flowers, filled with rows of columns made of various different kinds of precious substances, and populated by flocks of various different kinds of birds which have been manifested by the Tathāgata. Do you see all this, Ajita?"

The Bodhisattva Ajita replied, "I see it, Blessed One."

130. The Blessed One said, "Ajita, do you see the flocks of immortal birds all over that buddha-field? They sing with the voice of the Buddha, and because of them the bodhisattvas there constantly and uninterruptedly recollect the Buddha."

Ajita replied, "I see them, Blessed One."

131. The Blessed One said, "Ajita, do you see the living beings who ascend the sky in palaces a hundred thousand yojanas in size, and cross the sky to pay homage?"

Ajita replied, "I see them, Blessed One."

132. The Blessed One said, "Do you think, then, Ajita, that there is any difference between the gods who have power over the creations of others and the human beings in that world system of Sukhāvatī?"

Ajita replied, "Blessed One, I cannot think of a single difference. The human beings in that buddha-field possess great supernormal abilities."

133. The Blessed One said, "Ajita, do you see the human beings who are enclosed inside exquisite lotus flowers?"

He replied, "I see them, Blessed One. I see the human beings in the world system of Sukhāvatī who are enclosed inside exquisite lotus flowers. I see that they are able to move around, play, and enjoy themselves in palaces fifty, a hundred, or five hundred yojanas in size, palaces like those of the gods of the thirty-three, or of the yāma gods.

134. "However, Blessed One, there are other living beings who have manifested there spontaneously, sitting cross-legged on lotus flowers. Blessed One, what are the causes and conditions which result in some being enclosed inside exquisite lotus flowers, and some manifesting there spontaneously, sitting cross-legged on lotus flowers?"

135. The Blessed One said, "Ajita, the bodhisattvas who are enclosed inside lotus flowers are those who had doubts when they dwelt in other buddha-fields, and planted roots of virtue in order to be born in the world system of Sukhāvatī with such doubts in their minds. The ones

who have manifested there spontaneously, sitting cross-legged on lotus flowers, are those who had freed themselves from doubt and cut through their uncertainty when they planted roots of virtue in order to be born in the world system of Sukhāvatī. They are those who are devoted to the knowledge of the buddhas, the blessed ones, knowledge that is free from attachment. They are those who have faith in that knowledge, and who are committed to it.

136. "Ajita, bodhisattvas in other buddha-fields who think about being able to see the Tathāgata, the Arhat, the Perfectly Awakened Buddha Amitābha, who are free of doubt, who have no uncertainty about the knowledge of the buddhas that is free from attachment, and who have faith in their own roots of virtue, will manifest there instantly and spontaneously, sitting cross-legged on lotus flowers. They will have the same kinds of bodies as those living beings who were born there long before them.

137. "You see, Ajita, the wisdom of someone who has been deprived of the benefits of seeing buddhas and bodhisattvas, of hearing the Dharma, and of discussing it with others for five hundred years is ordinary, unexceptional, deficient, and limited. Someone like that has been deprived of the opportunity to practise and attain roots of virtue, all because they have fallen into doubt, and because their minds have become absorbed by such notions.

138. "Ajita, imagine that there was an anointed king, a *kṣatriya*, who had a prison which was covered in gold and lapis lazuli, with ropes made of strips of fine cloth and garlands of flowers hanging from the walls. Imagine that there were canopies everywhere, in a variety of different colours, and that the prison was covered in cotton and fine cloths. Imagine that there were flowers and blossoms scattered everywhere, and that the air was perfumed with the finest perfumes. Imagine that it had a great multitude of terraces, turrets, small windows, pavilions, and arched doorways, all made of the seven kinds of precious substances. Imagine that it was covered in nets of small bells, and that it had four corners, four pillars, four doorways, and four staircases. Imagine, then, that the king's son was thrown into this prison on account of some misdeed, and put into shackles made of gold from the Jambū River. Imagine that there was a couch prepared for him there with different kinds of woollen and cotton cloths spread over it, quilts from Kaliṅga thrown over it, a covering over the top, and a great multitude of beautiful red cushions at either end. He would either sit or lie on that couch, and

different kinds of pure food and drink of the highest quality would be offered to him. Do you think, Ajita, that the pleasures available to this prince would be exquisite?"

Ajita replied, "They would indeed be exquisite, Blessed One."

139. The Blessed One said, "Do you think though, Ajita, that he would enjoy them, that they would satisfy him and bring him contentment?"

He replied, "No, Blessed One. If the king had him led away and thrown into the prison, his only wish would undoubtedly be to be set free. He would strive to find nobles, princes, ministers, ladies of the court, merchants, householders, or castellans who could free him from the prison. The prince, Blessed One, would experience no pleasure in that prison, and he would not be set free until the king showed him mercy."

140. The Blessed One said, "In just the same way, Ajita, those bodhisattvas who have planted roots of virtue after having fallen into doubt, and who are uncertain about the knowledge of the buddhas, may be born in the world system of Sukhāvatī because they have heard the name of the Buddha, or simply because of a mental state of serene faith. However, they do not manifest there spontaneously, sitting cross-legged on lotus flowers, but will be enclosed inside lotus flowers. While they are inside the lotus flowers they perceive gardens and palaces, they do not produce faeces, urine, mucus, or snot, and nothing disagreeable appears in their minds. However, they are not able to see the Buddha, hear the Dharma, see bodhisattvas, discuss the Dharma with others and have it explained to them, cultivate any roots of virtue, or practise the Dharma in any way. They do not enjoy themselves or find contentment there. When that which has kept them there has been exhausted, however, they emerge from their lotus flower. When they emerge, they cannot tell whether they are emerging from the top, the bottom, or the side of the lotus flower.

141. "You see, Ajita, in the space of five hundred years a very great many countless hundreds of thousands of buddhas should be worshipped, and a great many roots of virtue, immeasurably many, innumerably many, uncountably many roots of virtue should be planted. Because they are afflicted by doubt, those bodhisattvas are deprived of all of this. You see, Ajita, what a great waste of time doubt is for bodhisattvas.

142. "Therefore, Ajita, bodhisattvas who are free of doubt should cultivate minds set on Awakening. So that they can quickly achieve their goal of being able to benefit all living beings effectively and bring them

happiness, they should dedicate all their roots of virtue to being born in the world system of Sukhāvatī, where the Blessed One, the Tathāgata, the Arhat, the Perfectly Awakened Buddha Amitābha dwells."

143. The Bodhisattva Ajita then said to the Blessed One, "Blessed One, how many of the bodhisattvas who will be born in the world system of Sukhāvatī attained perfection in this buddha-field, or in the presence of other buddhas, other blessed ones?"

144. The Blessed One replied, "Ajita, seven hundred and twenty trillion bodhisattvas who have attained perfection in this buddha-field will be born in the world system of Sukhāvatī. They attained perfection and became irreversible by planting roots of virtue with a very great many countless hundreds of thousands of buddhas. The number of bodhisattvas whose roots of virtue are more limited, then, is truly vast.

145. "A hundred and eighty trillion bodhisattvas who dwell in the presence of the Tathāgata Duṣprasaha, 'Awe-Inspiring', will be born in the world system of Sukhāvatī. A tathāgata named Ratnākara, 'Mine of Precious Substances', dwells to the north-east. Nine hundred million bodhisattvas who dwell in his presence will be born in the world system of Sukhāvatī. Two hundred and twenty million bodhisattvas who dwell in the presence of the Tathāgata Jyotiṣprabha, 'Brilliant Radiance', will be born in the world system of Sukhāvatī. Two hundred and fifty million bodhisattvas who dwell in the presence of the Tathāgata Amitaprabha, 'Infinite Radiance', will be born in the world system of Sukhāvatī. Six hundred million bodhisattvas who dwell in the presence of the Tathāgata Lokapradīpa, 'He Whose Luminescence Covers the World', will be born in the world system of Sukhāvatī. Six hundred and forty million bodhisattvas who dwell in the presence of the Tathāgata Nāgābhibhū, 'He Who Is Supreme Among the Nāgas', will be born in the world system of Sukhāvatī. Two hundred and fifty million bodhisattvas who dwell in the presence of the Tathāgata Virajaḥprabha, 'Spotless Radiance', will be born in the world system of Sukhāvatī. A hundred and sixty million bodhisattvas who dwell in the presence of the Tathāgata Siṃha, 'Lion', will be born in the world system of Sukhāvatī. Eight hundred and ten trillion bodhisattvas who dwell in the presence of the Tathāgata Śrīkūṭa, 'Glorious Mountain Peak', will be born in the world system of Sukhāvatī. A hundred trillion bodhisattvas who dwell in the presence of the Tathāgata Narendrarāja, 'King and Lord of Men', will be born in the world system of Sukhāvatī. Twelve thousand bodhisattvas who dwell in the presence of the Tathāgata Balābhijña, 'He Who Possesses

Power and the Higher Forms of Knowledge', will be born in the world system of Sukhāvatī. Two hundred and fifty million bodhisattvas who dwell in the presence of the Tathāgata Puṣpadhvaja, 'Flower-Banner', who have roused their energy, who have set out on the same journey, and who have stood facing west for ninety quintillion aeons in the space of eight days will be born in the world system of Sukhāvatī. A hundred and twenty million bodhisattvas who dwell in the presence of the Tathāgata Jvalanādhipati, 'Blazing Supremacy', will be born in the world system of Sukhāvatī. Six hundred and ninety million bodhisattvas who dwell in the presence of the Tathāgata Vaiśāradyaprāpta, 'He Who Has the Self-Confidence of a Buddha', will be born in the world system of Sukhāvatī. They will take birth there in order to see the Tathāgata Amitābha, to worship him, attend him, put their queries to him, and ask him questions.

146. "Ajita, I could continue to list the names of the tathāgatas from whose buddha-fields bodhisattvas travel to the world system of Sukhāvatī in order to see the Tathāgata Amitābha, worship him, and attend him, but even if I were to do so for a great many countless aeons I would not be able to list them all.

147. "You see, Ajita, how many living beings gain great attainments with ease by hearing the name of the Tathāgata, the Arhat, the Perfectly Awakened Buddha Amitābha. The commitment of those living beings who experience even a single mental state of serene faith in that tathāgata, or in this discourse on the Dharma, will not be inferior.

148. "That is why I tell you, Ajita, that is why I am explaining to you before the world with its gods that one should be willing to plunge into threefold thousand great thousand world systems filled with fire without thinking of turning back even once – just to hear this discourse on the Dharma. Why should you be willing to do this? You should be willing to do this, Ajita, because countless bodhisattvas have fallen back in their progress towards unsurpassed, perfect Awakening because they did not hear a discourse on the Dharma like this one.

149. "Therefore, you should engage with this discourse on the Dharma with determination so that you can hear it, grasp it, and bear it in mind. You should engage with it with great energy so that you can master it, explain it in detail, and cultivate it in meditation. You should copy it carefully into a book so that you can remember it, even if you only do so for a day and a night, or for the time it takes to milk the cows. Anyone

who wants to set an unlimited number of living beings irreversibly on the path to unsurpassed, perfect Awakening, anyone who wants to see the buddha-field of the Blessed One, the Tathāgata Amitābha, and anyone who themselves wants to bring into being the exceptional abundance of wonderful qualities that adorn it, should see this discourse on the Dharma as their teacher, as their preceptor.

150. "Ajita, there will be some living beings in the future, in the time when the true Dharma is lost, who will gain extremely great attainments with ease because excellent discourses on the Dharma like this one will reach their ears – discourses which are celebrated by all the buddhas, praised by all the buddhas, approved of by all the buddhas, and which quickly bring about the great knowledge through which one understands everything. They will be those living beings who have planted roots of virtue, offered service to victorious ones of the past and been blessed by the buddhas. When they hear these discourses, they will experience unparalleled joy and gladness, grasp them, bear them in mind, recite them, master them, explain them to others in detail, and find satisfaction in cultivating them in meditation. Even if they only copy them and worship them, they will create a great deal of merit – so much merit, in fact, that it cannot easily be calculated.

151. "Ajita, I have done what a tathāgata should do. You[170] must now engage in the kind of spiritual practice which is free from doubt.[171] Have no uncertainty about the unobstructed knowledge of the buddhas, which is free from attachment. Do not enter the prison made of jewels possessing all of the finest qualities. It is rare, Ajita, for a buddha to come into being. It is rare for the Dharma to be taught. It is rare to be born in favourable conditions. I have now explained, Ajita, how to successfully perfect all of your roots of virtue. Now apply yourselves to practice. I entrust this discourse on the Dharma to you, Ajita. You must go forward with courage, Ajita, so that the Dharma of the buddhas is not lost, so that it does not disappear. Do not waver from the Tathāgata's instructions."

152. The Blessed One then spoke these verses:

(1) "Those who have not created merit
will not hear me.
Those heroes who have attained their goal[172]
will hear these words.

(2) "Those who have seen a perfect buddha,
a protector of the world, a radiant one,

and who have listened to the Dharma with reverence
will attain supreme joy.

(3) "Inferior people, or those who are lazy in their thinking,[173]
will not be able to develop serene faith in the Dharma of the buddhas.
Those who are drawn to make offerings in buddha-fields
train in the practice of the protectors of the three worlds.

(4) "Just as a blind person in the dark
cannot point out the way to others,
no śrāvakas have an understanding of the knowledge of a buddha –
and ordinary living beings even less so.

(5) "Only a buddha can understand the good qualities of a buddha,
not gods, nāgas, titans, yakṣas, or śrāvakas.
Even pratyekabuddhas cannot comprehend
the knowledge of a buddha when it is explained to them.

(6) "If all living beings were equal in the purity of their understanding
and if they were all proficient in the ultimate truth,
they could speak for countless aeons and more
and still not fully describe the good qualities of just one buddha.

(7) "They would attain nirvana in the course of
these many countless aeons of explanation,
but they would still not be able to encompass the knowledge of a buddha.
That is how extraordinary the knowledge of the victorious ones is.

(8) "Therefore, someone who is learned and intelligent
should have faith in what I have said.
Then they will see the path of the knowledge of the victorious ones
before their very eyes, and exclaim, "The Buddha understands!"

(9) "Only very rarely is one born as a human being.
Only very rarely do buddhas appear.

It takes a long time to attain the wisdom which has faith as its goal.
You should rouse your energy to attain this goal.

(10) "Those who have heard excellent discourses on the Dharma like this one
experience joy when they recollect the sugatas.
They were our friends in times past,
and they aspire to Awakening."

153. While this discourse on the Dharma was being spoken, a hundred and twenty trillion living beings attained the purified, untainted Dharma-vision[174] of phenomena, free of impurities; twenty-four quadrillion attained one of the fruits of spiritual practice; the minds of eight hundred monks became free of grasping, and were liberated from the corruptions; two hundred and fifty million bodhisattvas attained patient acceptance of the fact that all phenomena are unarisen; and forty quintillion gods and human beings who had not previously done so developed minds set on unsurpassed, perfect Awakening. They planted roots of virtue dedicated to being born in the world system of Sukhāvatī because of their longing to see the Blessed One, the Tathāgata Amitābha. After they have been born there, they will all be born again in turn in other buddha-fields, as tathāgatas by the name of Mañjusvara, "Gentle Voice". Eight hundred trillion who attained patient acceptance with the Tathāgata Dīpaṃkara, whose progress towards unsurpassed, perfect Awakening is irreversible, who have been brought to maturity by the Tathāgata Amitāyus, and who practise in the same way as the bodhisattvas of the past will complete the practice of the vows that they have made when they are born in the world system of Sukhāvatī.

154. The threefold thousand great thousand world systems then shook in six different ways, and various different kinds of miraculous occurences could be seen. The earth became completely flawless. Musical instruments both human and divine played music, and the delightful melodies were heard all the way up to the realm of the *akaniṣṭha* gods.

155. This is what the Blessed One said. The hearts of the bodhisattva, the Great Being Ajita, of Ānanda, of everyone who was present, indeed of the whole world with its gods, human beings, titans, garuḍas, and gandharvas were filled with joy, and they rejoiced at the words of the Blessed One.

This concludes the Mahāyāna Sutra on the Abundance of Wonderful Qualities of Sukhāvatī, the book about Amitābha, which praises and celebrates the good qualities of Sukhāvatī, the buddha-field of the Blessed One, the Tathāgata Amitābha, and by means of which bodhisattvas can attain the stage of irreversibility.

The Tathāgata has explained the cause
of those phenomena which arise from a cause.
He has also explained how they cease.
This is how the Great Renunciant teaches.

The Sutra on the Visualization of the Buddha Amitāyus

Fó shuō guān wúliàngshòu fó jīng
佛說觀無量壽佛經

Translated from Sanskrit[175] into Chinese by the Central Asian Tripiṭaka Master Kālayaśas

Translated from Chinese by Dharmacārī Śraddhāpa

1. This is what I have heard. Once, the Buddha was staying in Rājagṛha, on Vultures' Peak, with a great sangha of 1,250 monks. There were also 32,000 bodhisattvas there, who were led by Mañjuśrī, the youthful prince of the Dharma.

2. At that time there was a prince in Rājagṛha called Ajātaśatru. Under the influence of his evil friend Devadatta he captured his father, King Bimbisāra, locked him in the seventh floor of the prison tower, and ordered his ministers to have no contact with him. The king's concubine Vaidehī was so devoted to him that, after she had bathed, she covered her body with a mixture of ghee, honey, and flour, filled her jewellery with grape juice, and visited the king in secret. The king ate the flour-paste and drank the juice. When he had rinsed his mouth with water he thanked her with folded hands, and then turned to face Vultures' Peak. He bowed to the far-off Blessed One and said, "Mahāmaudgalyāyana is my dear friend. I would ask him to give me the eight precepts, out of compassion." Mahāmaudgalyāyana then flew to the king as swiftly as a falcon. He came to the king in the same way every day, to give him the eight precepts. The Blessed One also sent the Venerable Pūrṇa to talk to the king about the Dharma. All of this continued for three weeks. Because he was eating the flour-paste and was able to hear the Dharma, the king looked happy and contented.

3. Ajātaśatru asked the guard, "Is my father, the king, still alive?" The guard replied, "Your Majesty, the king's concubine has been covering her body with flour-paste, filling her jewellery with grape juice, and visiting the king. The monks Mahāmaudgalyāyana and Pūrṇa have been coming to the king, flying through the air, to talk to him about the Dharma. It has not been possible to stop them." When he heard this, Ajātaśatru became furious with his mother. He said, "My mother is a traitor and is in league with a traitor. These monks are evil, and they have been keeping the king alive all this time with their sorcery." He then drew his sword to kill his mother.

One of his ministers, Candraprabha, was intelligent and wise. Together with Jīvaka, he bowed to the king and said, "Your Majesty, we have heard in the Vedic texts that since the beginning of this aeon there have been 18,000 evil kings who have killed their fathers in order to take the throne for themselves. However, we have never heard of any king who has gone as far as to kill his own mother. If Your Majesty carries out this unspeakable deed, you will bring dishonour to the *kṣatriya* class. We could not abide this. You would then be untouchable, and it would not be appropriate for us to remain in your service."

When the two ministers had spoken these words, they drew their own swords and stepped back a pace. Frightened and shaken, Ajātaśatru said to Jīvaka, "Are you not on my side?"

Jīvaka replied, "Restrain yourself, Your Majesty. Do not kill your mother." When the king heard these words, he regretted what he had done, and asked for forgiveness. He threw down his sword and, instead of killing her, ordered his mother to be cast into the deepest dungeon and never released.

4. The imprisoned Vaidehī, emaciated with worry, turned to face Vultures' Peak, bowed to the Buddha, and said, "The Blessed One, the Tathāgata, used to send Ānanda to comfort me. Now I am filled with anxiety and unease. As I am not able to gaze upon the face of the Blessed One, it is my heartfelt desire that the Venerable Maudgalyāyana and Ānanda come to me here."

Her tears fell like rain. She turned towards the far-off Buddha, bowed down in reverence, and lay there unmoving. On Vultures' Peak, the Blessed One understood Vaidehī's wish. He asked Mahāmaudgalyāyana, as well as Ānanda, to fly to her through the air. The Buddha himself vanished from Vultures' Peak and appeared in the royal palace.

When Vaidehī raised her head, she saw the Blessed One, the Buddha Śākyamuni. His body was the colour of pure gold, and he was seated on a lotus flower made of a hundred different kinds of precious substances. Maudgalyāyana stood to his left, and Ānanda to his right. Śakra, Brahmā, the protectors of the world, and all the other gods surrounded him in the air, showering him with heavenly flowers.

When Vaidehī saw the Buddha, the Blessed One, she took off her jewellery and threw herself on the ground at his feet. Through her tears, she addressed the Buddha. "Blessed One, what evil have I done that has resulted in me giving birth to such a wicked child? What kinds of causes and conditions have resulted in you, Blessed One, being born into the same family as Devadatta?

5. "Blessed One, it is my heartfelt desire that you would reveal to me a place free of sorrow, free of the defilements. In my future lives, I do not wish to try to find happiness in this world of confusion and evil. This place of confusion and evil is filled with hell-realms, hungry ghosts, and animals. It is filled with misery. It is my heartfelt desire that in the future I will not see any evil people, or hear any evil words. I now prostrate myself to you, Blessed One. I repent, and ask you to take pity on me. My only heartfelt desire is that the Buddha, who is like the sun, might teach me how to visualize a place where the effects of all actions have been purified."[176]

The Buddha then sent forth a ray of golden light from between his eyebrows, which illuminated innumerable world systems in the ten directions of space. The light then returned to the Buddha and gathered at the top of his head, where it was transformed into a golden platform which resembled Mount Sumeru. All of the wondrous, pure buddha-fields in the ten directions of space appeared there. Some were made of the seven kinds of precious substances, some of nothing but lotus flowers. Some resembled the palaces of gods who have power over the creations of others, and some were like crystal mirrors in which all the other buddha-fields in the ten directions of space appeared. In this way, Vaidehī was able to see[177] an infinite number of buddha-fields, in all their majesty.

Vaidehī then said to the Buddha, "Blessed One, although all of these buddha-fields are pure and radiant, I wish to be born in Sukhāvatī, where the Buddha Amitābha dwells. My only heartfelt desire, Blessed One, is that you would teach me how to contemplate that buddha-field and attain meditative concentration by doing so."

6. The Blessed One smiled. Rays of light of five different colours came from his mouth, and each shone on the head of King Bimbisāra. Although

the great king was imprisoned, he could see the Blessed One from afar in his mind's eye without hindrance. He bowed down to the Blessed One in reverence, and attained the state of a non-returner naturally and spontaneously.

7. The Blessed One then said to Vaidehī, "You do not know it yet, but the Buddha Amitābha is not far away. You should concentrate your awareness[178] on that buddha-field, and visualize it with great care. I will now reveal to you in comprehensive detail how you can purify the effects of your actions by doing so, so that in the future any ordinary person who wishes to purify the effects of their actions will be able to be reborn in the western buddha-field of Sukhāvatī. Those who wish to be born in that buddha-field should cultivate merit in three ways. Firstly, one should respect and support one's parents, honour and serve one's teachers, cultivate a mind filled with compassion and refrain from taking life, and practise the ten kinds of skilful action. Secondly, one should hold fast to the Three Refuges, observe all the precepts, and conduct oneself properly. Thirdly, one should cultivate a mind set on Awakening, and a deep faith in cause and effect. One should read and recite the Mahāyāna sutras, and encourage others in their practice. This is what is meant by purifying the effects of one's actions."

The Buddha then said to Vaidehī, "You do not know it yet, but it is by acting in these three ways that all the buddhas of the past, the present, and the future purify their actions."

8. The Buddha then said to Ānanda and Vaidehī, "Listen closely. Listen closely, and reflect carefully on what I am about to tell you. The Tathāgata will now explain how to purify the effects of one's actions, for the sake of all of the living beings in the future who will be tormented by the defilements. It is good, Vaidehī, it is excellent that you have asked me about this. Ānanda, you should bear what I am about to say in mind, and spread these words of the Buddha widely, sharing them with a great many living beings. The Tathāgata will now explain how to visualize Sukhāvatī, for the benefit of Vaidehī and all living beings in the future. Through the power of the Buddha, they will all be able to see this pure buddha-field as clearly as looking at their own face in a mirror. They will see the extraordinary, exquisite happiness that is to be found in that buddha-field, and because of the joy that will fill their hearts thereby, they will attain patient acceptance of the fact that all phenomena are unarisen."

The Buddha then said to Vaidehī, "You are an ordinary person, with a weak and feeble mind. You do not have the power of the divine eye, and so you cannot see things which are far away. All buddhas, all tathāgatas have a range of skilful means at their disposal which they can use to enable you to see."

Vaidehī said, "Blessed One, I have been able to see that buddha-field through the power of the Buddha, but when the Buddha has attained cessation, how will living beings in the future, living in a degenerate age and oppressed by the five kinds of suffering,[179] be able to see Sukhāvatī, the buddha-field of the Buddha Amitābha?"

9. The Buddha said to Vaidehī, "You, and all other living beings, should concentrate your mind, and gather your attention[180] in one place. You should then focus your mind on the west. How should you focus your mind? All living beings, except those who were born blind or whose vision is impaired, should look at the setting sun. Gather your attention, sit upright, and gaze unwaveringly at the sun. Do not let your mind wander. Concentrate your mind without getting distracted, and look at the setting sun, which is like a drum suspended in the air. When you have looked at the sun in this way, you should be able to see it clearly, whether your eyes are open or closed. This is the first visualization, where the mind is focused on the sun. This is the correct way to perform the visualization. Doing it in any other way is not correct."

10. The Buddha then said to Ānanda and Vaidehī, "When you have completed the first visualization, you should focus your mind on water. Focus your mind and picture everything to the west as being covered by a great body of water. See the water as clear and pure. You should be able to picture it clearly, with undivided attention. When you can see the water in your mind, imagine it freezing and turning to ice, brilliant and shining to its very depths. Then picture the ice turning into lapis lazuli. When you have completed this visualization, picture the lapis lazuli ground as being brilliant and shining to its very depths, both on the inside and on the surface. The lapis lazuli ground is supported from below by golden pillars inlaid with diamonds and the seven kinds of precious substances. These pillars have eight sides and eight corners, and each side is adorned with a hundred different kinds of precious substances. Each precious stone gives off a thousand rays of light, and each ray of light shines forth in eighty-four thousand different colours. When this light is reflected by the lapis lazuli ground, it becomes as brilliant as a hundred thousand million suns, so that it is impossible to look at it.

"The lapis lazuli ground is divided into different sections by a network of golden cords. The ground is divided neatly into sections, each made of one of the seven kinds of precious substances. Each of these precious substances gives off light in five hundred different colours, and this light can resemble flowers, the moon, or stars. This light remains suspended in the air, and turns into a platform made of light. On this platform, there are ten million palaces made of a hundred different kinds of precious substances. Both sides of the platform are adorned with ten billion flower-banners and innumerable musical instruments. The light also emits eight kinds of pure breezes which make the musical instruments sound. They play songs of suffering, of emptiness, of impermanence, and of no self. This is the second visualization, where the mind is focused on water.

11. "When you have successfully focused your mind in this way, make sure you visualize everything completely clearly, so that whether your eyes are open or closed, the image does not fade. Break off the practice only when it is time to eat. Keep the image constantly in your awareness. This is the correct way to perform the visualization. Doing it in any other way is not correct."

The Buddha then said to Ānanda and Vaidehī, "When you have successfully focused your mind on water in this way, you have attained what is known as the vision of the ground of Sukhāvatī. If you attain a state of samādhi in the course of this practice, you will see the ground of that buddha-field so clearly and in such detail that you will not be able to fully describe it. This is the third visualization, where the mind is focused on the ground."

The Buddha then said to Ānanda, "You should bear these words of the Buddha in mind, and communicate the Dharma of visualizing the ground of Sukhāvatī to all of the many living beings in the future who want to be free from suffering. Those who visualize the ground of Sukhāvatī will free themselves of the effects of previous unskilful actions[181] that would have kept them in samsara for eight billion aeons, and when they pass away they will undoubtedly be born in that pure buddha-field. Have no doubt about this. This is the correct way to perform the visualization. Doing it in any other way is not correct."

12. The Buddha then said to Ānanda and Vaidehī, "When you have successfully focused your mind on the ground in this way, next visualize the trees made of precious substances. When you visualize the trees made of precious substances, visualize them each individually, and then picture seven rows of trees in your mind. Each tree is eight thousand yojanas high, and all of the flowers and leaves without exception are

made of the seven kinds of precious substances. Each flower and each leaf emits a different kind of jewelled light. Those made of lapis lazuli emit a golden light. Those made of quartz emit a red light. Those made of agate emit a mother-of-pearl-coloured light. Those made of mother-of-pearl emit an emerald-coloured light. Coral, amber, and all of the other kinds of precious substances shine forth with great beauty. The trees are adorned with nets made of exquisite jewels. Seven rows of nets hang from each tree, and between each row of nets there are fifty billion wondrous palaces, each one equal to the palace of Brahmā, the King of the Gods. These palaces are inhabited by gods who naturally and spontaneously take up residence there. Each of these gods has fifty billion necklaces made of jewels the like of those worn by Śakra. The light from these jewels radiates a hundred yojanas in all directions, shining as brightly as ten billion suns and moons, such that they cannot be described in detail. The light from this great mass of jewels intermingles, producing exquisite colours.

"The trees made of precious substances are evenly spaced, and their leaves are evenly spaced as well. Exquisite flowers grow from between the leaves, and these flowers naturally and spontaneously produce fruit made of the seven kinds of precious substances. Each of these leaves is twenty-five yojanas long, and twenty-five yojanas wide. Like heavenly ornaments, they are a thousand different colours, and are decorated with a hundred different patterns. The many exquisite flowers are the colour of gold from the Jambū River. They spin like wheels of fire, and as they turn all kinds of fruit spring forth from among the leaves, as if from Śakra's vase. Great floods of light pour forth from them, and turn into banners and innumerable jewelled canopies. Within these jewelled canopies, the activities of all the buddhas in a billion worlds are reflected. All of the buddha-fields in the ten directions of space can been seen within them as well.

"When you are able to see the trees in this way, you should then visualize each of the individual elements of the trees in turn. Visualize the trunks of the trees, the branches, the leaves, the flowers, and the fruit, making them all clear in your mind. This is the fourth visualization, where the mind is focused on the trees. This is the correct way to perform the visualization. Doing it in any other way is not correct."

13. The Buddha then said to Ānanda and Vaidehī, "When you have successfully focused your mind on the trees in this way, next focus your mind on the ponds. You should focus your mind on the ponds in the following way. In Sukhāvatī, there are ponds filled with water which

possesses eight good qualities. Each pond is made of the seven kinds of precious substances, which are soft and beautiful. Fourteen streams of water flow forth from the Wish-Fulfilling Jewel, the King of Gems. These streams of water shine with the colours of the seven kinds of precious substances, and flow along channels made of yellow gold. The base of each of these channels is covered with diamond sand, and shines with a great multitude of colours. Each pond is filled with six billion lotus flowers made of the seven kinds of precious substances. Each lotus flower is a perfect circle twelve yojanas in diameter. The water from the Wish-Fulfilling Jewel swirls around the lotus flowers and flows between the trees. The exquisite, subtle sounds made by the water tell of suffering, of emptiness, of impermanence, of no self, and of the perfections.[182] They also intone the praises of the major and minor physical characteristics of the buddhas. Exquisite, subtle, golden light springs forth from the Wish-Fulfilling Jewel, the King of Gems. This light turns into birds the colours of a hundred different kinds of precious substances. They sing haunting, elegant songs, endlessly praising the practice of recollecting the Buddha, recollecting the Dharma, and recollecting the Sangha. This is the fifth visualization, where the mind is focused on the ponds filled with water which possesses eight good qualities. This is the correct way to perform the visualization. Doing it in any other way is not correct."

14. The Buddha then said to Ānanda and Vaidehī, "In each region of that buddha-field filled with precious substances there are fifty billion palaces made of precious substances. Innumerable gods dwell in these palaces, playing heavenly music. There are also musical instruments suspended in the air like heavenly banners made of precious substances, which produce music even though there is no one playing them. All of this music tells of the practice of recollecting the Buddha, recollecting the Dharma, and recollecting the Monastic Sangha.

"This is the sixth visualization, where the mind is focused on Sukhāvatī in a broad way, encompassing the trees, the ground, and the ponds, all of which are made of precious substances. The mind should be focused on a visualization which includes all of these elements. If you practise the visualization in this way, you will free yourself from the effects of previous extremely serious unskilful actions which you have performed over the course of a hundred million aeons, and you will undoubtedly be born in that buddha-field when you die. This is the correct way to perform the visualization. Doing it in any other way is not correct."

15. The Buddha then said to Ānanda and Vaidehī, "Listen closely. Listen closely, and reflect carefully on what I am about to tell you. I will give you a Dharma teaching on how to free yourself from suffering and from the defilements. You should bear what I am about to say in mind, and spread this teaching widely, sharing it with a great many living beings."

As he spoke these words, the Buddha Amitāyus appeared in the air above him, with the two great beings Avalokiteśvara and Mahāsthāmaprāpta on either side. They were blazing with light so brilliant that it was impossible to see them properly. Even the radiance of gold from the Jambū River multiplied a hundred thousand times could not compare with it.

When Vaidehī saw the Buddha Amitāyus, she bowed down at the Buddha's feet and said, "Blessed One, through the power of the Buddha I have now obtained a vision of the Buddha Amitāyus, along with his two attendant bodhisattvas. Please tell me how living beings in the future can visualize the Buddha Amitāyus, along with his two attendant bodhisattvas."

The Buddha said to Vaidehī, "Those who wish to visualize this Buddha should gather their attention, and focus their minds on a lotus flower made of seven kinds of precious substances growing from the earth. They should picture each petal of this lotus flower as being the colours of a hundred different kinds of precious substances, with eighty-four thousand veins running through it. Light shines forth from each vein in eighty-four thousand colours, like a heavenly painting. They should be able to see all of this clearly. The smaller petals of the lotus are two hundred and fifty yojanas long, and two hundred and fifty yojanas wide. The lotus flower has eighty-four thousand large petals and it is adorned with jewels, kings among gems, which shine between each of its petals. Each of these jewels radiates a thousand rays of light. This light is like a canopy made of precious substances which covers the whole of the earth.

"There is a platform on the lotus flower made of jewels the like of those worn by Śakra, and adorned with eighty thousand diamonds, rubies, Brahma-jewels, and wondrous nets made of jewels. Four pillars decked in banners made of precious substances arise naturally and spontaneously from the platform. Each of these banners made of precious substances is as big as a hundred quadrillion Mount Sumerus. Above these is a canopy made of precious substances, like the one in the palace in the heaven of the yāma gods. It too is adorned with fifty billion fine and wondrous jewels. Each of these jewels emits eighty-four thousand rays of light, and each ray of light shines forth in eighty-four thousand shades of gold. The golden light covers the ground made of precious substances and everywhere takes on different forms – diamond platforms, nets made of jewels, or clouds of different kinds of flowers. As it spreads throughout the ten directions of space, it takes on whatever form one wishes, and performs the actions of a buddha. This is the seventh visualization, where the mind is focused on the lotus seat."

The Buddha then said to Ānanda, "This wondrous lotus flower was brought into being through the power of the monk Dharmākara's vow. Those who wish to recollect this Buddha should first focus their minds on this wondrous lotus throne. When you focus your mind in this way, do not visualize all the different elements at the same time, but visualize each element in turn. Visualize each petal, each jewel, each ray of light, the platform, and each banner, so that you can see them as clearly as if you were looking at your own face in a mirror. When you have successfully focused your mind in this way, you will free yourself from the effects of unskilful actions which you have performed over the course of fifty billion aeons, and you will undoubtedly be assured of being born in Sukhāvatī. This is the correct way to perform the visualization. Doing it in any other way is not correct."

16. The Buddha then said to Ānanda and Vaidehī, "When you have obtained a vision of these things, you should then focus your mind on the Buddha. Why should you do this? The body of all the buddhas, all the tathāgatas, is the realm of reality, and they enter into the focused minds of all living beings. Therefore, when you focus your mind on the Buddha, your mind takes on the thirty-two major physical characteristics, and the eighty minor physical characteristics of the Buddha. When your mind creates the Buddha, your mind becomes the Buddha. The ocean of all the perfectly awakened buddhas arises from the focused mind. Therefore, you should concentrate your attention with an integrated mind and visualize the Buddha, the Tathāgata, the Arhat, the Perfectly Awakened Buddha with great care.

"When you focus your mind on the Buddha, you should begin by focusing on his image. Whether your eyes are open or closed, you should be able to see his image sitting atop the lotus like a jewel, the colour of gold from the Jambū River. When you can see the image of the Buddha sitting there, your mind's eye will open, and you will be able to see him completely clearly. You will also see the adornments of Sukhāvatī, which are made of the seven kinds of precious substances, the ground made of precious substances, the ponds made of precious substances, the rows of trees made of precious substances, the heavenly cloth made of precious substances draped over the trees, and the abundant nets made of precious substances which fill the sky. Visualize all this completely clearly, so that you can see it all as distinctly as if you were looking at something in the palm of your hand.

"When you have attained a vision of all this, picture a great lotus flower to the left of the Buddha, exactly the same as the first one, and another to his right. Focus your mind, and visualize the Bodhisattva Avalokiteśvara seated on the lotus seat to the left. Picture him radiating golden light just like the Buddha. You should then focus your mind on the image of the Bodhisattva Mahāsthāmaprāpta seated on the lotus seat to the right.

"When you have successfully focused your mind in this way, picture the Buddha and the bodhisattvas radiating exquisitely beautiful light. This golden light illuminates the trees made of precious substances. There are three lotus flowers under each tree, and on these three lotus flowers sit the images of a buddha and two bodhisattvas. That buddha-field is filled with such images.

"When you have successfully focused your mind in this way, you will hear the streams of water, the rays of light, all of the trees made of precious substances, the cranes, the *haṃsa*-geese, and the ducks, all proclaiming the wondrous Dharma. Whether you are absorbed in samadhi or not, you will always hear the wondrous Dharma. When you come out of samadhi, you should remember what you have heard, bear it in mind, and not forget it. Check whether what you have heard accords with the sutras. If it does not, you should regard it as a false mental construction. If it does accord with the sutras, you should regard it as a general perception of Sukhāvatī. This is the eighth visualization, where the mind is focused on the images of the Buddha and the bodhisattvas. If you practise the visualization in this way, you will free yourself from the effects of previous extremely serious unskilful actions which you have performed over the course of countless hundreds of millions of aeons, and in this life you will attain the Samadhi of the Recollection of the Buddha. This is the correct way to perform the visualization. Doing it in any other way is not correct."

17. The Buddha then said to Ānanda and Vaidehī, "When you have successfully focused your mind in this way, you should then visualize the body, the major physical characteristics, and the radiance of the Buddha Amitāyus. Understand, Ānanda, that the colour of the body of the Buddha Amitāyus is a hundred quadrillion times more brilliant

than gold from the Jambū River in the heaven of the yāma gods. The height of the Buddha's body is a number of yojanas equal to the number of grains of sand in the River Ganges multiplied by sixty quintillion. Between his eyes there is a tuft of white hair that curls to the right, five times as big as Mount Sumeru. The Buddha's eyes are as clear as the pure, limpid waters of the four oceans. Light as magnificent as Mount Sumeru radiates from every pore on his body. The sphere of the Buddha's radiance envelops a billion world systems, each containing a billion worlds. Within the sphere of his radiance there are a number of emanation buddhas equal to the number of grains of sand in the River Ganges multiplied by a hundred trillion. Each of these emanation buddhas in turn is attended by an assembly of emanation bodhisattvas.

"The Buddha Amitāyus has eighty-four thousand major physical characteristics, and within each of these there are eighty-four thousand minor physical characteristics. Each of these minor physical characteristics emits eighty-four thousand rays of light, and each of these rays of light illuminates all of the world systems in the ten directions of space, shining upon all of those living beings who recollect the Buddha, without exception. It is impossible to describe his physical characteristics, his radiance, and his emanation buddhas, but by recollecting them and focusing one's mind upon them, it is possible see them clearly in one's mind.

"Those who see these things in their mind in this way will see all of the buddhas in the ten directions of space, and this is therefore known as the Samadhi of the Recollection of the Buddhas.[183] Those who perform this visualization will attain a vision of the bodies of all the buddhas. By attaining a vision of the bodies of the buddhas, they will perceive the mind of the buddhas. The mind of the buddhas is great compassion, an unconditioned compassion that embraces all living beings. Those who perform this visualization will be born in the presence of all the buddhas when they die, and attain patient acceptance of the fact that all phenomena are unarisen. Therefore, those who are wise should concentrate their minds and perform the visualization of the Buddha Amitāyus with great care.

"Those who visualize the Buddha Amitāyus should begin by becoming absorbed by one of his physical characteristics. They should begin by visualizing the tuft of white hair between his eyebrows clearly. Those who visualize the tuft of white hair between his eyebrows will naturally and spontaneously be able to see his eighty-four thousand other physical characteristics. Those who see the Buddha Amitāyus will be able to see all of the innumerable buddhas in the ten directions of space. When they see all of the innumerable buddhas, they will receive their prediction to Awakening in their presence. This is the ninth visualization, where the mind is focused on all of the physical characteristics of the Buddha in a broad way. This is the correct way to perform the visualization. Doing it in any other way is not correct."

18. The Buddha then said to Ānanda and Vaidehī, "When you are able to see the Buddha Amitāyus completely clearly, you should then visualize the Bodhisattva Avalokiteśvara. The height of this bodhisattva's body is a number of yojanas equal to the number of grains of sand in the River Ganges multiplied by eight quadrillion. His body is the colour of pure gold, and there is a protuberance on the top of his head. His throat is surrounded by a sphere of radiance which extends for a hundred thousand yojanas. Within this sphere of radiance, there are five hundred emanation buddhas, all resembling Śākyamuni. Each of these emanation buddhas is attended by five hundred bodhisattvas, and innumerable gods. The radiance emanated by his body reveals living beings in the five realms of existence, with all their different physical characteristics. On his head he wears a heavenly crown made of jewels the like of those worn by Śakra, within which there is an emanation buddha twenty-five yojanas in height.

"The face of the Bodhisattva Avalokiteśvara is the colour of gold from the Jambū River. The tuft of hair between his eyebrows is the colour of the seven precious substances, and it emits eighty-four thousand rays of light. Each of these rays of light contains innumerable, uncountable hundreds of thousands of emanation buddhas, and each of these emanation buddhas is attended by uncountable emanation bodhisattvas. They all manifest naturally and spontaneously, filling all of the worlds in the ten directions of space. His arms are the colour of red lotuses, and emit eight billion rays of beautiful, exquisite light in the form of jewelled necklaces. All of the adornments of Sukhāvatī are reflected in those jewelled necklaces. The palms of his hands are the colours of fifty billion different lotus flowers. On each of his ten fingertips, eighty-four thousand different patterns can be traced, and each of these patterns is in eighty-four thousand colours. Each of these colours emits eighty-four thousand rays of light. Each ray of soft, gentle light illuminates everything. With his precious hands, he guides living beings.

"When he lifts his foot, the mark of the thousand-spoked wheel on its sole naturally and spontaneously transforms into a platform which emits fifty billion rays of light. When he puts his foot down, lotus flowers made of diamond and jewels scatter everywhere. All of his other physical characteristics are exactly the same as those of the Buddha, except for his invisible protuberance, which is not equal to that of the Blessed One. This is the tenth visualization, where the mind is focused on the actual physical characteristics of the Bodhisattva Avalokiteśvara."

The Buddha then said to Ānanda, "If you wish to attain a vision of the Bodhisattva Avalokiteśvara, you should visualize him in this way. Those who visualize him in this way will not encounter any misfortune. They will free themselves of the effects of previous unskilful actions that would have kept them in samsara for countless aeons. Simply hearing the name of this bodhisattva brings incalculable merit, and visualizing him with great care even more. Those who wish to obtain a vision of the Bodhisattva Avalokiteśvara should begin by visualizing the protuberance on the top of his head. They should then visualize his heavenly crown, and all of his other physical characteristics in turn. They should visualize this completely clearly, so that they can see it all as distinctly as if they were looking at something in the palm of their hand. This is the correct way to perform the visualization. Doing it in any other way is not correct."

19. The Buddha then said to Ānanda and Vaidehī, "You should then visualize the Bodhisattva Mahāsthāmaprāpta, whose body is the same size as that of Avalokiteśvara. The sphere of radiance which surrounds his face extends for two hundred and twenty-five yojanas, it sheds its light over two hundred and twenty-five yojanas. The radiance that emanates from his body illuminates the buddha-fields in the ten directions of space, such that they shine with the colour of pure gold. Any living being who knows him will be able to see him. Even if one only sees the light radiating from a single pore on his body, one will thereby be able to see the exquisite, pure radiance of all the buddhas in the ten directions of space. That is why this bodhisattva is known as Anantaprabha, 'Boundless Radiance'. He illuminates all living beings with his wisdom, leading them from the three states of misfortune to the attainment of unsurpassed power. That is why this bodhisattva is known as Mahāsthāmaprāpta, 'He Who Possesses Great Strength'.

"He possesses a crown of five hundred lotus flowers made of precious substances. On each of these lotus flowers there are five hundred platforms made of precious substances. On each of these platforms all the buddhas of the ten directions of space appear, surrounded by their vast pure buddha-fields, each adorned with their wondrous qualities.

"The protuberance on the top of his head is like a jewelled lotus bud, and is surmounted by a vase made of precious substances. It is filled with light in which all the activities of the buddhas appear. All of his other physical characteristics are exactly the same as those of Avalokiteśvara. When this bodhisattva walks, all of the worlds in the ten directions of space tremble, and wherever the earth moves, fifty billion lotus flowers made of precious substances spring up. Each of these lotus flowers is as majestic as those in Sukhāvatī. When this bodhisattva sits, seven precious buddha-fields quake, from the Buddha-Field of Golden Radiance to the nadir, to the Buddha-Field of the King of Radiance to the zenith. In the space between these buddha-fields, manifested bodies of the Buddha Amitāyus, of Avalokiteśvara, and of Mahāsthāmaprāpta appear, as innumerable as particles of dust. All of these manifested bodies gather in great clouds in Sukhāvatī. They fill the sky on all sides, and seated on lotus flowers they teach the wondrous Dharma in order to save living beings who are suffering. The visualization of this bodhisattva is the eleventh visualization, which is known as the visualization of the Bodhisattva Mahāsthāmaprāpta, or the visualization of the physical characteristics of the Bodhisattva Mahāsthāmaprāpta. It will free those who perform it of the effects of previous unskilful actions that would have kept them in samsara for innumerable aeons, and they will never again be born from a womb. They will be able to go to the wondrous, pure buddha-field of any buddha, whenever they wish. These visualizations are known as the complete visualizations of Avalokiteśvara and Mahāsthāmaprāpta. This is the correct way to perform the visualizations. Doing it in any other way is not correct."

20. The Buddha then said to Ānanda and Vaidehī, "When you have visualized these things, you should focus your mind and imagine yourself being born in Sukhāvatī, sitting cross-legged on a lotus flower. Imagine that the lotus flower is closed, and then that it opens. When the lotus flower opens, imagine five hundred rays of coloured light shining forth from your body. Imagine your eyes opening, so that you can see the buddhas and bodhisattvas filling the sky. Imagine hearing the sounds of the birds, the trees, and all the buddhas, every sound proclaiming the wondrous Dharma in accordance with the twelve divisions of the sacred scriptures.[184] When you come out of samādhi, remember the things you have seen – do not forget them. This is known as the vision of the Buddha Amitāyus and of Sukhāvatī. This is the twelfth visualization, where the mind is focused on a broad visualization.

"Countless emanation bodies of the Buddha Amitāyus, and of Avalokiteśvara and Mahāsthāmaprāpta, will invariably congregate wherever this practice is being done. This is the correct way to perform the visualization. Doing it in any other way is not correct."

21. The Buddha then said to Ānanda and Vaidehī, "Those who sincerely wish to be born in Sukhāvatī should visualize an image sixteen feet tall, seated on the surface of a pond. As I have already said, the size of the body of the Buddha Amitāyus is beyond measure, beyond the grasp of ordinary immature beings. However, because of the power of the vows that that Tathāgata took in the past, those who focus their minds on him will nonetheless be able to perform the practice. The merit gained by focusing the mind on the Buddha in this way is immeasurable, and the merit gained by visualizing all of his physical characteristics is even greater.

"The Buddha Amitābha can use his supernormal abilities[185] whenever he wishes, to manifest himself naturally and spontaneously anywhere in the ten directions of space. He can manifest a gigantic body which fills the sky, or a smaller body, eight or sixteen feet high. Wherever and however he manifests himself, his form is the colour of pure gold. The spheres of radiance of the emanation buddhas and the lotus flowers made of precious substances are like the ones I described earlier.

"The bodies of the Bodhisattvas Avalokiteśvara and Mahāsthāmaprāpta have the same appearance no matter where they are. Living beings can only tell them apart by examining their physical characteristics. These two bodhisattvas help the Buddha Amitābha in the task of transforming all living beings. This is the thirteenth visualization, where the mind is focused on a number of different things. This is the correct way to perform the visualization. Doing it in any other way is not correct."

22. The Buddha then said to Ānanda and Vaidehī, "The ordinary immature beings who are born in Sukhāvatī fall into nine categories. The highest level of the highest category is comprised of those living beings who have a heartfelt desire to be born there. They cultivate three kinds of mental states, and are then born in Sukhāvatī. What are these three kinds of mental states? The first is a clear mind. The second is a mental state of determination. The third is a mental state of cultivating a heartfelt desire, such that one dedicates the merits of one's skilful actions to the attainment of one's goal. Those who dwell in these three mental states will undoubtedly be born in that buddha-field.

"There are three other kinds of living beings who will be born in Sukhāvatī. What are these three kinds of living beings? The first kind is living beings who have minds filled with compassion, who do not take life, and who practise all the precepts. The second kind is living beings who recite the extensive Mahāyāna sutras. The third kind is those who practise the six recollections,[186] and whose heartfelt desire is such that they dedicate the merit they gain by doing so to being born in that buddha-field. If they do this for between one day and seven days, they will be born in Sukhāvatī.

"When people like this are born in that buddha-field because of the energy and effort they have put into their practice, the Tathāgata Amitābha will appear to them together with Avalokiteśvara, Mahāsthāmaprāpta, innumerable emanation buddhas, a hundred thousand monks, a great assembly of śrāvakas, and countless gods with their palaces made of the seven kinds of precious substances. The Bodhisattva Avalokiteśvara will be bearing a diamond platform, and will appear before the practitioner together with the Bodhisattva Mahāsthāmaprāpta. The Buddha Amitābha will illuminate the practitioner's body with a great flood of light and, together with all the bodhisattvas, extend his hands in welcome. Avalokiteśvara and Mahāsthāmaprāpta, along with countless other bodhisattvas, will praise and encourage the practitioner. When the practitioner sees all of this, they will jump for joy. They will seat themselves on the diamond platform and, following after the Buddha, instantly be born in that buddha-field.

"When they are born in that buddha-field, they see the body of the Buddha, as well as the bodies of all the bodhisattvas, with all their major and minor physical characteristics. They see the radiant trees made of precious substances proclaiming the wondrous Dharma, and when they hear it they attain patient acceptance of the fact that all phenomena are unarisen. In a single moment, they appear before each of the buddhas dwelling in the ten directions of space, and receive their prediction to Awakening. When they return to their own buddha-field, they receive innumerable hundreds of thousands of dhāraṇīs, each one a doorway into the Dharma. People like this belong to the highest level of the highest category.

23. "The middle level of the highest category is comprised of those living beings who do not necessarily accept and recite the extensive Mahāyāna sutras, but who have a good understanding of the ultimate truth and do not find it disturbing. They have a deep faith in the law of cause and effect, and they do not disparage the Mahāyāna. They dedicate the merit they gain thereby to being born in Sukhāvatī, because this is their heartfelt desire.

"When the life of a practitioner who has practised in this way is at an end, the Buddha Amitābha will appear to them together with Avalokiteśvara and Mahāsthāmaprāpta, surrounded by a great assembly, and bearing a platform of pure gold. He will speak words of praise to the practitioner, saying, 'Child of the Dharma, because you have practised the Mahāyāna and gained an understanding of the ultimate truth, I have come to welcome you.' A thousand emanation buddhas will then extend their hands to the practitioner at the same time. The practitioner will seat themselves on the platform of pure gold, and praise all the buddhas with folded hands. In an instant, they will be born in that buddha-field, in one of the ponds made of seven kinds of precious substances.

"The platform of pure gold then turns into a great lotus flower made of precious substances, which opens after one night. The body of the practitioner becomes the colour of pure gold, and lotus flowers made of the seven kinds of precious substances appear under their feet. The Buddha and the bodhisattvas all emit rays of light that illuminate the practitioner, who then opens their eyes. Because of the practice they have done during the night, they are able to hear the great swell of sounds proclaiming the pure, profound, ultimate truth. Descending from the golden platform, they venerate the Buddha, praising the Blessed One with folded hands. After seven days, their progress towards unsurpassed, perfect Awakening becomes irreversible. Moreover, they immediately gain the ability to fly through the air in any direction. They praise all the buddhas, and learn many samadhis from them. After an intermediate aeon, they attain patient acceptance of the fact that all phenomena are unarisen, and receive their prediction to Awakening. People like this belong to the middle level of the highest category.

24. "The lowest level of the highest category is comprised of those living beings who also have faith in the law of cause and effect, and do not disparage the Mahāyāna. They have cultivated a mind set on unsurpassed Awakening, and they dedicate the merit they gain thereby to being born in Sukhāvatī, because this is their heartfelt desire.

"When the life of a practitioner who has practised in this way is at an end, the Buddha Amitābha will appear to them together with Avalokiteśvara and Mahāsthāmaprāpta, surrounded by a great assembly, bearing a golden lotus, and manifesting five hundred emanation buddhas who will come to welcome this person. The five hundred emanation buddhas will then extend their hands to the practitioner at the same time and speak words of praise, saying, 'Child of the Dharma, because you have cultivated a mind set on unsurpassed Awakening, I have come to welcome you.'

"When the practitioner sees all of this, they will find themselves seated on the golden lotus, which will then close around them. Following after the Buddha, they will be born in a pond made of the seven kinds of precious substances. The lotus flower opens after a day and a night, and after seven days they are able to see the Buddha. Although they are able to see the body of the Buddha with all its physical characteristics, their minds are not clear. Only after three weeks are they able to see the Buddha completely clearly and hear the great swell of sounds all proclaiming the wondrous Dharma. They are then able to travel in all of the ten directions of space, worship all the buddhas, and hear them teaching the profound Dharma. After three intermediate aeons, they attain the doorway into the Dharma which consists of an understanding of all phenomena, and dwell in the stage of joy. People like this belong to the lowest level of the highest category. This is the fourteenth visualization, where the mind is focused on those who belong to the highest category. This is the correct way to perform the visualization. Doing it in any other way is not correct."

25. The Buddha then said to Ānanda and Vaidehī, "The highest level of the middle category is comprised of those living beings who observe the five precepts and the eight precepts, who practise all the precepts, and who have not committed any of the five acts which have immediate consequences, or any of the many other evil acts. They dedicate the merit they gain thereby to being born in Sukhāvatī, because this is their heartfelt desire.

"When the life of a practitioner who has practised in this way is at an end, the Buddha Amitābha will appear to them together with a great assembly of monks and illuminate the practitioner with golden light. He will then teach them about suffering, emptiness, impermanence, and no self. He will praise the act of going forth from home into homelessness to attain freedom from all suffering.

"When the practitioner sees all this, their hearts will be filled with great joy. They will then find themselves seated on the lotus platform and, kneeling, they will bow to the Buddha with folded hands. Before they have raised their heads, they will be born in Sukhāvatī in an instant. Their lotus soon opens, and when it unfolds, they hear the great swell of sounds praising the Four Truths of the Noble Ones. When they hear this, they immediately attain arhatship, acquire the three forms of knowledge, the six higher forms of knowledge, and the eight kinds of liberation. People like this belong to the highest level of the middle category.

26. "The middle level of the middle category is comprised of those living beings who observe the eight precepts, the precepts of a novice, or the full monastic precepts for at least a day and a night without violating any of the rules of conduct. They dedicate the merit they gain thereby to being born in Sukhāvatī, because this is their heartfelt desire.

"When the life of a practitioner whose mind has been perfumed by the practice of the precepts in this way is at an end, they will see the Buddha Amitābha before them, surrounded by a great assembly, radiating golden light, and bearing a lotus flower made of the seven kinds of precious substances. They will hear a voice coming from the sky, saying, 'Child of good family, as you have lived skilfully and followed the teachings of the buddhas of the three times, I have come to welcome you.' The practitioner will find themselves seated on the lotus flower, which will then close around them. They will be born in the world system of Sukhāvatī, in a pond made of the seven kinds of precious substances. After seven days the lotus flower opens, and the practitioner opens their eyes and praises the Blessed One with folded hands. They rejoice at hearing the Dharma, and attain stream-entry. After half an aeon, they attain arhatship. People like this belong to the middle level of the middle category.

27. "The lowest level of the middle category is comprised of children of good family who respect and support their parents and who act in a just and humane way. When the life of someone like this is at an end, they may meet a spiritual friend who will explain to them the happiness to be found in the buddha-field of the Buddha Amitābha, and the forty-eight vows of the monk Dharmākara. Because they have heard this, when they die they will be born in the world system of Sukhāvatī – in the space of time it would take for a strong man to bend his arm. After seven days they encounter Avalokiteśvara and Mahāsthāmaprāpta. They rejoice at hearing the Dharma, and attain stream-entry. After an intermediate aeon, they attain arahatship. People like this belong to the lowest level of the middle category. This is the fifteenth visualization, where the mind is focused on those who belong to the middle category. This is the correct way to perform the visualization. Doing it in any other way is not correct."

28. The Buddha then said to Ānanda and Vaidehī, "The highest level of the lowest category is comprised of those living beings who have acted

unskilfully in many different ways, although they have not disparaged the extensive sutras. When the life of a foolish person like this – who has cultivated unskilful qualities with no remorse – is at an end, they may meet a spiritual friend who will praise the names of the twelve divisions of the Mahāyāna scriptures. Hearing the names of all the different kinds of scriptures will free them from the effects of previous extremely serious unskilful actions that would have kept them in samsara for a thousand aeons. This wise friend also teaches them to recite 'Namo Amitābhāya Buddhāya' with folded hands. Reciting the name of the Buddha will free them from the effects of previous extremely serious unskilful actions that would have kept them in samsara for five billion aeons.

"The Buddha Amitābha will then send an emanation body, as well as emanations of Avalokiteśvara and Mahāsthāmaprāpta to appear before the practitioner. He will praise the practitioner, saying, 'Excellent, child of good family. By reciting the name of the Buddha, the effects of all your previous unskilful actions have been eliminated. I have come to welcome you.' When they have heard these words, the practitioner will see a light radiating from the emanation buddha, filling the room, and die filled with joy at this sight. Seated on a lotus flower made of precious substances, they will follow the Buddha, and be born in a pond made of precious substances. After seven weeks the lotus flower opens, and when it does the Bodhisattva of Great Compassion, Avalokiteśvara, and the Bodhisattva Mahāsthāmaprāpta appear before this person emitting a great flood of light. They explain all twelve divisions of the profound scriptures. When the practitioner hears this, faith arises in them, and they develop a mind set on unsurpassed Awakening. After ten intermediate aeons they will attain the doorway into the Dharma which consists of an understanding of all phenomena, and enter onto the first stage of the bodhisattva path. People like this belong to the highest level of the lowest category. They hear the word 'Buddha', the word 'Dharma', and the word 'Sangha'. They hear the names of the Three Jewels, and are born in Sukhāvatī."

29. The Buddha then said to Ānanda and Vaidehī, "The middle level of the lowest category is comprised of those living beings who break the five precepts, the eight precepts, or the full monastic precepts – foolish people who steal from the Sangha, who take the Sangha's property, or who teach the Dharma with impure motives, with no remorse. These wicked people adorn themselves with unskilful qualities, and because of their unskilful actions they are destined to fall into hell. When the life of someone like this is at an end, and the roaring inferno of hell is

close at hand, they may meet a greatly compassionate spiritual friend who will explain to them the ten great powers of the Buddha Amitābha. This spiritual friend will praise at length the radiance of the Buddha Amitābha, the higher forms of knowledge he possesses, his ethical conduct, his samadhi, his wisdom, his liberation, and his knowledge and vision of liberation. Hearing this person's words will free them from the effects of previous unskilful actions that would have kept them in samsara for eight billion aeons. The flames of hell will be transformed into a cool breeze, on which floats a heavenly flower. Upon this flower sit emanation buddhas and bodhisattvas to welcome the practitioner.

"In an instant, they will be born inside a lotus flower in a pond made of the seven precious substances. After six aeons, the lotus flower opens and, when it does, Avalokiteśvara and Mahāsthāmaprāpta will comfort them with their noble voices, and explain the profound Mahāyāna sutras. As soon as the practitioner hears the Dharma, they develop a mind set on unsurpassed Awakening. People like this belong to the middle level of the lowest category."

30. The Buddha then said to Ānanda and Vaidehī, "The lowest level of the lowest category is comprised of those living beings who act unskilfully, performing the five acts which have immediate consequences and the ten kinds of unskilful action, indulging in every possible kind of unskilful behaviour. Because of their unskilful actions, these foolish people are destined to be born in the three states of misfortune and experience immeasurable suffering for a great many aeons. When the life of a foolish person like this is at an end, they may encounter a spiritual friend who is able to comfort them in many ways, explain the wondrous Dharma to them, and teach them how to recollect the Buddha. This good friend will say, 'If you are not able to recollect the Buddha, you should recite the name of the Buddha Amitāyus with devotion.' If the practitioner then recites 'Namo Amitābhāya Buddhāya' with sincerety ten times in a row, then with each repetition they will free themselves of the effects of previous unskilful actions that would have kept them in samsara for eight billion aeons. When their life is at an end, they will see a golden lotus flower before them, blazing like the sun, and they will be born in Sukhāvatī in an instant. They remain inside the lotus flower for a full twelve aeons. When the lotus flower opens, they hear the voices of Avalokiteśvara and Mahāsthāmaprāpta, filled with great compassion, explaining how one can rid oneself of the effects of previous unskilful actions by realizing the actual nature of all phenomena. They rejoice at hearing this, and immediately develop a mind set on Awakening. People like this belong to

the lowest level of the lowest category. This is the sixteenth visualization, where the mind is focused on those who belong to the lowest category."

31. While the Buddha was speaking these words, Vaidehī and her five hundred ladies in waiting listened to what he was saying. They were immediately able to see Sukhāvatī, with all of its many different features, and they attained a vision of the body of the Buddha and the two bodhisattvas. Vaidehī exclaimed, "I have never experienced anything like this before!" Her mind became clear, and she attained great realization, and patient acceptance of the fact that all phenomena are unarisen. Her five hundred ladies in waiting developed minds set on unsurpassed perfect Awakening and a heartfelt desire to be born in that buddha-field arose in them. The Blessed One gave each of them a prediction that they would undoubtedly be born there and that, when they were, they would attain the Samadhi of Being in the Presence of All the Buddhas. Innumerable gods also developed minds set on unsurpassed Awakening.

32. Ānanda then rose from his seat, approached the Buddha, and said, "Blessed One, what is the name of this sutra, and how should we bear in mind the essence of the Dharma it contains?"

The Buddha replied to Ānanda, "The name of this sutra is 'The Visualization of Sukhāvatī, the Buddha Amitāyus, the Bodhisattva Avalokiteśvara, and the Bodhisattva Mahāsthāmaprāpta'. It is also called, 'Purifying and Freeing Oneself from the Effects of One's Previous Actions and Being Born in the Presence of All the Buddhas'. This is how you should bear it in mind, forgetting nothing. Those who practise this samādhi will attain a vision of the Buddha Amitāyus and the two great beings in their present body. If a child of good family simply hears the name of the Buddha, or the names of these two bodhisattvas, they will free themselves of the effects of previous unskilful actions that would have kept them in samsara for countless aeons. How much more effective will it be, then, if they recollect them? You should understand that those who recollect the Buddha are like the white lotus flowers of humanity. The Bodhisattva Avalokiteśvara and the Bodhisattva Mahāsthāmaprāpta are their closest friends. They will sit on the seat of Awakening and be born into the family of all the buddhas."

The Buddha continued, "Remember what I have said. Remember the name of the Buddha Amitāyus."

While the Buddha was speaking these words, the Venerable Maudgalyāyana, the Venerable Ānanda, and Vaidehī listened to what he was saying, and great joy arose in them.

33. The Blessed One then returned to Vultures' Peak by walking through the air. Ānanda told the great assembly gathered there what had happened. Countless human beings, gods, nāgas, and yakṣas rejoiced when they heard what the Buddha had said. They venerated the Buddha, and left.

This is the Sūtra on the Visualization of the Buddha Amitāyus, as spoken by the Buddha Śākyamuni.

Glossary

The glossary includes a substantial number of Sanskrit terms from the two *Sukhāvatīvyūha Sūtras*, and Chinese terms from the *Visualization Sūtra*, along with references to where in the texts these terms can be found. References are not provided for terms which occur frequently. In the case of terms which only occur in the *Visualization Sūtra*, the standard Sanskrit translation of Chinese terms is often given in brackets.

The abbreviations used are:
SSV: *Shorter Sukhāvatīvyūha Sūtra*
LSV: *Longer Sukhāvatīvyūha Sūtra*
VS: *Visualization Sūtra*

abode *vihāra*
This is the most common word used in Sanskrit for a dwelling place, and is also the standard term for a Buddhist monastery.
LSV 6, 8

absorbed *see* **mind absorbed by**

abundance *vyūha*
SSV 3–7, 9, 20; LSV 16, 20–2, 25–6, 28, 28 (Vow 38), 95, 129, 149, 155
see also **good qualities**

action *karma*, 業 *yè*
This is moral action which creates **happiness** or **suffering** depending on whether the action is an expression of positive or negative mental states.
see also **skilful**, **unskilful**

acts which have immediate consequences *ānantarya*, 五逆
These are: intentionally killing one's mother, one's father, or an **arhat**; shedding the blood of a **buddha**; or causing a schism in the **sangha**.
LSV 28 (Vow 19); VS 25, 30

aeon *kalpa*, 劫 *jié*
see also **intermediate aeon**

***akaniṣṭha* gods** *akaniṣṭha*
The highest gods of the pure abodes. The term *akaniṣṭha* means something like "nothing higher".
LSV 62, 129, 154
see also **god**, **gods of the pure abodes**

all-knowing one *sarvajña*
see **buddha**, **knowledge**

analysis *prabheda*
LSV 103

arhat *arhat*, 阿羅呵 *āluóhē*
Arhatship is the ultimate goal for the non-Mahāyāna Buddhist, but, in the Mahāyāna, it came to be seen as inferior to the goal of becoming a **bodhisattva**. It is also used as an epithet of a buddha.
see also **buddha**

aspiration *chanda*
LSV 19 (v.9)

austerities *tapas*
LSV 29 (v.9)

awakened *see* **buddha**

Awakening *bodhi*
This is the goal of all Buddhists, whether conceived of as the Awakening of an arhat in non-Mahāyāna schools or as the unsurpassed perfect Awakening of a buddha which is the goal of the Mahāyāna practitioner.
see also **buddha**

blessed one *bhagavat*, 世尊 *shìzūn*
This is one of the most common epithets of a buddha. The Chinese 世尊 *shìzūn* is a rather loose translation of the Sanskrit *bhagavat* and in translations into English from Chinese it is often rendered as "world-honoured one".
see also **buddha**

bodhi tree *bodhivṛkṣa*
A tree under which a bodhisattva attains Awakening, and becomes a buddha.
LSV 28 (Vow 27), 97–9

bodhisattva *bodhisattva*, 菩薩 *púsà*
The ideal of the bodhisattva is what defines the Mahāyāna and sets it apart from other Buddhist schools. The bodhisattva aims not to gain Awakening in a time and place where the Dharma is already available, but to discover it afresh and become a **perfectly awakened buddha**. In order to accomplish this, the bodhisattva must spend an inconceivable length of time engaging in spiritual practice in order to acquire the merit and wisdom required to make such a breakthrough.
see also **mind set on Awakening**, **path of the bodhisattva**

Brahmā 梵 *fàn*
The creator god in Indian religion.
see also **god**

Brahman *brāhmaṇa*
The priestly class in Hinduism, often mentioned along with, and in contrast to, **renunciants**.
LSV 31

branches of learning *pratisaṃvid*
These are: Dharma, wealth (*artha*), etymology (*nirukti*), and eloquence (*pratibhāna*).
LSV 28 (Vow 28), 68

bright and tranquil *viprasanna*
LSV 5–6
see also **clear mind**, **tranquility**

bring to mind *samanusmarati*
This comes from the same root as *anusmṛti*, which is translated as **recollection**.
LSV 6, 8

buddha *buddha*, 佛 *fó*
In some contexts, the word *buddha* is translated as "awakened".
see also **all-knowing one**, **arhat**, **blessed one**, **guide**, **knower of the world**, **perfect in wisdom and conduct**, **perfectly awakened buddha**, **pratyekabuddha**, **sugata**, **tathāgata**, **teacher of gods and human beings**, **three refuges**, **victorious one**

buddha-field *buddhakṣetra*, 國土 *guótǔ*
This is the field in which a buddha's influence can be felt. The phrase 淨國土 *jìngguótǔ*, "pure buddha-field" (often abbreviated to 淨國), is translated into English as "pure land".

***cakravāka*-bird** *cakravāka*
This is *Anas Casarca*, pairs of which are said to mourn when separated at night.
LSV 67

calm concentration *śamatha*
LSV 19 (v.5)

category *rāśi*
This refers to a threefold categorization of living beings: those who are fixed in wrong views and cannot learn the Dharma (*mithyātvaniyata*), those who are fixed in perfection and who will learn the Dharma whether they are taught it or not (*samyaktvaniyata*),

and those who are not fixed and who will learn the Dharma if it is taught to them, but not otherwise (*aniyata*). The word "category" only translates *rāśi* in LSV. The word translated as "category" in VS (生 *shēng*) is unrelated.
LSV 85

cessation *nirodha*, 滅 *miè*
This is synonymous with **Awakening**.
LSV 68, 82; VS 8

child of good family *kulaputra/ kuladuhitā*, 善男子 *shànnánzǐ* / 善女人 *shánnǚrén*
SSV 10; VS 26, 28, 32

child of the buddhas *buddhasuta*
LSV 96 (v.13)

child of the Dharma 法子 *fǎzi*
VS 23–4

clear mind *prasannacitta*, 至誠 *zhìchéng*
The principal meanings of the word *prasanna* are "clear", "bright", "pure", "true", "right", "tranquil", "kind", and "gracious".
LSV 28 (Vow 18), 91, 111; VS 22

compassion *karuṇā*, 慈 *cí* / 慈悲 *cíbēi*
The Chinese character 慈 *cí* can also be used to translate *maitrī* (**loving-kindness**).
LSV 12, 16, 22, 68; VS 2, 7, 17, 22, 28–30

complete nirvana *parinirvāṇa*
This is the final nirvana attained by a buddha upon the death of their physical body.
LSV 28 (Vows 11, 20), 40, 100
see also **nirvana**

consequences *vipāka*
These are the results that naturally flow from **actions** – skilful actions create **happiness** and negative actions create **suffering**. The word "consequences" translates *vipāka*, except in the phrase five **acts which have immediate consequences**.
LSV 63

contemplate 思惟 *sī wéi* (*cintanā*)
Thinking about or reflecting on.
VS 5

contentment *virāga*
This is the opposite of **greed** (*rāga*).

corruption *āsrava*
The corruptions are what prevents one from attaining Awakening. When they have been destroyed or removed, one is awakened. The corruptions are: the inclination towards sensual desire (*kāmāsrava*), the inclination towards continued existence (*bhavāsrava*), and the corruption of spiritual ignorance (*avidyāsrava*). The corruption of wrong views (*dṛṣṭyāsrava*) is sometimes added to this list.
LSV 2, 153
see also **higher forms of knowledge**

cruelty *vihiṃsā*
LSV 32

cultivate in meditation *bhāvanā*
The word *bhāvanā* literally means something like "bringing into being", but in Buddhist contexts it refers specifically to cultivating positive states in meditation.
LSV 149–50
see also **meditation, samadhi**

cyclic existence *bhava*
LSV 2
see also **samsara**

dedicate *pariṇāma*
In order to become a **perfectly awakened buddha**, a **bodhisattva** must accumulate vast quantities of **merit**, which they then dedicate to the goal of Awakening.
see also **roots of virtue**

defilement *kleśa*, 煩惱 *fánnǎo*
The defilements are what hold us back from Awakening. This term is very common, but not usually precisely defined. One description of the defilements includes: **greed** (*rāga*), enmity (*pratigha*), pride (*māna*), spiritual ignorance (*avidyā*), wrong views (*kudṛṣṭi*),

and doubt (*vicikitsā*).
SSV 18–19; LSV 2, 116; VS 5, 8, 15

degenerate/degeneration *kaṣāya*, 濁 *zhuó*
SSV 18; LSV 104; VS 8

delusion *moha*
LSV 29 (v.5), 119, 120

dhāraṇī 陀羅尼 *tuóluóní*
A *dhāraṇī* is a formula, often without conceptual meaning, which is recited in order to bring spiritual or material benefit. *Dhāraṇī*s are closely related to mantras, but tend to be longer.
LSV 28 (Vow 33); VS 22

Dharma 法 *fǎ*
The teaching of the **Buddha**, and the sum total of all methods which lead to **Awakening**.
see also **phenomenon, three refuges**

Dharma life *see* **lived the Dharma life**

dhyana *dhyāna*
The word *dhyāna* is usually translated as **meditation**, except where it refers to a state of meditative absorption, in which case it is left untranslated.
LSV 28 (Vow 37)

diamond 金剛 *jīngāng* (vajra)
The word vajra / 金剛 *jīngāng* is either translated as "diamond" or left untranslated as **vajra**, depending on the context.
VS 10, 13, 15, 18, 22

discourse *paryāya*
SSV 11–17; LSV 45, 147–51, 152 (v.10)

divine *divya*, 天 *tiān*
The word *divya* is also translated as "heavenly", depending on the context.
see also **god, higher forms of knowledge**

divine ear *divyaśrotra*
This is the power of clairaudience, the ability to hear things in other places and times.
LSV 28 (Vow 8), 68, 96 (v.16)

divine eye *divyacakṣus*, 天眼 *tiānyǎn*
This is the power of clairvoyance, the ability to see things in other places and times.
LSV 28 (Vows 7, 26), 96 (v.16)

the doorway into the Dharma which consists of an understanding of all phenomena 百法明門 *bǎifǎmíngmén*
In *A Dictionary of Chinese Buddhist Terms*, Soothill and Hodous translate this phrase as "the door to the knowledge of universal phenomena" and comment that it is "one of the first stages of Bodhisattva progress". They give no Sanskrit equivalent.
VS 24, 28

Earth *sahā*
The word *sahā* refers to the **world system** in which we live, and in which the Buddha Śākyamuni has taught the Dharma.
SSV 18–19; LSV 128

elder *sthavira*
LSV 1–3

emanation *nirmita*
LSV 93
see **emanation body**

emanation body 化身 *huàshēn* (*nirmāṇakāya*) **buddhas** and **bodhisattvas** have the ability to manifest multiple physical forms simultaneously in order to maximize the number of living beings they can help.
VS 28

emanation buddha 化佛 *shāhuà* (*nirmāṇabuddha*)
VS 17–18, 21–4, 28, 29

embraced *parigraha*/*parigṛhīta*/*pratigṛhṇīyuḥ*, 攝 *shè*
SSV 11–17; LSV 28 (Vow 24), 108; VS 17

empathy *anukampā*
The word *anukampā* literally means "to tremble with" or "to

resonate with".
LSV 9, 12, 22, 28 (Vow 24), 96 (v.14)

emptiness *śūnyatā*, 空 *kōng*
This is the central philosophical idea in Mahāyāna Buddhism that all phenomena are empty of independent existence or unchanging essence. It is one of the three forms of liberation, along with **freedom from characteristics** and **freedom from desire**. It is attained through insight into **no self**.
LSV 33, 68; VS 10, 13, 25

energy *vīrya*, 精進 *jīngjìn*
SSV 12; LSV 19 (v.2, 5, 7, 9), 36, 43, 145, 149, 152 (v.9); VS 22
see also **factors of Awakening, spiritual faculties, spiritual powers**

equanimity *upekṣā*
LSV 68
see also **factors of Awakening**

ethical conduct *śīla*, 戒 *jiè*
Ethical conduct is the first part of the threefold way of ethical conduct, **samadhi**, and **wisdom**. It is often defined in terms of a set of **precepts**, such as the **ten kinds of skilful/unskilful action**. The Chinese 戒 *jiè* is translated as both "precept" and "ethical conduct" according to context.
LSV 19 (v.2, 5), 36, 118; VS 29

ethically sensitive *hrīmat*
The word *hrīmat* literally means "possessing *hrī*". The word *hrī* refers to a positive sense of shame and regret for the **unskilful** actions one has performed.
LSV 119, 120

evil 惡 *è* (*pāpa*)
VS 2–5, 25

extensive 方等 *fāngděng* (*vaipulya*)
This refers to a category of Mahāyāna sutras which include texts such as the *Avataṃsaka Sūtra*, the *Saddharmapuṇḍarīka Sūtra*, and the *Ratnakūṭa Sūtra*.
VS 22–3, 28

eye of the Dharma *dharmacakṣu*
In LSV 153, *dharmacakṣu* is translated as "Dharma-vision".
LSV 112

factors of Awakening *bodhyaṅga*
These are **mindfulness**, analytical understanding of mental states (*dharmapravicaya*), **energy**, **joy**, **tranquility** (*praśrabdhi*), **samadhi**, and **equanimity**.
SSV 6; LSV 111

faculties *indriya*
This word can refer both to the sense faculties and to faculties in a more general sense.
LSV 5, 11, 28 (Vow 39), 103, 118
see also **spiritual faculties**

faith *śraddhā*, 信 *xìn*
The word *śraddhā* literally means "to place (*dhā*) the heart (*śrad*) upon". It represents an emotional response to the Buddha and his teaching, rather than a blind faith based on a belief in unprovable assertions.
SSV 17; LSV 87 (v.5), 135–6, 152 (v.8); VS 7, 23–4, 28
see also **serene faith, spiritual faculties, spiritual powers, wisdom which has faith as its goal**

false mental construction 妄想 *wàngxiǎng* (*kalpa*/*vikalpa*)
VS 16

feelings *vedanā*
The word *vedanā* doesn't refer to feelings in the sense of emotions, but rather to the pleasant, unpleasant, or neutral feeling of sense experiences. (This includes mental sense experience – the pleasant, unpleasant, or neutral feeling of thoughts and emotions).
LSV 69

focus the mind 想 *xiǎng*
The word 想 *xiǎng* is used frequently in the VS. It is the standard Buddhist Chinese translation for *saṃjñā*, but "perception" or "notion" (which is how *saṃjñā* is most usually

translated) wouldn't have fitted in the contexts in which 想 *xiǎng* is used in the VS. In the end, I felt that the phrase "focus the mind" best captured the meaning of the word in context, but something like "form a perception in the mind" might have been a slightly more literal option.
see also **notion**

folded hands *añjali*, 合掌叉手 *hézhǎng chāshǒu*
Placing the hands together, with the fingertips and the bases of the palms touching, is the traditional Buddhist gesture of respect and reverence.
LSV 5, 19, 122; VS 2, 23, 25–6, 28

fond of solitude *pravivikta*
LSV 33
see also **solitude**

forms of mastery *vaśitā*
A bodhisattva has ten *vaśitā*s or "forms of mastery": mastery of one's lifespan (*āyurvaśitā*), mastery of one's mind and mental states (*cittavaśitā*), mastery of one's **tools** (*pariṣkāravaśitā*), mastery of the **Dharma** (*dharmavaśitā*), mastery of **supernormal abilities** (*ṛddhivaśitā*), mastery over where one takes birth (*janmavaśitā / upapattivaśitā*), mastery of one's commitment (*adhimuktivaśitā*), mastery of one's **vows** (*praṇidhānavaśitā*), mastery of one's **actions** (*karmavaśitā*), and mastery of one's **knowledge** (*jñānavaśitā*).
LSV 39

four great kings *cāturmahārājakāyikā devāḥ*
These are the lowest of the **gods**, the ones closest to the human realm. They act as protectors of the world.
LSV 62

freedom from accumulation *anabhisaṃskāra*
This means that one no longer carries out karmic **action**, and so one is no longer "accumulating" actions which will have an effect in the future.
LSV 33, 68

freedom from characteristics *ānimitta*
This is one of the three forms of liberation, along with **emptiness** and **freedom from desire**. It is attained through insight into **impermanence**.
LSV 33, 68

freedom from desire *apraṇihita*
This is one of the three forms of liberation, along with **emptiness** and **freedom from characteristics**. It is attained through insight into **suffering**.
LSV 33, 68

fundamental nature *prakṛti*
LSV 114

gandharva *gandharva*
These are celestial musicians.
SSV 20; LSV 44, 125, 155

garuḍa *garuḍa*
Garuḍas are mythical birds, and the mortal enemies of the **nāgas**.
LSV 44, 117, 125, 155

gladness *pramodya*
LSV 28 (Vow 42), 44, 68, 108, 150

god *deva / devaputra*, 天 *tiān*
In Buddhism, the cosmos is filled with beings who exist on higher, more refined planes than human beings. However, these gods are seen as ultimately mortal, albeit fantastically long-lived, and most importantly lacking in **wisdom**. They are thus unable to give human beings the kind of assistance and guidance they would seek from buddhas and bodhisattvas.
see also **divine**, **four great kings**, **gods led by Brahmā**, **gods of the pure abodes**, **gods of the thirty-three**, **gods of the Tuṣita Heaven**, **gods who delight in creation**, **gods who have power over the creations of others**, **sunirmita gods**

gods led by Brahmā *brahmapurohita*
A class of gods.
LSV 62

gods of the pure abodes *śuddhāvāsa*
The pure abodes are where non-returners (those who are considered in non-Mahāyāna Buddhism to have attained the highest stage short of becoming an **arhat**) are reborn and where they attain **Awakening**.
LSV 43

gods of the thirty-three *trāyastriṃśa*
A class of gods.
LSV 62, 133

gods of the Tuṣita Heaven *(su)tuṣita*
A class of gods. The Tuṣita Heaven is where the Bodhisattva Maitreya resides until the time is right for him to take his final rebirth and rediscover the Dharma.
LSV 37, 62

gods who delight in creation *nirmāṇarati*
A class of gods.
LSV 62

gods who have power over the creations of others *paranirmitavaśavartin*, 自在天 *zìzai tiān*
In LSV this is sometimes abbreviated to *vaśavartin*.
LSV 37, 62, 71, 79, 132; VS 5

good qualities *guṇa*
I have translated *guṇa* as **wonderful qualities** when it occurs in combination with the word *vyūha*, as I felt that the phrase **abundance of wonderful qualities** better captured the sense of majesty in the phrase *guṇavyūha* as a whole.

grasping *upādāna*
LSV 114, 153

great being *mahāsattva*, 大士 *dàshì*
This is an epithet commonly applied to **bodhisattvas**.

great disciple *mahāśrāvaka*
SSV 1
see also **śrāvaka**

great person *mahāpuruṣa*
A "great person" in this context is one who has thirty-two major **physical characteristics**, and eighty minor ones, which mark their greatness. One who possesses these characteristics is either a **buddha** or a **king of the entire world**.
LSV 60, 103

greed *rāga*
LSV 29 (v.5), 120
see also **contentment**

guide *nāyaka*
An epithet of the **buddha**, this can also be translated as "leader".
see also **buddha**, **unsurpassable guide for those who wish to train**
LSV 29 (v.10), 96

***haṃsa*-geese** *haṃsa*, 鴈 *yàn*
These are mythical birds which are reputedly able to drink only the milk from a mixture of milk and water.
SSV 6; LSV 67; VS 16

happiness sukha, 樂 *lè*

hatred *doṣa*
LSV 19 (v.3), 29 (v.5), 119–20

heartfelt desire *praṇidhāna/praṇidhi*, 願 *yuàn*
This term is translated as both "heartfelt desire" and "vow" according to context.
Translated as "heartfelt desire": SSV 10, 17; LSV 91; VS 4–5, 22–6, 31
Translated as "vow": LSV 25, 27–31, 33, 42, 96 (v.17–18), 99–100, 108, 119, 153; VS 15, 21, 27

hearts filled with joy *āttamāna*
The word *āttamāna* is translated as "hearts filled with joy", whereas elsewhere **joy** is used to translate *prīti*.
SSV 20; LSV 155
see also **joy**

heavenly *see* **divine**

higher forms of knowledge *abhijñā*, 通具 *tōngjù* / 神通 *shéntōng*
These are the **divine eye** or

clairvoyance (*divyacakṣus*), the **divine ear** or clairaudience (*divyaśrotra*), knowledge of the thoughts of others (*paracittajñāna*), the **recollection** of previous states of existence (*pūrvanivāsānusmṛti*), **supernormal abilities** (*ṛddhi*), and the knowledge that the **corruptions** have been destroyed (*āśravakṣayajñāna*).
SSV 1; LSV 2, 3, 16, 103, 114, 119, 145; VS 25, 29
see also **knowledge**

hindrance *nīvaraṇa*
This is specifically what hinders a meditator from accessing the **dhyanas**, states of meditative concentration. They are desire for sensual pleasure (*kāmacchanda*), **ill-will** (*vyāpāda*), sloth and torpor (*styāna-middha*), restlessness and anxiety (*auddhatya-kaukṛtya*), and doubt (*vicikitsā*).
LSV 69

hungry ghost *preta*, 餓鬼 *èguǐ*
The realm of the hungry ghosts is one of the six realms into which one can be reborn. The hungry ghosts' experience is dominated by insatiable greed. They are pictured with large stomachs, thin necks, and mouths the size of pinholes. They are constantly hungry and thirsty, but whatever food and drink they do manage to consume only causes them more suffering.
LSV 28 (Vows 1, 2), 52; VS 5
see also **state of misfortune**, **world governed by Yama**

ill-will *vyāpāda*
A malicious attitude towards others.
LSV 32, 34

impermanence *anitya*, 無常 *wú cháng*
One of the three characteristics of conditioned existence, along with **suffering** and **no self**.
LSV 65; VS 10, 13, 25

Indra
The lord of the gods, also known as **Śakra**.
SSV 1; LSV 16

inferior *hīna*
The word *hīna* occurs three times in the LSV. The pejorative and polemic term *hīnayāna* is not found in the *Sukhāvatīvyūha Sūtras*, entering into Mahāyāna literature at a later stage of its development. The word *hīna* is often translated as "small" or "lesser", but in fact its connotations are stronger, such that "inferior", or even "defective" or "vile", better reflects its meaning.
LSV 79, 147, 152 (v.3)

initiation *abhiṣeka*
Initially, *abhiṣeka* was the ritual to anoint a king. The idea of *abhiṣeka* as a religious ritual which made the recipient into a kind of spiritual king can be found in the LSV, and became a central metaphor in later, Vajrayāna, Buddhism.
LSV 68

intellect *buddhi*
LSV 16, 19, 111, 115

intermediate aeon 小劫 *xiǎojié* (*antarakalpa*)
This is a subdivision of a kalpa (more properly *mahākalpa*) or **aeon**.
VS 23–4, 27–8

irreversible *avinivartanīya / avaivartika / avaivartya*, 不退轉 *bùtuìzhuǎn*
This is the point at which one can no longer fall back in one's practice of the Dharma, and further progress is assured. In non-Mahāyāna terms, this represents the attainment of **stream-entry**, but in the Mahāyāna it refers to the point at which one can no longer "fall back" from pursuing the goal of becoming a **perfectly awakened buddha** and be content to aim to become an **arhat**.
SSV 10, 17; LSV 28 (Vow 45), 46, 90,

94, 96 (v.18), 99, 144, 149, 153, 155; VS 23
see also **patient acceptance of the fact that all phenomena are unarisen**

jewel *maṇi*, 珠 *zhū*
see **precious substance** or **precious stone**

joy *prīti*
The word *prīti* has connotations of a joy which is physical and bodily, not simply mental and emotional. In VS, the word "joy" mostly translates 歡喜 *huānxǐ*. This can translate a wide range of Sanskrit terms, including *prīti*, but more commonly *pramoda* or *prasāda*.
LSV 28 (Vow 42), 44, 68, 96 (v.6, 15), 108, 150, 152 (v.2, 10)
see also **factors of Awakening, hearts filled with joy**

***kācilindika* cloth** *kācilindika*
A very soft, fine kind of cloth.
LSV 81

king of the entire world *cakravartin*
This is more literally a "wheel-turner", but refers to a king whose domain encompasses the whole world. The *cakravartin* is the only one apart from a **buddha** who possesses the **physical characteristics** of a **great person**.
LSV 79

kinnara *kiṃnara*
A mythical creature not unlike a centaur. They have either human bodies and horses' heads, or horses' bodies and human heads.
LSV 44, 125

knower of the world *lokavid*
This is an epithet of a **buddha**.
LSV 17
see also **knowledge**

knowledge
This mostly translates a range of words that share the root *jñā*, including *jñāna*, *ājñātā*, and *sarvajña*, but is also used to translate terms such as *lokavid* **knower of the world** in LSV 17, and *gatimat* "knowledgeable" in LSV 120. Depending on context, words derived from *jñā* are also translated as **understanding**.
see also **all-knowing one, higher forms of knowledge, three forms of knowledge**

knowledge that is free from attachment *asaṅgajñāna*
This could also be translated as "knowledge of non-attachment", or "unimpeded knowledge/ understanding".
LSV 19 (v.10), 29 (v.10), 113, 135–6, 151
see also **knowledge**

kṣatriya 剎利 *shālì*
The *kṣatriya* class are the rulers and warriors in the Hindu caste system.
LSV 138; VS 3

lapis lazuli *vaiḍūrya*, 琉璃 *liúlí*
There has been much debate as to what substance *vaiḍūrya* actually refers to. Monier-Williams has "cat's eye gem", but most translators seem to opt for lapis lazuli.

liberated *vimukta*
LSV 114, 153
see also **liberation**

liberation *vimokṣa*
The eight kinds of liberation (*aṣṭavimokṣa*) are: possessing form and perceiving form; not perceiving internal form, but perceiving external form; perceiving beauty; dwelling in the sphere of infinite space; dwelling in the sphere of infinite consciousness; dwelling in the sphere of nothingness; dwelling in the sphere of neither perception nor non-perception; dwelling in the cessation of perception and feeling.
LSV 2; VS 25, 29
see also **liberated**

lived the Dharma life *uṣitavat*
This is more literally "those who have lived", but I feel that this somewhat more interpretive

translation captures what is being got at.
LSV 2

living being *sattva*, 衆生 *zhòng shēng*

longer *vistara*
This is the "longer" in the title of the *Longer Sūtra*. In LSV 70, however, the word "detailed" also translates *vistara*.

loving-kindness *maitrī*
LSV 68, 96 (v.9), 111, 117

Mahāyāna *mahāyāna*, 大乘 *dàshèng*
Literally the "Great Way" or "Great Vehicle", the Mahāyāna encourages Buddhist practitioners to aim to become **bodhisattvas** rather than **arhats**.
SSV 20; LSV 155; VS 7, 22–4, 28–9

Maheśvara
Literally "Great Lord", this is most often used of Śiva and Kṛṣṇa.
LSV 43

mahoraga *mahoraga*
A mythical creature, literally "great serpent".
LSV 44, 125

māndārava flowers *māndārava* (also spelled *māndarava* and *mandārava*)
A kind of heavenly flower, which often rains down on buddhas or bodhisattvas in salutation.
SSV 5

mastery *see* **forms of mastery**

meditation *dhyāna*
LSV 19 (v.5), 28 (Vow 37), 36, 98, 103
see also **cultivate in meditation, dhyana, factors of Awakening, meditative concentration, samadhi, spiritual faculties**

meditative concentration 正受 *zhèng shòu* (*samāpatti*)
VS 5

mental construction *see* **false mental construction**

mental object *dharma*
LSV 35
see also **Dharma, phenomenon**

merit *puṇya*, 福 *fú*
This is the benefit or spiritual momentum that comes from **skilful** actions. A **bodhisattva** needs to make vast amounts of **merit** in order to attain **unsurpassed perfect Awakening**, and they **dedicate** all the merit they generate to that goal.
LSV 63, 71, 87 (v.4, 5, 10), 120, 150, 152 (v.1); VS 7, 18, 21–6

mind absorbed by *manasikāra*
This literally means "making to be (*-kāra*) in (*-i-*) the mind (*manas-*)".
SSV 6; LSV 14, 91, 93–4, 137

mind set on Awakening *bodhicitta*, 菩提心 *pútíxīn*
The arising of the mind set on Awakening is what makes one a **bodhisattva**. It is the overwhelming inspiration to commit oneself to attaining Awakening not for one's own sake but in order to be of benefit to all living beings. It has also been translated as "Awakening mind" or "will to Enlightenment".
LSV 20, 28 (Vow 34), 92, 142, 153; VS 7, 24, 28–31

mindful *smṛtimat*
The word *smṛtimat* literally means "possessing *smṛti*".
LSV 18, 120

mindfulness *smṛti*, 念 *niàn*
LSV 28 (Vow 34), 29 (v.4), 93, 120
see also **factors of Awakening, spiritual faculties, spiritual powers**

miraculous powers *prātihārya*
LSV 79

monk *bhikṣu*, 比丘 *bǐqiū*, 沙門 *shāmén*

Mount Meru/Sumeru 須彌山 *xūmíshān*
This is the mythical mountain which lies at the centre of our world in traditional Buddhist cosmology. It is often used as a paradigm of great size and majesty.

nāga *nāga*, 龍神 *lóngshén*
These are mythical serpents or serpent-demons who are associated with wisdom and with the depths. Traditionally, the *Prajñāpāramitā Sūtras* are believed to have been entrusted to nāgas for safekeeping by the Buddha Śākyamuni, and recovered by Nāgārjuna. The **garuḍas** are their mortal enemies. The word *nāga* can also mean "elephant", and is translated as such in LSV 2, 117, and 118. In LSV 6 it is somewhat ambiguous as to whether *nāga* refers to mythical serpents or to elephants. Gomez has "elephants", whereas I've left it as "nāgas".
LSV 6, 16, 44, 125, 145, 152 (v.5); VS 33

Nārāyaṇa
The son of the original man, often identified with one of the Hindu gods, and used as a paradigm of strength.
LSV 28 (Vow 25)

naturally and spontaneously *svayaṃbhu*, 自然 *zì rán*
This is more literally "self-existent" or "independent".
LSV 29 (v.9); VS 6, 12, 15, 17, 18, 21
see also **spontaneously**

nirvana *nirvāṇa*
This is a synonym for **Awakening**. It literally means "extinguishing (the fires of craving)".
LSV 19 (v.8), 85, 152 (v.7)
see also **complete nirvana**

no self anātman, 無我 **wú wǒ**
One of the three characteristics of conditioned existence, along with **suffering** and **impermanence**.
LSV 65; VS 10, 13, 25

noble one *ārya*
The noble ones are those who have attained at least the stage of **stream-entry**.
LSV 1

non-arising *anutpāda*
LSV 33, 68
see also **patient acceptance of the fact that all phenomena are unarisen**

non-human being *amanuṣya*
This can indicate any non-human being but is often used to refer to gods.
LSV 44, 125

notion *saṃjñā*
The word *saṃjñā* can often be translated as "perception" but, in the contexts in which it is used in LSV, "notion" fits better.
LSV 28 (Vow 10), 32, 83, 110, 137
see also **focus the mind**

nymph *apsaras*
LSV 77, 84

ordinary immature beings 凡(夫) *fán(fū)* (*bālapṛthagjana*)
All those who have not attained the stage of **stream-entry** are considered "ordinary, immature beings".
VS 21–2

path of the bodhisattva *bodhisattvacarya*
The phrase *bodhisattvacarya* is more literally the conduct or practice of a **bodhisattva**. The verb used with this phrase is from the root *car*, as is *carya*, so in the Sanskrit there's a repetition that is lost in my translation. What I have translated as "practising the path of the bodhisattva" could be translated more literally as something like "practising the bodhisattva practice".
LSV 28 (Vows 20, 35, 42), 34, 36–7, 39

patient acceptance *kṣānti*, 忍 *rěn*
The three kinds of patient acceptance mentioned in LSV 28 (Vow 46) are: the patient acceptance of the knowledge of the truth of suffering (*duḥkhe dharmajñānakṣānti*), the patient acceptance of the knowledge

of what follows from suffering (*duḥkhe anvayadharmajñānakṣānti*), and the patient acceptance of the knowledge of the truth of the origin of suffering (*samudaye dharmajñānakṣānti*).
see also **patient acceptance of the fact that all phenomena are unarisen**

patient acceptance of the fact that all phenomena are unarisen *anutpattikadharmakṣānti*, 無生法忍 *wúshēngfǎrěn*
This is the insight through which a **bodhisattva** becomes **irreversible**.
LSV 68, 99, 153; VS 8, 17, 23, 31
see also **non-arising, patient acceptance**

peace/peaceful *śānta*
The word *śānta* is also translated as "calmed" in LSV 119.
LSV 65, 68, 119, 120

perfect in wisdom and conduct *vidyācaraṇasaṃpanna*
The word "wisdom" here translates *vidyā* rather than *prajñā*.
see also **buddha**

perfectly awakened buddha *samyaksaṃbuddha*, 三藐三佛陀 *sānmiǎo sānfótuó*
This is the **Awakening** attained by a **buddha**, who rediscovers the **Dharma** in a place and time where it is not known.

phenomenon *dharma*, 法 *fǎ*
LSV 68, 99, 113–14, 116, 153, 155; VS 8, 17, 22–4, 28, 30–1
see also **Dharma**, **mental object**, **patient acceptance of the fact that all phenomena are unarisen**

physical characteristics *lakṣaṇa*, 相 *xiāng* / *(anu)vyañjana*, 好 *hǎo*
A **great person** – i.e. either a **buddha** or a **king of the entire world** – has thirty-two major **physical characteristics** (*lakṣaṇa*, 相 *xiāng*) and eighty minor ones (*anuvyañjana*, 好 *hǎo*), which mark their greatness. Most suggest elegance and beauty, but a few are odd or even grotesque, such as hands which reach below the knees.

pratyekabuddha *pratyekabuddha*
This is a theoretical category of awakened being who has attained **Awakening** but lacks either the skill or the motivation (or both) to teach the **Dharma**.
LSV 1, 28 (Vow 12), 152 (v.5)
see also **buddha**

precept 戒 *jiè*
The word 戒 *jiè* is translated either as "precept" or as **ethical conduct** according to the context.
VS 2, 7, 22, 25, 26, 29

preceptor *upādhyāya*
LSV 33, 149

precious substance or **precious stone** *ratna*, 寶 *bǎo*
see also **jewel**

prediction to awakening 記 *jì* (*vyākaraṇa*)
VS 17, 22–3

protector *nātha*
The phrase "protectors of the world" translates *lokapāla* at LSV 37, 43, and the equivalent Chinese phrase 護世 *hùshì* at VS 4.
LSV 19 (v.6), 29 (v.3), 96 (v.11, 13), 152 (v.2, 3)
see also **buddha**

protuberance 肉髻 *ròujì* (*uṣṇīṣa*)
This is a kind of bump on the top of the head – one of the **physical characteristics** of a buddha.
VS 18–19

rākṣasa *rākṣasa*
A rākṣasa is a kind of demon.

realm of reality *dharmadhātu*, 法界 *fǎjiè*
This can also be translated as "the realm of the Dharma" or even "the totality of phenomena".
LSV 113; VS 16

recollect/recollection *anusmṛti*, 念 *niàn* / 憶 *yì*
see **higher forms of knowledge**, **mindfulness**

reflections *mīmāṃsā*
LSV 7–8

renunciant *śramaṇa*
A wandering ascetic who rejected the norms of Brahmanical religion. Often contrasted with **Brahman**.
LSV 31, 155

roots of virtue *kuśalamūla*
"Planting" or "cultivating" roots of virtue is a common metaphor in Buddhism for accumulating **merit**.

Śakra 釋迦 *shìjiā*
The lord of the gods, also known as **Indra**.
LSV 37, 43, 79, 97; VS 4, 12, 15, 18

samadhi samādhi, 三昧 *sānmèi* / 定 *dìng*
This is the absorption or concentration attained through meditation. The word *samādhi* literally means something like "gathering the mind together".
LSV 11, 19 (v.2), 28 (Vows 40, 43), 93; VS 11, 16, 17, 20, 23, 29, 31–2
see also **cultivate in meditation, meditation, spiritual faculties, spiritual powers**

samsara *saṃsāra*, 生死 *shēngsǐ*
The Chinese translation of *saṃsāra* literally means "birth-death".
VS 11, 18, 19, 28–30, 32

sangha *saṃgha*, 衆 *zhòng*
The sangha is first and foremost the *āryasaṃgha* or sangha of the **noble ones**. It is sangha in this sense that is one of the **three refuges**. The term "sangha" is often used to refer exclusively to the sangha of **monks**, but it is, in principle, the entire Buddhist community.

self-confidence *vaiśāradya*
A **buddha** or **bodhisattva** possesses four kinds of self-confidence: the confidence of being perfectly **awakened** to all **phenomena** (or Dharma teachings) (*sarva-dharmābhisaṃbodhi-vaiśāradya*), the confidence that comes from knowing that all of the **corruptions** have been destroyed (*sarvāśrava-kṣaya-jñāna-vaiśāradya*), the confidence that comes from having clearly understood all phenomena which could cause distress or be an obstacle (*antarāyika-dharmānanyathātva-niścita-vyākaraṇa-vaiśāradya*), and the confidence that his methods of practice lead to success (*sarvasaṃpadadhigamāya nairyāṇika-pratipattathātva-vaiśāradya*).
LSV 68, 121, 145

sensual desire *kāma*
In LSV 29 (v.4), *kāma* is translated as "sense pleasures", and at LSV 96 (v.6) it is translated as "love".
LSV 32

serene faith *prasāda*
The word *prasāda* is in some ways synonymous with *śraddhā* (**faith**), but it has particular connotations of brightness and clarity. In LSV 139, *prasāda* is translated as "mercy", as the translation "serene faith" does not fit the context.
LSV 90, 93, 140, 147, 152 (v.3)

shorter *saṃkṣipta*
This is the word that means "shorter" in the title of the *Shorter Sūtra*. In LSV 70, the word "short" translates *saṃkṣipta*.
SSV 1

skilful *kuśala*
Skilful **actions** are those which are expressive of positive mental states – **loving-kindness, compassion, contentment**, etc.

skilful means 方便 *fāng biàn* (*upāya*/ *upāya-kauśalya*)
This is an important Mahāyāna concept, and expresses the idea that **buddhas** and **bodhisattvas** are creative and skilled in their use of a wide range of different methods to help living beings – even if certain methods may sometimes breach ethical norms and social conventions.
VS 8

solitude *viveka*
At LSV 68, *viveka* is translated as

"inclination towards solitude".
LSV 119
see also **fond of solitude**

soothe the mind *manojña*
SSV 7; LSV 28 (Vow 31), 53, 58, 65, 67, 68, 80

spiritual faculties *indriya*
The five spiritual faculties are **faith**, **energy**, **mindfulness**, **samadhi**, and **wisdom**.
SSV 6
see also **faculties, spiritual powers**

spiritual friend *kalyāṇamitra*, 善知識 *shànzhīshí*
LSV 33; VS 27–30

spiritual powers *bala*, 力 *lì*
The five spiritual powers are the same as the five **spiritual faculties**.
SSV 6; LSV 2, 68

spontaneously *aupapāduka*
More literally, "self-produced".
LSV 134–6, 140
see also **naturally and spontaneously**

śrāvaka *śrāvaka*
More literally, a "hearer" or "listener" – someone who has heard the **Dharma** taught by a **buddha**.
see also **great disciple**

stage *bhūmi*, 地 *dì*
LSV 68, 155; VS 24, 28

state of misfortune *akṣana/durgati*, 塗 *tú*
The three states of misfortune are being born as an animal, as a **hungry ghost**, or in hell.
LSV 52, 69; VS 19, 30

stream-entry 須陀洹 *xūtuóhuán* (*srotāpatti*)
In non-Mahāyāna Buddhism, the point at which one attains stream-entry is the point at which one's progress towards **Awakening** becomes **irreversible**.
VS 26–7

strength *sthāman*, 勢 *shì*
LSV 28 (Vow 25), 71; VS 19

suffering *duḥkha*, 苦 *kǔ*
Perhaps more precisely, "unsatisfactoriness"; this is one of the three characteristics of conditioned existence, along with **impermanence** and **no self**.
SSV 2; LSV 29 (v.2, 8), 69; VS 8, 10–11, 13, 15, 19, 25, 30

sugata *sugata*
This is an epithet of a **buddha**. The word *gāta* literally means "gone" but, when it is used in a compound in this way, it indicates being in a particular state. The prefix *su-* simply means "good" or "well", so *sugata* simply means "he who is well" or "he who is in a good state".
LSV 17, 96 (v.21), 152 (v.10)

sukha *see* **happiness**

Sukhāvatī *sukhāvatī*, 極樂世界 *jílè shìjiè*
The Realm of Happiness.

sunirmita gods *sunirmita*
A class of gods; *sunirmita* means "well-formed" or "well-manifested".
LSV 37

supernormal abilities *ṛddhi*, 神通 *shéntōng*
LSV 28 (Vow 5), 47, 49, 79, 96 (v.16, 21), 132; VS 21
see also **higher forms of knowledge**

suyāma gods *suyāma*
A class of gods.
LSV 37

swastika *svastika*
The swastika has extremely negative connotations in the West, but in Buddhism (and Hinduism) it is an ancient symbol for the sun and a sign of good fortune.
LSV 97

sympathetic joy *muditā*
This is the delight taken in the happiness of others.
LSV 68

tathāgata *tathāgata*, 如來 *rúlái* / 多陀阿伽度 *duōtuóāgādù*
This is an epithet of a **buddha**,

and is often translated as "thus-come" or "thus-gone", which makes little sense. The word *gāta* literally means "gone" but, when it is used in a compound in this way, it indicates being in a particular state. The word *tathā* means "like this", and in this context indicates "things the way they are" or "reality". So *tathāgata* can mean "he who dwells with things the way they are" or "he who dwells in reality".

teacher of gods and human beings *śāstṛ devānāṃ ca manuṣyāṇāṃ*
This is an epithet of a **buddha**.
LSV 17

ten kinds of skilful action *daśakuśalakarmapatha*, 十善業 *shí shànyè*
These are to abstain from taking life, taking anything which is not given, sexual misconduct, false speech, harsh speech, frivolous speech, slanderous speech, covetousness, ill-will, and wrong views.
VS 7

ten kinds of unskilful action *daśākuśalakarmapatha*, 十惡 *shí è*
These are to engage in taking life, taking anything which is not given, sexual misconduct, false speech, harsh speech, frivolous speech, slanderous speech, covetousness, ill-will, and wrong views.
VS 30

ten powers *daśabala*
For a description of the ten powers, see e.g. *Aṅguttara-nikāya*, Book of the Tens, Sutta 90.
LSV 29 (v.1)

three forms of knowledge 三明 *sānmíng* (*trividyā*)
This refers to knowledge of the future effects of actions, of the effects of actions performed in the past, and of illusion and liberation in the present.
VS 25

three refuges 三歸 *sān guī*
These are the **Buddha**, **Dharma**, and **Sangha**.
VS 7

three worlds *trailoka / traidhātu*
The three worlds or realms of Buddhist cosmology are the realm of sensual desire (*kāmadhātu*), the realm of form (*rūpadhātu*), and the formless realm (*arūpadhātu*). The phrase "three worlds" translates *traidhātu* in LSV 113 and *trailoka* in LSV 152.

threefold thousand great thousand *trisāhasramahāsāhasra*
While *trisāhasra* means "three thousand", the meaning of *mahāsāhasra* (literally "great thousand") is not clear. Edgerton suggests it may mean ten thousand, indicating a thirty-million-fold **world system**.
LSV 28 (Vow 12), 47, 148, 154

titan *asura / āsura*
The realm of the titans is located between the human realm and the god realms. The titans are sometimes described as "jealous gods" because they are engaged in constant and futile warfare with the gods to usurp their position in the cosmos.
SSV 20; LSV 28 (Vows 1, 2), 31, 44, 52, 125, 152 (v.5), 155

tools *pariṣkāra*
More literally "requisites" or "utensils".
LSV 39

trace perception *vāsana*
LSV 73

tranquility praśanta
LSV 68

transcendental *lokottara*
LSV 113

udumbara flower *udumbarapuṣpa*
A mythical flower which blooms extremely rarely.
LSV 12, 117

ultimate truth *paramārtha(satya)*, 第一義 *dìyī yì*
LSV 152 (v.6); VS 23

understanding
This mostly translates a range of words that share the root *jñā*, including *jñāna*, *ājñā*, and *jñatā*, but is also used to translate terms such as *abhisamaya* in LSV 79, and *upalabdhi* "have an understanding of" in LSV 113. Depending on context, words derived from *jñā* are also translated as **knowledge**.

unreceptive *vipratyayanīya*
This could be translated in even stronger terms – as "hostile", for example.
SSV 18

unskilful *akuśala*, 罪 *zuì*
Unskilful **actions** are those which are expressive of negative mental states – **greed**, **hatred**, **delusion**, etc.

unsurpassable guide for those who wish to train *anuttara puruṣadamyasārathi*
An epithet of a **buddha**.
LSV 17

unsurpassed perfect Awakening *anuttarā samyaksaṃbodhi*, 阿耨多羅三藐三菩提 *ānòuduōluó sānmiǎo sānpútí*
In the Mahāyāna, this is the full **Awakening** of a **buddha**, which surpasses that of an **arhat**. It is unsurpassed perfect Awakening which is the aim of the **bodhisattva**. In the translation, the verb "attained" is used with this phrase, but the Sanskrit *anuttarāṃ samyaksaṃbodhim abhisaṃbuddha* more literally means "awakened to unsurpassed perfect Awakening". The repetition of awakened/Awakening is clumsy in English, which is why I chose to render it as "attained". In Chinese, the verb used is 發 *fā*, which is closer in meaning to "attain".
SSV 8, 18, 19; LSV 31, 37, 51

untouchable 栴陀羅 *zhāntuóluó* (*caṇḍāla*)
Those who are outside the caste system, contact with whom is considered by orthodox Hindus to result in ritual pollution.
VS 3

vajra
This is left untranslated in LSV 28 (Vow 25) and 87 (v.2) and translated as **diamond** elsewhere.

victorious one *jina*
An epithet of a **buddha**.
LSV 6, 8, 29 (v.9), 87 (v.5), 99, 108, 120, 150, 152 (v.7, 8)

visualization, visualize 觀 *guān* (*darśana*, *vipaśyana*)
The character 觀 *guān* is often rendered as "contemplation" in translations of this sutra. I've gone for "visualization", as 觀 *guān* means quite literally "to see". It's often used in Buddhist Chinese to translate *darśana* or *vipaśyana*. The title of the *Visualization Sutra* is often reconstructed in Sanskrit as the *Amitāyur-dhyāna-sūtra*, but this seems unlikely, and I have not found any instances of 觀 *guān* being used to translate *dhyāna*. Paul Williams suggests the Sanskrit title *Amitāyur-buddhānusmṛti-sūtra*,[187] but the normal Chinese translation of *anusmṛti* is 念 *nian*, and this character is used in the *Visualization Sutra* in a way which strongly suggests that the meaning *anusmṛti* is intended. Given that the *Visualization Sutra* is unlikely to be a direct translation from an Indian language, I suspect that attempting to reconstruct a Sanskrit title is a fruitless endeavour, but on the basis of the Chinese I would suggest that *Amitāyur-darśana-sūtra* would be the most sensible and straightforward rendering.

vow *see* **heartfelt desire**

waste of time *anartha*
The word *anartha* literally means

"without purpose", "without meaning". The word *artha* (of which *an-artha* is the negation) has a wide range of meanings, and is variously translated elsewhere as "purpose", "meaning", "goal", "help", "matter", and "wealth".
LSV 141
see also **branches of learning**

water which possesses eight good qualities *aṣṭāṅgopetavāri*, 八功德水 *bāgōngdéshuǐ*
These eight qualities are that it is soothing, agreeable, mild, clear, not murky, pure, delicious, and not harmful even if enjoyed in excess.
SSV 4; VS 13

wisdom *prajñā*, 慧 huì
This is the direct insight into things the way they are which leads to Awakening. The verbal form *prajānāti* is translated as "come to an understanding" in LSV 7.
LSV 2, 19 (v.2), 36, 45, 87 (v.5), 103, 111–12, 115, 119–21, 137, 152 (v.9); VS 19, 29
see also **perfect in wisdom and conduct**, **spiritual faculties**, **spiritual powers**, **wisdom which has faith as its goal**

wisdom which has faith as its goal *śraddhārthaprajñā*
LSV 152 (v.9)
see also **faith**, **wisdom**

wish-fulfilling jewel *cintāmaṇi*, 如意珠 *rúyì zhū*
Rather like Aladdin's lamp, this is a jewel which will grant the one who possesses it anything they desire. It is commonly used as a metaphor for the **mind set on Awakening**.
LSV 97; VS 13

wonderful qualities *see* **good qualities**

world governed by Yama *yamaloka*
This is another term for the realm of the **hungry ghosts**.
SSV 6

world system *lokadhātu*, 世界 *shìjiè*
The meaning of this phrase does not map exactly onto any single concept in modern cosmology. Sometimes it seems to represent a galaxy, containing **threefold thousand great thousand** worlds. In other contexts, it refers to a region of a single world. Sukhāvatī is frequently described as a world system but, from the descriptions given, it seems to be a single world – or region – rather than a galaxy.

yakṣa *yakṣa* 夜叉 *yèchā*
Supernatural being or nature spirit.
LSV 44, 125, 152 (v.5); VS 33

Yama *Yama*
The Lord of Death, or of the Underworld.
see also **world governed by Yama**

yāma gods 夜摩天 *yèmótiān*
A class of gods.
LSV 37, 133; VS 15, 17

yojana 由旬 *yóuxún*
An Indian unit of measurement rougly equivalent to nine miles.

Notes

Introduction

1 Luis O. Gomez, *The Land of Bliss*, University of Hawai'i Press, Honolulu, HI 1996, pp.112–13.
2 Aaron Hughes, "Imagining the divine: Ghazali on imagination, dreams, and dreaming", *Journal of the American Academy of Religion* 70:1 (2002), pp.33–53, available at http://www.ghazali.org/articles/hughes.pdf, accessed on 8 October 2015.
3 "Hakuin's song of meditation", available at http://www.osholeela.com/poetry/hakuin.html, accessed on 8 October 2015.
4 *Samaññaphala Sutta, Dīgha-nikāya* 2, in *Thus Have I Heard: The Long Discourses of the Buddha, Dīgha-nikāya*, trans. Maurice Walshe, Wisdom Publications, London 1987, pp.104 and 108.
5 It also requires memory of course – we remember, for instance, ourselves and our contemporaries being younger, and things now old and battered being once new. Memory and imagination are in fact closely connected: the raw material of the imagination is memory, from which images, feelings, and thoughts are transformed into something new. To take the example of the Buddha's image of the beryl, cut into eight facets and strung on a blue, yellow, red, white, or orange cord: we may never have seen a necklace exactly like that, but because we've seen jewels and cord, and the colours blue and so on, we are able to imagine the necklace the Buddha describes.
6 *Vajracchedikā Prajñāpāramitā Sūtra* or *Diamond Sutra*, trans. Alex Johnson, ch.32, available at http://www.diamond-sutra.com/diamond_sutra_text/page32.html, accessed on 8 October 2015.
7 See for instance the *Ambattha Sutta*, DN 3, available at http://www.buddhasutra.com/files/ambattha_sutta.htm, accessed on 8 October 2015.
8 "The way things are" is a translation of *Dhamma*, which has a very wide range of meanings. In this context it means "reality" or "truth", but I prefer to use the less abstract phrase.
9 Marion Matics, *Entering the Path of Enlightenment: The Bodhicaryāvatāra of the Buddhist Poet Śāntideva*, Allen & Unwin, London 1970, p.67.

10 *Samaññaphala Sutta*, in *Thus Have I Heard*, p.102.
11 "Meditative concentration" is samādhi, which, in this context, is more or less synonymous with dhyāna. However, there are eight dhyānas, or levels of dhyāna, and, in the context of the threefold way, we could say that samādhi is the collective noun for all eight.
12 See for instance the *Ambattha Sutta*.
13 The compound Sanskrit term is *śraddhārthaprajñā* – *śraddhā*, *artha*, and *prajñā*.
14 To read Paul Harrison's translation, see http://lirs.ru/lib/sutra/Pratyutpanna_and_Surangama_Samadhi_Sutras,1998,BDK25.pdf, accessed on 8 October 2015.
15 John Carey, *What Good Are the Arts?*, Oxford University Press, New York 2006 (Kindle edition), ch.6, "Literature and critical intelligence".

Chapter 1

16 See, for instance David McMahan, "Orality, writing, and authority in South Asian Buddhism: visionary literature and the struggle for legitimacy in the Mahāyāna", *History of Religions* 37:3 (1998), pp.249–74, especially p.265: "it is clear to modern scholars, as it probably was to most Buddhists in ancient India, that the Mahāyāna sūtras were composed quite a long time after the death of Gautama and that it is highly unlikely that the 'historical' Buddha ever spoke any of them."
17 From the *Uttara Sutta*, *Aṅguttara-nikāya* 8.8, trans. Ṭhānissaro Bhikkhu, available at http://www.accesstoinsight.org/tipitaka/an/an08/an08.008.than.html, accessed 8 October 2015.
18 From the *Satthusāsana Sutta*, *Aṅguttara-nikāya* 7.79, trans. Hare (adapted by me).
19 The *Pratyutpanna-saṃmukhāvasthita-samādhi-sūtra* or *The Meditation in Which the Buddhas of the Present All Stand Before One*, ch.2, "The training", available at http://www.sutrasmantras.info/sutra22.html, accessed on 8 October 2015.
20 The story of Anāthapiṇḍada's meeting with the Buddha is from the *Vinaya*, ii.6.4.
21 The *Kāma Sutta*, the first sutta in ch.4, "Aṭṭhakavagga" or "The chapter of the eights", v.766–7, trans. Ṭhānissaro Bhikkhu, available at http://www.accesstoinsight.org/tipitaka/kn/snp/snp.4.01.than.html, accessed on 8 October 2015.
22 *Dhammapada: The Way of Truth*, trans. Sangharakshita, Windhorse Publications, Birmingham 2001, ch.21, "The Miscellaneous", v.290, p.99.
23 *The Niramisa Sutta*, *Saṃyutta-nikāya* 36.31.
24 William Blake, "Eternity", in *Blake, Complete Writings*, ed. Geoffrey Keynes, Oxford University Press, London 1985, p.179.

25 Paul Harrison, "Mediums and messages: reflections on the production of Mahāyāna sutras", *Eastern Buddhist* 35:1–2 (2003), pp.115–47 (especially p.122).

26 Most of the *kasiṇa*s are visual objects, but not all of them. The element air, for instance, can't be directly seen. One "sees" air by seeing plants and trees move in the wind. Alternatively, one can feel the wind on one's skin, in which case the *kasiṇa* is a physical sensation. For information on how to practise *kasiṇa* meditation, see http://www.wikihow.com/Practice-Kasina-Meditation, accessed on 8 October 2015.

27 This description of the *kasiṇa*s comes from a related teaching on the eight bases of transcendence. Numbers 5–8 of these are the colour *kasiṇa*s. See for instance the *Mahāparinibbāna Sutta, Dīgha-nikāya* xvi.3.29.

28 Buddhaghosa, *Visuddhimagga: The Path of Purification*, trans. Bhikkhu Ñāṇamoli, Singapore Buddhist Meditation Centre, Taiwan 1997, v.32–5.

29 *Visuddhimagga*, iv.31.

30 John Milton, *Paradise Lost*, Penguin Classics, London 2000, book 1, lines 254–5, p.9.

31 Wendell Berry, "Grace", in *Selected Poems*, Counterpoint, Berkeley, CA 1998, p.30.

32 The documentary about David Hockney was "The art of seeing", presented by Andrew Marr, shown on BBC2 on 27 February 2012. I haven't been able to access the programme to check that my memory of what Hockney said is correct.

33 From the *Zenrinkushu*, compiled by Eicho (1429–1504).

34 See, for instance, the *Desanā Sutta, Saṃyutta-nikāya* 42.7.

35 See, for example, Jan Nattier, *A Few Good Men: The Bodhisattva Path According to the Inquiry of Ugra (Ugraparipṛcchā)*, University of Hawai'i Press, Honolulu, HI 2005, pp.172–4.

Chapter 2

36 *Upaḍḍha Sutta, Saṃyutta-nikāya* 45.2.

37 *Dhammapada*, ch.1, "Pairs", p.13.

38 F. Max Müller and Bunyiu Nanjio, *Sukhāvatī-vyūha, Description of Sukhāvatī, The Land of Bliss*, Clarendon Press, Oxford 1883; see http://www.sacred-texts.com/bud/sbe49/sbe4927.htm, accessed on 13 October 2015.

39 John Dowland, the first line of his song "Come heavy sleep".

40 The *Dvedhāvitakka Sutta, Majjhima-nikāya* 19, trans. Bhikkhu Ñāṇamoli and Bhikkhu Bodhi.

41 This idea and image is from the *Dhammapada*, ch.9, "Evil", pp.48–9, v.121–2.

42 The *Nibbāna Sutta, Udāna* 8.1. I have combined translations by F.L. Woodward and John D. Ireland.

43 The *Bāhiya Sutta, Udāna* 1.10, trans. John D. Ireland, available at http://www.accesstoinsight.org/tipitaka/kn/ud/ud.1.10.irel.html, accessed on 8 October 2015.

44 The *Sutta-nipāta*, trans. K.R. Norman, in *The Rhinoceros Horn*, Pali Text Society, London 1985, p.184.

45 *Ibid*. The continuation of the quote is Norman's again, but adapted by me.

46 *Vakkali Sutta, Saṃyutta-nikāya* 22.87.

47 The *Caṅkī Sutta, Majjhima-nikāya* 95. I've quoted from Bhikkhu Ñāṇamoli and Bhikkhu Bodhi's translation *The Middle Length Discourses of the Buddha: A New Translation of the Majjhima-nikāya*, Wisdom Publications, Boston, MA 1995, p.780. Actually the Buddha says that there are five things that may turn out in two different ways, faith being just one of them. The other four are approval (of a teaching because we like it), tradition, reason, and a "reflective acceptance of a view" (that is, a conclusion we've come to after reflecting for some time).

48 Dilgo Khyentse Rinpoche's four levels of faith (from the book *The Excellent Path to Enlightenment: Oral Teachings on the Root Text of Jamyang Khyentse Wangpo*), available at http://quotes.justdharma.com/different-levels-of-faith-dilgo-khyentse-rinpoche/, accessed on 8 October 2015.

49 The distinction between naive realism, non-realism, and critical realism comes from the philosopher of religion John Hick. See, for instance, his book *The Fifth Dimension*, Oneworld, Oxford 1999, p.42.

50 Kenneth K. Tanaka, *The Dawn of Chinese Pure Land Doctrine*, State University of New York Press, Albany, NY 1990, p.6.

51 William Wordsworth, *The Major Works*, ed. Stephen Gill, Oxford University Press, Oxford 1984, p.131.

52 Pierre Hadot, *Philosophy as a Way of Life*, Blackwell, Oxford 1995, ch.2, "Philosophy, exegesis, and creative mistakes".

53 Quoted in David J. Kalupahana, *Buddhist Thought and Ritual*, Motilal Banarsidass, Delhi 2001, p.73.

54 The book Sangharakshita refers to is *Pure-Land Zen, Zen Pure-Land* by Yin Kuang, available at http://www.buddhanet.net/pdf_file/yin_kuang.pdf, accessed on 8 October 2015. Sangharakshita's quote about self-power and other-power can be found in *Through Buddhist Eyes*, Windhorse Publications, Birmingham 2000, p.288. My friend who asked Sangharakshita for clarification is Dharmacārī Nagapriya, and Sangharakshita's quoted reply is from an email to Nagapriya, sent on 15 January 2014.

55 The *Pratyutpanna-saṃmukhāvasthita-samādhi-sūtra* or *The Meditation in Which the Buddhas of the Present All Stand Before One*, ch.2, "The training".

56 The *Vimalakīrti Nirdeśa*, ch.1, "The purification of the buddha-field", translated from Sanskrit by Dharmacārī Śraddhāpa.

57 Gomez, *The Land of Bliss*, p.24.

Chapter 3

58 Yaśas seems to be known as Yaśodeva in the *Longer Sukhāvatīvyūhaḥ Sūtra*.

59 *Mahā-parinibbāna Sutta, Dīgha-nikāya* 16, trans. Vajira and Francis Story, available at http://www.accesstoinsight.org/tipitaka/dn/dn.16.1-6.vaji.html, accessed on 8 October 2015.

60 *Sutta-nipāta*, ch.5, "Pārāyanavagga" or "The chapter on the way to the far shore", in *The Rhinoceros Horn*, p.170.

61 *Mahā-parinibbāna Sutta*.

62 "Aeon" is *kappa*, the Pali equivalent to the Sanskrit *kalpa*, which is an unimaginably long period of time (see the explanation on pp 84–5). However, because a *kappa* can also mean time in general, translators often understand it to mean simply longer than the usual lifespan, i.e. a hundred years.

63 Siri Hustvedt, "Variations on desire: a mouse, a dog, Buber, and Bovary", in *Living, Thinking, Looking*, Sceptre, London 2012 (Kindle edition).

64 P.B. Shelley, "A defence of poetry", available at http://www.bartleby.com/27/23.html, accessed on 8 October 2015.

65 *Mettā Sutta, Sutta-nipāta* 1.8, rendered into English by Dharmacārī Padmavajra.

Chapter 4

66 *Gārava Sutta, Saṃyutta-nikāya* 6.2, trans. Ṭhānissaro Bhikkhu, available at http://www.accesstoinsight.org/tipitaka/sn/sn06/sn06.002.than.html, accessed on 8 October 2015.

67 Wilfred Cantwell-Smith, *Faith and Belief: The Difference Between Them*, Oneworld, Oxford 1998, p.12.

68 *Ibid.*

69 *The Art of Reflection*, Windhorse Publications, Cambridge 2010, p.143.

70 *Cetanā Sutta, Aṅguttara-nikāya* 11.2, trans. Ṭhānissaro Bhikkhu, available at http://www.accesstoinsight.org/tipitaka/an/an11/an11.002.than.html, accessed on 8 October 2015.

71 *Cetanā Sutta*. The phrase "act of will" is a translation of *cetanā*, which the Pali–English dictionary defines as "thinking as active thought, intention, purpose, will", while "in the nature of things" is *dhammatā*, meaning "natural" or "the natural way of things".

72 This is my teacher Sangharakshita's interpretation, and differs from the more traditional view, which says that the *dharma-niyama* accounts for the miraculous events that occur when someone becomes a buddha, such as the shaking of the earth. For Sangharakshita's interpretation, see, for instance, "Revering and relying upon the Dharma" by Dharmacārī Subhuti, pp.8–9, available at http://subhuti.info/essays, accessed on 8

October 2015. For the more traditional interpretation, see the *Aṭṭhasālinī* by Buddhaghosa.

73 I have given only the translations of the Sanskrit names in this passage so that you can experience their poetic beauty directly (assuming that you don't know Sanskrit). In his translation Śraddhāpa includes the Sanskrit names as well as their translations.

74 The *Daśabhūmika vibhāṣā śāstra*, attributed to Nāgārjuna, trans. Hisao Inagaki, available at http://web.mit.edu/stclair/www/Nagarjuna_easypractice.html, accessed on 8 October 2015.

75 Juan Ramon Jimenez, "Oceans", trans. from the Spanish by Robert Bly, in *News of the Universe: Poems of Twofold Consciousness*, Counterpoint, Berkeley, CA 2015, p.96.

76 William James, *The Varieties of Religious Experience*, Penguin Classics, London 1985, p.205.

77 H.G. Wells, *Mr Britling Sees It Through*, Trajectory Classics, Marblehead, MA 2014 (Kindle edition), book 3, section 9, ch.2.

78 H.G. Wells, *God the Invisible King*, Echo Library, Cirencester 2005, p.38.

79 Donald Tovey describing the opening of the first movement of Beethoven's *Eroica* symphony. From *Essays in Musical Analysis*, quoted in Roger Scruton, *The Aesthetics of Music*, Oxford University Press, Oxford 1997, p.155.

Chapter 5

80 The *Mahāsakuludāyi Sutta*, *Majjhima-nikāya* 77, trans. Bhikkhu Ñāṇamoli and Bhikkhu Bodhi, in *The Middle Length Discourses of the Buddha*, p.640.

81 William Blake, "Auguries of innocence", in *The Complete Poetry and Prose of William Blake*, ed. David V. Erman, Anchor, Garden City, NY 1982, p.490.

82 *Pabhassara Sutta*, *Aṅguttara-nikāya* 1.49–52.

83 From the *Samaññaphala Sutta*, *Dīgha-nikāya* 2, trans. Ṭhānissaro Bhikkhu, available at http://www.accesstoinsight.org/tipitaka/dn/dn.02.0.than.html, accessed on 8 October 2015.

84 From *The Hundred Thousand Songs of Milarepa*, trans. Garma C.C. Chang, Shambala Publications, Massachusetts, MA 1989, pp.128–9.

85 Martin Gayford, *A Bigger Message: Conversations with David Hockney*, Thames & Hudson, London 2011, p.53.

86 The *Bāhiya Sutta*, *Udāna* 1.10, trans. John D. Ireland, available at http://www.accesstoinsight.org/tipitaka/kn/ud/ud.1.10.irel.html, accessed on 8 October 2015.

87 "Pārāyanavagga", in *The Rhinoceros Horn*, p.170.

88 Stephen Sutton, his death reported in the *i* newspaper, 30 May 2014.

89 Hadot, *Philosophy as a Way of Life*, p.222.

90 Last few lines of the poem "From blossoms" by Li-Young Lee, available at http://www.poetryfoundation.org/poem/171754, accessed on 8 October 2015.

91 Nattier, *A Few Good Men*, p.114.
92 See Sungtaek Cho, "The psycho-semantic structure of the word *kṣānti*", available at http://www.buddhism.org/board/read.cgi?board=BuddhistStudies&y_number=19, accessed on 8 October 2015, and Genjun H. Sasaki, *Linguist Approach to Buddhist Thought*, Motilal Banarsidass, Delhi 1986, pp.133–40.
93 Verses from "The confounder of hell", *Vajrasattva sadhana*, available at https://alanashley.wordpress.com/2011/03/10/verses-from-the-confounder-of-hell-vajrasattva-sadhana/, accessed on 13 October 2015.

Chapter 6

94 The *Vimalakīrti Nirdeśa*, ch.1, "The purification of the buddha-field".
95 Gomez, *The Land of Bliss*, p.248, n.21.
96 See http://lirs.ru/lib/sutra/Pratyutpanna_and_Surangama_Samadhi_Sutras,1998,BDK25.pdf, accessed on 8 October 2015.
97 The *Vimalakīrti Nirdeśa*, ch.1, section 12.
98 *Ibid.*, ch.8, "The family of the tathāgatas", p.68.
99 Shelley, "A defence of poetry", available at http://www.bartleby.com/27/23.html, accessed on 8 October 2015.
100 From the *Cūḷagosiṅga Sutta*, *Majjhima-nikāya* 31, trans. Bhikkhu Ñāṇamoli and Bhikkhu Bodhi, in *The Middle Length Discourses of the Buddha*, pp.206–7.
101 Parker J. Palmer, *The Courage to Teach*, Jossey-Bass, San Francisco, CA 1998, pp.95–6.
102 The *Ratnaguṇasaṃcayagāthā*, trans. Edward Conze, in *The Perfection of Wisdom in Eight Thousand Lines and Its Verse Summary*, Four Seasons Foundation, San Francisco, CA 1973, p.10.
103 Blake, "Eternity", p.179.
104 Walter J. Ong, *Orality and Literacy*, Routledge, New York 1988, pp.49–57.
105 See https://malaysia.answers.yahoo.com/question/index?qid=20070627035427AAF0P3H, accessed on 8 October 2015.
106 David Drewes, "Early Indian Mahāyāna Buddhism II: new perspectives", *Religion Compass* 4:2 (2010), pp.66–74 (p.69), available at https://www.academia.edu/9226471/Early_Indian_Mahayana_Buddhism_II_New_perspectives, accessed on 8 October 2015.

Chapter 7

107 *Vinaya*, ii.7.2, trans. F.L.Woodward, slightly adapted by me. See F.L.Woodward, *Some Sayings of the Buddha*, Oxford University Press, Oxford 1973, p.181.
108 *Samaññaphala Sutta*, *Dīgha-nikāya* 2.
109 See http://dictionary.reference.com/browse/escapism, accessed on 8 October 2015.

110 Tricia Ellen, *Widow's Voice: Seven Widowed Voices Sharing Love, Loss, and Hope*, available at widowsvoice-sslf.blogspot.com, accessed on 8 October 2015.
111 *Upajjhathana Sutta, Aṅguttara-nikāya* 5.57, translator unknown.
112 David Whyte, "Sweet Darkness", in *River Flow, New and Selected Poems*, Many Rivers Press, Langley, WA 2007, p.348.
113 See http://www.chinapage.com/confucius/xiaojing-be.html, accessed on 8 October 2015.
114 *Khaggavisāṇa Sutta, Sutta-nipāta* 1.3, in *The Rhinoceros Horn*, pp.9 and 8.
115 Commentary to the *Sallekha Sutta*, available at http://www.accesstoinsight.org/tipitaka/mn/mn.008.nypo.html#fn-mn-008-17, accessed on 8 October 2015.
116 The *Mahānāma Sutta, Aṅguttara-nikāya* 8.25, trans. Kumara Bhikkhu, available at http://www.accesstoinsight.org/tipitaka/an/an08/an08.025.kuma.html, accessed on 8 October 2015.

Chapter 8

117 *Visuddhimagga*, iv.31.
118 Tanaka, *The Dawn of Chinese Pure Land Doctrine*, p.56.
119 *Ibid.*, from Hui-Yuan's commentary, translated by Tanaka, p.122.
120 Barbara Kienscherf, "See this sound", available at http://www.see-this-sound.at/works/216, accessed on 8 October 2015.
121 *Mahānāma Sutta, Aṅguttara-nikāya* 11.13, trans. Ṭhānissaro Bhikkhu, available at http://www.accesstoinsight.org/tipitaka/an/an11/an11.013.than.html, accessed on 8 October 2015.
122 See http://oll.libertyfund.org/pages/blake-william-an-introduction, accessed on 13 October 2015.
123 Zhiyi, *Ten Doubts About Pure Land*, trans. Master Thich Thien Tam, available at http://www.purelandbuddhism.com/10Doubts.pdf, p.4, accessed on 8 October 2015.
124 Julian Pas, *Visions of Sukhavati*, State University of New York Press, Albany, NY 1995, p.46.
125 *Kakacūpama Sutta, Majjhima-nikāya* 21, trans. Ṭhānissaro Bhikkhu, available at http://www.accesstoinsight.org/tipitaka/mn/mn.021x.than.html, accessed on 8 October 2015.
126 The *Saddharma Puṇḍarīka Sūtra*, ch.3. The quote is translated by Burton Watson in *The Lotus Sutra*, Columbia University Press, New York 1993, p.58.

Introduction to the translations

127 *Vinaya-piṭaka, Cūḷavagga* 5.33 (trans. Śraddhāpa). "Faith" here translates *pasāda* (Skt *prasāda*), rather than *saddhā* (Skt *śraddhā*).

128 From "Translator for the Buddha: an interview with Bhikkhu Bodhi", *Inquiring Mind* (spring 2006), available at http://www.inquiringmind.com/Articles/Translator.html, accessed on 8 October 2015.
129 F. Max Müller, *The Larger Sukhāvatī-vyūha* and *The Smaller Sukhāvatī-vyūha*, in *The Sacred Books of the East*, vol.49, Clarendon Press, Oxford 1894, p.25.
130 This term was coined by the scholar Kwame Anthony Appiah; see his essay "Thick translation", in *The Translation Studies Reader*, ed. Lawrence Venuti, 2nd edn, Routledge, London 2004, pp.389–401.
131 See for example *A Comedy of Errors*, act IV, scene 3: "There's not a man I meet but doth salute me / As if I were their well-acquainted friend."
132 Sangharakshita, *A Survey of Buddhism: Its Doctrines and Methods Through the Ages*, Windhorse Publications, Birmingham 1997, p.41.
133 *Ibid.*

The Shorter Sūtra on the Abundance of Wonderful Qualities Which Adorn Sukhāvatī

134 In translating the titles of the *Longer* and *Shorter Sūtras*, I have interpreted the Sanskrit title *Sukhāvatīvyūha* (which on its own does not make a great deal of sense) as being an abbreviation of *Sukhāvatīguṇālaṃkāravyūha*, which can be translated as *The Abundance (vyūha) of Wonderful Qualities (guṇa) Which Adorn (ālaṃkāra) Sukhāvatī*. This is based on the phrases *buddhakṣetraguṇavyūhaiḥ samalaṃkṛtaṃ* and *buddhakṣetraguṇālaṃkāravyūhasaṃpada,* which occur repeatedly in the *Shorter* and *Longer Sūtra* respectively.
135 Ajita is the future Buddha, better known as Maitreya.
136 In the Sanskrit, there are three synonyms for "dwell" (*tiṣṭhati, dhriyate, yāpayati*), but I felt it would be so unnatural to try to replicate this in English that I just left it as one verb. The same three verbs occur in LSV 40 and 122.
137 Alternatively: "studded with" (*ratnamaya*).

The Longer Sūtra on the Abundance of Wonderful Qualities Which Adorn Sukhāvatī

138 As sandalwood is considered the most exquisite of fragrances, the term *candana* can also be used metaphorically in Sanskrit to indicate that something is the most excellent of its kind.
139 Merukuṭa is found in Müller, but not in Vaidya.
140 Following Müller (Vaidya has "Girirājaghoṣośvara").
141 Gomez adds Tagaragandha, "Fragrance of the Pinwheel Flower" here. Tagaragandha is not mentioned in Vaidya, but Müller mentions that the name "Taragandha" is found in one of the manuscripts.
142 Amended from Ratnābhibhāsa, following Gomez.

143 There is no word meaning "fragrance" in this name, but there is a Buddha named Tamālapatrachandanagandha who appears in the *Saddharma Puṇḍarīka Sūtra*, so I have chosen to interpret this name as Mahātamālapatracandanakardamagandha in order to make sense of it.
144 Amended from Kusukābhijña, following Gomez.
145 Amended from Kolendra, following Gomez.
146 Vaidya has Dharmaketu, but here I follow Müller.
147 The numbering and organization of Amitābha's vows are slightly different in the Sanskrit and Chinese versions of the text. Thus, the famous vow known as Amitābha's eighteenth primal vow in East Asian Buddhism is included along with the content of the twentieth vow of the Chinese text in the nineteenth vow of the Sanskrit text.
148 The phrase "unable to fall away" translates *avaivartika*, which is translated elsewhere as **irreversible**.
149 Here, "peace" translates *śiva* rather than *śānta*.
150 Here, "awareness" translates *saṃprajāna*.
151 In the Sanskrit, there are three synonyms for "dwell" (*tiṣṭhati, dhriyate, yāpayati*), but I felt it would be so unnatural to try to replicate this in English that I just left it as one verb. The same three verbs occur in SSV 2 and LSV 122.
152 Here, "power" translates *adhiṣṭhāna* rather than *bala*.
153 The word "abundance" here does not translate *vyūha*.
154 "Words" here translates *śabda*, which is translated as "sound" in the previous sentence. However, it was not possible to find a single English term which could be used to translate *śabda* in both contexts.
155 Here: *pāramitā*.
156 Here: *upaśānta*.
157 The phrase "form a perception in their minds" translates *saṃjānanti*. This is the verbal form of the word *saṃjñā*, which is translated as "notion" (see Glossary).
158 The word "see" here also translates *saṃjānanti*.
159 The word *jāla* normally means "net", but can also mean "any reticulated or woven texture, wire-mail, mail-coat, wire helmet" (Monier-Williams).
160 Again, *saṃjānanti*.
161 The phrase "enjoy themselves" here translates *ramante* – a word which can have quite strong sexual connotations.
162 The phrase "minds become absorbed" translates *manasikāra* here and elsewhere (see Glossary). Here, though, the Sanskrit uses it as a verb in the active voice, and the disadvantage of this translation is that is makes it seem a bit passive, whereas the Sanskrit here makes it clear that it is active – the living beings in question are actively making their minds become absorbed by the Tathāgata.
163 The phrase "cultivate a heartfelt desire" here translates *praṇidhāsyanti*, which is the verbal form of *praṇidhaṇa*. *Praṇidhaṇa* is translated as both "heartfelt desire" and "vow" according to context, but here the meaning

is somewhat ambiguous, so this phrase could just as well be translated as "vow to be born in that world system".

164 See SSV 18.

165 The phrase "minds which practise the perfection of wisdom" translates *prajñāpāramitācaryācaraṇacittāḥ*, which is very similar to the phrase used at the beginning of the *Heart Sūtra*.

166 Here, the phrase "good qualities" translates *dharma*, not *guṇa*.

167 Here, "greed" translates *lubdha*, not *rāga*.

168 In the Sanskrit, there are three synonyms for "dwell" (*tiṣṭhati*, *dhriyate*, *yāpayati*), but I felt it would be so unnatural to try to replicate this in English that I just left it as one verb. The same three verbs occur in SSV 2 and LSV 40.

169 This is another name for Maitreya.

170 In Sanskrit, the pronoun *yuṣmābhir* is used, which makes it clear that the "you" being addressed is plural, and hence not only Ajita.

171 This can also be interpreted as "the spiritual practice of freeing (yourselves) from doubt". The phrase "spiritual practice" here translates *yoga*.

172 The phrase "attained their goal" translates *siddhārtha*.

173 The word "thinking" translates *dṛṣṭi*, more literally "views".

174 The phrase "Dharma-vision" translates *dharmacakṣu*, which is translated more literally as "the eye of the Dharma" in LSV 112.

The Sūtra on the Visualization of the Buddha Amitāyus

175 In fact, although the name of the translator is given at the beginning of the sutra, this text is considered unlikely to be a direct translation from Sanskrit, but rather a Chinese composition (although it may well have been based on earlier, Indian material). Even if it was translated from an Indian language, it would more likely have been a Prakrit – one of the commonly spoken dialects – rather than Classical Sanskrit.

176 The phrase "the effects of all actions have been purified" translates 清淨業 *qīngjìng yè*. This phrase, or others very similar to it, occur repeatedly in the sutra, and it more literally means "pure (or purified) action (*karma*)". In the contexts in which it occurs, I feel 業 *yè* is most reasonably interpreted as the effects of actions, rather than the actions themselves, but the translation "all actions have been purified" would be equally valid.

177 Here, "see" translates 觀 *guān*, which is translated elsewhere as **visualization/visualize**.

178 The word "awareness" here translates 念 *niàn*, which is the standard Chinese term for *smṛti* (**mindfulness**) and *anusmṛti* (**recollection**).

179 The suffering of (1) birth, old age, sickness, and death; (2) being separated from what you like; (3) having to deal with what you dislike; (4) not being able to get what you want; and (5) the suffering inherent

in the five *skandhas* (physical form, sensations, perception, habitual tendencies, and consciousness).

180 The word "attention" here translates 念 *niàn*, which is the standard Chinese term for *smṛti* (**mindfulness**) and *anusmṛti* (**recollection**).

181 The phrase "the effects of … **unskilful actions**" translates 罪 *zuì*, more literally simply "unskilfulness".

182 Here, "perfections" translates 波羅蜜 *bōluómì* (*pāramitā*).

183 This translates 念佛三昧 *niàn fó sānmèi*, which is exactly the same phrase which was translated as "Samādhi of the Recollection of the Buddha" at the end of section 16. In Chinese singularity/plurality is generally not explicitly indicated, and has to be inferred from the context.

184 These are: sutras (*sūtra*), songs (*geya*), verses (*gāthā*), stories (*nidāna*), morality tales (*itivṛttaka*), *jātaka* tales (*jātaka*), tales of wonder (*adbhutadharma*), legends (*avadāna*), extensive teachings (*vaipulya*), discourses on the Dharma (*upadeśa*), inspired utterances (*udāna*), and prophecies (*vyākaraṇa*).

185 The Chinese here, 神通 *shéntōng*, can translate both *ṛddhi* (**supernormal abilities**) and *abhijñā* (**higher forms of knowledge**). I'm interpreting it as *ṛddhi* here.

186 Recollection of the Buddha, the Dharma, the Sangha, ethical conduct, renunciation, and the gods.

Glossary

187 Paul Williams, *Mahāyāna Buddhism: The Doctrinal Foundations*, Routledge, London 2009, p.239.

Bibliography

Original texts

Müller, F. Max, *The Larger Sukhāvatī-vyūha* and *The Smaller Sukhāvatī-vyūha*, in *The Sacred Books of the East*, vol.49, Clarendon Press, Oxford 1894.

Müller, F. Max, and Bunyiu Nanjio, *Sukhāvatī-vyūha, Description of Sukhāvatī, The Land of Bliss*, Clarendon Press, Oxford 1883.

Taishō Shinshū Daizōkyō, vol.12, text 365 佛説觀無量壽佛經 *Fó shuō guān wúliàngshòu fó jīng*, available at http://21dzk.l.u-tokyo.ac.jp/SAT/ddb-bdk-sat2.php?lang=en, accessed on 9 October 2015.

Vaidya, P.L. (ed.), *Sukhāvatīvyūhaḥ (Saṃkṣiptamātṛkā) (Mahāyāna-sūtra-saṃgrahaḥ Part 1)*, The Mithila Institute of Post-Graduate Studies and Research in Sanskrit Learning, Darbhanga 1961, available at http://www.dsbcproject.org/node/6345, accessed on 9 October 2015.

Vaidya, P.L. (ed.), *Sukhāvatīvyūhaḥ (Vistaramātṛkā) (Mahāyāna-sūtra-saṃgrahaḥ Part 1)*, The Mithila Institute of Post-Graduate Studies and Research in Sanskrit Learning, Darbhanga 1961, available at http://www.dsbcproject.org/node/6346, accessed on 9 October 2015.

Reference works

Edgerton, Franklin, *Buddhist Hybrid Sanskrit Grammar and Dictionary*, Munshiram Manoharlal Publishers, Delhi 1953/2004, available at http://gandhari.org/n_dictionary.php (click on BHSD), accessed on 9 October 2015.

Hirakawa, Akira, *Buddhist Chinese–Sanskrit Dictionary*, The Reyukai, Tokyo 1997, available as part of the *Digital Dictionary of Buddhism* at http://www.buddhism-dict.net/ddb/ and the *Buddhist Door Glossary* at http://dictionary.buddhistdoor.com/en/, accessed on 9 October 2015.

Monier-Williams, Monier, *A Sanskrit English Dictionary*, Motilal Banarsidass Publishers, Delhi 1899/2002, available at http://gandhari.org/n_dictionary.php (click on MW), accessed on 9 October 2015.

Müller, Charles (ed.), *Digital Dictionary of Buddhism*, available at http://www.buddhism-dict.net/ddb/, accessed on 9 October 2015.

Soothill, William Edward, and Lewis Hodous, *A Dictionary of Chinese Buddhist Terms*, Routledge, London 1937/2004, available as part of the *Digital Dictionary of Buddhism* at http://www.buddhism-dict.net/ddb/ and the *Buddhist Door Glossary* at http://dictionary.buddhistdoor.com/en/, accessed on 9 October 2015.

Other translations of the Pure Land sutras

Gomez, Luis O., *The Land of Bliss*, University of Hawai'i Press, Honolulu, HI 1996 (includes translations of the *Longer Sutra* and the *Shorter Sutra* both from Sanskrit and from Chinese).
Inagaki, Hisao, and Harold Stewart (trans.), *The Three Pure Land Sutras*, rev. 2nd edn, Numata Center for Buddhist Translation and Research, Berkeley, CA 2003 (translations of all three sutras from Chinese), available at http://www.bdk.or.jp/pdf/bdk/digitaldl/dBET_ThreePureLandSutras_2003.pdf, accessed on 9 October 2015.

Studies of Pure Land texts

Pas, Julian, *Visions of Sukhavati*, State University of New York Press, Albany, NY 1995.
Tanaka, Kenneth K., *The Dawn of Chinese Pure Land Doctrine*, State University of New York Press, Albany, NY 1990.

Translations of Buddhist texts

Buddhaghosa, *Visuddhimagga: The Path of Purification*, trans. Bhikkhu Ñāṇamoli, Singapore Buddhist Meditation Centre, Taiwan 1997.
Chang, Garma C.C. (trans.), *The Hundred Thousand Songs of Milarepa*, Shambala Publications, Massachusetts, MA 1989.
Conze, Edward (trans.), *The Perfection of Wisdom in Eight Thousand Lines and Its Verse Summary*, Four Seasons Foundation, San Francisco, CA 1973.
Goddard, Dwight (ed.), *A Buddhist Bible*, Beacon Press, Boston, MA 1970 (translations of texts from various Buddhist traditions).
Harrison, Paul (trans.), *Pratyutpanna Samādhi Sūtra*, available at http://lirs.ru/lib/sutra/Pratyutpanna_and_Surangama_Samadhi_Sutras,1998,BDK25.pdf, accessed on 9 October 2015.
Matics, Marion, *Entering the Path of Enlightenment: The Bodhicaryāvatāra of the Buddhist Poet Śāntideva*, Allen & Unwin, London 1970.
Ñāṇamoli, Bhikkhu, and Bhikkhu Bodhi (trans.), *The Middle Length Discourses of the Buddha: A New Translation of the Majjhima-nikāya*, Wisdom Publications, Boston, MA 1995.
Nattier, Jan, *A Few Good Men: The Bodhisattva Path According to the Inquiry of Ugra (Ugraparipṛcchā)*, University of Hawai'i Press, Honolulu, HI 2005.

Norman, K.R., *The Rhinoceros Horn (Sutta-nipāta)*, Pali Text Society, London 1985.
Sangharakshita (trans.), *Dhammapada: The Way of Truth*, Windhorse Publications, Birmingham 2001.
Thurman, Robert (trans.), *The Holy Teaching of Vimalakīrti: A Mahāyāna Scripture*, Pennsylvania State University Press, University Park, PA 1976.
Walshe, Maurice (trans.), *Thus Have I Heard: The Long Discourses of the Buddha, Dīgha-nikāya*, Wisdom Publications, London 1987.
Watson, Burton, *The Lotus Sutra (Saddharma Puṇḍarīka Sūtra)*, Columbia University Press, New York 1993.

Scholarly articles and papers

Appiah, Kwame Anthony, "Thick translation", in *The Translation Studies Reader*, ed. Lawrence Venuti, 2nd edn, Routledge, London 2004, pp.389–401.
Drewes, David, "Early Indian Mahāyāna Buddhism II: new perspectives", *Religion Compass* 4:2 (2010), pp.66–74 (p.69), available at https://www.academia.edu/9226471/Early_Indian_Mahayana_Buddhism_II_New_perspectives, accessed on 9 October 2015.
Harrison, Paul, "Mediums and messages: reflections on the production of Mahayana sutras", *Eastern Buddhist* 35:1–2 (2003), pp.115–47.
Hughes, Aaron, "Imagining the divine: Ghazali on imagination, dreams, and dreaming", *Journal of the American Academy of Religion* 70:1 (2002), pp.33–53, available at http://www.ghazali.org/articles/hughes.pdf, accessed on 9 October 2015.
McMahan, David, "Orality, writing, and authority in South Asian Buddhism: visionary literature and the struggle for legitimacy in the Mahāyāna", *History of Religions* 37:3 (1998), pp.249–74

Miscellaneous

Cantwell-Smith, Wilfred, *Faith and Belief: The Difference Between Them*, Oneworld, Oxford 1998.
Carey, John, *What Good Are the Arts?*, Oxford University Press, New York 2006.
Gayford, Martin, *A Bigger Message: Conversations with David Hockney*, Thames & Hudson, London 2011.
Hadot, Pierre, *Philosophy as a Way of Life*, Blackwell, Oxford 1995.
Hick, John, *The Fifth Dimension*, Oneworld, Oxford 1999.
Hustvedt, Siri, *Living, Thinking, Looking*, Sceptre, London 2012.
James, William, *The Varieties of Religious Experience*, Penguin Classics, London 1985.
Kalupahana, David J., *Buddhist Thought and Ritual*, Motilal Banarsidass, Delhi 2001.

Kuang, Yin, *Pure-Land Zen, Zen Pure-Land*, available at http://www.buddhanet.net/pdf_file/yin_kuang.pdf, accessed on 9 October 2015

Palmer, Parker J., *The Courage to Teach*, Jossey-Bass, San Francisco, CA 1998.

Scruton, Roger, *The Aesthetics of Music*, Oxford University Press, Oxford 1997.

Shelley, P.B., "A defence of poetry", available at http://www.bartleby.com/27/23.html, accessed on 9 October 2015.

Wells, H.G., *God the Invisible King*, Echo Library, Cirencester 2005.

Wells, H.G., *Mr Britling Sees It Through*, Trajectory Classics, Marblehead, MA 2014.

Williams, Paul, *Mahāyāna Buddhism: The Doctrinal Foundations*, Routledge, London 2009.

Pronunciation guide

In Pāli and Sanskrit every letter is pronounced and there are no diphthongs. The short vowels a, i, and u are voiced more briefly than the others, which are known as long vowels. An approximate guide to pronunciation is as follows:

Vowels

a as in cut	*ā* as in cart	*ai* as in high	*au* as in out
e as in veil	*i* as in kick	*ī* as in bee	*o* as in low
u as in put	*ū* as in too	*ṛ* as the ri in trip	

Consonants

As in English, with the following qualifications:

c soft as in chat

d and *t* as in English, but with the tongue tip against the back of the upper front teeth

ḍ and *ṭ* as in *d* and *t*, but with the tongue tip curled up and backwards against the roof of the mouth

g hard as in good

ḥ at the end of a word has a slight echo of the preceding vowel

j as in jay unless followed by *ñ*, when it may be hard as in signal

ś and *ṣ* soft as in shin

v is pronounced somewhere between English *v* and *w*

Doubled consonants are pronounced as such, e.g. sadda as in midday, kṣ as in bookshop.

Nasal sounds

Before a consonant, make the natural sound associated with that consonant:

ṅk as in trunk	*ṅg* as in sang	*ñc* as in crunch	*nj* as in hinge
ṇṭ or *nt* as in tent	*ṇḍ* or *nd* as in bend	*mp* as in limp	*mb* as in limbo

Before vowels:
ñ as ny in banyan
ṃ at the end of a word nasalizes the preceding vowel, as in the French *bon*
n as in nit but with the tongue tip against the back of the upper front teeth
ṇ as in nit, but with the tongue tip curled up and backwards against the roof of the mouth

Aspirated consonants are shown followed immediately by the letter h, and should be pronounced with an audible out-breath. Note that *th* is always pronounced as in shorthand; *ph* is always pronounced as in haphazard.

For Chinese pronunciation, see http://pages.ucsd.edu/~dkjordan/chin/pinyin1.

Index

Introductory note

References such as '178–9' indicate (not necessarily continuous) discussion of a topic across a range of pages. Wherever possible in the case of topics with many references, these have either been divided into sub-topics or only the most significant discussions of the topic are listed. Because the entire work is about the *Sukhāvatīvyūhaḥ Sūtras*, the use of this term (and certain others which occur constantly throughout the book) as an entry point has been restricted. Information will be found under the corresponding detailed topics.

Dharma 34–9, 65–7, 69–71, 100–101, 243–7, 286–91, 296–9, 317–23
true 112, 258–9, 297
wondrous 213, 220, 222, 311, 315, 317, 319, 322
Dharmākara 89–96, 108–9, 123–4, 151, 195–6, 254–7, 266, 268
vows 88–90, 93, 95, 109, 113, 115, 126, 140
dharma-niyama 107–8, 111, 113, 116, 130, 140–1
dhyānas (absorbed meditative states) 6, 22–3, 26–30, 37, 50, 82, 124–5, 208
diamonds 205, 305, 308–10, 314, 317, 328, 340
Dīpaṃkara 38, 45, 84, 252, 299
disciples 7, 15, 17–19, 35, 38–40, 58–9, 121, 175–7
chief 20, 69, 77, 145, 175, 209
immediate 61, 98, 219
discipline 16, 151, 168, 265
discontent 159–60, 287
discontinuity 54, 133
discourse 1, 62, 70, 115, 169–70, 244–6, 296–7, 299
excellent 297, 299
graduated 5, 7, 28, 79, 129
disease 109, 137, 140–1, 284–5
disenchantment 16, 102, 106, 139, 148
disgust 35, 75, 146, 226–7
dispassion 16, 102, 139, 148
divine eye 28–9, 127, 258, 261, 283, 287, 328, 331
doorways 166, 293, 317, 319, 321, 328
Dowland, John 48
dreams 56–8, 281–2
dungeons 176–7, 182, 188–9, 227, 302

earth 28–9, 52–4, 133–4, 162–4, 204, 209–10, 291, 309
earth teaching, world system of 164, 291
echo 41, 151, 185, 290, 359
effort, skilful 105, 108, 119, 200, 218
elders 77, 191, 193, 241, 249–50
elephants 176, 289, 335
crazed 176
great 162, 249, 288
emanation buddhas 215–16, 312–13, 316, 318, 321–2, 328
emeralds 25, 126, 140, 242, 260, 272–3
emotions 101, 120, 141, 153, 329
positive 43, 161
empathy 76, 83, 159, 251, 256, 261, 283
emptiness 93, 206, 209, 267, 276, 306, 308, 329–30
enduring self 54, 67–8, 81, 87, 107, 154, 211–12, 214
energy 59–60, 81, 84, 86–7, 254–5, 296, 299, 329
great 110, 170, 269, 296
Enlightenment 1–2, 38–40, 52–4, 59, 61, 63, 65, 67
equanimity 22–4, 37, 132, 276, 329
escapism 185–7
religious 185–6
essence 101, 129–30, 211, 323, 329
eternalism 81, 135, 214
eternal life 55, 63, 89, 135
eternity 24, 123, 137, 160
ethical conduct/actions 45, 102, 107–8, 131, 254, 322, 329, 336
ethical practice 30, 52, 61, 104, 113–14, 190, 194, 201
ethical purity 3, 52, 114
ethics 7, 47, 51–2, 55, 66, 150, 179, 194
practice of 6, 30, 47–8, 51, 53, 180, 190, 193
pure 149, 183
events 54, 57, 68, 101, 130, 159, 175, 178
cosmic 18, 171
evil 177, 183, 187, 302–3, 329
existence 29–30, 52–3, 61, 80, 101, 129–31, 134, 137
conditioned 130, 332, 335, 338
cyclic 249, 327
experience 1–6, 22–3, 30–2, 53–4, 60–1, 116–19, 153–5, 214
of dhyāna 27, 29, 129
sense 6, 329
spiritual 43, 132, 213
visual 123, 205
eye
Dhamma 7, 28
divine 28–9, 127, 258, 261, 283, 287, 328, 331
eyebrows 218, 303, 312–13

faculties 2, 5, 59–60, 78–9, 84–5, 250–1, 286, 289
five spiritual 34–5, 55, 59, 111, 243, 338
imaginative 7, 88, 208, 210
spiritual 151, 329, 334, 337–8, 341
faith 7–8, 55–6, 58–61, 85, 99–100, 114–16, 149–50, 195–6
deep 190, 194–5, 304, 317
serene 113, 280–1, 294, 296, 298, 329, 337
false mental construction 213, 311, 334
family 151, 169, 180, 192–3, 231, 267, 303, 323
fantasy 88–9, 186, 213
fathers 21, 169, 175–7, 181–2, 192, 221, 225, 301–2
fear 19, 88, 92, 107, 141, 143, 285, 289
femininity 146–7, 262

five physical senses 23–4, 32–3, 43, 82
five spiritual faculties/powers 34–5, 55, 59, 111, 243, 249, 338
fixed and separate self 67–8, 87, 142
flags 94–5, 260–1, 268, 277, 279, 286
flowers 125–6, 133, 138–40, 271–3, 278, 286, 292–3, 306–7
fresh 133, 139, 278
garlands of 166, 181, 293
lotus 209, 220, 273, 291–4, 308–9, 311, 313–16, 318–22
sweet-smelling 123, 262, 281
focus 155, 203–4, 209–12, 217, 220–1, 305, 309–11, 315–16
folded hands 250, 254, 290, 301, 318–21, 330
followers 39, 41, 113, 175, 178, 187, 196–7, 207
food 30–1, 84, 94–5, 156, 161, 268, 271, 276
pure 166, 181, 294
formless world 23, 37, 53, 92
fragrances 85, 132–3, 252–3, 268, 271, 277–9, 285–6
freedom 22–4, 93, 102, 104–5, 167–8, 185, 267, 329–30
from accumulation 93, 267, 276
from birth 132, 276
from characteristics 93, 267, 276
complete 24, 131, 168
from desire 93, 132, 267, 276
friends 11, 31–2, 39, 44, 67, 69, 121–2, 143
spiritual 222, 320–2
friendship 44, 90, 159, 238
spiritual 44, 53, 159, 192
fruit 95, 126, 138–9, 141, 272–3, 284–5, 299, 307

gandharvas 71, 111, 247, 270, 291, 299, 330
Ganges, River 62, 86, 214–15, 244–5, 255, 269, 280–1, 312–13
gardens 95, 139, 276, 278, 291, 294
garlands 94, 140, 166, 260–1, 268, 277, 286, 293
garuḍas 111, 270, 289, 291, 299, 330
gender 147, 236
identity 236–7
generosity 5, 30, 95, 101, 139, 159, 161, 195–6
gentleness 161, 178, 244, 289
ghosts, hungry 29–30, 34, 37, 41, 257, 332, 338, 341
gifts 41, 76, 139, 161, 289
physical 161, 289
gladness 6, 111, 132, 264, 270, 276, 287, 297
goals 8, 104, 106, 140–1, 161, 299, 325–7, 341
gods 29–30, 146–7, 266–8, 274, 276–9, 291–2, 330–2, 337–9
akaniṣṭha 274, 292, 299, 325
jealous 29–30, 37, 41, 47, 106, 339
sunirmita 267, 330, 338
yāma 165, 214, 292, 309, 312, 341
going for refuge 48, 53, 66, 190, 194–6
gold 28–9, 40–1, 126, 147, 242, 272–3, 293, 309–10
colour of 79, 177, 182, 307, 310, 313–14, 316, 318
pure 79, 182, 250, 302, 313–14, 316, 318
golden appearance 80–1, 83, 178
golden colour 79, 147, 250, 253, 307, 313–14, 316, 318
golden light 303, 307, 310–11, 319–20
golden lotus 318–19, 322
Gomez, Luis 1, 72, 146, 237, 335
good family, children of 47, 70, 244, 246, 280, 320–1, 323, 327
good qualities 267, 280, 286–7, 289–90, 298, 300, 308, 341
inconceivable 62, 71, 244–6, 249
graduated discourse 5, 7, 28, 79, 129
grains of sand 62, 123, 214–15, 244–5, 255, 269, 280–1, 312–13
grape juice 176, 301–2
gravitational pull 106, 108, 180
Gṛdhrakūta, *see* Vultures' Peak
great assembly 163, 227, 291, 317–20, 324
great compassion 132, 217, 251, 256, 276, 312, 321–2
greatness 93, 266, 331, 336
Great Way, *see* Mahāyāna
Guān Jīng 9–10, 199, 202, 208, 216–17, 219, 222, 226–7

habitual karma 50–1
hair 149, 218, 270–1, 313
tufts of 215, 218, 312–13
haṃsa-geese 213, 243, 275, 311
hands, folded 250, 254, 290, 301, 318–21, 330
happiness 19–29, 31–5, 45–6, 87–8, 109, 137, 159–61, 165–8
abundant 22, 167–9
complete 150, 212
limited 22, 24, 167, 169
state of 15–42
unworldly 22–4, 26, 28, 37, 68, 109, 121, 167
worldly 21–3, 28, 88, 106, 167, 188, 201
hardship 115–16, 169
harmony 5, 34, 119, 168, 186, 243
harshness 161, 252–4, 289–90

head 124, 126, 215, 218, 256, 302–3, 313–15, 333
Bimbisāra's 177, 188–9
hearers 36, 40, 69, 122, 129, 338
heartfelt desire 43–5, 47–8, 87–8, 223–6, 244, 302–3, 316–20, 331
heaven 2, 31, 55, 85, 88, 189, 309, 312
hell realms 50, 112, 182, 221–2, 303
hells 2, 29–31, 41, 47, 257, 265, 271, 321–2
helpfulness 95, 139
higher forms of knowledge 85, 249–50, 252–3, 286, 288–9, 320, 322, 327–8
hindrances 130, 276, 304, 332
five 6
Hinduism 326, 338
Hockney, David 33, 127, 145
home 99–100, 107, 160, 169, 175, 186, 192–3, 206–7
honour 99–100, 190–1, 242, 261, 264, 280, 304
horses 57, 162, 289, 333
hostility 71, 158, 160–1, 194, 224, 287
householders 166, 193, 267, 294
Hughes, Aaron 2
Hui-Yuan 202
hungry ghosts 29–30, 34, 37, 41, 257, 332, 338, 341

ignorance 41, 49, 182, 211, 253
spiritual 327
illumined image 125–6, 137, 211–12
imagery 8, 29, 34, 121, 126, 131–2, 213, 215
images 1–2, 125, 164, 206–8, 212, 215, 306, 310–11
acquired 27–8, 200, 206, 208
counterpart 27–8, 200, 205, 208
illumined 125–6, 137, 211–12
preparatory 27, 200, 206
imagination 1–2, 4–8, 24–6, 28, 56–7, 85, 87–8, 208
imaginative faculty 7, 88, 208, 210
immature beings, ordinary 221, 316, 335
immeasurable buddhas 263–4
immediate consequences 112, 176, 221–2, 259, 319, 322, 325, 327
impermanence 4, 129–32, 206, 209, 306, 308, 330, 332
impure buddha-fields 21, 29, 31, 41–2, 71–2, 75–6, 124, 130
impure world 72, 148, 152
impurities 71, 87, 103, 162, 252–3, 255, 288–90, 299
incense 94–5, 140, 186, 260–1, 268, 277, 282, 286
inconceivable good qualities 62, 71, 244–6, 249
India 21, 32, 34, 100, 128, 162, 191–2, 231
Indra 17, 241, 246, 332, 337
infinite consciousness 24, 52, 92, 333
sphere of 24, 52, 92, 333
Infinite Life 81, 135, 243, 245, 271
infinite space 24, 52, 92, 333
sphere of 24, 52, 92, 333
initiation 276, 332
integrated mind 211, 310
intelligence 82, 183, 270, 290
intentions 11, 112, 122, 176, 194, 232, 256
irreversibility 106–8, 113, 115–17, 141–2, 150, 180, 300
irreversible bodhisattva 142, 200, 218–19, 225, 227

Jambū River 166, 209, 212, 214, 250, 307, 309–10, 312–13
James, William 117
Japan 103, 113
Japanese Pure Land 65, 92
jealous gods 29–30, 37, 41, 47, 106, 339
jealousy 30, 176
Jeta's Grove 18, 241
jewellery 139, 176–7, 250, 277–8, 301–3
jewels 35–6, 116, 194–6, 210, 260–3, 284, 307, 309–10
jewel trees 24–5, 44, 95, 111, 126–7, 201, 213
Jīvaka 177, 302
journeys 2, 56–7, 106, 238, 296
joy 22–4, 102, 105, 139, 160–1, 170–1, 331, 333
great 319, 323
sympathetic 132, 276, 338

kācilindika cloth 133, 278, 333
Kāla Mountains 274, 290
Kampila 155, 250
karma 45, 47, 49–51, 80, 141, 183–4, 187
death-proximate 50–1
habitual 50–1
law of 28, 52, 80, 107, 140, 179, 183–4, 195
skilful 50–1
unskilful 50, 176
weighty 50, 112–13, 208, 221
karma-niyama 107–8, 113, 116, 140
kasiṇa meditation 26–8, 121–2, 200, 203, 205
killing 50, 112, 177, 194, 221, 302, 325
kindness 43, 46, 49, 95, 98, 139, 156, 161
loving 89–90, 156, 276, 282, 287, 289, 334, 337
king of mountains 163, 274, 289, 291
kings 76, 166, 176–7, 252–4, 274, 288–9, 301–2, 330–3
knowledge 60–1, 251, 287–8, 293–4, 298, 332–3, 335–6, 339–40

knowledge (*cont.*)
higher forms of 85, 249–50, 252–3, 286, 288–9, 320, 322, 327–8
unobstructed 167, 297
and vision 83, 109, 148, 251, 266
kṣānti 142–3, 335
kṣatriya class 302, 333

lamps 125–6, 140, 260–1, 286
Land of Bliss, The 1, 72, 146, 237
language 2, 44, 57, 70, 131, 214, 231–7, 239
lapis lazuli 126, 201, 204–5, 242, 252–3, 272–3, 289, 305
law of karma 28, 52, 80, 107, 140, 179, 183–4, 195
legends 38–9, 182
Lennon, John 45, 49
liberation 232, 249, 320, 322, 329–30, 333, 339
knowledge and vision of 102, 322
life
eternal 55, 63, 89, 135
spiritual 3, 44, 95, 103–5, 115–17, 141, 152, 179–80
lifespan 135, 243, 256, 259, 271, 282, 290, 330
light 33–4, 89–90, 108–13, 204–6, 209–10, 214–16, 305–10, 312–15
golden 303, 307, 310–11, 319–20
rays of 161, 163, 210, 213, 283, 289–90, 303, 310–13
limited happiness 22, 24, 167, 169
limited mind 119, 182, 215
linear progression 116–17
lions 162, 245, 253, 257, 265, 289, 295
listeners 5, 7, 40, 55, 79, 129, 131, 163
literal-mindedness 77, 224
living beings 151, 254–60, 262–5, 274–6, 278–85, 287–90, 304–6, 312–22
Lokeśvararāja 86, 91, 254
lotuses 25, 27–9, 121, 127–8, 145, 209–10, 212–13, 309–10
blue 27, 242, 246, 268, 275, 291
closed 165–7, 182, 220–1
golden 318–19, 322
many-coloured 27, 242
red 27, 242, 275, 291, 313
lotus flowers 209, 220, 273, 291–4, 308–9, 311, 313–16, 318–22
lotus ponds 24–5, 27, 44, 199, 242
lotus seat 310–11
lotus throne 177, 201, 310
love 88–90, 116, 155, 159, 178, 181–3, 187, 191
unbounded 89, 128, 212
loving-kindness 89–90, 156, 276, 282, 287, 289, 334, 337

magical birds 2, 34–5, 44, 55, 59, 220
Mahāmaudgalyāyana 17, 77, 145, 149, 177, 241, 250, 301–2
Mahā-Parinibbāna Sutta 79–80, 84
Mahāsthāmaprāpta, Bodhisattva 201, 220, 311, 314–15, 317, 321, 323
Mahāyāna 39, 140, 170, 190, 195, 225, 317–18, 334
sutras 1, 8–9, 15–17, 39–40, 55, 89, 190–1, 194–5
Maheśvara 111, 270, 334
mahoragas 111, 270, 291
Maitreya 17, 62, 77, 170; *see also* Ajita
Mañjuśrī 17, 175, 241, 301
mano-niyama 107
mastery 257, 261, 268, 270, 283, 330, 334
Maudgalyāyana 175, 182, 193, 209, 270–1, 302–3, 323
meaning 100, 119–20, 130, 132, 232, 234–5, 250–1, 339–41
measurement 136–7, 341
meditation 23–5, 52–3, 59–60, 121–2, 201–6, 209, 219–21, 223–4
kasiṇa 26–8, 121–2, 200, 203, 205
practice 26, 36, 48, 114, 203, 207, 219, 223
meditative absorption 23, 26, 41, 43, 113–14, 124–5, 131–2, 137
meditative concentration 6, 84, 185, 303, 332, 334
meditators 17, 25, 28, 124, 199, 202–3, 205, 219–20
melodic sounds 129, 275
memory 5, 15, 77, 101, 208
mental constructs 68, 135–6, 213, 311, 329, 334
false 213, 311, 334
mental objects 267, 336
mental states 23, 29–30, 32, 113–14, 189, 194, 316, 329–30
negative 131, 325, 340
positive 95, 105, 139, 337
single 113, 115, 280, 296
skilful 101, 157, 165
unskilful 46, 106
merchants 166, 267, 294
mercy 166, 294, 337
merit 95, 139–40, 190, 194–5, 197, 280, 297, 316–20
accumulation of 276, 282, 337
Meru, Mount 244, 246, 252–3, 287, 291
metaphors 3, 51, 54, 106, 108, 116, 337, 341
Mettā Sutta 89, 128
midday 133–4, 278, 359
milk 156, 158, 296, 331
mind 3–7, 23–30, 32–6, 46–8, 121–5, 203–4, 209–14, 304–17

rays of light 161, 163, 210, 213, 283, 289–90, 303, 310–13
realism, naive 64, 72
reality 2, 5, 35, 111, 158–9, 161–2, 210–11, 215
realization 3, 54, 60, 109, 142, 154, 161, 184
rebirth 1–2, 45, 47–54, 112–13, 139–40, 216–17, 221, 224
recollection 25, 207, 216, 308, 311–12, 317, 326, 332
red lotuses 27, 242, 275, 291, 313
reflexive awareness 31, 87, 157
refuges 8, 36, 190, 194–5, 225, 326, 328, 337
  going for 48, 53, 66, 190, 194–6
religious escapism 185–6
remorse 102, 104–5, 179, 221, 321
renunciants 266, 326, 337
renunciation 5, 181
repetition 222, 322, 335, 340
resolution 44–5, 60, 93, 113, 255, 266
resonance 83, 119
  sympathetic 83–4
retreats 42, 68, 91, 94, 158, 196, 226, 237
reverence 98–9, 110, 186, 298, 302, 304, 330
rewards 29, 47, 51–2, 179–80, 189
rivers 53, 85, 128–9, 131, 142–3, 154, 163, 274–6
robes 140, 147, 250, 254, 260–1, 263, 267–8, 277
rocks 29, 35, 84–5, 118, 176
roots 45, 126, 138, 191, 193, 272–3, 280, 288
  of virtue 45, 47–8, 51–2, 112–14, 263–4, 280, 289, 293–5
rubies 25, 126, 140, 242, 260, 272–3, 309

Śakra 267, 270, 303, 307, 309, 313, 332, 337
Śākyamuni 25, 71, 98, 103–4, 110–11, 138, 164, 209
samādhi 84, 208, 213, 263–4, 311–12, 322–3, 329, 337–8
samsara 208, 211, 222–3, 306, 314–15, 321–3, 327, 337
sand, grains of 62, 123, 214–15, 244–5, 255, 269, 280–1, 312–13
sandalwood 85, 252–3, 260–1, 266, 268, 277, 279, 286
sangha 34–6, 149–50, 164, 176, 185–6, 243, 321, 337
  great 241, 249, 301
  of monks 163–4, 259, 281, 291, 337
  of śrāvakas 39, 47–8, 148, 244, 270–1
  symbol of 140, 145
Sangharakshita, Urgyen 66–7, 238–9
Sanskrit 9, 48, 85, 112, 175, 191, 234–8, 325
Śāriputra 20, 34, 36, 38–9, 69–71, 77–8, 241–4, 246–7
Sāvatthī 40–1
schism 176, 325
self 54, 68, 88–9, 119, 129–31, 142–3, 153–4, 211
  enduring 54, 67–8, 81, 87, 107, 154, 211–12, 214
  fixed and separate 67–8, 87, 142
self-awareness 31, 107, 157
self-confidence 162, 276, 289–90, 296, 337
self-help 64
selfhood 54, 88, 161, 211, 214, 221
self-power 64–8, 113, 117, 189
  practice 66, 115–16
sensations 92, 153–5, 276
sense experiences 6, 329
sense objects 43, 121, 204
sense pleasures 44, 265, 337
sensual desire 93–4, 266, 327, 337, 339
serene faith 113, 280–1, 294, 296, 298, 329, 337
serenity 23, 41, 92, 100, 102, 105
servants 18, 40, 55, 225
setting sun 63, 68, 201, 203–4, 210, 305
sexual craving 34
sexual misconduct 194, 339
silver 2, 25, 126, 140, 242, 260, 272–3
similes 4, 97, 149, 162
single mental state 113, 115, 280, 296
skilful actions 45, 47, 52, 95, 139, 190–1, 194, 337
skilful effort 105, 108, 119, 200, 218
skilful karmas 50–1
skilful mental states 101, 157, 165
skilful states 46, 48, 101–2, 104, 150, 211
skill 168, 238, 270, 275, 278–9, 336
sleep 41, 48–9, 56, 69
small bells, nets of 25, 36, 44, 166, 242–3, 284, 293
smells 122, 126, 129, 133, 141, 266–7, 273, 276–7
society, oral 69, 75, 162
solitude 40–1, 102, 132, 266, 276, 289, 330, 338
songs 34–5, 45, 206, 209, 260–1, 286–7, 306, 308
sons 166, 176, 178, 181–2, 189, 192, 225, 241
sorrow 100, 177, 184, 186, 217, 224, 289, 303
sounds 18–19, 111, 119, 140, 207–8, 220, 275–6, 315
  delightful 36, 243, 273
  melodic 129, 275
sovereignty 276, 278, 289

WINDHORSE PUBLICATIONS

Windhorse Publications is a Buddhist charitable company based in the UK. We place great emphasis on producing books of high quality that are accessible and relevant to those interested in Buddhism at whatever level. We are the main publisher of the works of Sangharakshita, the founder of the Triratna Buddhist Order and Community. Our books draw on the whole range of the Buddhist tradition, including translations of traditional texts, commentaries, books that make links with contemporary culture and ways of life, biographies of Buddhists, and works on meditation.

As a not-for-profit enterprise, we ensure that all surplus income is invested in new books and improved production methods, to better communicate Buddhism in the 21st century. We welcome donations to help us continue our work – to find out more, go to www.windhorsepublications.com.

The Windhorse is a mythical animal that flies over the earth carrying on its back three precious jewels, bringing these invaluable gifts to all humanity: the Buddha (the 'awakened one'), his teaching, and the community of all his followers.

Windhorse Publications
169 Mill Road
Cambridge
CB1 3AN
UK
info@windhorsepublications.com

Perseus Distribution
210 American Drive
Jackson TN 38301
USA

Windhorse Books
PO Box 574
Newtown NSW 2042
Australia

THE TRIRATNA BUDDHIST COMMUNITY

Windhorse Publications is a part of the Triratna Buddhist Community, which has more than sixty centres on five continents. Through these centres, members of the Triratna Buddhist Order offer classes in meditation and Buddhism, from an introductory to a deeper level of commitment. Members of the Triratna community run retreat centres around the world, and the Karuna Trust, a UK fundraising charity that supports social welfare projects in the slums and villages of South Asia.

Many Triratna centres have residential spiritual communities and ethical Right Livelihood businesses associated with them. Arts activities and body awareness disciplines are encouraged also, as is the development of strong bonds of friendship between people who share the same ideals. In this way Triratna is developing a unique approach to Buddhism, not simply as a set of techniques, but as a creatively directed way of life for people living in the modern world.

If you would like more information about Triratna please visit www.thebuddhistcentre.com or write to:

London Buddhist Centre
51 Roman Road
London E2 0HU
UK

Aryaloka
14 Heartwood Circle
Newmarket NH 03857
USA

Sydney Buddhist Centre
24 Enmore Road
Sydney NSW 2042
Australia

ALSO BY RATNAGUNA

The Art of Reflection

It is all too easy either to think obsessively, or to not think enough. But how do we think usefully? How do we reflect? Like any art, reflection can be learnt and developed, leading to a deeper understanding of life and to the fullness of wisdom. *The Art of Reflection* is a practical guide to reflection as a spiritual practice, about 'what we think and how we think about it'. It is a book about contemplation and insight, and reflection as a way to discover the truth.

'No-one who takes seriously the study and practice of the Dharma should fail to read this ground-breaking book.' – Sangharakshita, founder of the Triratna Buddhist Community

'The Art of Reflection *will give teachers insight into Buddhist practice. Even more importantly, it may help to develop the ability to engage in deeper personal and professional reflection.'* – Joyce Miller, *REtoday*

ISBN 9781 899579 89 1
£9.99 / $16.95 / €12.95
160 pages

Mind in Harmony: The Psychology of Buddhist Ethics

Subhuti

'It's not our bank balance, looks, social status or popularity that determines how happy, free and fulfilled we are in life. Finally, what really counts is our state of mind. Subhuti helps us to identify what's going on in our mind, including our moods and emotions, and see clearly what's helpful and what will end in tears.' – Vessantara, author of *The Breath* and *A Guide to the Buddhas*

'This is a refreshing approach to the classical Abhidharma material, relentlessly experiential and eminently practical. It offers a way of engaging directly with the sophisticated elements of Buddhist psychology that is immediately accessible and offers a real prospect of transformation. I heartily recommend it to anyone who wants to use Buddhist wisdom to explore and clarify their minds.' – Andrew Olendzki, author of *Unlimiting Mind*, senior scholar at Barre Center for Buddhist Studies

'What exactly should I be working on in my spiritual life?'

This is the question that Subhuti sets before us, along with what we most need to answer it for ourselves.

Long before the discoveries of contemporary neuroscience and psychology, the Buddha gained insight into the nature of mind. In early Buddhism this profound insight informed the Abhidharma – a 'training manual' to help us understand and transform our own minds. Subhuti brings this manual to life, and shows us the ways in which it illuminates our mind's patterns.

Outlining the processes whereby the mind attends to the world, and explaining how mindfulness fits into the pattern of spiritual development from the perspective of the Abhidharma, Subhuti guides us expertly to an appreciation of how mental states arise, and how to distinguish between skilful mental states and their opposites. In this way, we are given the means to live a happier and more fruitful life, and ultimately a pathway to liberation from all suffering. We are also offered a glimpse of how the enlightened mind of a Buddha works – the mind in its ultimate harmony.

Subhuti has led retreats in Europe, the United States and India on the Buddhist texts of the Yogacara Abhidharma, the source of this system of mind training. This book is the fruit of that teaching experience.

ISBN 978 1 909314 08 5
£12.99 / $19.95 / €12.95
272 pages

Compassion and Emptiness in Early Buddhist Meditation

Anālayo

Exploring the meditative practices of compassion and emptiness, Anālayo casts fresh light on their earliest sources in the Buddhist tradition.

'This book is the result of rigorous textual scholarship that can be valued not only by the academic community, but also by Buddhist practitioners. This book serves as an important bridge between those who wish to learn about Buddhist thought and practice and those who wish to learn from it. As a monk engaging himself in Buddhist meditation as well as a professor applying a historical-critical methodology, Bhikkhu Anālayo is well positioned to bridge these two communities.' – 17th Karmapa Ogyen Trinley Dorje

'In this study, Venerable Anālayo brings a meticulous textual analysis of Pali texts, the Chinese Āgamas and related material from Sanskrit and Tibetan to the foundational topics of compassion and emptiness. While his analysis is grounded in a scholarly approach, he has written this study as a helpful guide for meditation practice.' – Jetsunma Tenzin Palmo

'This is an intriguing and delightful book that presents these topics from the viewpoint of the early suttas as well as from other perspectives, and grounds them in both theory and meditative practice.' – Bhikshuni Thubten Chodron

'Anālayo holds a lamp to illuminate how the earliest teachings wed the great heart of compassion and the liberating heart of emptiness and invites us to join in this profound training.' – Jack Kornfield'

'This scholarly book is more than timely with its demonstrations that teachings on emptiness and compassion that are helpful to practitioners of any form of Buddhism are abundant in early Buddhist texts.' – Rita M. Gross

'Arising from the author's long-term, dedicated practice and study, this book provides a window into the depth and beauty of the Buddha's liberating teachings. Serious meditation students will benefit tremendously from the clarity of understanding that Venerable Anālayo's efforts have achieved.' – Sharon Salzberg

ISBN 978 1 909314 55 9
£11.99 / $17.95 / €16.95
232 pages

The Journey and the Guide: A Practical Course in Enlightenment

Maitreyabandhu

'This book feels contemporary and relevant – full of situations and anecdotes that you'll instantly recognize from your own life. But it also goes deep. Being both practical and profound, it really is what it says, "a practical course in Enlightenment".' – Vajragupta, author of *Buddhism: Tools for Living Your Life*

How can you make the most of your life? Maitreyabandhu – a prize-winning poet who has been sharing his experience of practising Buddhism for over 20 years – sets out to answer this most basic question. With humour and profundity, mixing poetry and myth with down-to-earth instruction, he describes what it means to set out on the Buddha's journey and how you can follow it – day by day and week by week.

'The natural mode of consciousness is to expand. In every moment we can either allow consciousness to unfold or we can make it "me" and "mine" and feel it shrink back to the level of egocentricity. It's as if we've identified with a tiny ripple on the surface of the ocean. Once we let go of that identification *there's the whole ocean:* centre-less, edgeless, completely free.'

Maitreyabandhu is an experienced teacher and a member of the Triratna Buddhist Order. Ordained in 1990, he has written two books on Buddhism, including the best-selling *Life with Full Attention*, as well as two collections of poetry. He lives and works at the London Buddhist Centre.

ISBN 978 1 909314 09 2
£11.99 / $18.95 / €14.95
344 pages

The Buddha on Wall Street: What's Wrong with Capitalism and What We Can Do about It

Vaḍḍhaka Linn

After his Enlightenment the Buddha set out to help liberate the individual, and create a society free from suffering. The economic resources now exist to offer a realistic possibility of providing everyone with decent food, shelter, work and leisure, to allow each of us to fulfil our potential as human beings, whilst protecting the environment. What is it in the nature of modern capitalism which prevents that happening? Can Buddhism help us build something better than our current economic system, to reduce suffering and help the individual to freedom? In this thought-provoking work, Vaḍḍhaka Linn explores answers to these questions by examining our economic world from the moral standpoint established by the Buddha.

'An original, insightful, and provocative evaluation of our economic situation today. If you wonder about the social implications of Buddhist teachings, this is an essential book.' – David Loy, author *Money, Sex, War, Karma*

'Lays bare the pernicious consequences of corporate capitalism and draws forth from Buddhism suggestions for creating benign alternatives conducive to true human flourishing.' – Bhikkhu Bodhi, editor *In the Buddha's Words*

'Questions any definition of wellbeing that does not rest on a firm ethical foundation, developing a refreshing Buddhist critique of the ends of economic activity.' – Dominic Houlder, Adjunct Professor in Strategy and Entrepreneurship, London Business School

ISBN 978 1 909314 44 3
£9.99 / $16.99 / €12.95
272 pages

Buddhist Meditation Tranquillity, Imagination & Insight

Kamalashila

First published in 1991, this book is a comprehensive and practical guide to Buddhist meditation, providing a complete introduction for beginners, as well as detailed advice for experienced meditators seeking to deepen their practice. Kamalashila explores the primary aims of Buddhist meditation: enhanced awareness, true happiness, and – ultimately – liberating insight into the nature of reality. This third edition includes new sections on the importance of the imagination, on Just Sitting, and on reflection on the Buddha. Kamalashila has been teaching meditation since becoming a member of the Triratna Buddhist Order in 1974. He has developed approaches to meditation practice that are accessible to people in the contemporary world, whilst being firmly grounded in the Buddhist tradition.

A wonderfully practical and accessible introduction to the important forms of Buddhist meditation. From his years of meditation practice, Kamalashila has written a book useful for both beginners and longtime practitioners. – Gil Fronsdal, author of *A Monastery Within*, founder of the Insight Meditation Center, California, USA

This enhanced new edition guides readers more clearly into the meditations and draws out their significance more fully, now explicitly oriented around the 'system of meditation'. This system provides a fine framework both for understanding where various practices fit in and for reflecting on the nature of our own spiritual experiences. Kamalashila has also woven in an appreciation of a view of the nature of mind that in the Western tradition is known as the imagination, helping make an accessible link to our own philosophical and cultural traditions. – Lama Surya Das, author of *Awakening the Buddha Within*, founder of Dzogchen Center and Dzogchen Meditation Retreats, USA

His approach is a clear, thorough, honest, and, above all, open-ended exploration of the practical problems for those new to and even quite experienced in meditation. – Lama Shenpen Hookham, author of *There's More to Dying Than Death*, founder of the Awakened Heart Sangha, UK

ISBN 9781 907314 09 4
£14.99 / $27.95 / €19.95
272 pages